The Essential
KARL
BARTH

A READER
AND COMMENTARY

Keith L. Johnson

Baker Academic
a division of Baker Publishing Group
Grand Rapids, Michigan

© 2019 by Keith L. Johnson

Published by Baker Academic
a division of Baker Publishing Group
PO Box 6287, Grand Rapids, MI 49516-6287
www.bakeracademic.com

Printed in the United States of America

Library of Congress Cataloging in Publication Data
Names: Barth, Karl, 1886–1968, author. | Johnson, Keith L., commentator.
Title: The essential Karl Barth : a reader and commentary / Keith L. Johnson.
Description: Grand Rapids : Baker Publishing Group, 2019. | Includes bibliographical references and index.
Identifiers: LCCN 2018034733 | ISBN 9781540960733 (cloth : alk. paper)
Subjects: LCSH: Barth, Karl, 1886–1968.
Classification: LCC BX4827.B3 A25 2019 | DDC 230/.044—dc23
LC record available at https://lccn.loc.gov/2018034733

In the introductory material and commentary, Scripture quotations are from the New Revised Standard Version of the Bible, copyright © 1989, by the Division of Christian Education of the National Council of the Churches of Christ in the United States of America. Used by permission. All rights reserved.

Scripture quotations labeled KJV are from the King James Version of the Bible.

19   20   21   22   23   24   25   7   6   5   4   3   2   1

\# 1039407554

To George and Bruce

Contents

Preface   ix

1. Introduction: The Life of Karl Barth   1

Part 1: Barth's Theological Development   13

   2. *The Epistle to the Romans*   23
   3. "The Word of God as the Task of Theology"   32
   4. An Answer to Professor Adolf von Harnack   44
   5. *The Resurrection of the Dead*   57
   6. *The Göttingen Dogmatics*   63
   7. "The Holy Spirit and the Christian Life"   69
   8. Preface to *Church Dogmatics* I/1   74
   9. Farewell   81
  10. "The Humanity of God"   93

Part 2: Barth's *Church Dogmatics*   103

  11. The Task of Dogmatics   109
  12. The Word of God   115
  13. Revelation and Faith   120
  14. The Doctrine of the Trinity   126
  15. The Missions of the Son and the Spirit   137
  16. The Knowledge of God   149
  17. The Reality of God   167

18. The Doctrine of Election   174

19. The Election of Jesus Christ   190

20. God's Decision for the World   200

21. Covenant and Creation   205

22. The Covenant Partner of God   211

23. God and Nothingness   224

24. God with Us   233

25. The Obedience of the Son of God   247

26. The Exaltation of the Son of Man   265

27. The Glory of the Mediator   278

28. The Scope of Salvation   287

29. Christian Community   290

Part 3: Barth's Political Engagement   301

30. A Brief Reminiscence of the 1920s   303

31. Sermon on Romans 15:5–13   308

32. The Barmen Theological Declaration   320

33. The Role of Christians in Wartime: "A Letter to American Christians"   325

34. "The Community of Christians and the Community of Citizens"   337

Conclusion: The Tradition of Karl Barth   347

Credits   366

Index   369

Preface

This book introduces readers to the theology of Karl Barth by presenting several of his most important writings in a single volume. The process of selecting these texts posed a challenge. Barth wrote millions of words in dozens of books, essays, sermons, and letters over many decades. This book contains approximately 100,000 of those words. Tough decisions had to be made, and I made them with two goals in mind. First, I wanted to assemble a collection that told the story of Barth's theology from the beginning to the end of his academic career. Barth lived a dramatic life, and I chose texts that captured the drama. Second, I selected texts that will help readers grasp the essence of Barth's theology. I wanted readers to know and understand what Barth thinks, but I also wanted them to be able to approach the rest of Barth's writings with confidence. As I look over the collection at the end of the process, I believe that this volume accomplishes both of these goals. But I could have reworked this volume several times over with completely different sets of texts and still have accomplished these same goals. This means that there is both good news and bad news for readers. The bad news is that many incredible texts were left on the cutting-room floor. The good news is that this book will prepare readers to spend a lifetime exploring them.

This book is divided into three parts, along with an introduction and conclusion on Barth's life and legacy. Part 1 provides an overview of Barth's theological development through texts that show how Barth refined his ideas over the course of his career. Part 2 features passages from Barth's *Church Dogmatics*, the work that occupied the majority of his life. Part 3 offers a sample sermon and other key texts that show how Barth responded to the threat posed by the Nazi government in Germany.

Each part opens with an essay that explains its purpose and structure. Each selection begins with an introduction that provides the context for that text and summarizes its argument. The selections also feature editorial footnotes designed to help the reader grasp Barth's claims more clearly. I wrote these footnotes with a particular audience in mind. The world of Barth scholarship contains many resources that are rich in content but also highly technical. Far fewer resources exist to help students learn how to read Barth. With this context in mind, I tried to avoid technicalities and the debates that occupy the time and energy of Barth specialists. My commentary instead is directed toward helping new readers of Barth to understand his work. My goal was to make Barth's thought accessible, to explain his ideas clearly, and to provoke further reading. I tried to offer the commentary I wish had been available to me when I first started reading Barth.

Memories of my initial encounter with Barth's work were on my mind when I agreed to take on this project. I read Barth's theology for the first time two decades ago as an undergraduate student. From the very first page, I felt like I had found a new friend. Barth put into words the theology I hoped was true. His work has often functioned in a pastoral way for me, both in my personal life and in my professional work. Academic theology is a difficult profession, and so is teaching. At key moments, reading Barth reminded me why I began studying theology in the first place. His work directs me to Jesus Christ and reminds me that Christ is for me and for the world. His confidence is reassuring when I lack my own. I am inspired by the way he grew and developed over the course of his career, especially after getting a late start. His love for his subject matter always cheers me up, and his joyous approach gives me hope as I face difficult questions.

My work on this project proved to me that, after over two decades of studying Barth, I am still only beginning to understand his theology. Some theologians are interesting for only a short time because there is little substance beneath the surface. Barth is different because he has become more interesting the longer I have studied him. Part of what makes Barth so fascinating is that he possessed a rare combination of intellect, eloquence, and courage. An initial reading of his theology reveals a passionate and engaging theologian confidently explaining his subject matter. A deep examination of these same passages shows a highly complex thinker who has constructed his theology with a level of originality, depth, and precision that has been matched only rarely in the history of theology.

Regardless of whether a reader finds the content of his claims compelling, Barth is an important theologian to study because of his significant influence on the discipline. By the coincidence of historical circumstance and the sheer force of personality, Barth changed the trajectory of the discipline of theology for both Protestantism and then, through his interpreters, Roman Catholicism. Reading his work puts readers in the middle of dozens of conversations that continue to influence the field. It also helps them understand many key movements that have shaped the last century, including liberation theology and apocalyptic theology. Even theologians who have strongly disagreed with Barth have often been affected by their encounters with his work and the challenge of opposing him. Thousands of different and diverse theologians have been forged on the anvil of Barth's *Church Dogmatics*, and the discipline of theology is stronger as a result.

In light of this influence, it is important to keep Barth's humanity in view. He struggled in many of his closest relationships, including his marriage. He had no trouble making friends, but he also had a tendency to lose friendships, including some of the most important ones in his life. His proclivity to issuing bold and definitive judgments sometimes produced unnecessary pain. For its power and eloquence, Barth's style sometimes leaves something to be desired. He often says in a thousand words what could have been said in ten. Many of his historical judgments are a product of his time, and they stand in need of correction by more recent scholarship and a global perspective. Barth tended to read major theological figures in light of their contemporary representatives, and this approach leaves his interpretations of some historical figures off the mark. His exegesis of Scripture is sometimes brilliant and breathtaking; at other times, his interpretations strain the biblical text beyond its limits.

But even these flaws give me hope. Barth regularly pointed out how much he had grown and changed over the course of his career. He found deep joy not only in offering answers but also in being formed by the difficult process of discovering them. He saw his written theological work as part of this process rather than the end of it. As I pick up the conversation Barth started and try to make my own contribution, I hope the process will expose and refine me as much as it did him.

I am grateful for several people who assisted me during the course of this project. Jeremy Lundgren helped by transcribing texts and checking translations in the midst of his busy doctoral duties. My teaching assistants Genevieve Austin Ellsworth and Anna Erickson scanned and transcribed several texts. The work was tedious, but they performed it with joy. They also took the lead in several other projects, both large and small, so that I would not be distracted from this one. Sarah DeGeus offered help during a busy time so that I could be free to focus on my writing, and her proofreading saved me from more than one mistake.

My friend Matthew Aragorn Bruce served as a valuable conversation partner as I worked on this project, and this book is much better because of his insights. I am particularly grateful for his permission to include two of his original translations in this volume. I also am thankful to Peter Zocher from the Karl Barth Archiv in Basel for the permission to use these two texts. Kait Dugan, from the Center for Barth Studies at Princeton Theological Seminary, provided helpful advice early in the project, and she encouraged the project at every turn. The same has been true for the team who originally asked me to take on this project: Paul Gavrilyuk, Paul Dafydd Jones, Karen Kilby, Kevin Hector, and Francesca A. Murphy.

I am blessed to have many friends who support me in my work. Particularly important during the time of this project were George Kalantzis, David Lauber, Vince Bacote, Gregory Lee, Beth Jones, Jeffrey Barbeau, Daniel Treier, Matthew Milliner, Timothy Larsen, Lynn Cohick, Gene Green, Gary Burge, Emily Langan, Shawn Okpebholo, Jamie Huff, Laura Yoder, Judi Nychay, and Krista Sanchez. I also want to recognize the members of the TPT: Wesley Keyes, Kevin Roberts, Sean Allen, Chris Thacker, Erin Conaway, Matthew Cook, Jausch Haynes, Matt Sciba, and Britt Young.

My wife, Julie, sacrificed her own interests more than once to give me the space to work on this project. Words cannot express my gratitude and love for her. The same applies to my sons, Everett and Blake. They bring immense joy to my life each day, and their presence reminds me that there are things far more important than theology.

Finally, I want to express my gratitude for the contributions that both George Hunsinger and Bruce McCormack have made to the study of Karl Barth's theology over the past three decades. Their work has transformed the discipline and enriched the legacy Barth left behind. I also am grateful for the role they have played in my life over the past fifteen years. They started out as my teachers but ended up as my friends. This book is dedicated to them.

CHAPTER 1

Introduction

The Life of Karl Barth

Karl Barth was born on May 10, 1886, in Basel, Switzerland, to Johann Friedrich (Fritz) and Katharina (Anna) Barth.[1] His parents' home was shaped by their intellectual interests and theological heritage. Fritz Barth served as a Reformed minister before joining the faculty of theology at the University of Bern, where he moved his family when Karl was three years old. He eventually became a well-respected professor of church history and New Testament, and he held the position for twenty-three years. His scholarly demeanor left a lifelong impression on his son, who respected him and looked up to him. Anna Barth was a well-educated pastor's daughter, and several of her family members had served as theologians in Basel. As the son of a professor, Karl spent much of his childhood reading, learning, and talking with the plethora of interesting guests who visited the Barth home. He received a good education, and later he described his younger self as a "bookworm."[2] Karl was most interested in studying literature, poetry, and history, and these subjects remained passions for his entire life. As he grew

1. The most significant collection of biographical material about Barth's life is Eberhard Busch's *Karl Barth: His Life from Letters and Autobiographical Texts* (Grand Rapids: Eerdmans, 1994). Much of the material used to create this account was drawn from Busch's volume.
2. Karl Barth, "Münster Faculty Album, 1927," in *Karl Barth–Rudolf Bultmann: Letters, 1922–1966*, trans. Geoffrey W. Bromiley (Grand Rapids: Eerdmans, 1981), 151.

into adulthood, he enjoyed reading detective novels before bed and studying the history of the American Civil War. He also developed a deep appreciation for music, particularly the work of Mozart.

His turn toward theology began at the age of thirteen as the result of his confirmation classes. Barth later recalled, "At the end of the classes I realized clearly the need to know more about the matter. On this rudimentary basis, I resolved to study theology."[3] In 1904, Barth enrolled at the University of Bern, where his father worked. He studied philosophy, the history of religion, church history, and Scripture. He proved to be a hardworking and intelligent student, and after two years in Bern, he sought advanced theological study in Germany. After some negotiation with his father, he ended up at the University of Berlin, where he studied under Adolf von Harnack. Barth spent the next few years moving around to different universities while interning at Swiss churches during the summers. After Berlin, he returned to Bern for a semester and then spent a semester in Tübingen before finally settling into the University of Marburg, where he studied with the theologian and ethicist Wilhelm Hermann. This tour of German universities exposed Barth to several major figures and ideas that shaped Protestant theology in the early years of the twentieth century. His teachers represented a mature and highly developed form of the liberal Protestant tradition that had been shaped by the thought of figures ranging from Immanuel Kant to Friedrich Schleiermacher to David Friedrich Strauss. Barth's university education gave him a strong background in the scientific method, a historical-critical approach to Scripture, and a liberal Protestant theology grounded on human religious experience.

After completing his university studies in 1908, Barth took a position as an assistant editor for the journal *Die Christliche Welt* (The Christian World) under the leadership of prominent liberal thinker Martin Rade. At this point in Barth's life, further academic work did not seem to be on the horizon. After being ordained for Christian ministry, Barth accepted his first church position by becoming the assistant pastor in a Reformed congregation in Geneva in 1909. He remained in Geneva for two years before accepting a pastorate in the small village of Safenwil, in the Aargau region of Switzerland, in 1911.

Barth stayed in Safenwil for over a decade, and these turned out to be among the most important years of his life. In 1913, Barth married Nelly Hoffmann, who had been a member of one of his confirmation classes in Geneva. They soon began a family that would grow to five children. In addition to his growing family responsibilities, Barth dedicated himself to his pastoral work. He found the realities of pastoral life both formative and surprising.

3. Barth, "Münster Faculty Album, 1927," 152.

He quickly learned that much of his classroom training did not translate into the village pulpit, and he found himself struggling to figure out what to say in his sermons. The disconnect between his training and ministry stemmed, in part, from the deep connection he felt with his congregants. Many of them worked in difficult conditions in local industries, and the bookish knowledge he had gained at the university provided little help as he sought to address the social and economic pressures they faced. He turned to the growing Christian socialist movement for insights, and soon he was taking an active role in workers' disputes on behalf of his congregants. Locals even began calling Barth "The Red Pastor" because of his political activities.

During these years the most significant theological event for Barth was the outbreak of the Great War in 1914. Barth strongly opposed the German rationale for the war, and as the horrific reality of the conflict become clear, everything Barth thought he knew about the progress of history and culture was challenged. He particularly was shocked to learn that many of his former teachers had signed a declaration of support for the German war policy. This action prompted him to question everything they had taught him. As Barth put it later, "An entire world of theological exegesis, dogmatics, and preaching, which up to that point I had accepted as basically credible, was thereby shaking to the foundations."[4] Barth found little recourse in his fellow socialists because many of them also were caught up in the fervor of the war. He began to feel isolated. The theological and political movements that had been the most central to his life no longer seemed viable for him, and he began to search for a new community and a fresh start in his theology.

During this period Barth developed a close friendship with neighboring pastor Eduard Thurneysen that would last the rest of his life. Through letters and conversations, they began to share their questions, discuss new ideas, and search for a fresh theological path. Thurneysen introduced Barth to the theology of Johann and Christoph Blumhardt. The Blumhardts' emphasis on eschatology and the kingdom of God exposed Barth to ideas and patterns of thought quite different from those he had encountered in the university. They also drove Barth to a new and deeper engagement with Scripture. He realized that he had taken the Bible for granted rather than seeking to understand it on its own terms. Now he read the text with care, and he found it invigorating.

In the summer of 1916, Barth began an intensive study of Paul's letter to the Romans. Instead of studying the historical context of the letter or

4. Karl Barth, "Concluding Unscientific Postscript on Schleiermacher," in *The Theology of Schleiermacher: Lectures at Göttingen, Winter Semester 1923/24*, ed. Dietrich Ritschl, trans. Geoffrey W. Bromiley (Grand Rapids: Eerdmans, 1982), 264.

examining critical or textual issues as he had been trained, Barth focused on Paul's message about God. He soon began to fill notebooks with his insights, and particular themes began to emerge. God could not be identified with any creaturely reality because he is totally distinct from every created thing. He breaks into the world from above in Jesus Christ, the revelation of God who reveals the true history while exposing the false one. The resurrection of Christ from the dead calls everything into question—every ideology and political movement and even religion itself.

As he continued to discuss these ideas with Thurneysen and a growing circle of friends, Barth began to share his insights in lectures delivered to churches and gatherings of pastors. During this same period, he edited his notebooks into a manuscript for a book, *The Epistle to the Romans*. When the first copies appeared in December 1918, Barth's hopes were modest. He thought his work might assist a few fellow pastors and thinkers who also were searching for a new way forward in postwar Europe. Barth was surprised when the book received a great deal of interest almost immediately. The boldness of its claims matched the times, and people began looking to this young pastor to see what else he had to say. As his reputation grew throughout 1919, Barth continued to lecture and develop his ideas. Near the end of that year, he delivered a powerful lecture, "The Christian in Society," at a conference of socialists in Tambach, Germany.[5] He proclaimed God as "Wholly Other" and drew a distinction between the kingdom of God and every creaturely ideal and human ideology. This lecture was widely discussed, and Barth acquired a new level of prominence. He later recalled, "I suddenly found a circle, and the prospect of further circles, of people to whose unrest my efforts promised answers which at once became new questions."[6]

From this point on, Barth's life began to change at a rapid pace. In light of responses he had received to his book as well as developments in his thinking, Barth began to revise his commentary on Romans to sharpen the argument. While these revisions were in progress, he received an invitation to serve as Honorary Professor of Reformed Theology at the University of Göttingen, a school shaped by the Lutheran tradition. Although the theological fit was tenuous, the position was the opportunity of a lifetime. Barth resigned from his pastorate in Safenwil and moved his family to Germany to begin his teaching career in 1921. This new position and the publication of the second edition of *The Epistle to the Romans* provided Barth with a new level of academic

---

5. See Karl Barth, "The Christian in Society," in *The Word of God and Theology*, ed. and trans. Amy Marga (London: T&T Clark, 2011), 31–70.

6. Barth, "Münster Faculty Album, 1927," 155.

prominence and credibility. His work began to receive responses from major scholars, many of them highly critical. Barth suddenly discovered that he was both the central figure in an exciting theological movement and the target of constant critique from the most significant scholars in the discipline.

That same year Barth partnered with his friends Thurneysen and Friedrich Gogarten to start the theological journal *Zwischen den Zeiten* (Between the Times). It would serve as an outlet for the writings of Barth and the other thinkers associated with what was now being called the "dialectical theology" movement. Through his essays in the journal and public lectures, Barth worked hard to defend the movement and his own views. "These were, of course, difficult years," he later recalled, "for I had not only to learn and teach continuously, but also, as the champion of a new trend in theology, I had to vindicate and protect myself in the form of lectures and public discussions of every kind."[7] He found his teaching particularly challenging since his lack of doctoral training left him unprepared to offer that level of instruction. Barth had to learn as he taught, and he often stayed up late into the night to prepare lectures he would deliver the following morning. He immersed himself in the theological tradition by teaching courses on the Reformed confessions and the thought of major figures like John Calvin and Friedrich Schleiermacher. He also conducted exegesis courses on several books of the Bible, and later he edited his lectures on 1 Corinthians and Philippians for publication. This historical and exegetical study proved helpful as Barth began teaching his first course on dogmatic theology in the spring of 1924. The experience of offering his own theology—of saying what he actually thought instead of merely criticizing others—was both invigorating and exhausting.

In 1925, Barth moved to the University of Münster to serve as Professor of Dogmatics and New Testament Exegesis. His thinking continued to develop as he taught new courses and repeated others for the second time. Münster was a Catholic city, and Barth took the opportunity to explore the Catholic tradition in depth. In addition to teaching seminars on Anselm and Thomas Aquinas, he participated in a Catholic reading group and invited several Catholic scholars to visit his seminars. He found his engagement with Catholic thinkers enriching because, unlike the Protestant liberals, they shared his interest in classical doctrines and the history of theology. They also raised questions about Barth's theology that prompted him to think more carefully about his claims. The fruit of this engagement is apparent in Barth's second cycle of lectures on dogmatic theology, which he delivered over the course of three semesters in Münster. Throughout these lectures, Barth drew from a

7. Barth, "Münster Faculty Album, 1927," 156.

wide range of sources and experimented with new forms of thought. He grew confident enough about his approach to make his dogmatics public. Barth revised the first part of these lectures for publication as a book titled *Die christliche Dogmatik im Entwurf* (Christian Dogmatics in Outline) in 1927. He planned for several others to follow this initial volume.

Barth soon reconsidered that plan. Once his dogmatics was published, he quickly realized that it did not accomplish his aims. "When the first volume was before me in print, it showed me plainly—whatever may be the experience of others, much more plainly than a manuscript lying in a cupboard could ever have done—how much I myself have still to learn both historically and materially."[8] He was especially disturbed by the way many of his allies within the dialectical theology movement responded to the book. Some of his allies received it positively but began to use Barth's arguments to support claims with which Barth himself strongly disagreed. This misuse of his ideas caused Barth to worry that his arguments had not been clear. Other allies sharply criticized the book. They thought Barth drew too deeply from the Christian past, focused on classical doctrines at the expense of existential realities, and offered an argument that was philosophically underdeveloped. A few even accused Barth's theology of prompting his readers to convert to Catholicism. While Barth did not agree with these criticisms, they helped him realize that he was moving in a different direction than many thinkers within the dialectical theology movement.

The following years were tumultuous for Barth personally, theologically, and politically. Barth's personal challenges involved his marriage. In 1925, Barth was introduced to Charlotte von Kirschbaum by their mutual contact Georg Merz, and a friendship soon developed. Over the next few years, Barth encouraged von Kirschbaum in her theological studies, and von Kirschbaum began to assist Barth with his work. She even spent holidays with Barth and his family. Their personal and professional relationship continued to deepen through 1926, when they realized that they had fallen in love. This created a tremendous crisis for Barth because he believed he faced an impossible choice. A divorce would have deeply negative ramifications for Nelly and his family, but he could not imagine living apart from the woman he loved. He also could not imagine pursuing his theological work without her help. Early in 1929, Barth invited von Kirschbaum to officially become his secretary and assistant. This decision raised tensions in Barth's marriage, and by that summer the situation became unbearable. Barth and Nelly discussed the possibility of a divorce, but they could not agree to it.

8. Karl Barth, *Church Dogmatics* I/1, rev. ed. (Edinburgh: T&T Clark, 1975), xi.

Instead, von Kirschbaum moved into the Barth house that October and dwelled with the family for the next three decades. "The result," Barth's biographer Eberhard Busch concludes, "was that they bore a burden which caused them unspeakably deep suffering."[9] While divorce remained a real possibility for several years, somehow they made the situation work. Nelly managed the household, and von Kirschbaum became "Aunt Lollo" to the children. She worked alongside Barth by handling administrative matters, performing research, editing his writings, and providing feedback on his ideas. Her work for Barth ended in 1964 when she moved to a nursing facility due to the onset of dementia. Together, Karl and Nelly visited her there every Sunday, and Nelly continued to do so in the years following her husband's death. After von Kirschbaum died in 1975, Nelly made the decision to bury her in the Barth family plot.

Barth's personal challenges were mirrored by theological ones, and they came as a result of Barth's realization that he again needed to rethink his theology from the ground up. One of the events that sparked this realization occurred in February 1929, when Barth invited Jesuit theologian Erich Przywara to visit Barth's seminar on Thomas Aquinas and talk about his doctrine of the analogy of being (*analogia entis*). Przywara's ideas deeply challenged Barth, and he realized that he had yet to offer a viable Protestant alternative to the rich theology of the Catholic tradition. So instead of spending the summer of 1929 writing the next volume of his dogmatics, as he had planned, Barth spent the summer reading and thinking. His goal was to figure out what a theology that begins with the Word of God looks like. "I had to learn," Barth later recalled, "that Christian doctrine, if it is to merit its name and if it is to build up the Christian church in the world as she must needs be built up, has to be exclusively and conclusively the doctrine of Jesus Christ—of Jesus as the living Word of God spoken to us."[10] His research produced immediate dividends, as can be seen in the bolder and more precise approach he deploys in his lecture "The Holy Spirit in the Christian Life" that October.[11]

Barth continued to refine his ideas over the next two years in conversation with Anselm's writings, on which he taught a seminar and then later wrote a book.[12] Anselm's account of the relationship between faith and reason

9. Busch, *Karl Barth*, 186.

10. Karl Barth, *How I Changed My Mind* (Richmond: John Knox, 1966), 43.

11. See Karl Barth, *The Holy Spirit and the Christian Life: The Theological Basis of Ethics*, trans. R. Birch Hoyle (Louisville: Westminster John Knox, 1993).

12. See Karl Barth, *Anselm: Fides Quaerens Intellectum; Anselm's Proof of the Existence of God in the Context of His Theological Scheme*, trans. Ian W. Robertson (Richmond: John Knox, 1960).

taught Barth how to build a theology on the basis of God's revelation in Jesus Christ. This theology would begin with the faith that comes in response to God's actions in history, and then it constantly would be tested by these divine actions to see if it corresponds to what God has revealed. The theologian would proceed with the goal of understanding what must be true about God's being in light of what God does in history. These insights served as the basis for Barth's revised lectures "The Prolegomena to Theology" that eventually would be revised as the text of *Church Dogmatics* I/1. He delivered these lectures at the University of Bonn, where he moved in the spring of 1930 to take up a new teaching position. In addition to his lecture courses in dogmatics, Barth continued to offer exegetical courses and seminars on major figures. He also added a series of courses on key topics—such as the doctrine of justification and the problem of natural theology—that were central to his refined approach.

The sharpened content of Barth's theology related directly to the political challenges he faced during this period. The early 1930s were a time of tremendous political turmoil in Germany; Adolf Hitler and his National Socialists preyed on this turmoil to advance their nationalist and anti-Semitic vision. After he came to power in 1933, Hitler moved to solidify his control of every facet of Germany society, including the Protestant church. There Hitler found a group of like-minded pastors and theologians known as the *Deutsche Christen* (German Christians). They defended Nazi policies on the basis of natural law and an idiosyncratic interpretation of Scripture, and they appealed to the authority of the new Nazi government to enforce their vision for the church. One of their key administrative decisions was to remove every Christian pastor with Jewish heritage from their church positions.

Barth's opposition to the German Christians was definitive and vocal. He began a new journal, *Theological Existence Today*, to serve as an outlet for writings that challenged their theology. With other pastors and theologians, he also began organizing to form a "confessing" alternative to the German Christians. In October 1933, due to the involvement of Gogarten and other dialectical theologians in the German Christian movement, Barth withdrew from the editorial board of his journal *Zwischen den Zeiten* and wrote a prominent farewell essay to the movement he had helped found.[13] Barth continued to speak and preach publicly in opposition to the German Christians throughout the end of 1933 and into the early months of 1934.[14] His activities

13. This essay can be found in chap. 9.
14. For an example of Barth's activities during this period, see his Advent sermon in chap. 31.

soon aroused the attention of the Nazi administration, and they brought him in for a three-hour interrogation in April 1934.[15]

The Nazi intimidation tactics did not slow Barth's work against the German Christians. In May 1934, he helped compose the Barmen Declaration, which was adopted as the foundational theological document of the Confessing Church at the end of that month. It begins with the unambiguous statement that "Jesus Christ, as he is attested to us in Holy Scripture, is the one Word of God which we have to hear, and which we have to trust and obey in life and in death."[16] The implication was clear: anyone who attempted to place the Word of God beneath the word of Adolf Hitler or any other figure is living a false Christian existence. Due to these activities and his refusal to take an oath of loyalty to Hitler, Barth was suspended from his teaching duties in November 1934. Soon he was banned from all public speaking before finally being dismissed from his teaching position in June 1935.

After his dismissal from Bonn, Barth was unemployed for less than a week before the University of Basel offered him a chair in systematic theology. Barth quickly accepted and returned to Switzerland with his family in July 1935. Once there, he dedicated himself primarily to his teaching and writing. He taught a variety of lecture courses and seminars for both undergraduate and graduate students, and he even served as a faculty administrator. Most of his energy, however, was devoted to working on his *Church Dogmatics*. He found the task all-consuming. He composed the material for delivery as lectures for his courses on dogmatics, which he taught every semester. He lectured for four hours during most weeks, requiring approximately thirty to forty hours of preparation. The average lecture consisted of about eight pages of text. After he delivered a lecture, there was little time for revision. He had to set them aside for publication and move on to the next lecture.[17]

In addition to his ever-growing list of publications, Barth traveled internationally several times in the years before World War II. Among other travels, he gave prominent lectures in Hungary, Scotland, the Netherlands, and Denmark; provided training courses for groups of pastors in France and Great Britain; and received honorary doctorates from the University of St. Andrews and Oxford University. These lectures and events cemented Barth's reputation as one of the world's most influential theologians. They also provided Barth with the opportunity to encourage his hosts to support the Confessing Church in its struggle against the German Christians and Adolf Hitler. Barth offered

15. See Busch, *Karl Barth*, 231.
16. For the text of this declaration, see chap. 32.
17. For these details, see Busch, *Karl Barth*, 373.

what support he could from his home in Switzerland. He started another journal, *Theologische Studien* (Theological Studies), to serve as an outlet for theological opposition to the Nazi government. After the war began, Barth wrote a series of open letters encouraging the Confessing Church and the various nations associated with the Allied cause.[18] At the same time, he criticized the neutral Swiss government and its people for not doing enough to help support those affected by the war. He acted to fill in the gap by raising funds for exiled German scholars as well as Jewish refugees who made it across the Swiss border.

When the war ended, Barth looked for ways to help the German people rebuild their nation and church. He criticized the Allied reconstruction efforts for being both insufficient and shortsighted because he thought the leaders of Germany were not being taught how to live in peace and freedom. Barth was concerned that many of the church administrators who supported Hitler remained in their positions, and he worried that the theological problems that had led to the German Christian movement had never been resolved. With these concerns in mind, Barth readily accepted the invitation to spend two semesters back at the University of Bonn as a guest professor. He lectured without notes in the ruins of the university, with his topics ranging from dogmatics to the relationship between the church and the state.[19] When he was not teaching, Barth traveled around Germany to preach, give lectures, and conduct radio interviews. His theme was political and theological reconciliation, and his goal was to lay the theological groundwork for a new vision of German society.

Barth's experiences in Germany and his growing concerns about the new atomic age convinced him that the world was entering a critical period. He wanted to do whatever he could to help the church lead the way toward peace. Barth used his stature to develop relationships with international church leaders and advocate for new avenues of cooperation among church bodies. Through these relationships, he helped lay the groundwork for the first assembly of the World Council of Churches in 1948, where he delivered the opening address. He also worked heavily behind the scenes to make preparations for the second assembly, which took place in 1954. During these years, Barth repeatedly was drawn into debates about the Cold War between the Western nations led by the United States and the Eastern bloc dominated by the Soviet Union. Many people wanted him to stand against communism in the same way that he had stood against the National Socialists, but Barth

18. For an example of these writings, see his "Letter to American Christians" in chap. 33.
19. For a selection from these lectures, see chap. 34.

refused to do so. Instead, he took the unpopular stance of criticizing both the capitalist excesses of the West and the totalitarianism of the East, and he argued that the church had no responsibility to choose one side over the other. Instead, the church should articulate and embody a third way that pointed beyond fear toward the peace of Christ.

As the 1950s continued, Barth began to feel the weight of his age and the pressure to complete his dogmatics. He began to turn down speaking engagements and travel opportunities to focus on his writing. His subject was the doctrine of reconciliation, and the volumes of the *Church Dogmatics* published during these years show Barth at the height of his theological power. His thinking is sharp and incisive, his tone confident and eloquent, and his ideas innovative yet steeped in biblical categories and exegesis. Along with his theological work, Barth's relationships also played an important part in his life during these years. He enjoyed being a grandfather and spending time with his family. Barth regularly preached on Sunday mornings to the inmates at the state prison of Basel.[20] He carried on lively correspondence with thinkers from around the world and welcomed a steady stream of visitors into his home for conversation. Students were coming to Basel in droves to study with him, and he invested in their work. He offered critiques of their writing, gave them theological and personal advice, and encouraged the development of their ideas. Barth found the work of younger Catholic theologians especially interesting because their innovative ideas gave him hope that the Catholic Church was moving in a positive direction.

After his retirement in 1962, Barth's pace of work slowed. He traveled to the United States to give a series of lectures that later would be published as *Evangelical Theology*.[21] When he returned home, he kept a busy schedule of correspondence, meetings, and writing until a series of health crises left him unable to work for much of the period between 1964 and 1966. During this same period, Charlotte von Kirschbaum began to show signs of illness and eventually entered a nursing home. From this point on, Barth's writing output nearly halted. He continued to read widely, however, and he paid especially close attention to the proceedings of the Second Vatican Council. In part due to his strong relationship with younger Catholic scholars, the Vatican invited Barth to serve as a Protestant observer to the council in 1965. He was unable to accept due to his health, but he recovered enough by the following summer to make a visit to Rome. In September 1966, Barth traveled to the Vatican to

20. For a collection of these sermons, see Karl Barth, *Deliverance to the Captives* (New York: Harper & Row, 1978).

21. Karl Barth, *Evangelical Theology: An Introduction* (New York: Holt, Rinehart & Winston, 1963).

spend a week dialoguing with Catholic officials, including Pope Paul VI, about the text of the Second Vatican Council. He later described his conversations that week as being marked by "brotherly trust, frankness, and relevance."[22]

After his return from Rome, Barth supervised the publication of one last volume of his *Church Dogmatics*, a fragment covering the doctrine of baptism, in 1967.[23] He would leave the rest of his planned volumes unfinished. Barth struggled with the new realities of his life, and he often found himself missing the excitement of his early years. He spent most of his time in his home reading, maintaining correspondence, and listening to music. But he also wrote and delivered lectures whenever he could. In February 1968, his interest in ecumenical work prompted him to deliver a lecture on the future of Protestant and Catholic theology in a joint appearance with Hans Urs von Balthasar. In that lecture he spoke of the ongoing work of the risen Christ to lead his people. "Life in the church," Barth says, "means existence in the renewal that he, Jesus Christ himself, carries out among and to his own people."[24] He decided to take up this theme again later that year, at what turned out to be the end of his life. Early in December 1968, he received an invitation to deliver a lecture to a gathering of Catholic and Protestant leaders that would take place the following month. Given his interest in ecumenical matters, Barth readily accepted the invitation and began writing the lecture on the evening of December 9. His argument focused on the centrality of Jesus Christ for the one church, both Catholic and Protestant. "He, Jesus Christ, is the old and is also new. He it is who comes [to the church] and to whom the church goes, but goes to him as him who was."[25] Late that evening—with this message about Jesus Christ and his church on his mind—Barth broke off writing and went to bed. He died peacefully during the night.

22. Karl Barth, *Ad Limina Apostolorum: An Appraisal of Vatican II*, trans. Keith R. Crim (Richmond: John Knox, 1968), 12.

23. See Karl Barth, *Church Dogmatics* IV/4 (Edinburgh: T&T Clark, 1969).

24. Karl Barth, "Kirche in Erneuerung," in *Einheit und Erneuerung der Kirche: Zwei Vorträge*, by Karl Barth and Hans Urs von Balthasar (Freiburg: Paulusverlag, 1968), 12.

25. Karl Barth, *Final Testimonies* (Grand Rapids: Eerdmans, 1977), 59.

PART 1

Barth's Theological Development

Karl Barth's theology developed in significant ways over the course of his career as he grew in knowledge, clarified his intentions, and considered new questions.[1] Discerning the nature of these changes is essential to an accurate interpretation of his work. Many, if not most, misinterpretations of Barth's theology result from a lack of attention to the details of his theological development. For example, consider Barth's argument in the second edition of *The Epistle to the Romans*, published in 1922 (chap. 2). It would be a mistake to cite a claim from *Romans* as "Barth's view" without accounting for the changes that took place in his theology in the decades that followed. Barth himself later remarked that his argument in *Romans* was both right and wrong. On the one hand, he always insisted that his criticism of Protestant liberalism in the book was correct: "We were certainly right! . . . There never could be a question of denying or reversing that change."[2] On the other hand, by the 1930s, Barth was warning his readers that his argument in *Romans* did

---

1. This introduction consists of a revised version of an earlier essay. See Keith L. Johnson, "A Reappraisal of Karl Barth's Theological Development and His Dialogue with Catholicism," *International Journal of Systematic Theology* 14, no. 1 (January 2012): 1–23.

2. Karl Barth, *The Humanity of God* (Richmond: John Knox, 1960), 41.

not do justice to the reality of the incarnation.[3] He also later admitted that he possessed "an uncertain grip" on Paul's letter when he wrote the book and that his misinterpretation of key passages produced a "one-sidedness" in his theology.[4] In his lecture "The Humanity of God" (chap. 10), Barth identifies the source of the problem: his early theology so strongly emphasizes God's distinction from humanity that it fails to account for the reality that God has decided to live together with humanity in Jesus Christ.

These qualifications mean that any interpretation of Barth's theology that appeals to *Romans* needs to account both for what Barth wrote in 1922 *and* the content of his later work. A failure to do so might lead an interpreter to read the text of *Romans* correctly but to misrepresent Barth's theology. To illustrate, a reader could cite a claim from *Romans* as "Barth's view" even though the later Barth would disagree with it. Or an interpreter could criticize Barth's argument in *Romans* and then dismiss "Barth's theology" even though the later Barth might agree with this criticism. Or a reader could cite a claim from *Romans* to make the case that Barth would support a particular view even though the later Barth might have strongly criticized such a view. The list of possible misinterpretations goes on—and *Romans* is just one of many works from Barth that could be misused in this way.

While the development in Barth's theology makes the interpretation of his work challenging, it also reflects Barth's core convictions about the practice of theology. He pursued his work with the awareness that, as a human, he was fallible and liable to make mistakes. Whenever Barth realized that he had fallen into an error—or if he learned something that altered his perspective—then he quickly adjusted his position. He did not see this willingness to change as a flaw or a sign of intellectual weakness. Barth described himself as "a good example of a theologian who is clearly a human being and who lives in time and moves with the time."[5] He also rejected the assumption that theologians should seek to create a comprehensive system where everything fits and every question is answered. In Barth's view, the theologian's primary task is to help the church think and speak rightly about the God revealed in Jesus Christ. "Theology is a science and a teaching," he says, "which feels itself responsible to the living command of this specific subject and to nothing else in heaven or on earth, in the choice of its methods, its questions and answers, in its concepts and language, its goal and limitations."[6] In

---

3. Karl Barth, *Church Dogmatics* I/2 (Edinburgh: T&T Clark, 1957), 50.

4. Karl Barth, *Church Dogmatics* II/1 (Edinburgh: T&T Clark, 1957), 634–35.

5. See Karl Barth, "Gespräch in Princeton II," in *Karl Barth Gesamtausgabe*, vol. 25, *Gespräche: 1959–1962* (Zurich: Theologischer Verlag Zürich, 1995), 521.

6. Karl Barth, *Dogmatics in Outline* (New York: Philosophical Library, 1949), 5.

line with this conviction, Barth believed that a theologian's method should not determine the content of the theology. Rather, the subject matter of theology—God's revelation in Jesus Christ—should shape the content of a theologian's method.

Two characteristics of Barth's theological development make it fairly straightforward to grasp. First, the majority of Barth's development takes place early in his career, with most of it happening in the years between 1920 and 1932. Close attention to Barth's writings from these years enables readers to understand the questions and answers that set the trajectory of Barth's thought as he begins his *Church Dogmatics*. Second, Barth's development occurs as a series of internal adjustments along a single christological trajectory. He begins his career with the conviction that God's revelation in Jesus Christ is the key to human knowledge of God, and he never wavers from this conviction. His development takes place because he gains a clearer understanding of the implications of this conviction over time. Barth described this process as gradual clarification of his thinking. He never concluded that his early theology was completely wrong; rather, he thought that he simply had failed to understand and express his convictions clearly. In his own words, he did not change his mind as much as he engaged in the "deepening and application of that knowledge which, in its main channels, [he] had gained before."[7] Or, as he put it when he explained why he decided to abandon his *Christian Dogmatics* in favor of a new *Church Dogmatics*, "I could still say what I had said. I still wished to do so. But I could not do it in the same way. What option had I but to begin again at the beginning, saying the same thing, but in a very different way?"[8]

The selections featured in part 1 provide glimpses into the different stages of Barth's development from the second edition of *The Epistle to the Romans* onward. When read alongside the selections from Barth's *Church Dogmatics* featured in part 2, the full range of Barth's development over the course of his academic career can be seen. This development can be divided into four distinct stages.

The first stage takes place from 1920, when Barth began writing the second edition of *Romans*, until the spring of 1924, when he began to compose his lectures on dogmatics in Göttingen. During this period Barth's goal is to confront the errors of Protestant liberalism by undermining its key claims. He believed his most pressing challenge was to explain why God— rather than the human experience of God—is the proper subject matter

7. Karl Barth, *How I Changed My Mind* (Richmond: John Knox, 1966), 42.
8. Karl Barth, *Church Dogmatics* I/1, rev. ed. (Edinburgh: T&T Clark, 1975), xi.

of theology. In the second edition of *Romans* (chap. 2), Barth answers this question by arguing that humans cannot know God on their own terms or by their own efforts. This knowledge comes strictly as the result of God's act to reveal himself in Jesus Christ. This revelation occurs definitively in the resurrection of Jesus, the moment in which the truth about history is unveiled. The resurrection is the crisis of history, the moment when the sovereign God judges and negates creation by revealing its true foundation in Christ.

During this same period, Barth also began to consider the question of how God can be the subject matter of theology without falling under human control. He addressed this question in his 1922 lecture "The Word of God as the Task of Theology" by advocating a dialectical approach (chap. 3). He argues that theologians ought to say something about God because people ask them questions that deserve answers. The problem is that they are unable to say anything about God because God is infinitely distinct from all human concepts or ideas. The proper response to these two realities is to live in the tension between them: "We ought to do both, to know the 'ought' and the 'not able to,' and precisely in this way give God the glory."[9]

Barth develops related ideas in his response to Adolf von Harnack's open letter (chap. 4). He challenges Harnack's scientific approach to Scripture because he thinks it treats the Word of God as a creaturely object accessible by human reason. Barth insists that God cannot be known through historical study or reason alone. Instead, this knowledge comes strictly as the result of God's act to reveal himself in and through creaturely history. Scripture testifies to this revelation, but it does so only because of God's action in his Word and Spirit. Barth adds depth to this argument in his book on 1 Corinthians, *The Resurrection of the Dead* (chap. 5). He argues that, because the resurrection of Jesus Christ unveils the true nature of creation, all Christian thinking should proceed on the basis of it. In this sense, even though the resurrection of the dead is an event that will happen one day in the future, it defines the meaning of history in the present. The real truth about creation is not accessed through historical investigation but is known only through God's revelation in Christ.

The second stage of Barth's development takes place from 1924 through the early part of 1929, when Barth made his first attempts to write his own dogmatic theology. Barth later recalled that these years were challenging because he could no longer simply attack "errors and abuses" but now had "to

---

9. Karl Barth, "The Word of God as the Task of Theology," in *The Word of God and Theology*, ed. and trans. Amy Marga (London: T&T Clark, 2011), 151.

say what [he] really thought."[10] This task was complicated by his convictions about God's transcendence and his worries about the human tendency to view God's revelation as an object to be possessed and controlled. Barth needed to show how God's revelation can take place *in* history without being transformed *into* history.[11]

Barth addresses this problem in his *Göttingen Dogmatics* (chap. 6). He argues that, while humans encounter God when God reveals himself to them in Jesus Christ, they do so only indirectly. God is present in Christ, but this revelation remains hidden in the veil of the human nature of Jesus of Nazareth. This dialectic enables Barth to affirm God's revelation in history while preserving God's distinction from history. Barth applies this doctrine through the phrase *Deus dixit* (God has spoken). God's revelation takes place as a Word-event, an address that occurs as an encounter between two subjects, God and the human. Since God is the primary subject in this encounter, his act of revelation is an eschatological event that cannot be defined or contained within the category of created history.

After developing these insights in his dogmatic lectures in Münster, Barth eventually came to the realization that he needed to refine his approach yet again. This realization inaugurates the third stage of Barth's development, which runs from 1929 through 1938. Barth's transition into this stage occurred after he invited the Jesuit theologian Erich Przywara to visit his seminar on Thomas Aquinas in February 1929. Przywara spent two days with Barth and his students, discussing his doctrine of the analogy of being (*analogia entis*) and its relationship to Catholic theology. Barth later described these conversations as "overwhelming," and it soon becomes clear why.[12] Like Barth, Przywara emphasized God's distinction from creation and the importance of God's revelation. But Przywara also emphasized that humans possess an intrinsic, created capacity to receive this revelation. While Barth explored the idea of such a capacity in his early dogmatics lectures, he had not definitively embraced or denied it.[13] Przywara's use of the concept provided Barth with the clarity he needed. Przywara appealed to this intrinsic human capacity to develop a comprehensive natural theology that draws all human thought about God into a theological metaphysics centered around the human

10. This remark is cited in Eberhard Busch, *Karl Barth: His Life from Letters and Autobiographical Texts* (Grand Rapids: Eerdmans, 1981), 156.

11. See Karl Barth, *The Göttingen Dogmatics: Instruction in the Christian Religion*, vol. 1 (Grand Rapids: Eerdmans, 1991), 58–59.

12. See Karl Barth and Eduard Thurneysen, in *Karl Barth Gesamtausgabe*, vol. 4, *Karl Barth–Eduard Thurneysen Briefwechsel: 1921–30* (Zurich: Theologischer Verlag Zürich, 1974), 652.

13. See Johnson, "Reappraisal of Karl Barth's Theological Development," 11–13.

consciousness.[14] This approach worried Barth because he thought it began from an abstract view of human being and produced a theology shaped by the limits of human subjectivity.[15]

Barth grew especially alarmed, however, when he realized that his own dogmatic theology had not closed the door to this kind of approach. He knew that he needed to refine his views in order to avoid confusion and error, but now he faced a new and complex problem. He had to describe God's relationship with humanity without presupposing that humans have an intrinsic capacity for this relationship by virtue of their creation by God, because he thought this kind of intrinsic capacity would leave God's revelation open to human manipulation. But he wondered how he could do so.

Barth found the answer in the Protestant doctrine of justification by grace alone through faith alone. He appealed to this doctrine just three weeks after Przywara's visit during his lectures "Fate and Idea in Theology," where he displays a new clarity on these issues.[16] The same patterns of thought show up in his lectures on ethics that same semester, where his approach is markedly different than it was the summer before. Whereas previously he had displayed an openness to the concepts of the orders of creation and natural law, Barth now concentrates on the sinful human's "hostility" to God, explaining to his students that "the concept of faith is the necessary turning point in [his] outlook."[17] The following summer, instead of continuing work on his dogmatics as planned, Barth spent his time reading the work of Martin Luther. He displays the fruit of this reading in his October 1929 lectures, "The Holy Spirit and the Christian Life" (chap. 7), where he draws on Luther's doctrine of justification to draw a sharp distinction between Przywara's analogy of being and his own "true" analogy of being.[18] Barth locates the distinction in the fact that Przywara's analogy begins with an *ideal* human, the human as created, while his begins with the *actual* human, the human as sinner. He thinks that while Przywara's starting point leads him to an abstract, general view of God and God's relationship with humanity, Barth's own starting

---

14. For the mature form of Przywara's argument, see Erich Przywara, *Analogia Entis: Metaphysics; Original Structure and Universal Rhythm*, trans. John R. Betz and David Bentley Hart (Grand Rapids: Eerdmans, 2014).

15. For a full account of Barth's assessment of Przywara's theology, see Keith L. Johnson, *Karl Barth and the Analogia Entis* (London: T&T Clark, 2010), 63–157.

16. See Karl Barth, "Fate and Idea in Theology," in *The Way of Theology in Karl Barth: Essays and Comments*, ed. H. Martin Rumscheidt (Allison Park, PA: Pickwick, 1986), 25–61.

17. Karl Barth, *Ethics*, ed. Dietrich Braun, trans. Geoffrey W. Bromiley (New York: Seabury, 1981), 270. For Barth's remarks on justification, see *Ethics*, 274–94.

18. Karl Barth, *The Holy Spirit and the Christian Life: The Theological Basis of Ethics*, trans. R. Birch Hoyle (Louisville: Westminster John Knox, 1993), 5.

point leads him to the particular relationship established in and through the Word of God. He concludes that the most important thing that can be said about humans is not that they have been created by God or have a capacity to be addressed by God but that they are sinners saved by grace alone, through faith alone, prompted by the Word alone. Any analogy between God and humans must start from the basis of this faith.

Barth continued to refine his views while thinking and writing about Anselm over the next couple of years. Anselm's theology teaches Barth that the knowledge of God that humans have through faith and thus the human relationship with God in faith are distinct from the knowledge of God and relationship with God that humans have by virtue of creation. Barth explains that since humans are "sinful by inheritance," knowledge of God cannot take place by the "actualization of that power to know which was originally created in [them]." Instead, this knowledge comes through a second act of grace that gives humans a "modified understanding," a new rationality that comes from faith alone. As Barth puts it, "The ultimate and decisive capacity for the understanding of faith [*intellectus fidei*] does not belong to human reason acting on its own but has always to be bestowed on human reason" by God.[19] This bestowing takes place through Jesus Christ, who personally guarantees that the human knowledge of God in faith is analogous to "the truth which belongs" properly only to God. Christ himself thus serves as the security that the knowledge of God humans have by faith "is determined primarily by its object, . . . [by] God himself."[20]

These insights led Barth to an important conclusion: human knowledge of God takes place in and through the person of Jesus Christ as he unites himself to humans for the sake of their salvation. This is the insight that propels Barth into his *Church Dogmatics*. In the preface to *Church Dogmatics* I/1 (chap. 8), Barth definitively rejects the Roman Catholic *analogia entis* and offers "a Protestant theology which draws from its own source, which stands on its own feet."[21] He then argues that the knowledge of God that Christ provides humanity takes the form of an analogy of faith (*analogia fidei*), which he describes in terms adopted from his interpretation of the Protestant doctrine of justification. Just as Protestants hold that humans do not contribute in any way to faith or salvation, Barth holds that intrinsic or created human capacities do not contribute in any way to the human's knowledge of God. He

19. Karl Barth, *Anselm: Fides Quaerens Intellectum; Anselm's Proof of the Existence of God in the Context of His Theological Scheme*, trans. Ian W. Robertson (Richmond: John Knox, 1960), 37–38.
20. Barth, *Anselm: Fides Quaerens Intellectum*, 46.
21. Barth, *Church Dogmatics* I/1, xiii.

explains that humans do have a capacity to receive God's revelation, but this capacity is "real only in faith. In faith, [the human] is created *by* the Word of God *for* the Word of God, existing *in* the Word of God and not in himself, not in virtue of his humanity and personality, not even on the basis of . . . creation, for that which by creation was possible for [the human] in relation to God has been lost by the fall."[22] So instead of making an intrinsic human capacity the presupposition of the reception of God's Word, Barth now holds that God's Word himself is the presupposition of the human capacity. This capacity is extrinsic to humans because it exists properly only in Christ and becomes operative only through the human's participation in Christ as a result of Christ's saving work.

These insights explain Barth's argument in his farewell letter to the dialectical theologians, written as he resigned from the editorial board of the journal *Zwischen den Zeiten* in 1933 (chap. 9). Barth had long worried that, even though many of his former allies affirmed the centrality of God's revelation in Jesus Christ, they believed this revelation could stand alongside insights drawn from natural theology. The consequences of this belief became apparent for Barth when Friedrich Gogarten and others offered theological justification for their support of the Nazi administration by appealing to insights drawn from their reflections on natural law. Barth's definitive rejection of their arguments and his unwillingness to associate with them flow directly out of the convictions he outlines in *Church Dogmatics* I/1.

Even though Barth's rejection of the idea that humans have an intrinsic capacity for God addresses the challenge of Przywara's theology and the errors of the German Christians, he soon realized that it opens up yet another problem. His attempt to address this new problem leads to the fourth and final stage of this thinking, which begins in 1938 and continues until his death in 1968. Catholic scholar Gottlieb Söhngen pointed out this new problem to Barth in 1934. Söhngen argued that, even though Barth concedes the existence of an analogous relationship between God and humans, by making this analogy extrinsic to human being, he ends up setting faith against being.[23] This opposition undermines his claims about the Christian's participation in Christ, since a participation in Christ is by definition a participation in *being*—namely, God's being—in and through Christ. For Barth's claims about humanity's participation in Christ and the analogy of faith to work, therefore,

---

22. Barth, *Church Dogmatics* I/1, 239.
23. See Gottlieb Söhngen, "The Analogy of Faith: Likeness to God from Faith Alone?," trans. Kenneth Oakes, *Pro Ecclesia* 21 no. 1 (2012): 56–75; Söhngen, "The Analogy of Faith: Unity in the Science of Faith," trans. Kenneth Oakes, *Pro Ecclesia* 21 no. 2 (2012): 169–94. Both articles were originally published in the German periodical *Catholica* in 1934.

he must presuppose an already-existing analogy of being between God and humans. So even if Barth refuses to admit it, his theology still functions under an implicit assumption that humans have an intrinsic created capacity to receive God's revelation.

In *Church Dogmatics* II/1, Barth responds by conceding Söhngen's point: "We can only observe that there is every justification for the warning that participation in being is grounded in the grace of God and therefore in faith. . . . We certainly must not neglect to take heed to this warning and comply with it."[24] This concession marks the point at which Barth embraces the necessity of an intrinsic human capacity for God, and it leads to perhaps the most critical moment in Barth's theological development. In many ways, Barth faces the same question that has occupied him his entire career: How can a theologian speak about God's revelation in history without making God available to history and thus make God's revelation subject to human manipulation and control? Behind this issue is the question of the continuity between creation and reconciliation, between nature and grace. After Barth's encounter with Przywara, he sought to deny that humans possess an intrinsic capacity to receive God's revelation because he thought this capacity led directly to a natural theology based on God's revelation in creation. This kind of natural theology was problematic to him because he believed it allowed abstract ideas to be imported into the doctrine of God. Such abstraction undermined God's particular revelation in Christ and opened the door to the kind of theology he had argued against since *Romans*. Barth had tried to avoid talking about an intrinsic capacity for God by turning to the analogy of faith (*analogia fidei*), but Söhngen had shown him that this move simply left him on the same ground as before. Now the question Barth faced was this: How can a theologian affirm that humans possess an intrinsic human capacity for God while also holding that human knowledge of God is determined solely by God's revelation in Jesus Christ and not also by knowledge gained through the human act of reflecting on God's revelation in the created order and human history?

Barth's answer is to say that both the created order and human beings are intrinsically determined by God's decision to reconcile the world in Jesus Christ. This is the argument working in the background of Barth's lecture "The Humanity of God" (chap. 10). It is a development of his earlier argument in *Church Dogmatics* II/2 where he claims that Jesus Christ is both the subject and object of election and thus the beginning and end of all created works (see chaps. 18 and 19 in part 2). Barth argues that the created order

24. Barth, *Church Dogmatics* II/1, 82.

is intrinsically defined by God's covenant of grace in Jesus Christ because it exists precisely in order to be the space where the covenant is executed. Likewise, human being is intrinsically defined by the covenant since Jesus Christ himself is the true human in relation to whom all other humans realize their humanity (see chap. 22). The human relationship with God takes place by grace alone through Christ alone as humans participate in Christ and, through him, in God. What humans intrinsically *are* as humans is determined at every moment by their union with Christ, who as the fully human and fully divine mediator also remains utterly distinct from humanity in his unique relation to the Father. This means that, while Barth can say that humans have an intrinsic capacity for God, he can also hold that this capacity is not a possession given to humans in creation but resides in Christ himself. There is an analogy of being between God and humans, but this analogy is grounded in God's act of reconciliation rather than his act of creation.

With this argument, Barth's theology reaches its mature and final form. From the very beginning of his career, Barth practiced theology on the basis of the conviction that human knowledge of God comes as the result of God's revelation in Jesus Christ. As he tried to work out the implications of this conviction, he struggled to explain how humans can possess this knowledge without determining its meaning and content. From the second edition of *Romans* until the end of his career, Barth works out this explanation in four stages along a single, Christ-centered trajectory. In each of the latter three stages, Barth revises his views to address new questions and problems, but these revisions occur so that he can better achieve the goal that shaped the theology of the first stage. This reveals continuity within Barth's theology since he does not retract his most basic insights from stage to stage but instead deepens and refines them until they reach the crescendo of the fourth and final stage. It also shows, however, that interpreters need to pay careful attention to the subtle shifts in Barth's thought from stage to stage if they are to understand what Barth is saying in any given stage or text accurately.

CHAPTER 2

The Epistle to the Romans

Introduction

Barth began work on *The Epistle to the Romans* in the summer of 1916, but he initially had no idea he would be writing a book. He was simply looking for a fresh start. The liberal theology of his youth no longer seemed viable, but he still had to mount the pulpit every Sunday and say something to his congregation. What would he say? He turned to Paul's letter to the Romans for help. In conversation with his friend Eduard Thurneysen, he spent the summer studying the text and filling a notebook with insights. By the end of the summer, these notes had turned into longer reflections, and the idea for a book began to form. He spent the next two years working on the manuscript. The book was finally published in December 1918 with an initial run of a thousand copies and little expectation. To Barth's surprise, it quickly created a theological firestorm, drawing strong reactions from pastors and scholars alike. Their positive and negative responses helped Barth see ways he could improve his argument. When the publisher approached him about a second edition, Barth took the opportunity to rework the manuscript from the ground up. The second edition of *The Epistle to the Romans* was published in 1922, and it became a foundational text for the dialectical theology movement with which Barth initially identified. He made no significant revisions to the text in the subsequent editions, and it was translated into English in 1933.

This excerpt is drawn from the first chapter, where Barth offers commentary on Romans 1. It displays Barth's dialectical style as well as several themes he develops at length throughout the book. Underlying Barth's analysis of Romans is his conviction that the Bible is first and foremost a book about God. He criticizes the idea of religion, which he defines as the ideas and practices by which humans attempt to transcend the creaturely. Such religion is doomed to failure because it leaves humans merely talking about themselves rather than God. The result is idolatry rooted in the failure to recognize that eternity and time are distinct. The eternal God cannot be known through natural historical or material means like other things in creation. Rather, God is known only as he breaks into creation from beyond in Jesus Christ. The resurrection of Jesus Christ is the singular point where time and eternity meet and is thus the crisis of history. It is the revelation that calls all prior understandings of reality and history into question by exposing the truth about God's relationship to humanity. The proper response to this revelation is faith, which begins with our recognition that God determines our knowledge of him by making himself known within creation while remaining distinct from it.

The Epistle to the Romans[1]

Jesus Christ our Lord. This is the Gospel and the meaning of history.[2] In this name two worlds meet and go apart, two planes intersect, the one known and the other unknown. The known plane is God's creation, fallen out of its union with Him, and therefore the world of the "flesh" needing redemption, the world of men, and of time, and of things—our world. This known plane is intersected by another plane that is unknown—the world of the Father, of the Primal Creation, and of the final Redemption.[3] The relation between us and God, between this world and His world, presses for recognition, but the line of intersection is not self-evident. The point on the line of intersection at which the relation becomes observable and observed is Jesus, Jesus of Nazareth, the historical Jesus—**born of the seed of David according to the**

---

1. Karl Barth, *The Epistle to the Romans*, 6th ed., trans. E. C. Hoskyns (Oxford: Oxford University Press, 1933), 29–31, 35–39, 44–45.

2. This opening line summarizes Barth's central claim in this excerpt: Jesus Christ unveils the truth about created reality and history in relation to God.

3. Barth uses the imagery of the intersecting planes to illustrate the dynamic intersection between the known world of creation and the unknown world of God. The phrase "the world of the Father" is drawn from a 1901 book of sermons by that title by Hermann Kutter (1863–1931), a Swiss theologian and Christian socialist who influenced Barth after his break from liberalism.

flesh. The name Jesus defines an historical occurrence and marks the point where the unknown world cuts the known world. This does not mean that, at this point, time and things and men are in themselves exalted above other times and other things and other men, but that they are exalted inasmuch as they serve to define the neighborhood of the point at which the hidden line, intersecting time and eternity, concrete occurrence and primal origin, men and God, becomes visible.[4] The years AD 1–30 are the era of revelation and disclosure; the era which, as is shown by the reference to David, sets forth the new and strange and divine definition of all time. The particularity of the years AD 1–30 is dissolved by this divine definition, because it makes every epoch a potential field of revelation and disclosure. The point on the line of intersection is no more extended onto the known plane than is the unknown plane of which it proclaims the existence. The effulgence, or, rather, the crater made at the percussion point of an exploding shell, the void by which the point on the line of intersection makes itself known in the concrete world of history, is not—even though it be named the "Life of Jesus"—that other world which touches our world in Him. In so far as our world is touched in Jesus by the other world, it ceases to be capable of direct observation as history, time, or thing.[5] Jesus has been—**declared to be the Son of God with power, according to the Holy Spirit, through his resurrection from the dead.** In this declaration and appointment—which are beyond historical definition—lies the true significance of Jesus. Jesus as the Christ, as the Messiah, is the End of History; and He can be comprehended only as Paradox (Kierkegaard), as Victor (Blumhardt), as Primal History (Overbeck).[6] As Christ, Jesus is the plane which lies beyond our comprehension. The plane which is known to us, He intersects vertically, from above. Within history, Jesus as the Christ can be understood only as Problem or Myth. As the Christ, He brings the world of the Father. But we who stand in this concrete world know nothing, and are incapable of knowing anything, of that other world. The Resurrection from

4. This is the human problem: God is eternal, but human knowledge of God is constrained within the limits of time. The "good news" is that Jesus Christ makes this relationship visible by entering into created history as the eternal Son of God. He is the point of intersection between eternity and time, and so he is the revelation of the God who saves.

5. Barth's reference to the "Life of Jesus" recalls studies of the historical Jesus by scholars like David Friedrich Strauss and Albert Schweitzer. Barth's point is that even though God reveals himself in the man Jesus who lived during the years 1–30, this revelation is not accessible to the empirical methods of historians.

6. The references here are to the Danish philosopher Søren Kierkegaard (1813–1855) and the theologians Johann Christoph Blumhardt (1805–1880) and Franz Overbeck (1837–1905). The writings of all three figures influenced Barth as he sought a new way forward after turning from the liberal theology of his former teachers.

the dead is, however, the transformation: the establishing or *declaration* of that point from above, and the corresponding discerning of it from below. The Resurrection is the revelation: the disclosing of Jesus as the Christ, the appearing of God, and the apprehending of God in Jesus.[7] The Resurrection is the emergence of the necessity of giving glory to God: the reckoning with what is unknown and unobservable in Jesus, the recognition of Him as Paradox, Victor, and Primal History. In the Resurrection the new world of the Holy Spirit touches the old world of the flesh, but touches it as a tangent touches a circle, that is, without touching it. And, precisely because it does not touch it, it touches it as its frontier—as the new world.[8] The Resurrection is therefore an occurrence in history, which took place outside the gates of Jerusalem in the year AD 30, inasmuch as it there "came to pass," was discovered and recognized. But inasmuch as the occurrence was conditioned by the Resurrection, in so far, that is, as it was not the "coming to pass," or the discovery, or the recognition, which conditioned its necessity and appearance and revelation, the Resurrection is not an event in history at all.[9] Jesus is *declared to be the Son of God* wherever He reveals Himself and is recognized as the Messiah, before the first Easter Day and, most assuredly, after it. This declaration of the Son of man to be the Son of God is the significance of Jesus, and, apart from this, Jesus has no more significance or insignificance than may be attached to any man or thing or period of history in itself— *Even though we have known Christ after the flesh, yet now we know him so no longer* (2 Cor. 5:16). What He was, He is. But what He is underlies what He was. There is here no merging or fusion of God and man, no exaltation of humanity to divinity, no overflowing of God into human nature. What touches us—and yet does not touch us—in Jesus the Christ, is the Kingdom of God who is both Creator and Redeemer. The Kingdom of God has become actual, is nigh at hand (Rom. 3:21–22). And this Jesus Christ is—**our Lord.** Through His presence in the world and in our life we have been dissolved as

7. Note that the resurrection is the moment when God declares himself from above *and* is discerned by humans from below. This is why the resurrection is the revelation that transforms history: it is the movement when Jesus Christ unveils history's true relation to the God who otherwise would remain unknown.

8. Barth adopts the image of a tangent touching a circle from Kierkegaard. See Søren Kierkegaard, *Søren Kierkegaard's Journals and Papers*, vol. 1, *A–E*, ed. and trans. Howard V. Hong and Edna H. Hong (Bloomington: Indiana University Press, 1967), 138.

9. Barth is careful to define the precise sense in which the resurrection of Jesus can be considered historical. He affirms that Jesus of Nazareth was a real historical person and that the resurrection happened outside the gates of Jerusalem. At the same time, he also insists that Christ is the revelation of the eternal God who is infinitely distinct from creation and beyond time. This means that Jesus cannot be described in *merely* historical terms, as if the truth about him could be captured through direct historical observation.

men and established in God.[10] By directing our eyes to Him our advance is stopped—and we are set in motion. We tarry and—hurry.[11] Because Jesus is Lord over Paul and over the Roman Christians, the word "God" is no empty word in the Epistle to the Romans.

From Jesus Christ Paul has received—**grace and apostleship.** Grace is the incomprehensible fact that God is well pleased with a man, and that a man can rejoice in God. Only when grace is recognized to be incomprehensible is it grace. Grace exists, therefore, only where the Resurrection is reflected. Grace is the gift of Christ, who exposes the gulf which separates God and man, and, by exposing it, bridges it.[12] . . .

I am not ashamed. The Gospel neither requires men to engage in the conflict of religions or the conflict of philosophies, nor does it compel them to hold themselves aloof from these controversies. In announcing the limitation of the known world by another that is unknown, the Gospel does not enter into competition with the many attempts to disclose within the known world some more or less unknown and higher form of existence and to make it accessible to men. The Gospel is not a truth among other truths. Rather, it sets a question-mark against all truths. The Gospel is not the door but the hinge.[13] The man who apprehends its meaning is removed from all strife, because he is engaged in a strife with the whole, even with existence itself. Anxiety

10. Even though a natural historian cannot discern the meaning of the resurrection simply by observing it, this does not leave humans without knowledge. The true meaning of the resurrection is declared to humans by Christ "wherever He reveals Himself." And since the risen Christ's self-declaration unveils the truth about the Creator and Redeemer of history, Christ unveils the true meaning of creation and history. This is what Barth means by the phrase "dissolved as men and established in God." Christ shows humanity that true history is *salvation* history, determined from beginning to end by his reign as the risen Lord.

11. This is a reference to Peter's description of believers as "waiting for and hastening the coming of the day of God" (2 Pet. 3:12). Barth used this phrase to describe the theology of Christoph Blumhardt (1842–1919), the son of Johann, who influenced his thinking in the years leading to this commentary.

12. Note that Christ does not elevate or fulfill our preexisting capacities but completely resets them. We are dissolved and then established; we are stopped and then set in motion; we wait and then hurry. Throughout the book, Barth relates this sense of movement to our justification: to be justified is to break with the known realm of creation and to move into that which is unknown and not yet realized. His point is that Christ's resurrection does not reveal the end of created history as much as it inaugurates the beginning of its future. And it is this future in Christ that determines the shape of our lives in the present.

13. If the gospel reveals the basis and meaning of created history itself, then any comparison between it and another religious idea is by definition a category mistake. The proper response to the gospel is not to ask, "Is this the right door to enter?"—i.e., is the gospel better or more rational than the alternatives? Rather, the proper response is to recognize that the gospel undercuts every alternative because it is the very presupposition of their existence.

concerning the victory of the Gospel—that is, Christian Apologetics—is meaningless, because the Gospel is the victory by which the world is overcome. By the Gospel the whole concrete world is dissolved and established. . . .

The Gospel of the Resurrection is the—**power of God,** His *virtus* (Vulgate), the disclosing and apprehending of His meaning, His effective pre-eminence over all gods. The Gospel of the Resurrection is the action, the supreme miracle, by which God, the unknown God dwelling in light unapproachable, the Holy One, Creator, and Redeemer, makes Himself known: *What therefore ye worship in ignorance, this set I forth unto you* (Acts 17:23). No divinity remaining on this side the line of resurrection; no divinity which dwells in temples made with hands or which is served by the hand of man; no divinity which needs anything, any human propaganda (Acts 17:24–25)—can be God. God is the unknown God, and, precisely because He is unknown, He bestows life and breath and all things. Therefore the power of God can be detected neither in the world of nature nor in the souls of men. It must not be confounded with any high, exalted force, known or knowable. The power of God is not the most exalted of observable forces, nor is it either their sum or their fount. Being completely different, it is the KRISIS of all power, that by which all power is measured, and by which it is pronounced to be both something and—nothing, nothing and—something.[14] It is that which sets all these powers in motion and fashions their eternal rest. It is the Primal Origin by which they all are dissolved, the consummation by which they all are established. The power of God stands neither at the side of nor above—supernatural!—these limited and limiting powers. It is pure and pre-eminent and—beyond them all. It can neither be substituted for them nor ranged with them, and, save with the greatest caution, it cannot even be compared with them. The assumption that Jesus is the Christ (Rom. 1:4) is, in the strictest sense of the word, an assumption, void of any content that can be comprehended by us. The appointment of Jesus to be the Christ takes place in the Spirit and must be apprehended in the Spirit.[15] It is self-sufficient, unlimited, and in itself true. And moreover, it is what is altogether new, the decisive factor and turning point in man's

14. Barth draws a sharp distinction between the gospel and all forms of religion, particularly those rooted in natural theology or innate piety. He worries that every religious ideal or act begins within the confines of human subjectivity and remains trapped there. The result is an idol shaped by human imagination rather than the living God. The gospel marks God's undoing of all religious striving because Christianity is not a type of religion but a break with *all* human religiosity. This is the point of Barth's use of the word KRISIS. The gospel is not the source or the pinnacle of human religious impulses. It is the power that frees humanity from these impulses.

15. This sentence captures a central insight of Barth's theology: God is known only as a result of an act of God. Barth will develop this idea more concretely later in his career (see chaps. 12 and 13).

consideration of God. This it is which is communicated between Paul and his hearers. To the proclamation and receiving of this Gospel the whole activity of the Christian community—its teaching, ethics, and worship—is strictly related. But the activity of the community is related to the Gospel only in so far as it is no more than a crater formed by the explosion of a shell and seeks to be no more than a void in which the Gospel reveals itself. The people of Christ, His community, know that no sacred word or work or thing exists in its own right: they know only those words and works and things which by their negation are sign-posts to the Holy One. . . .

The Gospel speaks of God as He is: it is concerned with Him Himself and with Him only. It speaks of the Creator who shall be our Redeemer and of the Redeemer who is our Creator. It is pregnant with our complete conversion; for it announces the transformation of our creatureliness into freedom. It proclaims the forgiveness of our sins, the victory of life over death, in fact, the restoration of everything that has been lost. It is the signal, the fire-alarm of a coming, new world.[16] But what does all this mean? Bound to the world as it is, we cannot here and now apprehend. We can only receive the Gospel, for it is the recollection of God which is created by the Gospel that comprehends its meaning. . . .

The Gospel does not expound or recommend itself. It does not negotiate or plead, threaten, or make promises. It withdraws itself always when it is not listened to for its own sake. "Faith directs itself towards the things that are invisible. Indeed, only when that which is believed on is hidden, can it provide an opportunity for faith. And moreover, those things are most deeply hidden which most clearly contradict the obvious experience of the senses. Therefore, when God makes alive, He kills; when He justifies, He imposes guilt; when He leads us to heaven, He thrusts us down into hell" (Luther).[17] The Gospel of salvation can only be believed in; it is a matter for faith only. It demands choice. This is its seriousness. To him that is not sufficiently mature to accept a contradiction and to rest in it, it becomes a scandal—to him that is unable to escape the necessity of contradiction, it becomes a matter for faith. Faith is awe in the presence of the divine incognito; it is the love of God that is aware of the qualitative distinction between God and man and God and the world; it is the affirmation of resurrection as the turning-point

16. Note how Barth describes the effect of the gospel as the transformation of creatureliness into freedom. Salvation is conceived not as moving from one form of creaturely life to another but as the complete transformation of created being altogether.

17. Barth draws this quote from Martin Luther's *The Bondage of the Will*. Luther is quoting 1 Sam. 2:6. See Martin Luther, *Luther's Works*, vol. 33, *Career of the Reformer III*, trans. and ed. Philip S. Watson (Philadelphia: Fortress, 1972), 62.

of the world; and therefore it is the affirmation of the divine "No" in Christ, of the shattering halt in the presence of God.[18] . . . The believer is the man who puts his trust in God, in God Himself, and in God alone; that is to say, the man who, perceiving the faithfulness of God in the very fact that He has set us within the realm of that which contradicts the course of this world, meets the faithfulness of God with a corresponding fidelity, and with God says "Nevertheless" and "In spite of this." The believer discovers in the Gospel the power of God unto salvation, the rays which mark the coming of eternal blessedness, and the courage to stand and watch.[19] . . .

The wrath of God is revealed against all ungodliness and unrighteousness of men. These are the characteristic features of our relation to God, as it takes shape on this side of the resurrection. Our relation to God is *ungodly*. We suppose that we know what we are saying when we say "God." We assign to Him the highest place in our world: and in so doing we place Him fundamentally on one line with ourselves and with things. We assume that He *needs something*: and so we assume that we are able to arrange our relation to Him as we arrange our other relationships. We press ourselves into proximity with Him: and so, all unthinking, we make Him nigh unto ourselves. We allow ourselves an ordinary communication with Him, we permit ourselves to reckon with Him as though this were not extraordinary behavior on our part. We dare to deck ourselves out as His companions, patrons, advisers, and commissioners. We confound time with eternity. This is the *ungodliness* of our relation to God.[20] And our relation to God is *unrighteous*. Secretly we are ourselves the masters in this relationship. We are not concerned with God, but with our own requirements, to which God must adjust Himself. Our arrogance demands that, in addition to everything else, some super-world should also be known and accessible to us. Our conduct calls for some deeper sanction, some approbation and remuneration from another world. Our well-regulated, pleasurable life longs for some hours of devotion, some prolongation into infinity. And so, when we set God upon

18. Barth draws the ideas in this sentence from Søren Kierkegaard. See Søren Kierkegaard, *Kierkegaard's Writings*, vol. 20, *Practice in Christianity*, ed. and trans. Howard V. Hong and Edna H. Hong (Princeton: Princeton University Press, 1991), 131–32.

19. If the gospel of God is the crisis of all creation, then faith in God requires an acknowledgment of this crisis. Barth depicts it as the trust that God will save us precisely in and through his negation of our creaturely existence.

20. We are *ungodly* whenever we think we know God but do not. This self-delusion happens whenever we place God within the realm of creatures and then arrange our relationship to him as if our service to him leads to a mutually beneficial relationship. The result of this creaturely picture of God is idolatry and false religion.

the throne of the world, we mean by God ourselves. In "believing" on Him, we justify, enjoy, and adore ourselves. Our devotion consists in a solemn affirmation of ourselves and of the world and in a pious setting aside of the contradiction. Under the banners of humility and emotion we rise in rebellion against God. We confound time with eternity. That is our *unrighteousness.*—Such is our relation to God apart from and without Christ, on this side resurrection, and before we are called to order. God Himself is not acknowledged as God and what is called "God" is in fact Man. By living to ourselves, we serve the "No God."[21]

Who hold the truth imprisoned in unrighteousness. This second characteristic is in point of time the first. Men fall prey first to themselves and then to the "No-God." First is heard the promise—*ye shall be as God!*—and then men lose the sense for eternity. First mankind is exalted, and then men obscure the distance between God and man. The nodal point in the relation between God and man apart from and without Christ is the unrighteousness of slaves. Thinking of ourselves what can be thought only of God, we are unable to think of Him more highly than we think of ourselves. Being to ourselves what God ought to be to us, He is no more to us than we are to ourselves. This secret identification of ourselves with God carries with it our isolation from Him. The little god must, quite appropriately, dispossess the great God. Men have *imprisoned* and encased the *truth*—the righteousness of God; they have trimmed it to their own measure, and thereby robbed it both of its earnestness and of its significance. They have made it ordinary, harmless, and useless; and thereby transformed it into untruth. This has all been brought to light by their ungodliness, and this ungodliness will not fail to thrust them into ever new forms of unrighteousness. If mankind be itself God, the appearance of the idol is then inevitable. And whenever the idol is honored, it is inevitable that men, feeling themselves to be the true God, should also feel that they have themselves fashioned the idol. This is the rebellion which makes it impossible for us to see the new dimensional plane which is the boundary of our world and the meaning of our salvation. Against such rebellion there can be revealed only the wrath of God.[22]

---

21. We are *unrighteous* whenever our religious impulses become the focus of our relationship with God. This leaves us with false worship, in part because we inevitably use our creaturely concept of God to facilitate our innate desires. The result of this religion is the exaltation of ourselves, which marks our rebellion against God.

22. Our unrighteousness and ungodliness go together, resulting in the "secret identification of ourselves with God" in the pattern of Adam and Eve. Not only does this sin evoke God's wrath, but it also leaves humans incapable of seeing Christ apart from the Spirit's help.

CHAPTER 3

"The Word of God as the Task of Theology"

Introduction

Barth delivered this lecture at a conference in Elgersburg, Germany, on October 3, 1922, at the invitation of his former teacher Martin Rade, who was the editor of the influential theological journal *Die Christliche Welt*. The conference gathered three to four hundred liberal Protestant academics and pastors associated with the journal. During the previous year's meeting in the fall of 1921, scholars Erich Foerster and Reinhard Liebe had issued strong criticisms of Barth's *The Epistle to the Romans*, and their essays later were published in the journal. Rade invited Barth to respond to his critics at the 1922 meeting. This event gave Barth the opportunity to defend himself, and it also gave him a chance to present his theology to some of the most influential thinkers in Germany.

Barth labored over the lecture and finished it only a few hours before he delivered it. His primary goal was to explain and defend the dialectical method he employs in his Romans commentary. Barth's practice of dialectic—which involves moving back and forth between claims while stressing their opposition to one another—challenges the liberal premise that we can speak correctly about God on the basis of a scientific account of history or religious experience. Barth rejects this premise on the basis of the distinction between time and eternity. His conviction is that, because theologians are constrained within creaturely time, they cannot know and speak the truth about the eternal God on their own. At the same time, however, he acknowledges that theologians have to say *something* about God, if only because people are constantly asking them to do so. The only way forward, as Barth sees it, is for theologians to account for God's distinction from creation and in that way to bear witness to God's revelation in Christ. Barth declares, "As theologians, we ought to speak of God. But we are humans and cannot speak of God. We ought to do both, to know the 'ought' and the 'not able to,' and precisely in this way give God the glory."[1]

This excerpt picks up in the middle of the lecture, where Barth is discussing the theologians' inability to speak about God. He explores three ways that theologians might attempt to speak about God: the ways of dogmatism, self-criticism, and dialectic. While each way has its own unique strengths and weaknesses, Barth's description of the way of dialectic provides one of the clearest accounts of his early theological method.

─────────── **"The Word of God as the Task of Theology"**[2] ───────────

We cannot speak of God. To speak of God in all seriousness would mean to speak on the grounds of revelation and faith. To speak of God would mean to speak that Word which can only come from God himself: the Word, *God becomes man.* We can say these three words, but it does not mean we have spoken the Word of God that contains the *truth.* Our theological task is to say that *God* becomes *human* and to say it as the Word of *God,* as *God* would say it. This would be the answer to the question put to us by terrified consciences. It would be the answer to the human's question about the redemption of his humanity. It is precisely this which must be sounded with trumpets in our churches and in our lecture halls—but differently than the way we scribes are used to—beyond the churches and lecture halls, out into the streets where people today are waiting for it. We stand in our pulpits and lecterns in order to say *this* to them. As long as we do not say *this* to them, we are speaking past them, and thus disappoint them.

This alone—note, God's Word alone—is the answer that possesses genuine transcendence and thus has the power to solve the riddle of immanence. This answer does not eliminate the question, nor merely underline and sharpen it,

1. Karl Barth, "The Word of God as the Task of Theology," in *The Word of God and Theology,* ed. and trans. Amy Marga (London: T&T Clark, 2011), 177.
2. Barth, "Word of God as the Task of Theology," in Marga, *Word of God and Theology,* 185–98.

or even audaciously assert that the question itself is the answer. It is an assertion, which, although true, has a way of being too explicit or too ambiguous when it comes from our mouths. No, the question must *be* the answer. It must be the fulfillment of the promise, the satisfying of the hungry, the opening of the blind eyes and deaf ears (cf. Isa. 35:5). We must *give* this answer, but this very answer we cannot give.[3]

I see three ways in which we can attempt to provide this answer. All three end up with the insight that we cannot give the answer. They are the ways of dogmatism, self-criticism, and dialectic. But note that this differentiation is only a conceptual one. No actual, respected theologian has taken only one of the three ways. We will encounter Luther, for example, in all three.

The first way is the way of *dogmatism*.[4] This way seeks to properly understand the human in his need and questioning by leaning more or less explicitly upon the Bible and dogma, presenting the familiar Christological, soteriological, and eschatological perspectives that have been developed out of the claim that God became human. Being reminded of Luther's sermons, I consider it better to go down *this* way—if one does not know any better—than to revert back to cultivating the spiritual life and piety with the help of history, even biblical history. For when we revert back, we lose sight of the things that are necessary and *not necessary* for humanity, and thereby forget what people are really asking of us: that we as theologians ought to speak of God. It is true that there are things to question in orthodoxy. However, orthodoxy contains a powerful, living memory of what is necessary and not necessary—more so than some of its theological opponents. It is this particular memory, and not merely custom or laziness that allows orthodoxy to be so effective time and again, religiously, ecclesiastically, and even politically. . . .

Why is this not how it works? Because the human's question about God is abolished by this kind of answer. He no longer has a question, for an answer stands in its place. But he is a human and as such, he cannot let the question go. For he himself, the human, is the question. If there is an answer for him, then it must take on his nature: it must itself become a question. But this does not mean simply speaking of God, or placing something before the human, even if it is the word "God," and demanding that he believe it. This

---

3. People ask theologians questions about God—Who is God? How does God relate to us?—because they want comfort in the face of death. The problem is that theologians cannot answer these kinds of questions because they involve divine realities that transcend creaturely life. Only God can answer these questions. The question driving Barth's essay, then, is this: How should theologians go about answering questions to which only God can respond?

4. The way of *dogmatism* involves appealing to the claims of Christian orthodoxy represented in the church's tradition. This approach addresses questions about God by appealing to the authority of Scripture and the tradition on the basis of God's unique relationship to them.

is precisely the point: The human can*not* believe what merely stands *before* him, even if what was *there* is also *here*. The human can*not* believe what is not *revealed* to him, what does not have the power and perfection to come *to him*. God alone is not God. He might be something else. The God who reveals himself—this is God. The God who becomes human is God. Dogmaticians do not speak of this God.[5]

The second way is the way of *self-criticism*.[6] This way does indeed provide clear, terribly clear, statements about the incarnation of God. With this way, anyone who wants to participate in God is bid to die, to surrender all individuality, every sense of self, all egoism; he must fall silent, become simple and open in order to become as purely receptive as the Virgin Mary when the angel appeared to her: "I am the servant of the Lord; let it be according to your word" [Luke 1:38]! God is not a This or a That, an object, a thing, an opposite, or a second thing. God is pure, all-filling Being. God is without physical qualities. Only the particular individuality of the human stands in God's way. Were this obstacle to finally and ultimately be eliminated, the birth of God would certainly occur in the soul. Even the way of mysticism is truly remarkable! Who has a right to berate it outright, when even the young Luther enthusiastically played with the best of them in the Middle Ages for a while?

It is quite remarkable that even the mystical way possesses the insight that when it comes to speaking of God, it can in no way be about the building up of the human but must fundamentally be about helping in the deconstruction of his existence. It possesses the insight that when it comes to speaking of God, the human is asking for the one who is *not himself*.

That is why I call this way the way of mysticism, which can also be understood as a form of idealism. It is a self-critical way. For the human places himself under judgment, he negates himself, because it is seen so clearly here that what must be overcome is the human as human. . . .

But the human cannot speak of God even in this way. The mystic wants to *claim*—and we are all a little bit mystic—that *God* is that which wants to fulfill the human who is himself annihilated, that *God* is the abyss into which the human has collapsed, the darkness into which he gives himself, the "No" under which he ought to stand. But we are in no position to *demonstrate* this. The only thing we are *certain* of, that which we can *demonstrate*, is always

5. The strength of dogmatism is that the orthodox tradition contains concrete answers to the questions people are asking about God, life, and death. These answers fail to satisfy, however, because they are an insufficient substitute for a word that comes directly from God.

6. Barth identifies the way of *self-criticism* with Christian mysticism. This approach addresses questions about God by drawing conclusions about God on the basis of God's infinite distinction from creaturely being.

only the negation, the negativity of the human. When we consider that the human *emerges* precisely *from* this negativity of his existence, *from* this question mark on the other side of all that makes up his life, we are stunned to discover that we are doing nothing else by following the self-critical way but making the question mark even more gigantic.[7] . . .

The third way is the way of *dialectic*.[8] It is by far the best way, not only because it is the Pauline-Reformation way, but also because the content is superior. This way presupposes the great truths of both dogmatism as well as self-criticism in their fragmentary nature and relative sufficiency. From the outset, this way takes seriously the positive unfolding of the thought of God on the one side and the critique of the human and all things human on the other. Neither one, however, happens on its own accord but with constant reference to their common presupposition, to the living truth itself, which itself is naturally not a reference. Rather, it stands in the center and gives each one its position and its negation, its sense and meaning. Here we consistently see the living truth, the decisive content of a genuine speaking of God—that God (really God!) becomes human (really human!).[9]

But how should we establish the necessary relationship of each side to the center? The true dialectician knows that this center is incomprehensible and invisible. He will let himself get carried away into direct communication as seldom as possible, for he knows that every direct communication about it, whether it is positive or negative, is *not* communication *about it*. Instead, it will always be *either* dogmatism *or* self-critique.[10] Only along this narrow

7. Even though the way of self-criticism accounts for God's distinction from creatures, it fails to address ultimate questions because it offers no way to receive an address directly from God. Instead, the questioner is left with a creaturely answer derived from the negation of creaturely being. No personal speech from God to the human occurs, and so the questioner is left with merely human answers.

8. Barth frames the way of *dialectic* as the higher synthesis of the previous two methods: it offers the positive claims of dogmatism while also maintaining a self-critical approach to creaturely being and life. By labeling it the "Pauline-Reformation way," he is both defending the integrity of his Romans commentary against its critics and claiming that it stands in line with the core convictions of the Protestant Reformation.

9. The central presupposition of the dialectical method is that God speaks personally to humans. The theologian's task is to bear witness to this divine speech, in part by not trying to replace it with human speech.

10. Direct communication about God is impossible because God's distinction from creation means that God always remains beyond the theologian's grasp. Dogmatism fails to uphold this distinction by saying too much—and doing so with great certainty. Self-criticism fails to maintain this distinction because it purports to be speaking directly about God when its insights are based on the negation of created being. No direct speech from God occurs, because God is merely identified as the being that exists beyond the limits of the creaturely. Creaturely being thus still determines the parameters of the theological claim.

cliff ridge can we walk—and keep walking, for if we stand still we will fall. It might be to the right or to the left, but it will definitely be down. Thus the only thing left is an appalling spectacle for all those overcome by dizziness, where we *keep looking* from one side to the other, from the position to its negation and the negation to its position. The only thing to do is to clarify the "Yes" in the "No" and the "No" in the "Yes," pausing no longer than a moment in the gaze of the "Yes" *or* the "No."[11] The only thing to do is to speak of the glory of God in creation (recalling Rom. 8:19–22) only to swiftly and strongly emphasize the complete hiddenness in which we perceive God in the natural world; to speak of death and transitoriness only to remember the majesty of an entirely different life that meets us in death. In the same way, the image of God in humans is by no means to be spoken of apart from the warning once and for all that the human as we know him is a fallen creature, whose misery we know more about than his glory.[12] That being said, however, sin should not be spoken of except to point out that we would not recognize it if it were not already forgiven us. According to Luther, that God has made the human righteous means nothing else than imputed righteousness [*justificatio impii*; Rom. 4:5 in the Vulgate]. Once the impious person realizes that he is impious and nothing more, he can then hear that he is righteous and nothing more. The only possible answer to the genuine insight into the imperfection of every human work is to eagerly get back to work. However, even after we have done everything we are required to do, we will still have to say that we are worthless slaves [Luke 17:10]. The present is only worth living in view of the eternal future, the beloved Last Day. But we are mere dreamers if we think that the future of the Lord is not standing right outside our door, today. "A Christian is a

11. Barth uses the image of the ridge to capture the reality that theology takes place as an *event*. Theologians are able to speak about God only as they "keep walking" forward while declaring both the "Yes" (that God speaks in created history) and the "No" (that the God who speaks cannot be grasped in creaturely terms). In this sense, theology involves the movement of faith as the theologian obediently traces out what God has revealed.

12. Barth illustrates the dialectical approach by responding to two common objections to the claim that God's infinite distinction from creation means that God is incomprehensible to us. The first objection insists that, because God reveals his eternal nature within the created order, humans must be able to know something true about God by reflecting on this order. Barth responds by saying that, while God does reveal his glory in creation (yes), humans are unable to perceive the truth about God on their own (no). The second objection appeals to the idea that humans were created in God's image to claim that humans can know something of God by reflecting on their own human nature, particularly the human conscience. Barth rejects this idea by arguing that, while humans are in God's image (yes), their fallen nature leaves them unable to derive any positive knowledge of God by reflecting on their own human being (no).

free lord over all things, subject to none. A Christian is a perfectly dutiful servant in all things, subject to all."[13]

I need not continue. Whoever has ears to hear will understand what I am getting at here. He understands that the question is the answer because the answer is the question. The moment the answer becomes audible to him, he becomes more eager than ever to ask new questions. Indeed, he would not have had the answer if he did not continue to have the question.

Faced with all this, an onlooker—a "prairie dweller" probably—will stand there confused, not understanding a thing.[14] Maybe he will whine about supernaturalism or atheism. He will see old Marcion emerging from his grave, and after him, Sebastian Franck, who are actually not the same. Perhaps he will even see it as Schelling's philosophy of identity. He will be shocked about the negation of the world that is so terrible that he no longer knows what is happening to him, and then he will be annoyed about the fact that an affirmation of the world ought to be possible precisely by this means, in a way he never could have dreamed of. He will rise up against the positive, then against the negative, and then again against the "unforgivable contradiction" with which each confronts the other.

What should the dialectician—a "son of the mountains" probably—answer, except to say: "My friend, you must understand that when you ask about *God*, when the talk is really from *God*, then you ought not to expect anything different from *me*. I have done all I could to alert you to the fact that my affirmation, like my negation, does not claim to be the truth of God. It only claims to be a *witness* to the truth of God who stands in the center, on the

13. Barth draws a link between his dialectical method and Martin Luther's doctrine of justification, because he thinks this method simply works out the implications of Luther's doctrine for the task of theology. In *The Freedom of the Christian*—the text that Barth cites here—Luther argues that Christians are simultaneously righteous and sinful, and that both truths must be affirmed in their fullness. He also insists that the dialectical reality of justification activates rather than paralyzes the Christian, since we will be free to serve our neighbor only when we know that our good works do not contribute to our salvation. In a similar way, Barth thinks that theologians are free to speak about God only when they realize that the truth of their speech rests with God rather than their own actions. See Martin Luther, *Luther's Works*, vol. 31, *Career of the Reformer I*, trans. and ed. Harold J. Grimm (Philadelphia: Fortress, 1957), 329–77.

14. The phrases "prairie dweller" and "son of the mountains" refer to the criticisms leveled against Barth by Erich Foerster at the previous year's conference. Foerster accused Barth, the "son of the Swiss mountains," of offering a theology that was impossible for everyday Christians living in the "flat land" to understand or implement. This charge of spiritual elitism prompted him to accuse Barth of Marcionism. A related charge of "supernaturalism" was issued at the same conference by Reinhard Liebe. Barth has both criticisms in his mind in this section. See Erich Foerster, "Marcionitisches Christentum: Der Glaube an den Schöpfergott und der Glaube an den Erlösergott," in *Die Christliche Welt* 35 (1921), cols. 809–27; Reinhard Liebe, "Der Gott des heutigen Geschlechts und wir," in *Die Christliche Welt* 35 (1921), cols. 850–53, 866–68, 883–89.

other side of every 'Yes' and 'No.' For this very reason, I have never affirmed without negating, never negated without affirming, because the one, like the other, is not the ultimate thing. I apologize if my *witness* to the ultimate thing is not enough for you and the answer you seek. It could be that I have not yet given clear enough witness to prevent any misunderstanding; that I have not yet lifted up the 'Yes' strongly enough through the 'No' and the 'No' strongly enough through the 'Yes.' It could be that you in fact could see nothing but that upon which the 'Yes' and the 'No' depend.[15]

"It could be, however, that my failure lies in the fact that you have not yet properly *asked*, that is, that you have not yet properly asked about *God*. If you had, we would have understood each other." Such is the way the dialectician could answer the onlooker, and he would probably be right.

He would *probably* be right, but maybe he *wouldn't* be—even in the face of the onlooker! For even dialectical speaking suffers from an inherent weakness. This becomes apparent when the dialectician wants to persuade, for then he is dependent upon having his conversation partner *first approach* him with the question of God. If he really speaks of God here, his answer will be the question at the same time. If he really speaks of God here, he will not be allowed to leave his conversation partner standing there shaking his head at the message that he does not yet have the right question. The dialectician would be better off shaking his own head about the fact that *he* apparently does not yet have the right *answer*, the answer which is the very question of his conversation partner. The dialectician's speaking would rest precisely on a very significant presupposition, namely, on the living, original truth, there in the center. His speaking itself is not, could not be, and should not be the framework for this presupposition. Rather, it should be an affirmation and a negation that obviously refers to this presupposition, this origin. But it must come primarily in the form of a *claim* that it is all this. The claim will sound *clear* to the right and to left, but a final claim showing that the right and the left are saying the same thing will sound *ambiguous*, very ambiguous.

How does human speaking become meaningful in a necessary and compelling way? How does it come to have power as a witness?[16] This is the problem that arises with particular force out of the dialectical method, because

15. Note how Barth's appeal to the category of "witness" changes the nature of the theological task. When the theologian receives a question about God, her task is not to answer it directly but instead to direct the questioner to God. This redirection does not mean that the theologian is idle, but, rather, it means that she has to do the hard work of declaring both the "Yes" and the "No" that must be said in order to prevent creaturely misunderstandings of God's speech.

16. This question flows out of the observations of the previous paragraph. If the dialectical theologian's task is simply to bear witness to God, what is the content of this witness? A

everything that could be done to make human speaking carry meaning and bear witness is done. On those occasions when dialectical speaking *has* proven itself to be meaningful and bear witness—as in the case of several interlocutors of Plato, Paul, and of the Reformers—it did not do so on the basis of the abilities and activities of the dialectician or his claims, which are in fact questionable, more questionable than any indignant onlooker could imagine. When it happens, it is because the dialectician's unambiguous and ambiguous claims allow the living truth in the center, the reality of God, to assert *itself*. It creates the question that is raised about it, and gives the answer that the human is looking for, because it already *is* precisely both: the right question and the right answer.

But the possibility that God *himself* speaks when the human speaks of him is not contained in the dialectical way as such. It arises where even this way *comes to an end*.[17] It is evident that one can also elude the claims of the dialectical theologian. In this respect, the dialectical theologian himself is no better than the dogmatic or self-critical theologian. The actual weakness of the dogmatic and self-critical theologian, his own inability to truly speak of *God*, and his compulsion to speak always about something else, appear in even more pronounced ways in the dialectical theologian. Precisely *because* he wants to say *it all*, and in view of the living truth itself no less, he becomes only more painfully aware of the unavoidable *absence* of this living truth in his saying it all. Even if God were to suddenly speak his own Word and give a sense and meaning to everything, beyond anything his conversation partner could say about it all, even then, *precisely* then, the dialectical theologian as such is proven wrong, and can only confess: "We cannot speak of God." Even if God himself speaks, it can only happen beyond that which could be said by the dogmaticians and the self-critics, and perhaps even more primitive speakers.

There is no reason why dialectical theology should be the *preferred* leader, even if it simply leads *up to* the front of this door that can only be opened from the inside. If it somehow imagines itself to be of special importance, even if only as preparation for that which God does, let it be clear that with

---

theologian who says too much or too little will fall off the ridge into the abyss. What, then, does true and faithful theological speech look like?

17. Barth answers the question about the nature of true theological speech by explaining that the theologian's task is to affirm what can and cannot be said about God *and then stop*. God's act of revealing himself to the questioner is not included within the method because God's speech cannot be contained within, or guaranteed by, any human act. From one perspective, this is the weakness of the dialectical method: at the end of the day, it gives the theologian no answers of her own to address the questions she receives. But this weakness is also a great strength because the theologian's silence is an acknowledgment that such questions can be answered by God alone.

all its paradoxes it can do no more *to this end* than a simple, direct word of faith and a humility.[18] In relation to the kingdom of God, any pedagogy can be good or bad—a stool may be high enough and the longest ladder may be too short to take the kingdom of heaven by force.

Now who—and this is more or less clearly every theologian—after seeing all this, after testing all the possibilities available in these three ways (and I have only given the viable possibilities) would not be distressed?

I now turn to the third claim which I would like to use to characterize our situation: *We ought to do both*. We ought to speak of God but cannot, and *precisely in this way, give God the glory*. There is not much to say about this statement. It can only stand there as a concluding stroke and confirm that everything is meant the way it all has been said.

The Word of God is the necessary but impossible task of theology. This is the conclusion to everything I have said up until this point. It is actually all I have to say on this topic. Now what? Does it mean a return to the low country where one appears to be a theologian but in reality is actually something completely different, something that others can be too, causing them to fundamentally *not* need us? I am afraid that even if we were capable of such a tour de force, the logic of the matter would soon lead us right back to where we stand now. Or should we move from a service of the *word* to a service of *silence*? As if it were easier and more possible to be still before God (really before *God*), than to speak of him! What kind of game is this supposed to be? Should theology just bid its farewell? Should we hang up our hats and become happy, like other people? But people are not happy. If they were, we would not be here. The pressure of our task is a sign of the plight of every other human task. If we were not here, other theologians would then be in the same situation. A mother cannot walk away from her children, and the shoemaker cannot walk away from his block, and we cannot be convinced that the dialectic of the children's nursery is any less effective than the dialectic of our theological study halls. Giving up theology makes as little sense as taking of one's life—nothing will come of it, and nothing will change by doing so. So, persevere. That is all. We ought to *know* both the necessity and the impossibility of our task.[19] What does this mean?

18. These two words—"faith" and "humility"—define the posture of the dialectical theologian. The theologian proceeds with faith that God will act and a humility to point in the direction of God without seeking to replace God's speech with the theologian's own words.

19. Barth paints a bleak picture of the task of theology here. As he sees it, the theologian is to be called to a task that is necessary but impossible, and so she lives in "distress" while unhappily persevering through hardships. It is interesting to compare this gray, almost bureaucratic depiction of the theologian to the depictions of the glad and playful theologian found in his later work. The difference between these depictions follows the trajectory of Barth's own

It means we hold our gazes steadfastly on that which is expected of us since we have been set in the place where we are now standing. The question is not what will come of it, and whether people will be satisfied with us. Our task only makes sense within the context as we know it of human life in its entirety, only in nature and culture, where questions arise about how this entirety as such makes sense within the world and God's creation. This question can only arise in the human. Therefore our task can be categorized only as that which cannot be categorized. Such logic, such a categorical imperative of objectivity, is a part of our vocation just like any other vocation.[20] But ours has *this* particular content. We must fix our eyes on this categorical imperative, like every railroad conductor does. More cannot be demanded from us; neither can any *less*.

As we consider our task, it must be equally remembered that only *God* can speak of God. The task of theology is the Word of God. This means the certain *defeat of all* theology and *of every* theologian. Even here we must not avoid the things that are meant to be seen, or divert our attention to one side or the other, toward the array of enlightening or unenlightening veiling and disguising of the facts of the matter. We must be clear about the fact that no matter which way we pursue, even if our names were Calvin or Luther, we would no more reach the goal than Moses did the Promised Land [cf. Deut. 34:4]. Even though it is truly worthwhile to be careful about choosing the way we must go, not settling for the first thing we find, we must keep in mind that our goal is the speaking of *God himself*. So we ought not to wonder when at the end of our ways, even if we have performed our task well (especially if we have done it well) our mouths *close*. . . .

All of my thoughts circle around the one point which is called "Jesus Christ" in the New Testament. Whoever says "Jesus Christ" may not say, "It might be possible," but, rather, must say, "It *is*." Yet which one of us is in the position to say "Jesus Christ"? *We* must satisfy ourselves with the fact that "Jesus Christ" *has been said* by his first witnesses. Our task is to believe in their witness, to believe in the promise, and to be witnesses of their witness—to be theologians of *Scripture*. My lecture today is given in the vein of the Old Testament and Reformed theology. As a Reformed theologian (and in my opinion, of course, not only as that), I must maintain a certain distance toward the Lutheran concept of real presence—the Lutheran "is"—as well

---

theological development. As he grows more confident in his thinking, his description of what it looks like to do theology becomes more joyful.

20. This idea of "objectivity" will become an important concept in Barth's later work. Here his point is that the theologian's primary subject matter is God, and her task is to bear witness to him in service to others.

as toward the Lutheran *certainty of salvation*. The question now is whether theology can and ought to get out beyond being a prolegomena to Christology. It could also indeed be the case that with the prolegomena *everything* is already said.[21]

21. With this ending, Barth gestures back toward one of the key themes of *The Epistle to the Romans* while also anticipating the focus of his later dogmatic work.

An Answer to Professor Adolf von Harnack

Introduction

This letter is the fourth in a series of five exchanges between Karl Barth and Adolf von Harnack that were published in the prominent magazine *Die Christliche Welt* in 1923. The history behind these exchanges begins nearly two decades earlier, when Barth was a student at the University of Berlin. Harnack was one of Barth's favorite professors at the university, and despite his young age, he secured a coveted spot in one of Harnack's seminars on church history. There he learned the rigors of the scientific method that dominated the modern discipline of theology. For his part, Harnack regarded Barth as a promising student.

Barth grew disillusioned with Harnack when he found his name among the signatories on a manifesto supporting the German war policy during World War I. This event, and Barth's turn from liberal theology, prompted the theological search that eventually led to the publication of *The Epistle to the Romans*. Barth crossed paths with Harnack again at a conference in 1920 where Barth was lecturing on his approach to the Bible. During this lecture, Barth emphasized the importance of God's distinction from creation as well as the use of dialectic.[1] Harnack struggled to make sense of Barth's claims, and he strongly disagreed with the parts he could understand. He later wrote

1. See Karl Barth, "Biblical Questions, Insights, and Vistas," in *Theology and the Word of God*, ed. and trans. Amy Marga (London: T&T Clark, 2011), 71–100.

to a friend: "Not one word, not one sentence, could I have said or thought."[2] His worries prompted him to publish "Fifteen Questions to the Despisers of Scientific Theology" in *Die Christliche Welt*. Sensing that these questions were aimed primarily at him, Barth responded with "Fifteen Answers to Professor Adolf von Harnack." Two open letters followed, including the response from Barth printed below. The exchange concluded with a short postscript by Harnack politely ending the conversation.

In his questions and open letter, Harnack seeks to demonstrate that Barth's rejection of the scientific method opens the door to subjectivism and disfigures the "simple gospel" preached by Jesus Christ. In contrast to Barth's claims about God's otherness, he insists that historical study of the Bible can lead to reliable knowledge of Christ, and thus of God. This critical approach also enables Christians to demonstrate that their faith corresponds to the morality of culture centered around the highest ideals of truth, goodness, and beauty. Harnack worries that Barth's emphasis on the difference between human reason and divine truth robs Christians of their certainty, undermines their ability to communicate the faith to the culture, and opens the door to spiritual fanaticism. The result is the undermining of historic Christianity.

Barth's response emphasizes that a truly scientific method must be determined by the subject matter of theology, which is nothing other than God himself. We know God only as God reveals himself to us, and we respond in faith through the Spirit's power. Starting with revelation does not mean rejecting historical-critical study, but it does place such study in its proper context. While historical-critical study can remove obstacles that keep us from recognizing God's revelation when it comes, God alone gives us knowledge of the truth about his eternal being and our relationship to him.

——— "An Answer to Adolf von Harnack's Open Letter"[3] ———

Esteemed Dr von Harnack,

It is not necessary to state explicitly that your extensive discussion of my answers to your questions is an honor for which I am grateful to you.

2. This remark comes from a letter to Eberhard Vischer. See Agnes von Zahn-Harnack, *Adolf von Harnack* (Berlin: Hans Bott Verlag, 1935, 1951), 532; cited in H. Martin Rumscheidt, ed., *Revelation and Theology: An Analysis of the Barth-Harnack Correspondence of 1923* (New York: Cambridge University Press, 1972), 15.

3. Karl Barth, "An Answer to Adolf von Harnack's Open Letter," in Rumscheidt, *Revelation and Theology*, 40–48, 50–52.

Nevertheless, I enter with hesitation upon the task of giving more information to you about my theological thoughts. The editor thought it something
which in view of your letter was the natural thing to do. But you yourself have
stated that my answers have shown you only the gap that divides us. Is it not
pointless and annoying to pose further riddles to you now and more than
likely to most of the readers of *Die Christliche Welt*? My position is unpleas-
ant in yet another way: the first time you posed real questions to which I, as
one of those to whom they were addressed, had to answer as well or as badly
as I could. In your letter, however, you confront me as someone—and I have
absolutely no intention of challenging your right in this, you, who are one of
my revered teachers of former times—who has accomplished his tasks, has
obtained knowledge, and who, because of the experience and the reflections
of a rich life, has not time and no ear not only for answers different from those
he would himself give, but also for questions other than his own. Is there any
further answer to be given to questions? Is the discussion not over? But since
you wanted to tell me that it was not my answers you had in mind when you
raised your original questions—something I never doubted—I think that I
owe it to you and to our listeners to confess that I do consider my answers
open to debate, but that still for the time being and until I am shown a better
way I reserve all else to myself.[4] Nonetheless, your objections cannot deter me
from continuing to ask along the line of those answers. Allow me therefore
to touch again on every point and to draw some of them together. For a real
understanding of my continued opposition I would refer to my publications
as well as to those of my friends Gogarten and Thurneysen, something you
would do also were you in a similar situation.[5] (For the other group of those to
whom you addressed yourself I assume no responsibility.) More to the general
public as to you I would like to say that in the end no effective repudiation
of our views will be possible without a serious study of our point of view.

　　You see in what you call "scientific theology" "the only possible way of
grasping the object epistemologically" and you call it "new because it has

4. Barth wants to open up a debate about the proper method for theology. In his letter to
Barth, Harnack presumes that the scientific method centered on historical-critical inquiry is the
only way to properly know an object. He also presupposes that theology should operate with
the same criteria as other disciplines, because only one true science governs each era. While
Harnack considers these claims essential for rational inquiry, Barth rejects them. He insists that
disciplines can be scientific (i.e., rational and ordered) in different ways. Theology is distinct from
other disciplines because God is its subject matter. Since we know God only through revelation,
theology cannot be based on historical-critical inquiry, as Harnack presumes.

5. Barth here is referring to Friedrich Gogarten and Eduard Thurneysen, both of whom are
associated with the dialectical theology movement. While Barth's friendship with Gogarten
would fray within a decade (see chap. 9), he would remain lifelong friends with Thurneysen.

attained to greater clarity and maturity only since the eighteenth century, old since it began when man started to think."[6] I hope that I am not reading anything into your position when I assume, based on that explicit reference to the eighteenth century, that the Reformers Luther and Calvin (together with that unfortunate tribe of "revival preachers") would fail to qualify as "scientific theologians," whereas Zwingli and Melanchthon might not. I would also assume that for you the idea of considering the Apostle Paul (in addition to whatever else he was) as one of those theologians is quite out of the question. Be that as it may, I believe I know "thinking men" in earlier and later centuries who as theologians pursued wholly different ways from those which since the eighteenth century have been regarded as normal, men whose scientific quality (should "scientific quality" mean objectivity) it would in my opinion be hazardous to doubt. The appeal to Paul's or Luther's theology is for you nothing but a presumptuous attempt at imitation. On this side of the "gap" the process looks relatively simple. We have been irresistibly impressed by the material superiority of those and other older theologians, however little they may fit into the present scheme of the guild. We, therefore, cannot feel ourselves relieved, by the protest of the spirit of modern times (which perhaps has to learn to understand itself first!) nor by the faith in the forgiveness of sins (!) which you invoked, of our duty to consider the fundamental point of departure of those theologians more seriously in regard to its total justification than was done especially in recent theology in spite of all the research into Paul and the enthusiasm for Luther. There can be no question of any repristination here whatsoever. It is my private view that the exercise of repristinating a classical theological train of thought, which in the days of medieval and Protestant scholasticism was known as "theology," is probably more instructive than the chaotic business of today's faculties for which the idea of a determinative *object* has become strange and monstrous in face of the determinate character of the *method*. But I also think I know that this *same* kind of thing can and should not return and that we must think *in* our time *for* our time.[7] Actually the point is not to keep the historical-critical method of

---

6. Harnack argued that an accurate interpretation of Scripture requires historical-critical reflection because the Bible is diverse in both genre and content. Rational judgments must be made about *how* to read Scripture, and only a historical-critical reading of the text can make these kinds of objective judgments. Since the claims of theology are drawn from the Bible, theology also must be based in historical-critical reflection if it is to explain and defend the Christian faith within the modern world. The alternative would be to embrace a naive biblicism shaped by the subjective experiences of the interpreter, and the result would be a theology incapable of supporting the faith of the church or convincing the skeptic.

7. Barth emphasizes the material superiority of the Reformers' theology in order to raise doubts about the supposed methodological superiority of modern theology. Barth is not

biblical and historical research developed in the last centuries away from the work of theology, but rather, to fit that method, and its refinement of the way questions are asked, into that work in a meaningful way. I think I said this in my answers 2, 3, and 14 and may thus be permitted to express astonishment that you still accuse me of regarding critical biblical science as something "devious," of wishing to be "rid of it," and must therefore be threatened with the punishment of occultism which is decreed by "divine order" for despisers of reason and science.[8] What I must defend myself against is not historical criticism but rather the foregone conclusiveness with which—and this is characteristic also of your present statements—the task of theology is *emptied*, that is to say, the way in which a so-called "simple gospel," discovered by historical criticism *beyond* the "Scriptures" and *apart from* the "Spirit," is given the place which the Reformers accorded to the "Word" (the correlation of "Scripture and Spirit"). Such a gospel can be called "God's Word" only metaphorically because it is at best a human impression of it.[9] The sentence so repugnant to you and others, to the effect that the task of theology is one with the task of preaching, is for me an *inevitable* statement of the *program* (in the carrying out of which, of course, many things must still be considered). In this, I assume it is conceded that the preacher must by right proclaim "the Word" and not perhaps his own heuristic knowledge, experiences, maxims and reflections. You have said that the truth of preaching and of faith come about "through the Word of the Christ." (The definite article before "Christ" is of no consequence to me at all.) If the transmission of this "Word" is the preacher's task, then it is also that of the theologian (who finds himself at least in virtual personal union with the former). The tactical and practical differences in accomplishing this are obvious as is the

---

abandoning the modern historical-critical method, as if he thinks theologians should turn back the clock and operate in the same way as earlier figures. Instead, he is trying to relativize the importance of this method in light of the presupposition that he thinks has undergirded faithful Christian theology both past and present: the notion that God's revelation is the starting point for the knowledge of God.

8. This sentence captures one of the key questions at stake in the debate between Harnack and Barth—namely, whether Harnack's historical-critical method or Barth's dialectical approach should be primary. Harnack sees the question as an *either-or*, and he contends that Barth's views should be wholly rejected. Barth sees the question as a *both-and*. He does not reject historical-critical reflection, but he thinks it should operate within the context of a dialectical approach that begins with God's revelation received in faith.

9. Harnack criticized Barth's difficult, paradoxical style by contrasting it with the "simple gospel" preached by Jesus. His point is that Barth undermines the power of this gospel by making the truth of God impossible for creatures to understand on their own. Barth's response is that Harnack's "simple gospel" is at best metaphorical, because the divine content has been replaced by human claims.

understanding that some of the things which belong to the lectern are to be left out of the pulpit and vice versa. The *theme*, however, which the theologian must pursue in history and which he must strive to express in a manner appropriate to his situation, cannot be a *second* truth *next to* that which he is obliged to present as a preacher. That was self-evident in the beginnings of Protestant theology (I think especially of Zurich and Geneva). I cannot see how the subsequent abstract separation of "scholarly" and "edifying" thought and speech can be derived from the essence of the matter. However, if it be right to assume the unity of the theologian's and the preacher's task, what is completely ruled out as a theme for one as well as for the other, along with everything that is merely human impression and not God's Word, is a "simple gospel" which as alleged "revelation" remains in the Bible, after the sufficient ground of cognition for all revelation, given in the correlation of "Scripture" and "Spirit," has been radically eliminated.[10]

But at this point arises your categorical declaration that my "*concept of revelation*" is "*totally*" (the italics are yours!) "incomprehensible" to you. You had asked in question 1 how one might come to find out what the content of the gospel is without historical knowledge and critical reflection. I answered in the first instance that the gospel itself tells us that this understanding occurs exclusively through an action (through deed and word) of this very "content" (of God or Christ or the Spirit). Surely you will not demand individual citations for this thesis. In the second instance, I said concerning critical reflection that it cannot be good to reverse the order and turn "Thus says the Lord" into "Thus hears man." If there is a way to *this* "content," then the content itself must be the way; the speaking voice must be the listening ear. All other ways do not lead to this goal, all other ears do not hear this voice. The fact that God is himself the goal as well as the way is something—and I gladly concede this—which to *me* as to *you* is *totally* incomprehensible, not only "fog," but, to speak with Luther, darkness. If you were to tell me that one cannot believe in a way from God *to us*, to which there does not correspond apparently any way from us *to God* (for it is always most exclusively God's way *to us*), I could only reply that deep down in my heart I think exactly the same.[11] But then,

---

10. Consistent with his rejection of the primacy of the modern historical-critical method, Barth pushes against the distinction between academic and pastoral thought. In his view, the task of the preacher is to proclaim the Word of God rather than merely talk about her own human ideas or experiences. The theologian has a nearly identical task. While practical differences exist between the two occupations, they stand united in this singular purpose. This union alarmed Harnack because he worried that it undermined the scientific character of theology.

11. Harnack accused Barth of leaving believers in a "fog" by portraying God as incomprehensible to humans. Barth concedes this point because he thinks it's true. The distinction between God and creation means that God is unknowable by us until God acts to reveal himself

is it not already included, quite apart from what the Bible says about it on every page, in the concept of revelation (and really not only in *my* concept!) that one cannot "believe" it? Would it not be better to renounce this high-sounding word if revelation were only the designation of a very sublime or a very deep but still a possible human discovery? Or should we theologians, if we do not wish to do this, not get up enough courage to let our theology begin with the perhaps essentially skeptical but nevertheless clear reminder of the "totally incomprehensible," inaudible and unbelievable, the *really* scandalous testimony that God himself has said and done something, something *new* in fact, outside of the correlation of all human words and things, but which *as* this new thing he has injected into that correlation, a word and a thing next to others but *this* word and *this* thing? I am not talking now of the possibility of accepting this testimony. I only ask whether we should not for once *reckon* more soberly with the fact that what is called Christianity made its first and for us recognizable beginning with this testimony? This testimony, which historical criticism cannot analyze enough, and which will not cease being *this* testimony when thus analyzed, I call in its totality "the Scriptures." The delineation of "the Scriptures" over against other scriptures appears to me a secondary question. Should an extra-canonical writing contain in a notable fashion this very testimony, there can be no *a priori* impossibility of letting this testimony speak through it also, no, quite to the contrary. From this observation, however, to the canonization of *Faust*, for example, there is a long way which a discerning Church just will *not* travel.[12]

The Scriptures then witness to revelation.[13] One does not have to believe it, nor *can* one do it. But one should not deny that it witnesses to revelation, *genuine* revelation that is, and not to a more or less concealed religious possibility of man but rather to the possibility of God, namely that *he* has acted under the form of a human possibility—and this as *reality*. According to this testimony, the Word became flesh, God himself became a human-historical *reality* and that this took place *in the person of Jesus Christ*. But from this it by no means follows for me that this event can also be an object of

to us. Only God can clear away the fog, and any attempt by the human to do so inevitably places creaturely ideals about God at the center. The result is a theology that produces no real knowledge of God.

12. Barth is referring to Johann Wolfgang von Goethe (1749–1832), who is widely considered to be among the greatest German writers. Harnack had referred to him in a prior letter.

13. Barth appeals to "testimony" to challenge Harnack's assumptions about the Bible. Rather than approaching the Bible as a historical document to be critically excavated for insights, Barth sees the Bible as a witness to God's revelation. The object of this revelation cannot be captured by historical examination because it transcends created reality and history. To investigate the natural history of the text is merely to study the human lives of the witnesses, not the revelation itself.

human-historical *cognition*; this is excluded because and insofar as *this* reality is involved. The existence of a Jesus of Nazareth, for example, which can of course be discovered historically, is not *this* reality. A historically discernible "simple gospel," discernible because it is humanly plausible, a "simple gospel" which causes no scandal, a "simple," that is, in your sense, a word or a deed of this Jesus which would be nothing other really than the realization of a human possibility—would not be *this* reality.[14] I doubt whether it is possible at any cogent point to separate one word or one deed of Jesus from the background of this reality, even considered only historically, that is, from the Scripture which witnesses to revelation and so to the scandal it causes and then proceed to interpret it as the "simple gospel" in your sense. Why, for example, I regard this as impossible in reference to the command to love God and one's neighbor, I mentioned in my fifth answer, for which you have chastised but not refuted me. I can now only in passing enter protest against your description of the parables of Jesus [*die Gleichnisse Jesu*] as "'understandable and comforting" parables [*Parabeln*] and I hope to have in both cases at least some historians on my side.[15] But even if you could succeed in claiming some point or other in the tradition for your position, it would merely mean that this point is *not*, or is only in context with other points, the object of the testimony or the kerygma which is surely in your judgment also the sole issue for the New Testament writings. The object of the *testimony* has been made known by the apostles and evangelists to such an extent as *revelation*, as the action of God himself, it has been thrust back so deeply into an impenetrable hiddenness and *protected* so strongly from every desire for *direct* perception, that not only all statements which obviously refer to this "center of the gospel," found for example in that rather threatening bundle in the second article of the Creed, but in fact the "Sermon on the Mount" as well, the parabolic and polemical speeches of Jesus and the account of his passion, all leave the circumspect reader with the conclusion that there can be no question of speaking here of a direct historical *comprehensibility* of

---

14. Note how Barth challenges the very definition of "reality." True reality—the reality with which theology is concerned—is the reality of *God*. This reality cannot be known empirically because it transcends the capacities of human cognition. Harnack's historical-critical approach leads to a merely creaturely version of this reality and thus does not lead to knowledge of God.

15. The distinction here is between the usual German word for "parable" (*Gleichnis*) and Harnack's use of the word *Parabel*, which has the sense of a "tale" or "story." Barth's point is that Harnack is dismissing the parables as mere tales, while Barth sees the parables as God's own speech given to instruct and edify. The ironic implication is that it is Harnack (rather than Barth) who is driving a wedge between the everyday meaning of the biblical text and the reality of God.

this "historical" *reality* (revelation).[16] All that is comprehensible is always that other which makes up the historical context of the alleged revelation.

Beyond this "other" the barrier goes up and the scandal, the fable or the miracle threatens. The historical reality of Christ (as revelation, as "center of the gospel") is not the "historical Jesus" whom an all too eager historical research had wanted to lay hold of in disregard of the very warnings made in the sources themselves (coming upon a banality which has been and shall be proclaimed in vain as a pearl of great price). Nor is it, as you said, an imagined Christ but rather *the risen one*, or let us say with more restraint in view of our little faith: the Christ who is *witnessed to* as the risen one. That is the "evangelical, the historic Jesus Christ" and, otherwise, that is, apart from the testimony to him, apart from the revelation which must here be believed, "we know him no longer." In this sense I think I can legitimately appeal to 2 Corinthians 5:16. At this decisive point, that is, in answering the question: what makes Jesus the Christ? in terms of the reference to the *resurrection*, one is indeed left from man's point of view with what you called "totally" incomprehensible.[17] And I gladly confess that I would a hundred times rather take the side of the No, the refusal to believe which you proclaim on the basis of this fact, than the talents of a "positive" theology which ends up making what is incomprehensible altogether self-evident and transparent once again, for that is an emptying and a denying of revelation which with its apparent witness to the revelation is worse than the angriest refusal to believe which at least has the advantage of being suited to the subject matter. My declaration of sympathy for the "most radical" biblical science was meant in this sense. The theology of the Reformers did not need this negative discipline because it still had the courage not to avoid the scandal of revelation. It thus never raised the question of a historically discernible core of the gospel. *We* need it, however, because we have fallen into this impossible question through flight from the scandal.[18] I see the theological function of historical criticism

16. Barth's point in this long sentence is straightforward: the biblical writers' depictions of Jesus Christ preclude the possibility that anyone can comprehend him through direct historical observation.

17. This is a key question in the dispute between Harnack and Barth: Which "historical" Jesus should scholars be seeking? Should they seek the Jesus who lived and worked in the first century, or the risen Jesus who lives and works today? Barth insists that it must be the latter, in line with 2 Cor. 5:16: "From now on, therefore, we regard no one from a human point of view; even though we once knew Christ from a human point of view, we know him no longer in that way." If Barth is right, then a "historical" study of Jesus must proceed in a manner different from any other science because it starts from the basis of faith in the resurrected Jesus.

18. Barth insists that his claims about the historical incomprehensibility of Christ stand in line with the teaching of the Reformers, even though they did not emphasize this point. They never did so, Barth thinks, because they never considered the possibility that it could be

especially in the task of making clear to us *a posteriori* that there is *no road* this way, and that in the Bible we have to do with testimonies and *only* with *testimonies*. I notice that this is the function it has in fact fulfilled among us since David Friedrich Strauss, and done so excellently in its own way, even if it is not widely understood and above all unaware of what it was doing.[19]

The *acceptance* of this unbelievable testimony of the Scriptures I call *faith*. Again I do not claim that this is a discovery of my theology. I do ask, however, what else faith could be—disregarding sentimentalities—but the obedience I give to a human word which testifies to the Word of God as a word addressed to me, as if it were itself God's Word? Let no one have any delusions here about the fact that this is an unprecedented event, that here one must speak of the *Holy Spirit* if all the objections Herrmann rammed into our heads against a "mere credence" in historical facts *apart* from this basis of cognition are not to hold good.[20] Therefore I distinguish faith as *God's working* on us (for only he can say to us, in such a way that *we* will hear it, what we *cannot* hear, 1 Cor. 2:9) from all known and unknown human organs and functions, even our so-called "experiences of God." Is that such an unheard-of novelty? Must I, as one of the Reformed tradition, ask whether Luther's explication of the third article in the Small Catechism is valid or not? Do you really not see that through the rash abandonment of this concept of faith in favor of the lentilpottage of a less paradoxical one, the doors have been opened to the anthroposophic *tohuwabohu* of faith and occult "capabilities" of man, confronted with which official theology is simply at a loss?[21]

It has to be thus: whatever may be said against the possibility of revelation can with equal strength be said also against the possibility of faith. That leaves us with this as the *second* excluded possibility: God who according to the witness of the Scriptures has spoken "the Word of Christ" speaks that Word also to me through the witness of the Scriptures empowered through the internal

---

otherwise. Barth has to go beyond what the Reformers said and clarify an issue they never had to face in order to hold the same position they did.

19. Here we see Barth's account of the ongoing usefulness of the historical-critical method: it demonstrates that purely historical readings of the Bible cannot lead us to God because it shows that the Bible contains testimonies to a revelation that transcends natural history. Barth appeals to David Friedrich Strauss here because he was the founder of an especially influential stream of radical biblical criticism.

20. Wilhelm Herrmann (1846–1922) was a teacher of Barth who greatly influenced his early theological development.

21. The word *tohuwabohu* refers to the original Hebrew phrase in Gen. 1:2 that calls the earth a "formless void." Barth's point is that, because the Bible testifies to the living God, we will read it rightly only when we approach it spiritually (i.e., through the power of the Holy Spirit) on the basis of our faith in Christ. If we approach the text under our own power, then we inevitably will derive an account of God cast in our own image.

witness of the Holy Spirit (*testimonium Spiritus Sancti internum*), so that I hear it and by hearing it believe. Is this the "theory of the exclusive inner word" or one of the many "other subjectivistic theories"? In your third question, you yourself spoke of the *awakening* of faith. I agree, but hold that what we are concerned with here, as also in the "understandable and comforting parable" of the prodigal son, Luke 15:32, is the awakening of someone dead, that is, with *God's miracle* just as in revelation. Indeed, I have no confidence in any objectivity other than the one described in this way or in terms of the correlate concepts of "Scripture" and "Spirit," least of all in the pontifications of a science which would first have to demonstrate its absolute superiority over the subjectivist activity of the "preachers of awakening" by means of results.[22] . . .

Still in connection with the charge of Marcionism, you demand from me a full answer to the question "whether God is simply unlike anything said about him on the basis of the development of culture, on the basis of the knowledge gathered by culture and on the basis of ethics."[23] Very well, then, but may I ask you really to listen to my whole answer. NO, God is "absolutely not at all that," as surely as the Creator is not the creature or even the creation of the creature. But precisely in this NO, which can be uttered in its full severity only in the faith in revelation, the creature recognizes itself as the work and the possession of the Creator. Precisely in this NO God is known as God, as the source and the goal of the *thoughts* of God which man, in the darkness of his culture and his decadence, is in the habit of forming. For this NO, posited with finality by revelation, is not without the "deep, secret YES under and above the NO" which we should "grasp and hold to with a firm faith in God's Word" and "confess that God is right in his judgment against us, for then we have won." This is how it is with that NO: "nothing but YES in it, but always deep and secretly and always seeming to be nothing but NO."[24] What lover

22. Here Barth appeals to the Reformed doctrine of the "internal witness of the Holy Spirit" (*testimonium Spiritus Sancti internum*). John Calvin deployed this doctrine to emphasize that the validity and truthfulness of Scripture depended on the testimony of the Spirit rather than the external authority of the church (see his 1559 *Institutes of the Christian Religion* 1.7). Barth draws on this idea to claim that Scripture does not need to be historically verified by us in order to be considered true. This Spirit-secured veracity of Scripture—rather than our own historical study—is the only truly objective basis for theological thinking.

23. Harnack insisted that the central claims of Christianity must stand in continuity with the highest moral ideals of a culture, because if no such continuity exists, then the gospel will be unintelligible. This claim is the basis of the charge of Marcionism leveled against Barth. As Harnack sees it, Barth's claim that divine revelation is distinct from history effectively erases the history of Israel and the church. The result is a cultural "blank slate" (*tabula rasa*) that then is filled in with new spiritual insights.

24. Barth responds to the charge of Marcionism by emphasizing that God's distinction from creation (the "NO") does not erase but establishes the creature's relationship with God (the

of contradictoriness might have said that? Kierkegaard or Dostoevsky? No, Martin Luther! Is Luther to be suspected then of Marcionism too? According to Zwingli, yes, but I think that you and I understand him better than that. So, why should you not understand *me* a little better at the same time? Does the human really become insignificant when, in the faith in revelation, its *crisis* occurs which makes forever impossible every identification between here and the beyond, excepting always the one which it does not become us to express (about the end of all things foreseen in 1 Cor. 15:28)? Does it really not become full of significance and promise, really serious and possible precisely through being moved out of the twilight of supposed fulfillment into the light of real *hope*? Is it really *not* enough for *us* to have and to behold in the transitory the parable of the intransitory, to live in it and to work for it, to be glad as men that we have at least the *parable* and to suffer as men under the fact that it is *only* the parable, *without*, however, anticipating the "swallowing up of death in victory" in a spurious consciousness of eternity exactly *because* the great temporal *significat* applies to the greater eternal *est* and nothing else? Have I really made *"tabula rasa"*?[25]

Yes, you say so, honored Sir, and you must know *why*, although you cannot deduce it from my statements. I am afraid that you *must* really misunderstand me *precisely at this point*, even if we could agree about revelation and faith.[26] Why is it that right here, where of all things the existential question of our relation to God and the world, where the confirmation in hope of faith in revelation is involved, you unambiguously exchange the role of the defender of *science* for that of the defender of the so-called "Christian" possession? Why the lament about the "sublimity" of my metaphysics and psychology, as if all of a sudden *popular intelligibility* were for you the standard of right theology? What is the meaning of measuring the distances which, more here and less there, separate me from the "Christianity of the gospels," as if the

---

"YES"). Only when we acknowledge that God is distinct from creation will we be in position to recognize the true nature of God's relationship to us in Christ.

25. Barth uses this series of questions to emphasize that, instead of erasing culture by turning it into a "blank slate" (*tabula rasa*), he is simply acknowledging the reality that God is distinct from creation. This position corresponds to, rather than contradicts, the orthodox Christian tradition. The quote "swallowing up of death in victory" comes from 1 Cor. 15:54. Barth's use of the words *significat* and *est* reflects their use in eucharistic theology: the former means that the elements *signify* the body and blood of Christ, while the latter means that the elements *are* Christ's body and blood.

26. The questions that follow emphasize Barth's account of the key difference between his and Harnack's approaches: while Barth begins with and upholds God's absolute distinction from creation, Harnack does not. The implication, barely veiled below the surface, is that Barth could pose questions about Harnack's adherence to Christian orthodoxy in much the same way that Harnack has raised such questions about Barth.

topic of our discussion were all of a sudden the *Christian nature* of my theology? What is the meaning of the charge of "commending" a "state of mind," unpalatable to you, when the point of your scientific misgivings was that neither revelation nor faith was made understandable by me in the familiar, "simple" fashion as a *state of mind*, when, in other words, the state of mind was introduced by you into our discussion? Why all those strong words about "illusion," "frivolity," "lover of contradictoriness," etc., when you have certainly not demonstrated, from my perhaps unsatisfactory, but nevertheless circumspect answers, the right to such tumultuous conclusions and accusations? How am I to explain the transition from instruction to admonition and how am I to answer it? You can surely guess that I, too, have angry thoughts about the connection between the *scientific* character of your theology, which causes you to repudiate what I (and not only I) call revelation and faith, and your own *Christian position*, which comes out into the open in the idea that Paul's "saved in hope" must be suspected as "problematical." I too would be in the position of registering strongest scruples and of uttering very sharp words where the misunderstanding between us seems so hopeless. Yet what else would I do then but seal this hopelessness, on my part too, something that must not be done? It is better in every respect to break off here.

Yet let me repeat: I do not intend to entrench myself in those positions in which you, honored Sir, and our voluntary-involuntary audience in this conversation have seen me, simply because I know how frighteningly relative *everything* is that one can *say* about the great subject which occupies you and me. I know that it will be necessary to speak of it in a way quite different from that of my present understanding. I would like to be able to listen attentively in the future to whatever *you* also will have to say. But at this time I cannot concede that you have driven me off the field with your questions and answers, although I will gladly endure it when it really happens.

Respectfully yours,
Karl Barth

CHAPTER

5

The Resurrection of the Dead

Introduction

Throughout the 1920s, Barth taught courses on Scripture alongside his regular offerings in dogmatic and historical theology. At the University of Göttingen, these courses included studies of Ephesians, Philippians, Colossians, James, 1 John, and the Sermon on the Mount (Matt. 5–7). He lectured on 1 Corinthians during the summer semester of 1923. These lectures were important enough to Barth that he revised them for publication the following year under the title *The Resurrection of the Dead*. The selections here are drawn from the English translation of that book released in 1933.

Barth's key claim is that Paul's account of the resurrection in 1 Corinthians 15 is the lens through which the entire letter should be interpreted. He argues that Paul approaches creaturely reality and history eschatologically, which means that he defines them in light of the future. The theological and ethical instructions Paul gives to the Corinthians reflect the reality that they live in the time between Christ's resurrection and their own resurrection in the future. Barth thinks this life "in between" should determine how Christians approach God and their own creaturely existence. Christians should not think about the resurrection merely as an event that will take place some day in the future. Rather, they should view the resurrection as a future event that determines the reality of the present.

One of the most interesting aspects of Barth's reading of 1 Corinthians is the way he utilizes historical-critical scholarship. On the one hand, Barth is suspicious of the primacy given to the historical-critical method among modern interpreters. He makes it clear that *God* speaks through Paul's text and that this divine Word remains beyond the reach of the historical critic. On the other hand, Barth draws on the resources of historical scholarship to describe the situation in Corinth and the context in which Paul's claims are made. The result is a theological interpretation of the text that incorporates historical-critical insights without giving them primacy. In this way, Barth's exposition of 1 Corinthians both corresponds to and moves beyond his reading of Romans, and it hints at the direction Barth would be moving in the years to come.

———————————— *The Resurrection of the Dead*[1] ————————————

If the assumption is correct upon which we have so far proceeded in our commentary, that the discourse of the apostle in the whole Epistle proceeds from a single point and harks back again to this same point, and that 1 Corinthians 15 is to be understood as an attempt to express in words this one single point in itself, severed from the relationships in which it had up till now almost only been visible, then the doctrine of the Resurrection of the Dead which he expounds here is in no case an "eschatology" in the sense which attaches to this word in ordinary dogma, that is an attempt, after speaking of everything else possible, to bring forward something about death, the beyond and world perfection, but we have to do here with the doctrine of the "End," which is at the same time the beginning, of the last things, which are, at the same time, the first.[2] . . . Truly, this is not a recollection among other recollections: it is *the* recollection which Paul wants to awaken. But the theme is to be the *resurrection* of the dead. Only that gives meaning and emphasis to the recollection. What is the end, if it be only the end? What is eternity, if it

1. Karl Barth, *The Resurrection of the Dead*, trans. H. J. Stenning (New York: Revell, 1933), 107–9, 133–34, 151–52, 167–68, 201–2.
2. Barth thinks that Paul's entire argument in 1 Corinthians reflects the reality that Christ has been raised from the dead. Paul's discussion of the resurrection in 1 Cor. 15 thus is the heart of his letter and the basis for his other claims in it. Barth builds on this idea to make a more general observation: our resurrection is not merely an event that will take place in the future, but it also is the future event that wholly determines the reality of the present. This claim matches his argument in *The Epistle to the Romans* that the resurrection is the point where eternity touches creation and reveals its true meaning and basis.

be only eternity? What can touch us, when we are *not*, when we do not know, when we cannot have? With the word "resurrection," however, the apostolic preaching puts in this empty place against all that exists for us, all that is known to us, all that can be possessed by us, all things of all time—what? not the non-being, the unknown, the not-to-be-possessed, nor yet a second being, a further thing to become known, a higher future possession, but the source and the truth of all that exists, that is known, that can belong to us, the reality of all *res*, of all things, the eternity of time, the *resurrection* of the dead. But be it understood: all this exactly where only the indifferent conception of the non-existent, unknown, inconceivable seems to have room, where only the dissolution of all things and phenomena seems to be in question, where only the contradictory assertion of the infinity of time seems to be left, where death seems to be the last word. The dead: that is what we are. The risen: that is what we are not. But precisely for this reason the resurrection of the dead involves that that which *we are not* is equivalent with that which *we are*: the dead living, time eternity, the being truth, things real.[3] All this is not given except in hope, and therefore, this identity is not to be put into effect. The life that we dead are living here and now is not, therefore, confounded with *this* life, of which we can only ever say that we are not yet living in it; the endlessness of time is not to be confused with eternity; the corporeality of phenomena is not to be confused with *this* reality; the being that we know or can know is not to be confused with *this* its origin, in its truth, the sharp fundamental step which parts the latter from the former, as the impossible from the possible, is not to be removed, but *given* in hope—in hope, in the identification of the former with the latter, the resurrection of the dead already *effected* in God.[4] . . .

The whole meaning of verses 12–28 is, indeed, this—that this historical fact, the resurrection of Jesus, stands and falls with the resurrection of the dead generally. What kind of historical fact is that reality of which, or at any rate the perception of which, is bound up in the most express manner with the perception of a general truth, which by its nature cannot emerge in history, or to speak more exactly, can only emerge on the confines of all history, on the

3. Barth's point here is that the resurrection changes everything because it reconfigures the way we understand our lives. If our lives end in death—and if death is something completely distinct from life—then what difference does our impending death make for our present lives? But if our future involves our resurrection, then our future life completely determines the reality of our present lives. We *are* the people who *will be* resurrected.

4. Even though we will be raised from the dead, this future has not yet happened, and we cannot confuse it with the present. Just as God remains infinitely distinct from creaturely being even as he completely determines it, so the future remains distinct from the present even as it defines and shapes every aspect of it.

confines of death? As little, at any rate, as this general truth is itself *fact*, for the reality of which the same man who wrote verses 12–19 will adduce *historical proof* in verses 3–7. As really chronological information only a phrase is left to us in verses 3–7, and that is in the words "and was buried" in verse 4; but is it perchance possible from this sentence to understand historically the frontier of history looming before and behind, or would this not be the worst interpretation of the real facts: that rather *history*, which undoubtedly speaks in these words "and was buried," is here illuminated in the most dazzling manner, from the *frontier* of history, which is described by the words "who died" on the one hand, by the words "he rose again" on the other hand, while the words "he was seen" is the rendering of the many-voiced testimony (v. 15) that this boundary has been seen? In history, to be sure! But *in* history, the *frontier* of history, and indeed—and this is the vital point—not only from the one side, not only from the "he died"—the death of Christ alone would not, in fact, be the frontier of history becoming visible; this fact alone would coincide with the second, the phrase "he was buried"—but also from the other side, that "God raised up Christ" (v. 15). This is in truth the *substance* of the testimony, and the origin of the testimony is just that the fourfold "he was seen." This, then, is how the four facts are to be interpreted: not as a monotonous chronological recital of things of the same kind, but extremely graduated in a series several times interrupted: Like two massive pillars: Christ *died* for our sins; and: Christ *rose again* on the third day; both being asserted, "according to the scriptures," as historical facts, to be sure, but *what kind* of historical facts? *This* end, the end of our sins, which yet can only end when history ends, and *this* beginning, the beginning of a new life, which yet can only begin when and where a new world begins.[5] . . .

If that be true, if the end of history set by God is here, if the new eternal beginning placed by God appears here, then that which has appeared from God applies to the whole of history within the scope of this horizon, then the miracle of God to Christ is immediately and simultaneously the miracle of God *to us*, and not a miracle about which it may, at any rate, still be asked: What has it to do with us? If we see God at work there, then what is true there is also serious for us here and now, then our life, too, it goes without

5. Here we see Barth tracing out the implications of Paul's claim that Christ's resurrection is related to the "historical fact" of the resurrection generally. He focuses on a key question: Precisely what kind of "historical fact" are we talking about when it comes to the resurrection? He argues that it cannot be like other "facts" because the resurrection occurs on the very boundary of created reality itself. Instead, the "fact" under discussion here is a unique act of God. The implication is that we are able to recognize the *true* facts of history—the facts that reflect the reality of God—only when we view history in light of divine revelation. To see history in this way is to view it through the lens of faith rather than our own empirical perception.

saying, is placed in the light which proceeds from that horizon of all that we call life. Not yet in fulfillment. We are indeed, still living this life, as yet, we, indeed, only know time; it is the "not yet" which separates us from the resurrection. But we are living the life limited by that horizon, we are living in time for eternity, we are living in the hope of the resurrection, it is that which cannot be denied, if Christ's resurrection is to be understood, not as miracle or myth or psychic experience (which all come to the same thing), but as God's revelation.[6] . . .

Waiting means really *looking towards* something that is just coming, and here it is only Paul's intention to testify vigorously to this coming as such. It is the arrival, nay, the presence, of the hidden Christ and His victory, with which the resurrection even of His own is occurrence. Christ's *parousia* is nothing different, second next to His resurrection, only the definite coming-to-the-surface of the same subterranean stream which in revelation for the first time became perceptive in time, the *fulfillment* of that which in time can only be grasped as a *promise*. In order to understand, we must here, as in the case of the resurrection, try to form the idea of a *boundary* of all time, except it is now not merely revealed and believed, but—and with this our idea of time loses all intelligibility—finally *marked*, the "God is God" without any dialectical tension as *given*. This is the general victory of Christ announced in the resurrection, which, once known in its absoluteness, although never and nowhere present, is yet always and everywhere to be conceived of as the crisis of every human temporal thing.[7] . . .

We thus stand in the connection of salvation history, which is a real history: the perishing of an old, the becoming of a new, a path and a step on this path, no mere relationship, but history which is not enacted in time, but between time and eternity—the history, in which the creation, the resurrection of Christ, and the End, as verse 48 indicates, are one day . . . And thus [Paul] places man forcibly in the light, or rather, twilight, of the truth that he is created by God in the middle between Adam and Christ, and tells him: Thou art *Both*, or rather, thou *belongest* to both, just as both jointly describe God's way, from the old to the new creature, so thy life also is the scene across which this path leads, so must thou, too, make the journey *from* here *to* there.

---

6. If the resurrection is the revelation of God, then our most important task is to order our view of reality so that it begins with and proceeds from this event. Since the resurrection can be acknowledged by faith but not historically demonstrated, our view of reality should proceed from the starting point of faith.

7. If Christ's resurrection reveals the true nature of reality and history, then our present lives will be determined by God's promise about Christ's return and our future resurrection. We have faith when we trust that the God who issued this promise will be faithful to carry it out even though it has not yet been fulfilled.

In other words, he jerks the questioner and spectator out of his comfortable position and sets him right in the middle of the *struggle*, in which the resurrection is truth.[8]

8. When God revealed the truth about created reality and history in the resurrection of Jesus Christ, he also revealed that our lives are determined by Christ's life. This determination is shaped not by our experience of Christ but by the reality that his life serves as basis and limit for our lives even as we remain "in Adam." Our task is to think and live in the reality of Christ by tracing out what must be true about reality, history, and human being in light of the future he brings.

CHAPTER 6

The Göttingen Dogmatics

Introduction

Barth delivered his first series of lectures on dogmatic theology during the spring and summer of 1924 while teaching at the University of Göttingen. He found the work difficult because instead of merely repeating or criticizing what other people taught, Barth now had to say what he believed. "What are *you* going to say?" Barth asked his students during the opening lecture. "Not as one who knows the Bible or Thomas or the Reformers or the older Blumhardt, but responsibly and seriously as one who stands by the words that are said: *you*? And *what* are you going to say?"[1]

As Barth figured out how to answer these questions for himself, he drew deeply from the wells of the Reformed tradition. Later in his career, he specifically credited Heinrich Heppe's *Reformed Dogmatics*—a collection of excerpts from post-Reformation theologians covering major areas or doctrine—for showing him the way forward during this period.[2] He was impressed with the way the older Reformed theologians oriented their theology toward the church, and he also found many of the categories and distinctions they used to organize their claims helpful for his own thinking. He adopted many

1. Karl Barth, *The Göttingen Dogmatics: Instruction in the Christian Religion*, vol. 1, trans. Geoffrey W. Bromiley (Grand Rapids: Eerdmans, 1991), 6.
2. See Karl Barth, foreword to *Reformed Dogmatics*, by Heinrich Heppe (Grand Rapids: Eerdmans, 1978), v.

of these distinctions as his own, although he often reconfigured their meaning so that they fit his own ideas and aims.

This selection comes from one of Barth's opening lectures where he is explaining the implications of an idea he adopted from the work of the Dutch theologian Herman Bavinck: *Deus dixit*, "God has spoken." His key point is that dogmatic theology should reflect the reality that God's revelation is God's speech to the believer in the *present*. Dogmatic theologians cannot operate on the basis of the church's claims from the past; nor do they operate in a vacuum, as if they can simply generate their own ideas on their own terms. Instead, they offer their claims about God as a response to their specific and concrete encounter with God as God speaks his Word to them here and now. In these paragraphs, Barth is particularly interested in explaining the relationship between this present-tense divine speech and the historical text of the Bible. Many themes from his debate with Adolf von Harnack can be seen here, although they now take a new form as Barth reframes them in the service of a constructive account of God's revelation to the church. Barth will develop many of these same ideas more fully in his *Church Dogmatics*.

―――――――――――――― *The Göttingen Dogmatics*[3] ――――――――――――――

In distinction from scripture, however, revelation is God's Word itself, God's own speaking in which he alone is the subject, in which no flesh also speaks, but he and he alone. This is found in scripture, this pregnant *Deus dixit*, God speaking personally as the subject, God as the author, God not only giving authentic information about himself but himself speaking about himself. This is what makes scripture the Word of God.[4] This is the living hand which imperiously waves the rod, the canon. This is the authority of the canon, the unconditional constraint which issues from it. This is what makes the historical heteronomy in the relationship between the church and the Bible into an

―――――――――――――――――――――――――――

3. Karl Barth, *Göttingen Dogmatics*, vol. 1, 57–63.

4. In these opening sentences, Barth affirms that Scripture *is* the Word of God and also is *distinct from* the Word of God. These two claims correspond to each other because of Barth's particular definition of divine revelation. For Barth, revelation takes place when God personally acts to reveal himself to us. So Scripture *is* the Word of God because God personally speaks in and through it. This is what Barth means by the phrase *Deus dixit* (God has spoken). At the same time, Scripture remains *distinct from* the Word of God because Scripture is merely the creaturely medium through which God reveals himself. Taken together, these two claims summarize Barth's view of Scripture: God speaks his Word through the human words of Scripture even as these words remain fully human.

absolute heteronomy.[5] The fact that God himself is on the scene, speaking about himself, is an adequate reason to speak about him. It is the permission and command to do so. God in his revelation, God as speaking subject, is a possible object of human speech which at once becomes a necessary object. This is *how* scripture bears witness to him. This is *why* it does. This is *how* he speaks through the medium of scripture. This is how the permission and command to speak about God come into history at the start of the series to which we ourselves belong. God's own speaking is the final authority, the summit of the mountain above which there is only heaven, the summit to which we are led when, directed by preaching to the church and by the church to the Bible, we come up against the direction that the Bible itself gives us. It directs us to God. But God can and will direct us only to himself.[6] . . .

We have now reached the point from which we can survey to some extent the situation of Christian preaching. But before we do this, we must make sure by a few small delimitations that we are not mistaken, that we have really reached this point together. What can this *Deus dixit* mean to which we have been driven? What must it mean?[7]

1. Obviously, it is an address. The presupposition of the Bible is not that God is but that he spoke. We are directed, not to God in himself, but to God communicating himself. What makes scripture holy scripture is not the correctness of the prophetic and apostolic statements and thoughts about God but the I-Thou encounter, person to person, about which these thoughts and statements tell us. Only within this I-Thou relation, in which one speaks and another is spoken to, in which there is communication and reception, only in full *action* is revelation revelation. When we do not think of revelation as such, that is, one person speaking and another spoken to, God revealing himself to us and we to whom he reveals himself; when revelation is seen from the standpoint of the noninvolved spectator, then it amounts to non-revelation. God is completely inconceivable, concealed, and absent for those whom he does not address and who are not addressed by him. To receive revelation is to be addressed by God.[8]

5. Heteronomy is the opposite of autonomy. It refers to a state of being ruled or governed by an authority rather than by oneself. Barth's point is that the Bible has authority over the church because God exercises his own divine authority through it.

6. Note the interplay of the concepts of permission and command. We are permitted to speak about God because he has spoken to us, and this revelation compels us to speak to others so that they also might hear God's speech.

7. Another way to put this question is this: What precisely do we mean when we say that divine revelation takes place only when God speaks to us?

8. This first point emphasizes that divine revelation is personal in nature. God speaks to us in order to disclose himself to us. We cannot seek out and then observe God's revelation on

2. Obviously, too, revelation means disclosure, *apokalypsis, phanerosis, revelatio*. Being revelation only in action, in the event of address, revelation is not a direct openness on God's part but a becoming open. God tears away the veil, the husk, the concealment when he reveals himself. He removes the incomprehensibility. He makes impossible the possibility of taking offense, of not believing. These things are essentially related to revelation. Later Protestant orthodoxy did incalculable damage with its doctrine of inspiration in which it did not accept the paradox that in scripture God's Word is given to us in the concealment of true and authentic human words, when it removed the salutary barrier between scripture and revelation, when it adopted pagan ideas and made the authors of the Bible into the *amanuenses*, pens, or flutes of the Holy Spirit, and thus found in the Bible an open and directly given revelation, as though this were not a contradiction in terms. Long before the Enlightenment this meant no more and no less than a pitiful historicizing of revelation, which then continued if in another form. To deny the hiddenness of revelation even in scripture is to deny revelation itself, and with it the Word of God. For God's Word is no longer God's Word when the truth that is new every morning (cf. Lam. 3:23) is made into a sacred reality, when the miracle of God that is encircled with the possibility of offense is made into a marvel to which one may quietly point. The same applies, of course, to modern theories of revelation which in place of the supposed sacred letter posit a supposed sacred history as the palpable reality. The holy that is obvious, the sacral, is never the true holy. The true holy is spirit, not thing. The *Deus dixit* is revelation, not revealedness.[9]

3. Obviously, too, the *Deus dixit* means a here and now. Or rather a then and there, for it is better to say that there is no avoiding the offensive *"there in Palestine"* and *"then in the years AD 1–30"* if we are really to think the thought of Christian revelation. I have chosen the Latin *Deus dixit* not least because of the Latin perfect tense (*dixit*), which expresses something that the translations do not. To be sure, we have here a remarkable and unique perfect. What is denoted is an eternal perfect. But in the first instance it takes

---

our own. Nor can we identify it with some specific quality, such as historical truthfulness, as if divine revelation could be described or defined on creaturely terms. Revelation must be seen strictly as the event in which God personally addresses us and we hear God's voice.

9. In this second point, Barth criticizes the "historicizing of revelation" that occurs whenever we identify revelation directly with a creaturely thing or event. He worries that this kind of direct identification leaves us in control because it presumes we have the ability to seek and know God by utilizing our own creaturely capacities. But God is distinct from creation and cannot be identified with any historical creaturely thing—even the Bible itself. We know God, even in and through the Bible, only because God personally breaks into creation from the outside to reveal himself to us.

the form of the usual perfect, and the meaning cannot be separated from this form. The contingent fact that the church finds the witness to revelation in these specific writings, and that in the witness it finds revelation, is no accident. The contingency lies in the nature of revelation. *Deus dixit* indicates a special, once-for-all, contingent event to which these specific writings rather than any possible writings bear witness.[10] . . .

4. Obviously, too, the concealed and unique address that we call God's revelation is *qualified* history. What I mean by that is as follows. The "oracles of God" (Rom. 3:2), that which are disclosed out of hiddenness, the here and now of revelation, are an event in time and space (otherwise there would be no here and now), but as revelation they are not in sequence with all else in time and space. Their relation to the whole of contingent reality (to which they belong) is similar (I glance aside to a philosophical correlation only by way of analogy) to that of the concept of limit or idea to the concept of reason. They do not negate it, but they bracket it—provisionally, we should not say more . . . The history of *Deus dixit* has, as qualified history, no such links with the rest of history. It must either be understood in and for itself or not at all.[11]

5. Obviously, too, *God* is always the subject, and God the *subject*, in this concealed and singular address which is not in continuity with other events. Only revelation in the strict sense overcomes the dilemma which haunts all religious philosophy, namely, that the object escapes or transcends the subject. Revelation means the knowledge of God through God and from God. It means that the object becomes the subject. It is not our own work if we receive God's address, if we know God in faith. It is God's work in us. Our own work either breaks down here or it succeeds and the result is—an idol. But revelation means that God's work is done in us whose own work would necessarily end

10. This third point offers a qualification about the relationship between God's speech in the present ("here and now") and the history depicted in Scripture ("there and then"). On the one hand, God's revelation in the present cannot be collapsed into his revelation in the past, as if our task is to discover the events God performed in history and then apply the "truths" about these events to our lives in the present. Barth thinks this kind of approach inevitably leaves the human interpreter in control, and so he argues that God's revelation takes place in the present only as God personally encounters us in his Word. On the other hand, we cannot focus on God's speech in the present to such an extent that we ignore or contradict what God said and did in the history recorded in Scripture. The God who speaks here and now is the same God who spoke there and then, and so the Word that God speaks to us in the present will correspond to the Word that God spoke through the prophets and apostles in the past.

11. The fourth point builds on the third. God's words and deeds in Scripture are historical in the sense that they occurred in time and space, but they are distinct from all other historical things because they are the words of *God* and thus transcend the limits of creaturely history. They must be seen as "qualified history" because they remain beyond the reach of a historical-critical investigation.

either the one way or the other. The modern locating of revelation in feeling or experience or what is called inwardness is so terrible just because in relation to God it ascribes to us an organ, and the use of an organ, which is ours apart from God; just because it makes God an object *without* God, and in so doing it denies revelation, in which the *Deus dixit* never ceases to be *Deus dixit* even when we believe, even when we think we feel and experience it, even when we try to speak about God. *God* is the subject even when we hear his Word in the witness of the prophets and apostles. To honor heroes, even the man Jesus of Nazareth, is to deny revelation, for it forgets the *Deus dixit*, the divine nature in Christ, to which alone honor and worship belong. *God* is subject even in what we try to say about him. Only improperly and representatively, as it were, may we feel that we ourselves are the subjects of what is said if every word that we think we may and can say objectively about God is not to be again a denial of revelation. Nowhere and never is the *Deus dixit* a reality except in God's own most proper reality.[12]

6. Obviously, too, the process of God's self-revealing is a *dicere*, its content is Word. It is indeed *God's* Word, which we may not take on our own lips or repeat. It differs radically from all the words that we speak. Yet it is not matter, thing, or nature. It is word, *logos*, intellectual communication, a revelation of reason, and our being addressed by God is in the most pregnant sense knowledge, appropriation of word, thinking the thoughts of God that are communicated to us and that demand our hearing and obedience. To be sure, these are God's thoughts and God's reason. . . . Its real content, however, is the truth, and it thus comes to us in a form that corresponds to the truth: not in the form of an ambivalent being, but in the form of the Word which seeks to be known as the bearer of the truth, which gives itself to be known, spirit speaking to spirit through the Spirit.[13]

---

12. Barth's fifth point focuses on questions related to human subjectivity, particularly those that arise as a result of Kantian philosophy. Barth insists that God is not merely the object but also the subject of our knowledge, because God must act to reveal himself to us in order for us to know him. In this way, God overcomes the limits of our subjectivity and enables us to truly know him despite his difference from us. If *we* were the subject responsible for seeking and then knowing God, then we would remain trapped within the limits of our own subjectivity because we never would know if our knowledge of God reflected the reality of God or merely our own human categories.

13. Barth's sixth point explores themes he will later develop at length in his *Church Dogmatics*. God reveals his own divine thoughts to us in human words that are true—not because they are identical to God's thoughts but because they correspond to God's thoughts in a creaturely way. The basis of this correspondence is God's speaking of his Word and our faithful response to it by the power of the Spirit.

CHAPTER 7

"The Holy Spirit and the Christian Life"

Introduction

The summer of 1929 was pivotal in Barth's development. During the winter semester of that year, he taught a seminar on Thomas Aquinas's *Summa Theologiae*. Along with a close reading of the primary text, Barth and his students read secondary works by Catholic thinkers who represented the best of the Thomistic tradition. One of the books they read was by the Jesuit theologian Erich Przywara (1889–1972).[1] Przywara argued for the existence of an analogy of being (*analogia entis*) between God and creatures based on God's act of creation, and he used this idea as the basis for vigorous defense of the Catholic faith. Barth was so intrigued by Przywara's arguments that he invited him to visit the seminar to discuss his ideas. Over the course of two days, Przywara delivered a public lecture and then met with Barth privately at his home to talk about theology. Barth later wrote to a friend that Przywara "overwhelmed" him during this visit.

This exposure to a sophisticated and powerful Catholic theology deeply challenged Barth. Based on the mixed reactions to his 1927 volume of dogmatics, he had already concluded that his theology needed to change if he was going to achieve the aims he had set out to accomplish. Now he realized,

1. The book was Erich Przywara, *Religionsphilosophie katholischer Theologie* (Munich: Oldenburg, 1926). It was translated into English as *Polarity: A German Catholic's Interpretation of Religion*, trans. A. C. Bouquet (London: Oxford University Press, 1935).

perhaps for the first time, just how challenging it would be to offer a theology of his own that could stand alongside the great Catholic thinkers.

In order to find a way forward, Barth decided to spend the summer of 1929 reading rather than writing. He focused particularly on the works of Augustine, who deeply influenced Przywara, as well as the writings of Martin Luther. He hoped Luther would show him a new and distinctively Protestant way to respond to the challenge posed by Catholicism. He put the fruit of his summer reading on display during his lecture "The Holy Spirit and the Christian Life," delivered to a meeting of pastors in Elberfeld, Germany, on October 9, 1929. In this lecture, he draws a stark contrast between Przywara's theology and his own. While Przywara had argued that God's act of creation establishes a relationship of continuity between Creator and creature, Barth rejects this idea. Humans do not relate to God as the result of an "original endowment" given to them in creation. Rather, the human relationship with God is determined at every moment by God's act of grace in the Word and Spirit. This argument—and the clarity and conviction with which Barth delivers it—displays some of the key convictions shaping Barth's theology as he begins the task of writing his *Church Dogmatics*.

-------------- **"The Holy Spirit and the Christian Life"**[2] --------------

The discontinuity between God the Creator and man, when one considers the relation of Creator and creature, must mean that between being Lord and being lorded over there exists an irreversibility such as excludes the idea of God as an object of whom, in Platonic fashion, we have a reminiscence, as "Ancient Beauty." It denotes the knowledge of God, which man obtains as revelation, of what is really and utterly new, and which no innate awareness of beauty on man's part has ever seen objectively.[3] If the creature is to be strictly understood as a reality willed and placed by God in distinction from God's own reality, that is to say, as the wonder of a reality which by the power of God's love, has a place and persistence alongside God's own reality, then the continuity between God and it (the true *analogia entis*, by virtue of which he, the uncreated Spirit, can be revealed to the created

2. Karl Barth, *The Holy Spirit and the Christian Life: The Theological Basis of Ethics*, trans. R. Birch Hoyle (Louisville: Westminster John Knox, 1993), 5–7.

3. Barth rejects the idea of a natural theology. Humans do not possess an innate sense of God, nor can they know God by reflecting on their own created being. The distinction between God and creatures makes this kind of natural knowledge of God impossible.

spirit)—this continuity cannot belong to the creature itself but only to the Creator *in his relation* to the creature. It cannot be taken to mean that the creature has an original endowment in his makeup, but only as a second marvel of God's love, as the inconceivable, undeserved, divine *bestowal* on his creature. Man as *creature* is not in a position from which he can establish and survey (e.g., in a scheme of the unity of like and unlike) his relation to God and thereby interpret himself as "open upward," as Erich Przywara says, and consequently describe his own knowledge as if it meant that God's revealedness were within the compass of his own understanding by itself.[4] The sayings "God has made us for himself" and "man made in the image of God" are not to be taken as meaning an abiding and sure fact of revelation that we have once and for all made our own, but it is a process of revelation, which, in the strictest sense, is first coming to us and to come, moment by moment, if, as we should, we have taken seriously what is meant by the *Deity* of the *Creator* Spirit. Then revelation is to be understood as the occurrence of the Creator Spirit's coming to us in the future, of him-who-exists-for-us, and so it is not a *datum* but a *dandum* (Lat.: "to be given"), not as fulfillment but as promise. Grace is our having been created, but it is also "created for God." But grace is ever and in all relations God's *deed* and *act*, taking place in this and that moment of time in which God wills to be gracious to us, and is gracious, and makes his grace manifest. It is never at all a quality of ours, inborn in us, such as would enable us to know of it in advance.[5] . . .

4. Barth is drawing a contrast between his views and those of Erich Przywara, a Catholic theologian with whom Barth dialogued. Przywara argued that creatures have an intrinsic relationship with God by virtue of their creation by God, because they exist by participating in the being of God. While they do not possess their being in the same way God does—since God is eternal and they are not—they do possess it in a manner analogous to God's being. This is the *analogia entis*, the "analogy of being." Przywara argued that reflection on this innate relationship between divine and creaturely being can lead to knowledge of both God and our relationship with God. Barth rejects this idea. He argues that God's act of creation establishes a discontinuity between divine and creaturely being because creation is a divine act in which the creature does not participate. And if God is distinct from creatures, then the relationship between God and creatures is not determined by any intrinsic quality they both possess—such as being—but by God's unique decision to personally relate to creatures in love. This relationship takes place in a distinct event as a result of the unique work of Christ and the Spirit.

5. Barth insists that our account of how we know God must be based on God's relationship with us rather than our own human capacities. Even though humans were created in the image of God for the sake of their relationship with God, this does not mean they have an innate ability to know God. Creaturely being and divine being are infinitely distinct from one another, and so reflection on created being will not give us knowledge of God. Likewise, while God certainly relates to his creatures, this relationship is not a general feature of creaturely existence but a unique, particular act of grace that stands in line with God's decision to relate to us through Christ and his Spirit.

"What does 'Christian life' mean?" When, where, how, and by whom was that which is called "Christian" lived? We have to give answer, not historically, psychologically, nor in sociological terms, but theologically. And then the answer cannot be ambiguous. It runs thus: then, and just then, when God wills to be and is gracious to man and makes his grace manifest to him. Therefore then, and just then, when God speaks his Word to him, when Christ, as the crucified and risen One, is present there for him, indeed on his behalf. We can describe the same moment chosen by God—the same event taking place in God's freedom—as man's openness or preparedness for God's grace, as his existence for Christ, as his hearing God's Word. In saying this we have not spoken of any of man's own autonomous actions. But when we keep in view the subjective aspect of the central concept of revelation, we have spoken then of the special work of God the *Spirit*, of the wonder of the love in *the outpouring of the Holy Spirit*. When revelation takes place, the Holy Spirit is, according to a figure of speech much cherished in the ancient church, "the finger of God by whom we are sanctified." He is the Paraclete who is not only speaking on our behalf but speaking to us so that we have to hear him, the speaking God. For it does not enter into consideration that we somehow open, prepare, and equip ourselves for taking part in this event at all. The fundamental significance of the Holy Spirit for the Christian life is that this, our participation in the occurrence of revelation, is just our *being grasped* in this occurrence which is the effect of the *divine* action.[6]

In any case, Christian life is now also *created* life. The Christian, constituted such by the action of the divine Word and Spirit, is not in the first place the child of God, nor in the first place is he the justified sinner, but simply this and that human creature. And as the Word of God always approaches him in his human creatureliness, because it is in any case the Word of his Creator, so the preparedness which the Holy Spirit makes always affects his human creatureliness as such. For he, the Paraclete, is at all events the Creator Spirit as well, as we sought to understand him previously in his distinction from the human spirit. And our theme is just this: What is the significance of the *Spirit* of God for the Christian life?

6. This paragraph outlines Barth's description of what it means to speak about God on Christian terms. Christians know God as a result of the work of Jesus Christ, who reveals the truth about God to them by establishing a saving relationship with them; and they know God as a result of the work of the Holy Spirit, who gives them the capacity to receive God's revelation and then respond faithfully to it. A Christian knowledge of God thus is derived from the saving work of Christ and the Spirit rather than general insights derived through the exercise of innate human capacities.

It can be said with confidence that this significance means that man as he is, in his creaturely existence as man and as an individual, is opened, prepared, and made fit by God for God.[7]

7. Barth argues that God's saving action in Christ and the Spirit both defines and determines what it means for us to be a creature. We become the creatures God created us to be as the Spirit opens our lives so that we might relate to God through Christ.

CHAPTER 8

Preface to *Church Dogmatics* I/1

Introduction

In 1925, Barth moved from Göttingen to the University of Münster. The city had a strong Catholic heritage, and Barth quickly found himself with new dialogue partners. For example, he participated in a Catholic reading group and taught seminars on Anselm and Aquinas so that he could learn more about the Catholic tradition. This engagement with Catholic theology, along with his ongoing conversations with thinkers like Erich Przywara, shaped his thought in new ways. Instead of drawing primarily from the Protestant tradition, Barth now appealed to sources from the whole Christian tradition. "It would seem that Church history no longer begins for me in 1517," he later wrote. "I can quote Anselm and Thomas with no sign of horror. I obviously regard the doctrine of the early Church as in some sense normative."[1]

These new influences were apparent in his lectures. Barth had delivered a full cycle of dogmatic lectures while at Göttingen, covering everything from prolegomena to eschatology. Now in Münster, he began again. The manuscripts from this second cycle of dogmatic lectures reveal how much Barth had learned over the decade. The thunderous Barth of *The Epistle to the Romans* now was more refined and careful. While he still offered strong criticisms, he

---

1. Karl Barth, *Church Dogmatics* I/1, rev. ed. (Edinburgh: T&T Clark, 1975), xiii.

also drew from a wide variety of thinkers and ideas in his attempt to construct a viable theology of his own.

Barth decided to publish these lectures as a series of volumes on dogmatic theology. The first volume containing his lectures on theological prolegomena appeared in 1927 as *Die christliche Dogmatik im Entwurf* (Christian Dogmatics in Outline).[2] It received a mixed reception, including from Barth himself. Seeing the volume in print was a humbling experience because he saw every flaw and realized that he still had much to learn. He also was surprised at the way other scholars responded to the book. He had expected his critics to point out every mistake, which they did. But he was shocked by the way his allies appealed to his book for support as they took positions that Barth himself thought were clearly mistaken. Barth worried that he had not communicated his ideas clearly enough.

Soon Barth realized that he needed to start over again. He had originally planned to write a second volume of dogmatics in 1929. He abandoned that project and instead spent the time reading and thinking about how he might clarify his thought. After he moved to the University of Bonn in 1930, he took the opportunity to begin his dogmatic lectures all over again. Now he called them a *church* dogmatics.

This first volume of this third cycle of dogmatics was published in 1932, and this selection is drawn from the preface to that volume. Barth explains why he abandoned his former project and started again. He also takes the opportunity to respond to critics who accused him of turning toward Catholicism. Barth makes it clear that he is offering a distinctively Protestant theology that stands on its own in conversation with the entire church tradition.

Church Dogmatics I/1[3]

When five years ago I published *The Doctrine of the Word of God* as the first volume of a *Christian Dogmatics in Outline*, I had many serviceable materials to hand and thought that I should and could finish the promised whole within the time which has now elapsed.[4] Things turned out differently.

---

2. Karl Barth, *Die christliche Dogmatik im Entwurf* (Munich: Christian Kaiser Verlag, 1927). This volume has never been translated into English.

3. Barth, *Church Dogmatics* I/1, xi–xvi.

4. Barth is referring to his 1927 book based on theological lectures at the University of Münster. For the critical edition of this book, see *Karl Barth Gesamtausgabe*, vol. 14, *Die Christliche Dogmatik im Entwurf I: Die Lehre vom Worte Gottes, Prolegomena zur christlichen Dogmatik 1927* (Zurich: Theologischer Verlag Zürich, 1982).

When the first volume was before me in print, it showed me plainly—whatever may be the experience of others, much more plainly than a manuscript lying in a cupboard could ever have done—how much I myself have still to learn both historically and materially. The opposition which it encountered at least amongst colleagues was too general and vehement, the intervening changes in the theological, ecclesiastical and general situation gave me so much to think about, and the need for my little work on Anselm of Canterbury was so pressing, that I could not pay any attention to the gradually increasing chorus of friendly or ironical enquiries as to what had happened to the second volume, nor even think of continuing on the level and in the strain of the initial volume of 1927.[5] This first became clear to me, of course, when the four thousand copies of the first edition of what had been published as the first volume began to run out, and I was faced with the task of preparing a second edition. My experience of twelve years ago in re-editing the *Römerbrief* was repeated. I could still say what I had said. I wished to do so. But I could not do it in the same way. What option had I but to begin again at the beginning, saying the same thing, but in a very different way?[6] Hence I must gratify or perhaps in part annoy my readers by giving them a revision of the old book instead of the expected new one. May some at least believe that from my own standpoint at any rate this change of plan has been forced on me by the pressure of outer and inner necessities! And may it be clear to some at least that there are good reasons for this unusual arrest or change of direction!

The alteration which I have made consists first and formally in the fact that I have thought it good to make my exposition much more explicit. This emerges at once in the relationship between the size of the book and the material covered. The book is much larger, and it has been severely compressed in places, but it covers only half the material treated in the first edition, and is thus only a half-volume. But what else can I do? In the last five years all the problems have assumed for me a far richer, more fluid and difficult aspect. I have had to make more extensive soundings and lay broader foundations. And yet I venture to hope that the result has been to make everything simpler and clearer.[7] . . .

5. Barth's "little work on Anselm" is his 1931 book, *Fides Quaerens Intellectum: Anselm's Proof of the Existence of God in the Context of His Theological Scheme*, trans. Ian W. Robertson (Richmond: John Knox, 1960). His engagement with Anselm shaped his thought as he began working on his *Church Dogmatics*.

6. The phrase "begin again at the beginning" reflects one of Barth's core convictions. Right theological thinking involves an ongoing attention to God's Word, which confronts us again and again each day in distinct ways. We respond to this Word faithfully by evaluating and then correcting the whole of our thinking in light of what God says.

7. These remarks show that, after nearly a decade of working as a professional theologian, Barth had a clearer grasp of how challenging it can be to offer one's own theology. This new

The facts as to the change in content between the first and this second edition, the reader may gather from the book itself. I may content myself here with some general observations.

In substituting the word Church for Christian in the title, I have tried to set a good example of restraint in the lighthearted use of the great word "Christian" against which I have protested. But materially I have also tried to show that from the very outset dogmatics is not a free science. It is bound to the sphere of the Church, where alone it is possible and meaningful.[8] As laments have accompanied the general course of my development, they will undoubtedly increase at this obvious alteration. But some will see what I have had in view when in recent years, and indeed even in this book, I have often had to speak with some vigor against, or rather on behalf of, the Church. Be that as it may, it will be found that in this new edition the lines are drawn more sharply in the direction indicated by this alteration.

This means above all that I now think I have a better understanding of many things, including my own intentions, to the degree that in this second draft I have excluded to the very best of my ability anything that might appear to find for theology a foundation, support, or justification in philosophical existentialism. "The Word or existence?" The first edition gave to acumen, or perhaps stupidity, some ground for putting this question. I may hope that so far as concerns my own intentions the answer to it is now clear. In the former undertaking I can see only a resumption of the line which leads from Schleiermacher by way of Ritschl to Herrmann. And in any conceivable continuation along this line I can see only the plain destruction of Protestant theology and the Protestant Church.[9] I can see no third alternative between that exploitation of the *analogia entis* which is legitimate only on the basis of Roman Catholicism, between the greatness and misery of a so-called natural knowledge of God in the sense of the *Vaticanum*, and a Protestant theology which draws from its own source, which stands on its own feet, and which is finally liberated

---

awareness stemmed, in part, from his deep engagement with Catholic theologians while teaching in Münster.

8. The idea that dogmatics is a science bound to the Word of God is not new for Barth. Yet the idea that the *church* is the location from which dogmatics is practiced marks a shift from his earlier work, which largely depicted the task of theology in the light of God's encounter with individuals.

9. Barth offers a remarkable criticism of his own 1927 book on dogmatics in these lines. He admits that, despite his intentions, he depicted the event of God's revelation in a way that made the capacities of the human recipient of this revelation essential to the event. This error left God's revelation conditioned by human subjectivity. He realized he had made this mistake only after other theologians began to cite his work in support of views that were recognizably liberal. Later in *Church Dogmatics* I/1 (140), he expresses astonishment that he made such a mistake, and he works throughout the volume to correct it.

from this secular misery. Hence I have had no option but to say No at this point. I regard the *analogia entis* as the invention of the Antichrist, and I believe that because of it it is impossible ever to become a Roman Catholic, all other reasons for not doing so being to my mind short-sighted and trivial.[10]

To say this is to clarify my attitude to the charge which I clearly foresaw five years ago and which has been raised at once all along the line and in every possible tone from friendly concern to downright anger, namely, that historically, formally and materially I am now going the way of scholasticism. It would seem that Church history no longer begins for me in 1517. I can quote Anselm and Thomas with no sign of horror. I obviously regard the doctrine of the early Church as in some sense normative. I deal explicitly with the doctrine of the Trinity, and even with that of the Virgin Birth. The last-named alone is obviously enough to lead many contemporaries to suspect me of crypto-Catholicism.[11] What am I to say? Shall I excuse myself by pointing out that the connection between the Reformation and the early Church, trinitarian and christological dogma, and the very concepts of dogma and the biblical Canon, are not in the last resort malicious inventions of my own? Or shall I oppose to indignation my own indignation at the presumption which seems for its own part to regard the necessity of ignoring or denying these things, and therefore an epigonous fideism, as dogmas whose despisers are at once open to the charge of Catholicism? Or shall I ask, perhaps mentioning names, why none of the so-called positive theologians of whom there are still supposed to be several in German universities—they or their predecessors ran a fairly lively campaign for the "confession" only twenty years ago—have sprung to my assistance in this matter? Or shall I ask what or what sort of teaching they now think should be given concerning the Trinity and the Virgin Birth? Or shall I merely be astonished at the Philistinism which thinks it should bewail

10. Barth's harsh remark about the Roman Catholic *analogia entis* (analogy of being) would spark intense debate in the years to come. Yet his main point here is that he sees no alternative to the distinctly Protestant theology he offers in this volume. He cannot adopt the path of Protestant liberalism since its account of God is determined by human subjectivity. He also cannot go in the direction of Catholic natural theology in the tradition of the First Vatican Council because it makes a similar mistake. His harsh statement that such theology is the "invention of the Antichrist" indicates how clearly Barth sees the choice. In his view, an account of God can be determined either by the limits of creaturely being—as it is in Protestant liberalism and Roman Catholicism—or by God's revelation in Christ and the Spirit. He chooses the latter.

11. Barth's strong condemnation of the Catholic analogy of being stems, in part, from his desire to reject the spurious charge—made by Barth's former colleague Georg Wobbermin just a few months prior—that Barth's theology had been prompting Protestants to convert to Catholicism. Barth strongly rejected the charge, and he labors here to show that, even though he draws from the insights of traditionally Catholic thinkers, his theology remains starkly distinct from Catholicism.

"speculation" when it does not recognize its own ethicism, and fails to see that not merely the most important but also the most relevant and beautiful problems in dogmatics begin at the very point where the fable of "unprofitable scholasticism" and the slogan about the "Greek thinking of the fathers" persuade us that we ought to stop? Or shall I laugh at the phonetically ridiculous talk about *fides quae* and *fides qua* by which many obviously think that they can dismiss the whole concern of scholasticism at a single stroke, promptly dealing with me at the same time? Or shall I rather bemoan the constantly increasing confusion, tedium and irrelevance of modern Protestantism, which, probably along with the Trinity and the Virgin Birth, has lost an entire third dimension—the dimension of what for once, though not confusing it with religious and moral earnestness, we may describe as mystery—with the result that it has been punished with all kinds of worthless substitutes, that it has fallen the more readily victim to such uneasy cliques and sects as High Church, German Church, Christian Community and religious Socialism, and that many of its preachers and adherents have finally learned to discover deep religious significance in the intoxication of Nordic blood and their political *Führer*? However right these various courses might be, I can only ignore the objection and rumor that I am catholicizing, and in face of the enemy repeat the more emphatically and expressly whatever has been deplored in my book in this respect. It is precisely in relation to this disputed aspect that I am of particularly good courage and sure of my cause.[12]

A final remark may be made concerning the present theological situation. Whether in agreement or opposition this book will be the better understood the more it is conceived, as I have already said in the preface to the first edition, as standing on its own, and the less it is conceived as representing a movement, tendency, or school. In this sense, too, it aims to be a Church dogmatics. I may take it as well known that there exists between Eduard Thurneysen and myself a theological affinity which is of long standing and has always shown itself to be self-evident. Again, among theological colleagues, ministers and non-theologians I know many men and women towards whom I am conscious of being wholeheartedly sympathetic in general outlook. But this does not constitute a school, and I certainly cannot think in this emphatic way of those who are commonly associated with me as leaders or adherents of the

12. These series of questions are aimed at Wobbermin and others who questioned Barth's use of patristic and medieval theology as well as his affirmation of traditional doctrines like the Virgin Birth of Christ. Barth insists that, while his approach stands in line with the Reformers and the best insights of the orthodox Christian tradition, his critics' theology is historically tendentious, theologically vacuous, and susceptible to the influence of the latest social and political winds in Germany. Given this contrast, Barth feels comfortable with the path he has chosen.

so-called "dialectical theology." It is only fair to them as well as to me that in its new form, too, this book should not be hailed as the dogmatics of dialectical theology. The community in and for which I have written it is that of the Church and not a community of theological endeavor. Of course, there is within the Church an Evangelical theology which is to be affirmed and a heretical non-theology which is to be resolutely denied. But I rejoice that *in concreto* I neither know nor have to know who stands where, so that I can serve a cause and not a party, and mark off myself from a cause and not a party, not working either for or against persons. Thus I can be free in relation to both ostensible and true neighbors, and responsible on earth only to the Church. I only wish I could make things clear to those who would like to see me walking arm in arm with X or Y.[13]

---

13. As we will see in the next chapter, Barth's relationship with many of the so-called dialectical theologians became strained at the end of the 1920s into the early 1930s. His remarks here mark an important clarification about Barth's relationship to the movement. Rather than offering a theology identified with any particular group, Barth is writing theology for the entire church. This marks a change in focus for Barth. Rather than focusing primarily on what he is against or acting in support of a movement, Barth is going to carve his own path and make an offering for the church as a whole.

Farewell

Introduction

In August 1922, Karl Barth and his friends Eduard Thurneysen and Friedrich Gogarten decided to create a new academic journal. They wanted to provide an outlet for the writings of the thinkers associated with the dialectal theology Barth had helped start. They named their new journal *Zwischen den Zeiten* (Between the Times) and commissioned Georg Merz to serve as its founding editor. Soon they signed a contract with the publisher Christian Kaiser Verlag, and the first issue appeared that October. Over the next decade, *Zwischen den Zeiten* published dozens of essays and sermons from its founders as well as other thinkers, including Rudolf Bultmann and Emil Brunner. The journal provided the dialectal theologians a place to share their ideas, receive feedback, and respond to criticism. In many ways, it set the agenda for the movement and was the source of its unity.

The problem was that, while the dialectical theologians were united about what they rejected, they had different visions for what they supported. As the decade progressed, Barth grew worried that many of his colleagues were falling back into old errors. He particularly was concerned that many of them were basing their theological claims on the basis of general historical and anthropological starting points. For example, Barth worried that Gogarten directly identified divine revelation with natural history and the human subject. This enabled humans to know God by reflecting on their own created being or the movement of history apart from a unique act of God. Barth thought Bultmann's description of the historical Jesus relied too heavily on the historical-critical method, and he worried that his theology was too closely tied to philosophical existentialism. Brunner fell into similar errors when he affirmed that humans could know God by means of their rationality or from natural law viewed in distinction from Jesus Christ. Barth described all these ways of thinking as "returning to the fleshpots of Egypt" because they were too close to the Protestant liberalism they had initially rejected.

At the same time, these same thinkers were growing concerned about Barth's theology. They worried he was drawing too deeply from the Christian tradition and that his theology was becoming a type of Reformed Scholasticism. They also criticized his theology for being philosophically underdeveloped. In their eyes, Barth's insistence on the uniqueness of divine revelation left him unable to address the needs of contemporary society and undermined the church's mission. These impressions were solidified by Barth's first volume of dogmatic theology, *Die christliche Dogmatik im Entwurf* (Christian Dogmatics in Outline). After it was published in 1927, many of his colleagues issued public or private criticisms of the book. Even Merz thought it signaled that Barth had abandoned the prophetic posture that had defined the movement and the journal.

It was clear that Barth and the dialectical theologians were moving in different directions, but he kept publishing in the journal through the end of the decade. Then in the early 1930s, the German Christian movement developed in support of the ideology of the Nazi Party. When Gogarten publicly identified with this movement in 1933, Barth found the situation unbearable. He was not willing to be associated with thinkers who embraced this kind of thinking. It was time to bid both the journal and his former friends farewell. Barth wrote this essay on October 18, 1933, and it was quickly published in *Zwischen den Zeiten*. It appears here for the first time in English.

------------------------------ Farewell[1] ------------------------------

When Gogarten, Eduard Thurneysen, and I, along with Georg Merz as editor, founded *Zwischen den Zeiten* [ZdZ] in the Fall of 1922, we were, so we thought, relatively agreed in terms of what we wanted. In opposition to the positive-liberal or liberal-positive theology of the Neo-Protantism of the beginning

1. Karl Barth, "Abschied," in *Zwischen den Zeiten* 11, no. 6 (1933): 536–44. The critical edition is found in *Karl Barth Gesamtausgabe*, vol. 49, *Vorträge und Kleinere Arbeiten 1930–1933*, ed. Michael Beintker, Michael Hüttenhoff, and Peter Zocher (Zurich: Theologischer Verlag Zürich, 2013), 492–515; translation by Matthew J. Aragon Bruce. Information in several of the notes below has been adapted from the notes found in the critical edition.

of the century and its anthropocentric god which we thought we recognized as its sanctuary, we sought to develop a theology of the Word of God, which had gradually imposed itself upon us as young pastors, as commanded by the Bible and as we found it commendably cultivated by the Reformers. (The name "dialectical theology" had been affixed to us that same year by a spectator.)[2] However, after the completion of a few volumes of our journal, no amount of skillfulness could conceal the fact that there were significant differences in regard to how we understood this tacitly presupposed program, especially between Gogarten and me. For a good while, though, we could smooth things over and even rejoice at the fact that it might arguably be a sign of the energy and riches of our circle, if the one side was seen to be almost continuously occupied with the issues of our supposedly common task that bordered on the philosophical or, to be precise, the ethical, while the other side was nearly just as continually occupied with the history of theology and dogmatics.

Yet, the question hung there from the very beginning: Why are you failing to pursue the necessary task of clearly defining your presuppositions? And the counterquestion: Will you ever actually get to the subject matter? Still, why would it not be thoroughly interesting and advantageous to allow this reciprocal exchange of questions to continue on and on? And if one increasingly got the impression that, with the advancing years, there was something like an occasionally implicit or even explicit polemical back and forth, if the anthropological direction of the one over time was as unmistakable as the theological direction of the other—if then, only in appearance or truly, a third, and fourth, and fifth voice joined the fray independent of this opposition, or even in conscious sympathy for one side or the other, and, supposedly still in the same basic key, sang its special song more or less admirably, edifyingly, and instructively in between them—well, then all this could and might indeed be the case, for those years were intellectually stimulating; still they did not exactly provoke anyone to make a decision. The singular deprecating assertion made by a mischievous little imp five years ago, that the leaders of the dialectical theology were as at variance with one another as the generals of the Chinese revolution, could be laughed at and set aside as a tasteless joke.[3] The existing tensions, of which we were well aware, were endured because they were not intolerable, and they apparently not only were endured by some of our readers but in fact

2. This unnamed spectator is thought to have been present for Barth's lecture "The Word of God as the Task of Theology" (see chap. 3).

3. Barth is referring to a remark by Hans Michael Müller: "*The* dialectical theology is a phantom. Barth formerly called it into life. But today there is more methodological disunity among its leaders than among the political generals in China." See Müller, "Credo, ut intelligam: Kritische Bemerkungen zu Karl Barths Dogmatik," *Theologische Blätter* 17 (1928): 175.

were highly valued on account of the diverse and, consequently, stimulating contents, which, on account of these tensions thus seemed to characterize the journal as a whole. Moreover, Georg Merz, who was equipped by nature and by grace for precisely such an office, was forced, by means often laborious and self-sacrificial, to encourage and to mediate wherever it was urgently needed; he also supplemented it with his own work in a highly successful manner and gathered together and presented the results in ever new formations. And our publisher too, from his special position, could certainly only have been pleased with the course of events.[4] It may well have continued for far longer.

But would it be honorable for things to continue so? That is the question which has acutely preoccupied me; the first time was a year ago and then again throughout the whole of last winter. Readers of *Church Dogmatics* I/1 know the question that I think should be directed to Gogarten—the text on pages 125 and following was already written in 1931, and Gogarten was immediately informed—to what degree might his present anthropological underpinning of theology really differ from that of Catholicism and Neo-Protestantism?[5] To this day, I have never received an answer. However, the answer emerges in what he has published since then, his *Politischen Ethik* [Political Ethics], and the articles "Staat und Kirche" [State and Church] and "Schöpfung und Volkstum" [Creation and Cultural Identity] published in *ZdZ* in 1932, which, in light of that unanswered question, filled me with a grief that could no longer be suppressed.[6] Where, where has this development led, which—beginning with the investigations concerning the authentic concept of history—has now led to the dogma of the orders [of creation] becoming ever more forceful? In which possible sense, so I now retrospectively asked myself, had Gogarten already prefixed [as an epigraph] the Thomistic statement "grace does not destroy but perfects nature" to his "Religiösen Entscheidung" [Religious Decision] of 1921?[7] It also happened that, both inside and outside of our journal, I saw Emil Brunner, who was also considered part of our group, put forth a theology which I could increasingly still only judge as, in effect, a grievous return—by the light of my understanding of our common departure—under

---

4. The publisher is Albert Lempp.

5. See Barth's criticisms of Gogarten in *Church Dogmatics* I/1, rev. ed. (Edinburgh: T&T Clark, 1975), 125–31.

6. See Friedrich Gogarten, *Politische Ethik: Versuch einer Grundlegung* (Jena: Eugen Diederichs, 1932); Gogarten, "Staat und Kirche" *ZdZ* 10 (1932): 390–410; Gogarten, "Schöpfung und Volkstum," *ZdZ* 10 (1932): 481–504.

7. Barth is referring to the Roman Catholic dictum *gratia non tollit naturam sed perficit*, which is drawn from the theology of Thomas Aquinas (see *Summa Theologiae* I, q. 1, a. 8, ad. 2). Gogarten placed this quote as the epigraph of his book *Die religiöse Entscheidung* (Jena: Eugen Diederichs, 1921).

a new banner, to the abandoned fleshpots of Egypt [cf. Exod. 16:3]—namely, to the Neo-Protestant or Catholic schema of "reason and revelation," as it was openly proclaimed for the first time within Protestantism by the so-called rational orthodoxy at the turn of the seventeenth to the eighteenth centuries.[8] But I was also astonished to see that the crowd of our closer and wider circle of readers, and not least our editor, did not feel themselves to be called on by the increasingly evident conflict to make a decision, indeed, that they did not seem to feel the conflict much at all; but also that they were equally fond of appealing to me, through my manifestos—as they were understood—as to Gogarten, to obtain a kind of reassurance. In the more populist journal *Christentum und Wirklichkeit* [Christianity and Reality], which Christian Kaiser Verlag acquired a few years ago, I saw only too clearly the particular way that those in Franconia and other regions of central Germany sought to understand the new discovery of the "biblical-reformational insight," and the precise dosage they intended to give to the people.[9] There were certain hours last winter when I wondered in near despair whether the resulting lemonade would now really be worth all the work and the struggle which for nearly twenty years we thought was the task of a renewal of theological thinking and of church proclamation. It was a consolation to me, and at the same time a cause for concern, to hear Eduard Thurneysen repeatedly affirm that he shared my apprehension and that in any case the two of us had originally meant something rather different than the others.[10] Nonetheless, I still thought that after a slight change to the outward format of the journal, introduced at the beginning of the current volume year, that I could with a clear conscience, and with a not altogether impossible hope for new developments, be part of a circle within the group and still publish my work as before in this well-established journal with the expectation of at least *also* being heard.[11] It was, after all,

8. For an example of what Barth has in mind here, see Emil Brunner, "Die andere Aufgabe der Theologie," *ZdZ* 7 (1929): 255–76. Also see Barth's harsh critique of Brunner's position in his essay, "No! Answer to Emil Brunner," in *Natural Theology: Comprising "Nature and Grace" by Professor Dr. Emil Brunner and the Reply "No!" by Dr. Karl Barth*, trans. Peter Fraenkel (London: Centenary, 1946), 65–128.

9. *Christentum und Wirklichkeit* was founded in 1910 by Friedrich Rittelmeyer (1872–1938) and Christian Geyer (1862–1929). Georg Merz had a close relationship with both of them, and when Christian Kaiser Verlag took over the journal in 1932, he saw the potential for a complementary relationship between it and *Zwischen den Zeiten*. Barth worries that his ideas now will be associated with the content of this other journal.

10. Thurneysen had been Barth's close friend and theological confidant since they turned away from liberalism in 1914. Barth's point is that they both now worried that everything they had been trying to accomplish for nearly two decades was being undermined.

11. The change to which Barth refers is an alteration to the title page of *ZdZ*, which originally listed Georg Merz as the "general editor" and Barth, Gogarten, and Thurneysen as "regular

still peacetime, a time when it might appear permissible, or obligatory even, to take a more relaxed view toward such things. But the last months of this peacetime have, for me, truthfully no longer been pleasant ones.

Sometime this past summer, we read in the *Deutsches Volkstum* [German Folkdom] Gogarten's confession of Wilhelm Stapel's theologumenon that for us the law of God is identical with the law of the German people.[12] That Gogarten a little later also capitulated on church politics, along with ancillary issues, to the side of Ludwig Müller and Joachim Hossenfelder was and is to me relatively secondary next to the fact of his manifold repetition of this confession in his book *Einheit von Evangelium und Volkstum* [Unity of Gospel and Folkdom], pages 8 and 23.[13] With this remark, Gogarten had adopted as his own the fundamental thesis of the German Christians. This is not the place to discuss this thesis. I acknowledge without further qualification that Gogarten's entire path has led him with the highest degree of consistency to condone everything. This, and his adherence to the "movement of faith," is the unambiguous expression of what he has always meant and wanted.[14] After the event, we can and really must say that there is nothing more self-evident than that it was bound to happen with him. The "beer is now out of the barrel," as Luther used to say.[15]

However, my pointed, angry rejection of that thesis is equally consistent. I have always aimed straight at what we at that time, at the beginning of the

---

contributors." Barth worried that this title placed him in the position of implicitly endorsing everything published in the journal. On January 31, 1933—the day after Hitler seized power— Barth arranged to have this page eliminated so that he could not be associated with individual essays found in the journal.

12. Wilhelm Stapel (1882–1954) was the editor of the Germany monthly magazine *Deutsche Volkstum*. In a 1932 book on German political theology, Stapel argued that the law of God is one and the same as the law of the German people. In the June issue of *Deutsche Volkstum*, Gogarten publicly endorsed this idea. See Friedrich Gogarten, "Die Selbständigkeit der Kirche" *Deutsches Volkstum* 15 (1933): 448. Also see Wilhelm Stapel, *Der christliche Staatsmann: Eine Theology des Nationalismus* (Hamburg: Hanseatische Verlagsanstalt, 1932), 174–85.

13. Ludwig Müller and Joachim Hossenfelder were leaders in the German Christian movement, which sided with the Nazi Party. In the book Barth references, Gogarten says, "For the law is given to us in our cultural identity. Here I can only agree with Stapel completely." See Friedrich Gogarten, *Einheit von Evangelium und Volkstum* (Hamburg: Hanseatische Verlagsanstalt, 1933), 18, 23.

14. Gogarten publicly joined the German Christian movement in August 1933. Barth's point here is that Gogarten's decision to embrace this movement is the logical consequence of his theological trajectory over the past decade.

15. Barth probably is referring to a phrase used by Luther in a 1530 letter criticizing Zwingli's position on the Lord's Supper: "It is dangerous to accept such new teaching in contrast to lucid and open texts and the clear words of Christ. . . . I know for a fact that [our] opponents themselves cannot silence their consciences with [the poor biblical passages they quote], and I am convinced that, were the beer in the barrel again, they would now let it remain there." See Martin Luther, *Luther's Works*, vol. 49, *Letters II*, trans. and ed. Gottfried G. Kroedel (Philadelphia: Fortress, 1972), 302.

twenties, appeared to fight together, which is now the agenda, in concentrated form, in the doctrine, in the mentality, and in the attitude of the German Christians. I cannot see anything in German Christianity but the last, fullest, and worst spawn of the essence of Neo-Protestantism, which the Protestant church, if it is not to be overcome, must make ripe for Rome. I regard Stapel's dictum about the law of God as the complete betrayal of the gospel.[16] I believe that this dictum is today much worse because it is much more fundamental and much more concrete than it was in the era of Harnack and Troeltsch, which represents the erection of the anthropocentric god of the eighteenth and nineteenth centuries. Gogarten will be as little surprised by me as I am little surprised by him. The sun has brought things to light about me just as it has about him.[17] We are now both wiser than we were thirteen years ago or even a year ago. But this must mean that we are now as a divorced couple. It would not make any sense, but it could only mislead and confuse the theological and ecclesiastical public, if henceforth we desired to outwardly present ourselves as part of a united group and a front. Gogarten stands where Emmanuel Hirsch, where Wobbermin, where H. M. Müller, where Fezer, where Schumann, where they all stand.[18] But whoever stands there stands with those with whom I will never even appear to stand together and work together. I want this as much as the apostle John, if the report is true, wanted to be in the bathhouse with Cerinthus. In spite of, or precisely because of, his saying, "Children, love one another!"[19]

16. Note how Barth draws a link between the theological errors of the German Christians and the theological errors he had been fighting since the beginning of his career. He sees the ideology of German Christians as a new form of the old errors of Protestant liberalism. The implication for Gogarten is clear: he has turned away from the truth, embraced the theology of their opponents, and betrayed Jesus Christ.

17. It is likely that Barth is referencing the Brothers Grimm fairy tale "The Bright Sun Brings It to Light." In this story, a young and poor tailor's apprentice murders a Jewish traveler in order to steal his money. The Jewish man's dying words are "The bright sun will bring it to light." Many years later, the now-successful tailor sees the sunlight reflecting off his morning coffee and remembers the Jewish man's words. He says aloud that he wishes he could bring it to light, and he then tells his wife the story of the murder. She then tells other people, and eventually the tailor is arrested and sentenced. The reason Barth would apply this story to Gogarten in this circumstance should be clear.

18. Georg Wobbermin (1869–1943), Hans Michael Müller (1901–1989), Karl Fezer (1891–1960), and Friedrich Karl Schumann (1886–1960) were all professors of theology in German universities. They each were members of the Nazi Party and supported the German Christian movement. They criticized Barth in defense of the German Christian cause, and some of them served as advisers to Ludwig Müller, the leader of the German Church.

19. Barth is referring to a story told by the early Christian martyr Polycarp, as reported by Irenaeus. Polycarp said the apostle John once went to take a bath at Ephesus and saw Cerinthus already there. He left without bathing, saying, "Let us flee lest even the bathhouse collapse because Cerinthus the enemy of the truth is in there." See Irenaeus, *Against Heresies* 3.3.4. The biblical references are to 1 John 3:11, 18, 23; John 13:23; 15:12, 17.

This is the decision to which I have come regarding Gogarten and the German Christians. I assume that Gogarten himself will at least formally understand and agree. But, it is not the decision of the editor and the publisher, and if we are not deceived, it also is not the decision of the greatest part of the readership of the *ZdZ*. Their decision is that the ecclesial crisis of this year does not necessitate making a decision concerning the journal, that the sun has brought nothing to light about our circle, that henceforth theological essays based on Stapel's dictum could be placed and calmly read in the *ZdZ* beside an essay like mine on the first commandment—in short, that everything could go on as before in the *ZdZ* as if nothing had happened.[20] The basis for this decision that there be no decision is documented in issue 4 of this journal.[21]

On the basis of this decision, I have to regard my labor as part of *ZdZ* as finished. In a time like the present, where the field of theology and church has moved from a bare field for military exercises to the battlefield—as in those times which up until now we chiefly have known only from books—in such a time I must be able to assume full responsibility for the theological and ecclesiastical content of a journal for which I feel accountable as a cofounder coming both from Germany and outside of it. But I cannot do this if, from this moment onward, even a single individual belonging to the German Christians or from those who are close to them cooperate in this journal to any degree, if the editor has no sense that there can now no longer be any conviviality and forbearance, if I must thus fear that in the next issue I will be able to read, for example, some mildly clever apology of the Aryan paragraph on the basis of the orders of creation presented as an, at minimum, plausible contribution to the "biblical-reformational insight."[22] Because I cannot do this and because the editor and publisher cannot do anything else, I must therefore say farewell to the *ZdZ*.

20. See Karl Barth, "The First Commandment as an Axiom of Theology," in *The Way of Theology in Karl Barth: Essays and Comments*, ed. H. Martin Rumscheidt (Allison Park, PA: Pickwick, 1969), 63–78. It was published in *ZdZ* 11 (1933): 297–314.

21. Volume 11, issue 4 of *ZdZ* appeared in August 1933. In addition to Barth's essay on the first commandment, it contained a review by Hinrich Knittermeyer, who had joined the German Christians. It also contained a review of Barth's *Theological Existence Today!* by Georg Merz. In that review, Merz offers a qualified defense of the German Christians in response to Barth's harsh criticisms of them. Barth saw this mixed message as unclear and intolerable. *ZdZ* no longer could mediate between the various factions within dialectical theology.

22. The "Aryan Paragraph" was part of the Law for the Restoration of the Professional Civil Service passed by the Nazis in April 1933. It required members of certain offices to prove their Aryan heritage and promise to support the state. The clear intention was to exclude Jews and other undesirables from influential offices. The German Church utilized this paragraph to remove ethnically Jewish pastors from their churches and censure any pastor who officiated a mixed-race wedding.

Georg Merz, if I understand him correctly, wants to replicate on a small scale in the journal what exists on a large scale in the German Protestant Church: the interesting juxtaposition of yes *and* no.[23] I think that *ZdZ* should have left this to the *Christlichen Welt* or to the *Zeitwende* or some similar publication.[24] I think that the position from which anyone could regard such a synthesis as possible is a historical-philosophical one and not a theological one. I think that our journal could have been a truly ecclesiastical force in modern times if only it had proven itself to be a humble but unbreakable dam against the German Christian flood. Because this is not possible, I regret to say that I can have nothing to do with *ZdZ*. I would prefer that my voice no longer be heard than to aid and abet the opinion that henceforth one can leisurely listen to me with one ear and Gogarten with the other. Whoever wants *that* would do well today to listen entirely and only to Gogarten.

The foundation and existence of *ZdZ* rests on a misunderstanding. A productive misunderstanding, so much can and must be said today, despite everything. If the ways of providence could be grasped, we might say, even a necessary misunderstanding. But in any case, the irreconcilable opposition between my work and Gogarten's, as the light of day has now dawned, and moreover the lack of understanding between Georg Merz and me regarding the gravity of that opposition, proves that there is a misunderstanding. Misunderstandings exist in order to be eliminated. *ZdZ* will no longer be a source of misunderstanding after I have withdrawn from it.

Explanations such as those given here tend to be subjected, after the fact, to all sorts of interpretations, which are then used to produce an overly simplified version of the stated opinion. And who can defend himself against interpretations? But I may give a few warnings—to be clear I am not thinking here of either Gogarten and Merz—along the way to the interpreters.

There will be many people who will want to see my resignation from *ZdZ*, as well as my position on the present church crisis, as a result of my Reformed opposition to Lutheranism.[25] Be warned. It is obvious that I am

23. Barth is referring to an article written by Merz in the same issue in which this essay appears. Merz argues, "It would therefore have been dear to me, if the dispute about these things would have continued in *ZdZ* and carried out to their end. It is my firm conviction that not only our circle, but also the whole Church and its theology would have benefited from it." Barth clearly rejects this mediating position. See Georg Merz, "Abschied," *ZdZ* 11 (1933): 553.

24. *Christliche Welt* (The Christian World) was a magazine identified with Protestant liberalism. *Zeitwende* (Turning Point) was another magazine that provided a forum to discuss Protestant culture and art. During the Nazi period, it served as a sympathetic outlet for German Christian writings.

25. Gogarten and Bultmann were Lutheran, and they argued that their differences with Barth stemmed from the historic disagreements between the Lutheran and Reformed traditions. In

Reformed. But the Neo-Protestantism which culminates in the "Christian faith movement" destroys both Lutheranism and the Reformed Confession. So good a Lutheran, in his own way, as A. F. C. Vilmar, who was once in a not dissimilar situation, let himself be misrepresented by his interpreters as little as possible, just as I am able to do now.[26] Good Lutherans today do not stand among the German Christians, nor among the mediators between them and us others, but resolutely with us others! Moreover, there are plenty from the Reformed Confession who are corrupted and stand entirely or halfway among the German Christians. If there was ever a time for union between good Lutherans and good Reformed (I know how few and far between both are today)—namely, for a union in a new confessional struggle against the newest form of that ancient foe—then it is today.[27] Today the serious fronts actually cut diagonally across the boundaries of both traditional confessions.

There will be many people who, considering the content, will want to suggest that on this occasion the actual decisive factor that lies behind my theological and ecclesial judgment is my political thought concerning the events of the past year. Be warned. It is obvious that I have my own thoughts about it. But if I really could be interpreted from this point of view, then I hardly would have fouled so thoroughly the concept of German religious socialism (which, according to the unbesmirchable witness of Leonhard Ragaz, already happened in 1919); then my theological and ecclesiastical affinity for Marxism, liberalism, etc., would still also have had to become visible somehow during these fourteen infamous years; and then at this time—and I would add also in this year 1933—my listeners, most of whom are of a political persuasion altogether different than I, would have noticed something of this evil causal interconnection within my theology and acted accordingly. Prove to me this connection from my books, essays, and sermons; or, you may ask, if you wish, what I was doing and not doing in all these years in Göttingen, Münster, and Bonn, and then—but only then, if you are willing and able—may you

---

their view, these disagreements should remain historical since they reflected the theology of the Reformation rather than contemporary thought. To accuse Barth of emphasizing them is to charge him with historical obscurantism.

26. Barth is referring to August Vilmar (1800–1860), who rejected a proposed Lutheran-Reformed union by comparing the confessions of the two churches and then defending the accuracy of the Lutheran confession.

27. The phrase translated as "that ancient foe" is "des altbösen Feind," which would be more literally rendered as "the old, evil enemy." But since Barth likely is alluding here to the first verse of Luther's hymn "A Mighty Fortress Is Our God," the translation follows the traditional English version of that hymn: "For still our ancient foe, doth seek to work us woe."

continue to speak about my political background. Until then, I will regard it as derogatory gossip.[28]

And there will be many people who on this occasion will point out once again that I am a Swiss, and not, as Hirsch wrote so well, "from root to branch" a German.[29] Be warned. It is obvious that I am Swiss, and not only in part but wholly; just as I have also now lived my life in Germany and done my work in Germany not for half a year but for twelve whole years. But there are also Swiss, indeed Swiss who live in Switzerland, who do not swear on anything higher than Gogarten, and on the other hand good Germans, indeed Germans living in Germany, who would not even think of doing so. Since when is it customary to make the homeland of a person a decisive argument in a factual dispute? What does anyone actually think they can prove with this argument, in relation to the matter which concerns the theology and church today? Do they perhaps want to persuade me, and also a number of others who were born German citizens, that authentic Germanism only begins with Aryanism and with the profession of natural theology? That a seriously responsible contribution to the destiny of Germany would have to be reckoned by the bowing of the knee before the mysteries of the German Christians or at least proven by respecting their "concerns" as ostensibly legitimate?[30] I am well aware of the part which I am to play as Swiss citizen who, in the midst of German theology and the German church, also wants to remain totally and steadfastly Swiss. In the words of the very secular Gottfried Keller:

> "Free men, thank God, it's still our custom:
> In ardent words let freedom ring!"[31]

28. Barth's point is that his theological judgments here are not being shaped by his political beliefs. If that were the case, then his well-known political socialism would have been driving his theology all along. In fact, it is his theology that is shaping his politics.

29. The theologian Emanuel Hirsch, who strongly supported the German Christian movement, criticized Barth's *Theological Existence Today!* for failing to discern the needs of the contemporary church. In the midst of his critique, he said, "I would not think . . . [Barth] would be so blind here if he were a German from root to branch as we are, if he had lived the fate of our people in war and defeat and self-alienation as well as the rise of National Socialism with trembling and joy like us." See Emmanuel Hirsch, "Das kirchliche Wollen der Deutschen Christen: Zur Beurteilung des Angriffs von Karl Barth [*Theologische Existenz heute!*, Munich, 1933]," in *Das kirchliche Wollen der Deutschen Christen* (Berlin: Evangelischer Pressverband für Deutschland, 1933), 7.

30. Here Barth is referring to a remark from Hirsch: "It is our concern, as German Christians, that our Protestant Christianity does not fail to hear the call of the Führer for right cooperation in the nationalization of the Germans. This is why we demand a new formation of the concepts of the people, the state, and the church in the meaning of our directives." See Emmanuel Hirsch, "Volk, Staat, Kirche," in *Evangelisches Deutschland* 10 (1933): 204.

31. Barth here cites a stanza from the Swiss poet Gottfried Keller's *Wegleid*. Keller opens his novella *Das verlorene Lachen*—translated into English under the title *The Lost Smile*—with

And—if anyone should ask about my citizenship papers, I would certainly say that I am Swiss—I would also certainly say that I could not better prove my love for Germany, my belonging to it, than by the fact that I am in the thick of things in Germany, contrary to many Germans. Grant me the right to have my arguments rebutted!

And here is a word to the *laissez-faire*!—I know that there are also earnest people who with me are widely aware of what is at stake, including those who will abstain from the aforementioned, misguided argumentations, people who are also concerned, who are also opposed to the German Christians, who are opposed to the mediators, who will shake their head at my brusque posture on the present church situation and now also at my pointed letter of resignation. I admit that at the present moment, given the diversity of temperaments and ways of life, not everyone can be as focused on such matters as I seem to be. If only I could be convinced otherwise, by what inner law we *might* be less focused today! Until then I would like it if you believed me that I am loyal not only to the cause, to which we all must be devoted, but also and especially to all those to whom this cause is a serious matter, whether or not they understand me at this moment; that I am now focused and thus, for example, because the *ZdZ* cannot be made to be so focused, I say farewell to the *ZdZ*. It is my opinion that by saying farewell I can say much more clearly what I would like to say than if I were to add further *words* to the journal in its present form. And I am hopeful that this step will also be seen as sensible to those whose final impression is presently that I am simply being exceedingly stubborn.

My future publications will, for the time being, be published in a series, published at irregular intervals, titled *Theologische Existenz heute!* [Theological Existence Today!], from Christian Kaiser Munich, which Eduard Thurneysen and I have already begun to edit.[32]

---

the same poem. See Gottfried Keller, *Stories*, ed. and trans. Frank G. Ryder, German Library 44 (New York: Continuum, 1982), 190.

32. This concluding paragraph was set in a smaller font in the original text. The writings featured in the issues of *Theological Existence Today!* during this period mostly came from Barth. He includes lectures, essays, and sermons offering his commentary on the situation in Germany. His biographer Eberhard Busch notes that Barth asked his audience to read his contributions as if they bore the subtitle "between the lines." The German phrase for "between the lines"—*Zwischen den Zeilen*—differs from *Zwischen den Zeiten* by one letter. See Eberhard Busch, *Karl Barth: His Life from Letters and Autobiographical Texts* (Grand Rapids: Eerdmans, 1994), 230.

CHAPTER

10

"The Humanity of God"

Introduction

Barth delivered "The Humanity of God" to a gathering of pastors on September 25, 1956, in Aarau, Switzerland. According to his biographer, he composed the lecture "virtually at one sitting."[1] The event was significant for Barth because the venue brought back memories. In 1920, Barth had delivered his lecture "Biblical Questions, Insights, and Vistas" at the Aarau Student Conference in that same room.[2] Adolf von Harnack was in the audience that day, and he was shocked at the claims Barth made. He privately questioned Barth after his talk, and although Harnack was Barth's former teacher and a senior scholar, Barth defended himself vigorously. While their conversation remained cordial, the two men left their meeting with a clear sense that they sharply disagreed about matters of biblical interpretation. The stage was set for the public debate that would occur in the years to come.

Now over seventy years old, Barth could look back at this early period with a sense of perspective and humility. He now realized that while he was right in what he opposed in his early theology, he was wrong in what he affirmed. His goal in this lecture is to explain how he came to this realization,

1. Eberhard Busch, *Karl Barth: His Life from Letters and Autobiographical Texts* (Grand Rapids: Eerdmans, 1994), 423.
2. For a text of this lecture, see Karl Barth, "Biblical Questions, Insights, and Vistas," in *The Word of God and Theology*, ed. and trans. Amy Marga (London: T&T Clark, 2011), 71–100.

and he does so by offering a candid and self-critical assessment of his own theological development. He leaves no doubt that he still believes that his criticism of Protestant liberalism was well-founded and necessary. But he also admits that his early theology missed the mark in important ways. While he talked a lot *about* Jesus Christ during these years, he neglected to allow his theology to be shaped *by* Jesus Christ. He learned this lesson as he wrote his *Church Dogmatics* because the challenge of writing his own theology taught him that it was necessary to base every claim on the reality of the human Jesus Christ, the one true God. He describes his new focus on the humanity of God as a "genuine revision" in his theology. Yet he insists that this revision does not mark a retreat but an advance from his earlier position. It is a new way of saying the same ideas he had tried but failed to communicate in his early work.

This excerpt captures the heart of Barth's lecture and provides important insights into how Barth understood his own development. It also helpfully summarizes several key themes that stand at the center of Barth's *Church Dogmatics*.

"The Humanity of God"[3]

I

. . . Evangelical theology almost all along the line, certainly in all its representative forms and tendencies, had become *religionistic, anthropocentric,* and in this sense *humanistic.*[4] What I mean to say is that an external and internal disposition and emotion of man, namely his piety—which might well be Christian piety—had become its object of study and its theme. Around this it revolved and seemed compelled to revolve without release. This was true of evangelical theology in its doctrine of principles, in its presentation of the Christian past and its practical understanding of the Christian present, in its ethics and in that which perhaps was to be regarded as its dogmatics, in the proclamation and instruction of the Church determined by it—above all, however, in its interpretation of the Bible. What did it know and say of the *deity* of God? For this theology, to think about

3. Karl Barth, *The Humanity of God* (Richmond: John Knox, 1960), 39–46.
4. This excerpt begins in the midst of Barth's argument. He is describing the condition of Protestant theology in the early part of the twentieth century, before his break from liberalism. The word "evangelical" here means "Protestant," inclusive of both the Lutheran and Reformed traditions.

God meant to think in a scarcely veiled fashion about man, more exactly about the religious, the Christian religious man. To speak about God meant to speak in an exalted tone but once again and more than ever about this man—his revelations and wonders, his faith and his works. There is no question about it: here man was made great at the cost of God—the divine God who is someone other than man, who sovereignly confronts him, who immovably and unchangeably stands over against him as the Lord, Creator, and Redeemer. This God who is also man's free partner in a history inaugurated by Him and in a dialogue ruled by Him was in danger of being reduced, along with this history and this dialogue, to a pious notion—to a mystical expression and symbol of a current alternating between a man and his own heights or depths. But whatever truth was gained in this way could be only that of a monologue.

At this point some of us were appalled after we, along with everyone else, had drained the different chalices of this theology to the last drop. We then concluded (from approximately the middle of the second decade of our century on) that we could not side with it any longer. Why? Had the pious man and the religion of whose history and presence we had heard so many glorious things at the university and of which we ourselves thereafter had tried to speak, become a matter of question in our own person? Was it the encounter with socialism as interpreted by Kutter and Ragaz which opened our eyes to the fact that God might actually be wholly other than the God confined to the musty shell of the Christian-religious self-consciousness, and that as such He might act and speak?[5] Was it the suddenly darkened outlook for the world, in contrast to the long period of peace in our youth, which awakened us to the fact that man's distress might be too great for a reference to his religious potentiality to prove a comforting and prophetic word? Was it—this has played a decisive role for me personally—precisely the failure of the ethics of the modern theology of the time, with the outbreak of the First World War, which caused us to grow puzzled also about its exegesis, its treatment of history, and its dogmatics? Or was it, in a positive sense, the message of Blumhardt concerning the Kingdom of God which, remarkably enough, was only then becoming timely?[6] Was it Kierkegaard, Dostoevsky, Overbeck,

---

5. Hermann Kutter (1863–1931) and Leonhard Ragaz (1868–1945) were Swiss theologians who advocated distinct versions of Christian socialism in Switzerland during the period of Barth's ministry. Barth interacted with them as he worked out how his new theological convictions related to his long-standing commitment to socialism.

6. Barth is referring to the work of Johann Christoph Blumhardt (1805–1880), a Lutheran theologian who influenced Barth through his son Christoph (1842–1919) in the years after Barth's break from liberalism. Barth found hope in Blumhardt's account of the kingdom of

read as a commentary on that message, through which we found ourselves compelled to look for and set sail to new shores?[7] Or was it something more fundamental than all that, namely, the discovery that the theme of the Bible, contrary to the critical and to the orthodox exegesis which we inherited, certainly could not be man's religion and religious morality and certainly not his own secret divinity? The stone wall we first ran up against was that the theme of the Bible is the deity of *God*, more exactly God's *deity*—God's independence and particular character, not only in relation to the natural but also to the spiritual cosmos; God's absolutely unique existence, might, and initiative, above all, in His relation to man.[8] Only in this manner were we able to understand the voice of the Old and New Testaments. Only with this perspective did we feel we could henceforth be theologians, and in particular, preachers—ministers of the divine Word.

Were we right or wrong? We were certainly right! Let one read the doctrine of Troeltsch and Stephan! Let one read also the dogmatics of Lüdemann, in its way so solid, or even that of Seeberg! If all that wasn't a blind alley! Beyond doubt what was then in order was not some kind of further shifting around within the complex of inherited questions, as this was finally attempted by Wobbermin, Schaeder, and Otto, but rather a change of direction.[9] The ship was threatening to run aground; the moment was at hand to turn the rudder an angle of exactly 180 degrees. And in view of what is to be said later, let it immediately be stated: "That which is gone does not return." Therefore there never could be a question of denying or reversing that change. It was, however, later on and it is today a question of "revision." A *genuine* revision in no way involves a subsequent retreat, but rather a new beginning and attack in which what previously has been said is to be said more than ever, but now even better.[10] . . .

God, which was rooted in an eschatological vision of Christian knowledge and a distinct approach to the New Testament.

7. The references here are to the Danish philosopher Søren Kierkegaard (1813–1855), Russian novelist Fyodor Dostoevsky (1821–1881), and the German Protestant theologian Franz Overbeck (1837–1905). While quite distinct, each thinker raised questions about the relationship between faith and culture that influenced Barth as he rebuilt his theology.

8. This theme stands at the center of Barth's early theology, represented especially by chaps. 2–5 in this volume.

9. The references here are to the scholars Ernst Troeltsch, Horst Stephan, Hermann Lüdemann, Reinhold Seeberg, Georg Wobbermin, Erich Schaeder, and Rudolf Otto. All were influential thinkers who shaped the landscape of Protestant theology during the early period of Barth's theological development. His point here is that none of their theologies were satisfactory.

10. While Barth remains convinced that he and his allies were correct to reject liberal theology, he also believes that this rejection must be qualified by further insights. The German word for

It must now quite frankly be granted that we were at that time only partially in the right, even in reference to the theology which we inherited and from which we had to disengage ourselves—partially right in the same sense in which all preponderantly critical-polemic movements, attitudes, and positions, however meaningful they may be, are usually only partially in the right. What expressions we used—in part taken over and in part newly invented!—above all, the famous "wholly other" breaking in upon us "perpendicularly from above," the not less famous "infinite qualitative distinction" between God and man, the vacuum, the mathematical point, and the tangent in which alone they must meet. "And as she warbled, a thousand voices in the field sang it back."[11] There was also the bold assurance that there is in the Bible only *one* theological interest, namely, that in God; that only *one* way appears, namely, that from above downwards; that only *one* message can be heard, namely, that of an immediate forgiveness of sins both in prospect and in retrospect. The problem of ethics was identified with man's sickness unto death; redemption was viewed as consisting in the abolition of the creatureliness of the creature, the swallowing of immanence by transcendence, and in conformity with these the demand for a faith like a spring into the abyss, and more of the like! All this, however well it may have been meant and however much it may have mattered, was nevertheless said somewhat severely and brutally, and moreover—at least according to the other side—in part heretically. How we cleared things away! And we did almost nothing but clear away! Everything which even remotely smacked of mysticism and morality, of pietism and romanticism, or even of idealism, was suspected and sharply interdicted or bracketed with reservations which sounded actually prohibitive! What should really have been only a sad and friendly smile was a derisive laugh!

Did not the whole thing frequently seem more like the report of an enormous execution than the message of the Resurrection, which was its real aim? Was the impression of many contemporaries wholly unfounded, who felt that the final result might be to stand Schleiermacher on his head, that is, to make God great for a change at the cost of *man*? Were they wrong in thinking that actually not too much had been won and that perhaps in the final analysis it was only a new Titanism at work?[12] Was it only obduracy when, beside the

"revision" here is *Retraktation*. Barth's use of this word calls to mind Augustine's *Retractions*, in which Augustine makes a critical assessment of his own writing and theology near the end of his life.

11. This line comes from the poem "Spring's Revelation" by the German poet Emanuel Geibel. Barth cites it to emphasize how these phrases took on a life of their own in the early years of his theology.

12. The word "Titanism" refers to a rebellion against dominant social conventions that faces nearly impossible odds. Barth appeals to the idea here, in the midst of a long string of

many who to some extent listened with relief and accompanied us, so many others preferred to shake their heads, nonplused or—like Harnack at that time—even angry over such an innovation?[13] Was there not perhaps in their obduracy the dark presentiment that, in the religionism, the anthropocentrism, the ill-fated humanism of the earlier theology, there might have been something at work that could not be given up? Is it possible that, granted the unmistakable contestability, even perversity of their position, the *humanity* of God did not quite come into its rights in the manner in which we, absorbed as we were in contemplation of the mighty deployment of Leviathan and Behemoth in the book of Job, lifted up His deity on the candlestick?

Where did we really go astray? Where was and is the starting point for the new change of direction? The shrewd friend from another shore has, as is well known, laid his finger on the fact that at that time we worked almost exclusively with the concept of *diastasis*, only seldom and incidentally with the complementary concept of analogy.[14] That may be the case. But was not this formal principle merely a symptom of a more deep-seated, essential infirmity in our thinking and speaking at that time? I believe it consisted in the fact that we were wrong exactly where we were right, that at first we did not know how to carry through with sufficient care and thoroughness the new knowledge of the deity of God which was so exciting both to us and to others.[15] It was certainly good and proper to return to it and to make it known with greater power. Moreover, Master Calvin in particular has given us more than wise guidance in this matter. The allegation that we were teaching that God is everything and man nothing, was bad. As a matter of fact, certain hymns of praise to humanism were at that time occasionally raised—the Platonic in particular, in which Calvin was nurtured.

It is nevertheless true that it was pre-eminently the image and concept of a "wholly other" that fascinated us and which we, though not without examination, had dared to identify with the deity of Him who in the Bible is

---

self-criticisms, to raise questions about whether his early theology achieved what it set out to accomplish.

13. The reference to Adolf von Harnack concerns his exchange with Barth, discussed in chap. 4.

14. The word *diastasis* refers to God's infinite distinction from created being. This "shrewd friend" likely is the Catholic theologian Hans Urs von Balthasar, who described Barth's embrace of analogy in his theology in his 1951 book on Barth. See Hans Urs von Balthasar, *The Theology of Karl Barth: Exposition and Interpretation*, trans. Edward T. Oakes, SJ (San Francisco: Ignatius, 1992).

15. Barth's self-criticism on this point is important. While he still thinks his early theology was essentially correct, he admits that it remained unstable because he did not follow through on the implications of its governing convictions, particularly about God's revelation in Jesus Christ.

called Yahweh-Kyrios. We viewed this "wholly other" in isolation, abstracted and absolutized, and set it over against man, this miserable wretch—not to say boxed his ears with it—in such fashion that it continually showed greater similarity to the deity of the God of the philosophers than to the deity of the God of Abraham, Isaac, and Jacob. Was there not a threat that a stereotyped image would arise again? What if the result of the new hymn to the majesty of God should be a new confirmation of the hopelessness of all human activity? What if it should issue in a new justification of the autonomy of man and thus of secularism in the sense of the Lutheran doctrine of the two kingdoms? That was the concern and the objection of Leonhard Ragaz.[16] God forbid! We did not believe nor intend any such thing.

But did it not appear to escape us by quite a distance that the deity of the *living* God—and we certainly wanted to deal with Him—found its meaning and its power only in the context of His history and of His dialogue with *man*, and thus in His *togetherness* with man? Indeed—and this is the point back of which we cannot go—it is a matter of *God's* sovereign togetherness with man, a togetherness grounded in Him and determined, delimited, and ordered through Him alone. Only in this way and in this context can it take place and be recognized. It is a matter, however, of God's *togetherness* with man. Who God is and what He is in His deity He proves and reveals not in a vacuum as a divine being-for-Himself, but precisely and authentically in the fact that He exists, speaks, and acts as the *partner* of man, though of course as the absolutely superior partner. He who does *that* is the living God. And the freedom in which He does *that* is His deity. It is the deity which as such also has the character of humanity. In this and only in this form was—and still is—our view of the deity of God to be set in opposition to that earlier theology. There must be positive acceptance and not unconsidered rejection of the elements of truth, which one cannot possibly deny to it even if one sees all its weaknesses. It is precisely God's *deity* which, rightly understood, includes his *humanity*.[17]

16. To put this criticism differently: By so emphasizing God's distinction from the world, did the early Barth leave the world completely void of God's presence—thus opening the door to a truly secular world in which God has no relevance at all?

17. This paragraph contains the heart of Barth's critique of his early theology. While he was correct to emphasize God's distinction from created being, he failed to recognize that this infinitely distinct God has decided to live his own eternal life in relation to humanity. This decision to live together with humanity comes from God alone and corresponds to his divine being and character. There is no way to talk about God rightly in distinction from this decision because any attempt to do so is to talk about something other than the "living God" revealed in the Bible. For Barth's development of these themes in the *Church Dogmatics*, see chaps. 18, 19, and 24 in this volume.

II

How do we come to know that? What permits and requires this statement? It is a *Christological* statement, or rather one grounded in and to be unfolded from Christology. A second change of direction after that first one would have been superfluous had we from the beginning possessed the presence of mind to venture the whole inevitable counterthrow from the Christological perspective and thus from the superior and more exact standpoint of the central and entire witness of Holy Scripture.[18] Certainly in *Jesus Christ*, as He is attested in Holy Scripture, we are not dealing with man in the abstract: not with the man who is able with his modicum of religion and religious morality to be sufficient unto himself without God and thus himself to be God. But neither are we dealing with *God* in the abstract: not with one who in His deity exists only separated from man, distant and strange and thus a nonhuman if not indeed an inhuman God.[19] In Jesus Christ there is no isolation of man from God or of God from man. Rather, in Him we encounter the history, the dialogue, in which God and man meet together and are together, the reality of the covenant *mutually* contracted, preserved, and fulfilled by them. Jesus Christ is in His one Person, as true *God*, *man's* loyal partner, and as true *man*, *God's*.[20] He is the Lord humbled for communion with man and likewise the Servant exalted to communion with God. He is the Word spoken from the loftiest, most luminous transcendence and likewise the Word heard in the deepest, darkest immanence. He is both, without their being confused but also without their being divided; He is wholly the one and wholly the other. Thus in this oneness Jesus Christ is the Mediator, the Reconciler, between God and man. Thus He comes forward to *man* on behalf of *God* calling for and awakening faith, love, and hope, and to *God* on behalf of *man*, representing man, making satisfaction and interceding. Thus He attests and guarantees to man God's free *grace* and at the same time attests and guarantees to God man's free *gratitude*. Thus He establishes in His Person the justice of God vis-à-vis man and also the justice of man before God. Thus He is in His Person the covenant in its fullness, the Kingdom of heaven which is at hand, in which God speaks and man hears, God gives and man receives, God commands

18. In Barth's view, his early theology failed because its central claims were developed in distinction from the concrete relationship that God establishes with humanity in Jesus Christ.

19. In other words, a theology that begins with Jesus Christ will resemble neither the Protestant liberalism that Barth rejected nor the early theology he offered as an alternative.

20. Barth's appeal to the idea of a covenant is characteristic of his later work. In his account, Jesus Christ fulfills God's covenant with humanity on both the divine and the human side. This theme is developed most fully in Barth's discussion of the doctrine of election in *Church Dogmatics* II/2, discussed in chap. 18.

and man obeys, God's glory shines in the heights and thence into the depths, and peace on earth comes to pass among men in whom He is well pleased. Moreover, exactly in this way Jesus Christ, as this Mediator and Reconciler between God and man, is also the *Revealer* of them both.[21] We do not need to engage in a free-ranging investigation to seek out and construct who and what God truly is, and who and what man truly is, but only to read the truth about both where it resides, namely, in the fullness of their togetherness, their covenant which proclaims itself in Jesus Christ.

Who and what *God* is—this is what in particular we have to learn better and with more precision in the new change of direction in the thinking and speaking of evangelical theology, which has become necessary in the light of the earlier change. But the question must be, who and what is God *in Jesus Christ*, if we here today would push forward to a better answer.[22]

21. The last few sentences reflect the structure and themes Barth develops in the doctrine of reconciliation of *Church Dogmatics* IV/1–3, discussed in chaps. 24–29. Barth was in the midst of working on these volumes when he delivered this lecture.

22. As well as any other, this paragraph expresses the central convictions that shape Barth's theological method.

PART 2

Barth's *Church Dogmatics*

Karl Barth's *Church Dogmatics* fills 13 volumes along with an additional index volume. In its English translation, it contains 8,353 pages, over six million words, and approximately 15,000 biblical citations. Scholars rank it among the most significant works of theology ever produced. It changed the trajectory of twentieth-century theology by influencing key thinkers and sparking a variety of global movements within both the Protestant and Roman Catholic traditions. It continues to play an important role in contemporary theology, and its content and implications likely will be debated for centuries. Barth considered the *Church Dogmatics* his life's work. He approached the task of writing it as an act of obedience and his own way of taking "every thought captive to obey Christ" (2 Cor. 10:5). But he made a point of taking neither himself nor his dogmatics too seriously. "The angels laugh at old Karl," he once said. "They laugh at him because he tries to grasp the truth about God in a book of *Dogmatics*. They laugh at the fact that volume follows volume and each one is thicker than the previous one."[1] He also did not consider his *Church Dogmatics* to be the final word for every theologian. "I

---

1. This remark is cited in Robert McAfee Brown, introduction to *Portrait of Karl Barth*, by Georges Casalis (Garden City, NY: Doubleday, 1963), 3.

see . . . the *Church Dogmatics*, not as a conclusion, but as the opening of a new conversation."[2]

Barth organizes his dogmatics around paragraphs, which are long sections of text devoted to defending a thesis. The thesis is printed in bold font at the beginning of each paragraph, and it summarizes Barth's claim in that section. The *Church Dogmatics* contains 74 paragraphs along with an additional fragment on baptism.[3] Additional theses can be found in the posthumously published *The Christian Life*, which contains material from Barth's final dogmatic lectures that he did not edit for publication.[4] Some paragraphs in the *Church Dogmatics* run for hundreds of pages. Barth often organizes his argument around numbered subsections with distinct titles, but he does not always do so. Readers have to pay close attention to the flow of Barth's argument in order to note when he is transitioning between points. His constructive claims are featured in normal-size font, which runs throughout the paragraph. This text is interrupted by small-print sections where Barth offers in-depth examinations of primary or secondary sources, exegesis of key biblical passages, or surveys of historical figures, traditions, and movements. Both the normal and small-print sections are essential to grasping Barth's argument in a given paragraph.

Barth possesses a distinct style of argumentation. While his theses are precisely phrased, Barth's defense of them is marked by a repetitive and reflective approach that often is compared to a symphony. He might begin by making an initial claim that explains his thesis. He then will offer an extended reflection upon this claim that moves back and forth as he considers it from different angles. At a certain point, his argument will reach a crescendo, and he will draw the various parts of his argument together into a few sentences or paragraphs. Then Barth will start a *new* movement, only slightly different from the first, that extends or supplements his prior claim by examining it from a different perspective. He might go through this process several times from distinct vantage points before finally bringing the various parts of his argument together. This approach means that Barth does not try to present a linear proof of his thesis as much as he seeks to reflect and mediate on it in conversation with Scripture, church tradition, and contemporary thinkers. This style often makes Barth's position on a given topic difficult to summarize. Barth's entire

---

2. This remark is cited in Eberhard Busch, *Karl Barth: His Life from Letters and Autobiographical Texts* (Grand Rapids: Eerdmans, 1994), 488.

3. These theses are collected together in Karl Barth, *Church Dogmatics: Index Volume with Aids for the Preacher* (Edinburgh: T&T Clark, 1977), 1–13.

4. See Karl Barth, *The Christian Life: Church Dogmatics IV/4; Lecture Fragments*, trans. Geoffrey W. Bromiley (Grand Rapids: Eerdmans, 1981).

argument, in all its twists and turns, is what he thinks on a given topic, and his true position will be represented only when every part of his argument is held together at once.

Two things are helpful to remember when reading and interpreting Barth's *Church Dogmatics*. First, the text originally was written to be delivered as lectures in Barth's courses on dogmatics. Anyone who has participated in a lecture course knows that professors tend to repeat themselves when they want to emphasize a key point, and they often begin each class by summarizing the material they covered in the prior class before adding new material. These traits can be seen throughout Barth's *Church Dogmatics*. He argues like a professor who is leading a class week by week through a semester. Sometimes it becomes clear that Barth is picking up where he left off in a prior semester, this time with a completely different set of students who need to catch up with his argument. When this original classroom context is kept in mind, the organization and flow of Barth's argument—as well as his repetitive style—become more clear and understandable.

Second, most of Barth's students took his courses as part of their training for pastoral ministry. Barth did not deliver his material primarily for other theologians, although he knew they would be reading it. He wrote it to instruct future church leaders so they would be prepared for service in local parishes. The content and structure of his arguments often assume this pastoral context. Barth often talks about the proclaimed Word of God, and he makes a point of drawing connections between difficult dogmatic material and the practical concerns of the Christian life. This is one of the reason Barth believed that ethics always must be included within dogmatics: "I do not think it right to treat [ethics] otherwise than as an integral part of dogmatics, or to produce a dogmatics which does not include it."[5]

Barth organized his *Church Dogmatics* into five volumes, with each volume centered on a doctrine. The selections below span the entire *Church Dogmatics* and feature the backbone of Barth's argument throughout the whole project. While these selections do not cover every important topic that Barth discusses, they provide a helpful glimpse into several key arguments that make Barth's theology distinct.

Barth presents the prolegomena to his theology in his *Doctrine of the Word of God* (vol. I). The selections from *Church Dogmatics* I/1 begin with Barth's discussion of the task of dogmatic theology and the relationship between dogmatics and the church (chap. 11). Barth's account of the threefold Word of God is featured (chap. 12) along with his description of the relationship

---

5. Karl Barth, *Church Dogmatics* I/1, rev. ed. (Edinburgh: T&T Clark, 1975), xvi.

between divine revelation and human faith (chap. 13). The selections from this part-volume culminate with Barth's innovative account of the doctrine of the Trinity (chap. 14). The discussion then turns to Barth's exploration of the saving missions of the Son and the Holy Spirit in a selection from *Church Dogmatics* I/2 (chap. 15).

Barth's *Doctrine of God* (vol. II) stands at the heart of his *Church Dogmatics*. The opening section of *Church Dogmatics* II/1 is featured because it provides Barth's mature account of theological epistemology (chap. 16). His description of God as the One who loves in freedom is central to Barth's doctrine of God and many of the arguments found in later volumes (chap. 17). The selections then turn to Barth's doctrine of election developed in *Church Dogmatics* II/2. They begin with Barth's account of his approach to the doctrine (chap. 18), continue with his description of the election of Jesus Christ (chap. 19), and end with his "purified" version of supralapsarianism (chap. 20).

The Doctrine of Creation (vol. III) opens with an account of the relationship between God's covenant of grace and the created order in *Church Dogmatics* III/1 (chap. 21). Barth turns to the topic of theological anthropology in *Church Dogmatics* III/2 by showing how the elect human, Jesus of Nazareth, reveals the truth about every human (chap. 22). Barth explores the doctrine of providence in *Church Dogmatics* III/3. In the midst of his development of this doctrine, Barth offers a striking account of "nothingness," which is his preferred term to describe the powers identified with sin and evil (chap. 23). Barth turns to the special ethics of creation in *Church Dogmatics* III/4, where he focuses on humanity's freedom before God and their responsibilities in light of God's command.

Barth's *Doctrine of Reconciliation* (vol. IV) is the climax of his *Church Dogmatics* and contains some of his most powerful passages. He begins in *Church Dogmatics* IV/1 by drawing the argument from the earlier volumes together into a striking account of God's relationship with humanity in Jesus Christ (chap. 24). He develops this idea by turning to the priestly office of Jesus Christ and his death for human sins on the cross. He focuses particularly on the Son's humility and obedience and then works out the implications of his death for the church's understanding of the triune being of God (chap. 25). He then turns to the kingly office of Christ and discusses the exaltation of humanity that takes place in the resurrection of Jesus Christ (chap. 26). He moves to an account of the risen Christ's work in his prophetic office to reveal and proclaim his victory over sin and death (chap. 27). The selections then close with Barth's answer to questions about universalism (chap. 28) and his description of the basis and power of the Christian community (chap. 29).

Barth did not live to complete volume V of his *Church Dogmatics* on the doctrine of redemption. He found satisfaction in the fact that his life's work would remain unfinished, because he thought it testified to the human quality of all dogmatic theology. "I have called the attention of others to the fact that, not only in Holy Scripture, but also in *Church Dogmatics* II/1, perfection is the epitome of the divine attributes, so that it is better not to seek or imitate it in a human work."[6]

6. Karl Barth, *Church Dogmatics* IV/4 (Edinburgh: T&T Clark, 1969), vii.

CHAPTER

11

The Task of Dogmatics

Introduction

Barth outlines the task and proper procedure for dogmatic theology in this excerpt from the opening pages of *Church Dogmatics* I/1. While many of these insights have been present in Barth's theology for years, his description of them is now more refined and precise. They summarize the method Barth intends to follow throughout his dogmatics.

Three claims stand out. First, Barth places dogmatics in a secondary and subsidiary position by framing it as a self-critical enterprise oriented toward the service of the church. Rather than operating from a position of superiority, the theologian remains responsible to God, who is the primary subject matter of dogmatics. And instead of existing for its own sake, theology serves the church by seeking to clarify and enrich the church's speech about God. Second, Barth draws a sharp distinction between divine revelation and the content of dogmatics. His goal is to establish that God's Word—rather than judgment of the theologian—serves as the criterion of the dogmatics. It is in this context that Barth appeals to the analogy of faith (*analogia fidei*) as the basis for Christian talk about God. This concept plays an important role in the early volumes of the *Church Dogmatics*. Third, Barth frames the task of dogmatics as an act of obedience by arguing that it takes place as a theology of the cross (*theologia crucis*). Theologians proceed rightly when they reexamine their claims each day in light of a fresh hearing of the Word of God and their desire to "take every thought captive to obey Christ" (2 Cor. 10:5). This argument gives Barth a distinct approach to the creedal tradition, the role of dogma, and the exegesis of Scripture.

---------------------- *Church Dogmatics* I/1[1] ----------------------

Dogmatics is the self-examination of the Christian Church in respect of the content of its distinctive talk about God. The true content which is sought we shall call dogma. This term, and therefore the word "dogmatics," will be explained in §7.[2] In this initial approach we may simply say that when we describe the true content of the Church's talk about God as the object of human work or investigation, we presuppose that it has both the capacity and the need to serve as the object of human enquiry. In other words, we presuppose that the "science of dogma" is both possible and necessary. Neither proposition is self-evident. Each must be sustained.

1. Dogmatics as an enquiry presupposes that the true content of Christian talk about God can be known by man. It makes this assumption as in and with the Church it believes in Jesus Christ as the revealing and reconciling address of God to man. Talk about God has true content when it conforms to the being of the Church, i.e., when it conforms to Jesus Christ . . . "if prophecy, then in accordance with the analogy of faith" (Rom. 12:6).[3] It is in terms of such conformity that dogmatics investigates Christian utterance. Hence it does not have to begin by finding or inventing the standard by which it measures. It sees and recognizes that this is given with the Church. It is given in its own peculiar way, as Jesus Christ is given, as God in His revelation gives Himself to faith. But it is given. It is complete in itself. It stands by its claim without discussion. It has the certainty which a true standard or criterion must have to be the means of serious measurement. Dogmatics presupposes that, as God in Jesus Christ is the essence of the Church, having promised Himself to it, so He is the truth, not merely in Himself, but also for us as we know Him solely by faith in Jesus Christ. To the extent that dogmatics receives this standard by which it measures talk about God in Jesus Christ, in the event of the divine

---

1. Karl Barth, *Church Dogmatics* I/1, rev. ed. (Edinburgh: T&T Clark, 1975), 11–16.

2. For this paragraph, "The Word of God, Dogma, and Dogmatics," see *Church Dogmatics* I/1, 248–92.

3. Most translations of Rom. 12:6 are similar to the NRSV: "We have gifts that differ according to the grace given to us: prophecy, in proportion to faith." The Greek word translated as "proportion" is *analogia*, and given his emphasis on the "analogy of faith" throughout *Church Dogmatics* I/1, Barth offers a more literal rendering of that word.

action corresponding to the promise given to the Church, it is possible for it to be knowledge of the truth. What is or is not the true content of such talk about God is clear at once and with complete fullness and certainty in the light in which we are here set.[4] The fulfillment of this knowledge, the event of human action, the appropriation corresponding to this address in which, through the stages of intuitive apprehension to formulated comprehension, the revelation of the analogy of faith (*analogia fidei*) and the resultant clarity in dogmatics (in dogmatics too, but not first or solely in dogmatics) take creaturely form, is, of course, a second event compared with the divine action itself, united with it in faith, yet also in faith to be distinguished from it. The second event, however, does not abolish the first. In, with and under the human question dogmatics speaks of the divine answer. It knows even as it seeks. It teaches even as it learns. In human uncertainty like any other science, it establishes the most certain truth ever known. In relation to its subject, every statement in dogmatics, as a statement of faith, must be ventured with the assurance of speaking divine and not just human truth. In distinction from the academic reserve of, e.g., a philosophical proposition, it cannot evade the severity of the dogmatic. The necessary corrective is supplied by the matter itself: "in relation to its object . . . as a statement of faith." The intractability of faith and its object guarantees that divine certainty cannot become human security. But it is this intractable faith and its intractable object which make possible the certain divine knowledge which is at issue in dogmatics. "Those who are spiritual discern all things, and they are themselves subject to no one else's scrutiny. 'For who has known the mind of the Lord so as to instruct him?' But we have the mind of Christ" (1 Cor. 2:15–16).[5] . . .

2. Dogmatics as an enquiry presupposes that the true content of Christian talk about God must be known by men. Christian speech must be tested by its conformity to Christ. This conformity is never clear and unambiguous.

4. Barth insists that dogmatics does not need to prove itself by external standards, such as those operative in the academy. Theologians presuppose that God can be known because Christian dogmatics is the task of critically reflecting on the reality that the Word of God has been spoken to the church. To step outside this context by asking *if* God has revealed himself or *if* God can be known is to begin from another starting point and thus to engage in something other than dogmatics.

5. Note the distinction Barth draws between revelation and dogmatics. God's revelation is clear and certain, and it comes first; dogmatics occurs as a second event as theologians reflect on what God has revealed. Because it proceeds by faith, dogmatics does not possess the same level of certainty as revelation. The theologian cannot locate her security in her own claims because they are merely human reflections. Yet this reality does not undermine the certainty of God's revelation or the human ability to testify to it. Inasmuch as the content of dogmatics corresponds to what God has revealed, this content can be considered certain. Barth will explain how this content can be certain later in his *Church Dogmatics* (see chap. 16).

To the finally and adequately given divine answer there corresponds a human question which can maintain its faithfulness only in unwearied and honest persistence. There corresponds even at the highest point of attainment the open: "Not as though I had already attained" (Phil. 3:12). Dogmatics receives even the standard by which it measures in an act of human appropriation. Hence it has to be enquiry. It knows the light which is intrinsically perfect and reveals everything in a flash. Yet it knows it only in the prism of this act, which, however radically or existentially it may be understood, is still a human act, which in itself is no kind of surety for the correctness of the appropriation in question, which is by nature fallible and therefore stands in need of criticism, of correction, of critical amendment and repetition. For this reason the crea-turely form which the revealing action of God assumes in dogmatics is never that of knowledge attained in a flash, which it would have to be to correspond to the divine gift, but a laborious movement from one partial human insight to another with the intention though with no guarantee of advance. "For now we see in a mirror, dimly . . . now I know only in part" (1 Cor. 13:12). And with a similar application, we may also recall 2 Corinthians 4:7: "But we have this treasure in clay jars, so that it may be made clear that this extraordinary power belongs to God and does not come from us." . . .

The fact that it is in faith that the truth is presupposed to be the known measure of all things means that the truth is in no sense assumed to be to hand. The truth comes, i.e., in the faith in which we begin to know, and cease, and begin again. The results of earlier dogmatic work, and indeed our own results, are basically no more than signs of its coming. They are simply the results of human effort. As such they are a help to, but also the object of, fresh human effort. Dogmatics is possible only as *theologia crucis* (theology of the cross), in the act of obedience which is certain in faith, but which for this very reason is humble, always being thrown back to the beginning and having to make a fresh start. It is not possible as an effortless triumph or an intermittent labour. It always takes place on the narrow way which leads from the enacted revelation to the promised revelation . . . "through faith for faith" (Rom. 1:17).[6] . . .

Here our way diverges from that of Roman Catholic dogmatics, and we must also enter a warning against a certain tendency in the older Protestant tradition. Dogmatics is the science of dogma. Only in a subordinate sense,

---

6. Barth's description of the practice of theology over the last two paragraphs is striking. Theologians' claims about God must be tested again and again for their accuracy because humans are fallible and God is mysterious. They must persistently seek after God while con-stantly revising their ideas in light of a fresh encounter with God's revelation. Theology thus is a form of discipleship, a lifelong endeavor marked by humility, self-criticism, and correction.

and strictly in conjunction with the primary, is it also the science of dogmas. The task of dogmatics, therefore, is not simply to combine, repeat and transcribe a number of truths of revelation which are already to hand, which have been expressed once and for all, and the wording and meaning of which are authentically defined. . . .

This only too practicable view, by its direct equation of divine ascription and human appropriation in the dogmas, fails to recognize the divine-human character of the being of the Church. The being of the Church is Jesus Christ, and therefore an indissolubly divine-human person, the action of God towards man in distinction from which human appropriation as attested in the dogmas believed by the Church may be very worthy and respectable but can hardly be called infallible and therefore withdrawn from further enquiry whether this is how it should be. The concept of truths of revelation in the sense of Latin propositions given and sealed once for all with divine authority in both wording and meaning is theologically impossible if it is a fact that revelation is true in the free decision of God which was taken once for all in Jesus Christ, that it is thus strictly future for us, and that it must always become true in the Church in the intractable reality of faith. The freely acting God Himself and alone is the truth of revelation. Our dogmatic labors can and should be guided by results which are venerable because they are attained in the common knowledge of the Church at a specific time. Such results may be seen in the dogmas enshrined in the creeds. But at no point should these replace our dogmatic labors in virtue of their authority. Nor can it ever be the real concern of dogmatics merely to assemble, repeat and define the teaching of the Bible.[7] . . .

Exegetical theology investigates biblical teaching as the basis of our talk about God. Dogmatics, too, must constantly keep it in view. But only in God and not for us is the true basis of Christian utterance identical with its true content. Hence dogmatics as such does not ask what the apostles and prophets said but what we must say on the basis of the apostles and prophets. This task is not taken from us because it is first necessary that we should know the biblical basis. . . .

7. Barth's warning about the place of dogma in the church stems from his definition of dogmatics. Since dogmatics is a human enterprise distinct from God's revelation, it can never replace this revelation. Dogma does not carry the same authority as God's Word because it is the product of human reflection on that Word and is both fallible and in need of constant revision. Divine revelation can never be a once-for-all human possession, as if it were merely a collection of truths or ideas that could be grasped, organized, and then sealed in a final form. Rather, the form God's revelation takes is the event in which God personally addresses the church in Jesus Christ and the church responds in faith and obedience through the power of the Spirit. The pattern of the historical church's response in the past can serve a guide for the church's response in the present, but in no way can it stand alongside, or replace, God's revelation itself.

As the Church accepts from Scripture, and with divine authority from Scripture alone, the attestation of its own being as the measure of its utterance, it finds itself challenged to know itself, and therefore even and precisely in face of this foundation of all Christian utterance to ask, with all the seriousness of one who does not yet know, what Christian utterance can and should say today.[8]

8. These remarks about the role of Scripture in dogmatics emphasize that God's revelation involves his present-tense encounter with the church. God speaks in and through Scripture. Theologians are not called merely to investigate the history of texts but to listen to what God is saying here and now. This approach stands in line with Barth's early work, which does not dismiss the role of historical-critical exegesis but places it within the context of God's personal encounter with the church. See, e.g., Barth's engagement with Harnack in chap. 4.

CHAPTER

12

The Word of God

Introduction

Barth argues that God speaks in and through his Word. This Word is not something other than God, as if God merely transmits information to humans while staying in the background. Rather, the Word of God is the event in which God personally encounters humans and unveils himself to them. This self-revelation is the basis of the church's knowledge of God and the criterion of its speech about God. In the context of God's reconciliation of sinners, this revelation takes place in and through Jesus Christ, the Word of God made flesh.

In this excerpt, Barth explains how the Bible and proclamation relate to the event of God's self-revelation in Christ. He argues that the Word of God takes a "threefold form" as revealed, written, and proclaimed. Christ is the revealed Word of God; Scripture is its written form; and the church's preaching is the proclaimed form. These three forms are united by the fact that God has determined to speak in all three ways. There is no difference of degree or value among the three forms of the Word of God, and so the church rightly approaches each form with the same reverence. They are distinct, however, because they exist in an ordered relationship. Drawing on an analogy of the Trinity, Barth explains that Scripture is the Word of God because it testifies to Jesus Christ; and in turn, the church's proclamation is the Word of God because it faithfully corresponds to both Scripture and Christ.

Barth's account of the threefold form of the Word of God emphasizes that God's revelation to humans takes place in a present-tense encounter. When the church considers Christ or Scripture, the focus is not primarily on events that happened in the past but on Christ's speech to the church right now. This prevents the church from seeing God's revelation, whether in the historical Jesus or in Scripture, as an object that can be managed or possessed. The church is not the master of its knowledge of God, but instead this knowledge is something the church receives again and again in a free act of divine grace.

Church Dogmatics I/1[1]

Revelation, *revelatio*, ἀποκάλυψις, means the unveiling of what is veiled. If this is meant strictly and properly, then all that is distinct from revelation is concealment, the hiddenness of the veiled. . . . All revelation, then, must be thought of as revealing, i.e., as conditioned by the act of revelation. The event in which revelation occurs must be seen in connection with what has happened once and for all in this act. All fulfilled time must be seen as filled with the fullness of this time. Revelation itself, however, is not referred to anything other, higher, or earlier.[2] Revelation as such is not relative. Revelation in fact does not differ from the person of Jesus Christ nor from the reconciliation accomplished in Him. To say revelation is to say "The Word became flesh." To be sure, one can say something quite different by revelation, something purely formal, and relative as such. But to say this is not to say what the Bible means by the word or what Church proclamation is referring to when it refers to the Bible or what must be called revelation in Christian dogmatics if this is to take itself seriously as such. When in the word revelation we say "The Word was made flesh and dwelt among us" (John 1:14), then we are saying something which can have only an inter-trinitarian basis in the will of the Father and the sending of the Son and the Holy Spirit, in the eternal decree of the triune God, so that it can be established only as knowledge of God from God, of

1. Karl Barth, *Church Dogmatics* I/1, rev. ed. (Edinburgh: T&T Clark, 1975), 118–21.
2. Barth argues that revelation occurs when God unveils himself to us, and he makes two important qualifications in order to explain what this unveiling involves. First, the content of divine relation is not the unveiling of some higher truth behind what God shows us in Christ. God's revelation is personal in nature, and the content of divine revelation is nothing other than the living God himself. Second, while God reveals himself in the words and deeds described in the Bible, revelation does not refer to these earlier events. Revelation refers to God's unveiling of himself to us in Christ in the present. While the Christ who speaks to us in the present is one and the same as the Christ who spoke in the past, revelation refers to our personal encounter with Christ here and now.

light in light. The same applies if instead of Jesus Christ we say concretely "God with us." It is true that in the term revelation we might have something relative rather than this absolute in view, but the Bible is thinking only of this absolute, and in the knowledge of this absolute the Church with the help of the Bible recalls past revelation, and a dogmatics that works in the sphere of the Church and not in a vacuum has also to cling to it. But to say "God with us" is to say something which has no basis or possibility outside itself, which can in no sense be explained in terms of man and man's situation, but only as knowledge of God from God, as free and unmerited grace.[3] As the Bible bears witness to God's revelation and as Church proclamation takes up this witness in obedience, both renounce any foundation apart from that which God has given once and for all by speaking. The Bible and proclamation both appeal to this fact that has been given here and now. They cannot reproduce it as a given fact. They cannot bring it on the scene themselves. They can only attest and proclaim it. To bring it about that the *Deus dixit* is present with the Church in its various times and situations is not in the power of the Bible or proclamation. The *Deus dixit* is true—now the *where* and *when* must come into force again—where it *is* true, i.e., where and when God, in speaking once and for all, wills according to His eternal counsel that it be true, where and when God by His activating, ratifying and fulfilling of the word of the Bible and preaching lets it become true.[4] This being and becoming true of revelation consists, then, in the fact that the Church really recollects past revelation, and in faith receives, grasps and really proclaims the biblical witness of it as the real promise of future revelation, future revelation here

3. Barth's claims correspond to the account of revelation and history he developed early in his career. While the Bible gives us a record of the history of God's words and deeds in the past, we cannot access divine revelation simply by studying this history alone. If this were possible, then the human knower would be in control of the event of revelation. Instead, to speak of revelation is to refer to a unique and particular divine act that takes place as God unveils himself to us. Since this action reflects the will of the triune God as exercised in the saving work of the Son and Spirit, we have no access to it apart from this work.

4. Barth's remark about God's "eternal counsel" is the key to understanding his argument. His claim is that both the Bible and preaching fit within the context of the triune God's determination to reveal himself to us. He explains their place by appealing to the concept of the threefold Word of God: revealed, written, and proclaimed. As the written form of the Word of God, the Bible testifies to the revealed Word of God—Jesus Christ—and in turn this biblical testimony serves the criterion by which the human preacher proclaims the Word of God. Both the Bible and preaching are the Word of God because, and only because, God has sovereignly determined to use them in order to reveal himself to us in time. This "only" is important. Barth worries that, if the Bible or preaching were the Word of God because they possessed some other characteristic, such as historical accuracy, then revelation could be discovered on the basis of this characteristic in distinction from a unique act of God. The human then would be in control of the revelation, and the content of this revelation would be determined by human subjectivity.

being simply that which has taken place once and for all but is now directed to us too, just as the Christ who comes again is no other than the Christ who has come, but this Christ as the One who now comes also to us. The "God with us" becomes actual for us *here and now* as the promise received and grasped in faith because it is *there and then* a divine act. It is thus that which is true in and for itself, and it becomes true for us as recollection and also as promise, as recollection of Christ come in the flesh and as hope of Christ coming again in glory. It is Jesus Christ Himself who here speaks for Himself and needs no witness apart from His Holy Spirit and the faith that rejoices in His promise received and grasped. This independent and unsurpassable origin of the Word of God that comes to us is what we have in view when we speak of its third form, or materially we should rather say its first form, i.e., its form as the Word of God revealed.[5] . . .

We have been speaking of three different forms of the Word of God and not of three different Words of God. In this threefold form and not otherwise—but also as the one Word only in this threefold form—the Word of God is given to us and we must try to understand it conceptually. It is one and the same whether we understand it as revelation, Bible, or proclamation. There is no distinction of degree or value between the three forms. For to the extent that proclamation really rests on recollection of the revelation attested in the Bible and is thus obedient repetition of the biblical witness, it is no less the Word of God than the Bible. And to the extent that the Bible really attests revelation it is no less the Word of God than revelation itself. As the Bible and proclamation become God's Word in virtue of the actuality of revelation they are God's Word: the one Word of God within which there can be neither a more nor a less. Nor should we ever try to understand the three forms of God's Word in isolation. The first, revelation, is the form that underlies the other two. But it is the very one that never meets us anywhere in abstract form. We know it only indirectly, from Scripture and proclamation. The direct Word of God meets us only in this twofold mediacy. But Scripture too, to become God's Word for us, must be proclaimed in the Church.[6] So, to give a survey of the whole, the following brief schedule of mutual relations may be drawn up.

5. Note how the living Christ himself stands at the center of Barth's account of the threefold Word of God. As the church reads and proclaims the words of Scripture, God's words and deeds in the past become the means by which God speaks his promise to the church in the present. Christ is the agent of this divine speech: as the one who lived in the flesh and will come again, he speaks to the church in the present as the living Word who makes promises for its future. The church responds in faith and obedience when its claims about Christ correspond to Christ's own testimony in and through Scripture.

6. Barth emphasizes that each of the three forms of the Word of God—God's revelation in Christ, Scripture, and preaching—are rightly considered the Word of God because God has

The revealed Word of God we know only from the Scripture adopted by Church proclamation or the proclamation of the Church based on Scripture.

The written Word of God we know only through the revelation which fulfills proclamation or through the proclamation fulfilled by revelation.

The preached Word of God we know only through the revelation attested in Scripture or the Scripture which attests revelation.

There is only one analogy to this doctrine of the Word of God. Or, more accurately, the doctrine of the Word of God is itself the only analogy to the doctrine which will be our fundamental concern as we develop the concept of revelation. This is the doctrine of the triunity of God. In the fact that we can substitute for revelation, Scripture and proclamation the names of the divine persons Father, Son and Holy Spirit and *vice versa*, that in the one case as in the other we shall encounter the same basic determinations and mutual relationships, and that the decisive difficulty and also the decisive clarity is the same in both—in all this one may see specific support for the inner necessity and correctness of our present exposition of the Word of God.[7]

---

determined to use all three forms to speak to the church. This divine determination means that all three forms must be treated with the same sense of loyalty and reverence. No form can be valued over the others, nor can they be isolated from one another or pitted against each other. For example, the church cannot appeal to God's revelation in Christ to correct the words of Scripture, nor will faithful proclamation in the church contradict what God has revealed in Scripture or Christ.

7. While Barth emphases the unity of the three forms of the Word of God, he also insists the three forms exist in an ordered relationship: God's revelation in Christ is the source of the testimony of Scripture and the preacher. He draws an analogy to the Trinity in order to illustrate this relationship. In the triune life of God, the Son proceeds from the Father, and the Spirit proceeds from the Father and the Son. In an analogous way, the written Word proceeds from the revealed Word, and the proclaimed Word proceeds both from the written and revealed Word.

CHAPTER

13

Revelation and Faith

Introduction

Barth argues that humans know God by faith, which comes in response to hearing the Word of God. But this argument raises questions. If faith is a human act, does that not leave human subjectivity at the center of Barth's account of the knowledge of God? Is not human knowledge of God determined by the human capacity to receive and understand God's revelation? If so, then has Barth fallen into the very problem he has been trying to avoid since the beginning of his theological career?

Barth addresses these questions by describing precisely what kind of capacity the human exercises in the event of faith. His explanation is nuanced and dialectical. On the one hand, Barth insists that humans are incapable of receiving God's revelation on the basis of their created capacities. Their finitude leaves them unable to know God under their own power, and their fallenness leaves them liable to distort what God has revealed. He still affirms the claim that shaped the early part of his career: if an act of the human subject determines the human's knowledge of God, then the inevitable result is idolatry. On the other hand, Barth insists that God makes humans capable of receiving divine revelation. When God speaks his Word, God also establishes a "point of contact" with the human knower that makes the reception of this Word possible. The human receives a new capacity to receive God's revelation, but since this capacity exists by grace rather than nature, the knowledge that results is determined not by the human's subjectivity but by God's action.

When God unites himself to the human in the event of his self-revelation, God also evokes a response of faith and obedience from the human. Since this response is explained in terms of God's grace instead of the human's natural capacities, God remains the subject who determines the content of the knowledge that results from it. Barth describes this divine determination of human knowledge as the "conformity" of the human to God.

Church Dogmatics I/1[1]

If one asks about the reality of the knowledge of God, which is so inconceivable in its How, which can be revealed only by God, which can be proclaimed by man only in the service of God and in virtue of His presence; if one asks what this reality is in so far as the knowability of God is included within it, the only possible answer which is both accurate and exhaustive is that this reality is faith.[2] . . .

Faith is not one of the various capacities of man, whether native or acquired. Capacity for the Word of God is not among these. The possibility of faith as it is given to man in the reality of faith can be understood only as one that is loaned to man by God, and loaned exclusively for use. The moment we regard it as a possibility which is in some sense man's own, the opposite statement regarding man's incapacity comes back into force. We do not understand it as a possibility which is in any sense man's own.[3] But for this reason there can also be no objection from the standpoint of man's possibilities when we say that in faith there takes place a conformity of man to God. We do not say a deification but a conformity to God, i.e., an adapting of man to the Word of God. In faith, as he really receives God's Word, man becomes apt to receive it. If one were to deny this, one could no longer describe and understand faith as the act and experience of man nor man as the subject of

1. Karl Barth, *Church Dogmatics* I/1, rev. ed. (Edinburgh: T&T Clark, 1975), 228, 238–47.
2. Barth is addressing a key question in this excerpt: How can humans truly know God if the knowledge of God is beyond their capacity? Barth's answer is "faith," and his goal is to offer a specific account of what faith involves.
3. Barth's argument in this paragraph is dialectical, and both sides of the dialectic must be kept in view in order to understand what he is saying. On one side of the dialectic is one of Barth's central convictions: because God is distinct from creatures, humans cannot know God through the exercise of their natural capacities. If this kind of knowledge were possible, then humans themselves would determine both the event and content of divine revelation.

faith. But if we ascribe to man this aptness which is not his own but is loaned to him by God, which is not to be contemplated but simply used in faith, an aptness to receive the Word of God, then we cannot shrink from speaking of a conformity to God proper to him in faith.[4] Hearing the Word of God could not take place if there were not something common to the speaking God and the hearing man, an analogy, a similarity in and with this event for all the dissimilarity implied by the difference between God and man—if we may now adopt this term—a "point of contact" between God and man.[5] . . .

In faith, man is in conformity to God, i.e., capable of receiving God's Word, capable of so corresponding in his own decision to the decision God has made about him in the Word that the Word of God is now the Word heard by him and he himself is now the man addressed by this Word. One is not to seek this capability among the stock of his own possibilities. The statement about the indwelling of Christ that takes place in faith must not be turned into an anthropological statement. There must be no subtraction from the lostness of natural and sinful man, as whom the believer will for the first time really see himself. But this natural and sinful man that he is, and that in faith he must see himself to be, is dead in faith, in Christ, according to Romans 6:3ff., and I am alive in faith, a miracle to myself, another man, and as such capable of things of which I can only know myself to be absolutely incapable as a natural sinful man. Part of this capability is that the Word of God is knowable to man in faith, that it can be spoken to him, and that he can hear it, that he can receive it as a word, and indeed as God's Word. . . .

To the image of God in man which was lost in Adam but restored in Christ there also belongs the fact that man can hear God's Word. Only as the Word of God is really spoken in spite of his sin and to his sin, only in the

4. On the other side of the dialectic is the idea that God creates a "conformity to God" (*Gottförmigkeit*) in the recipient of divine revelation. This conformity does not involve a change in the creaturely being of the recipient, as if she now possesses new qualities or capacities. Rather, God lends the recipient of revelation a new aptitude (*Eignung*) that enables her to hear and respond to God's Word in faith. This aptitude, as Barth says in the following sentence, is the "point of contact."

5. This final sentence brings both sides of the dialectic together. The human is able to receive God's revelation, even though she remains naturally incapable of doing so, because God creates an aptitude for this revelation in her when he reveals himself to her. In the event of God's revelation, a "point of contact" exists between God and the human, an analogy of faith, as God gives the human the capacity to know him that in no way changes the reality that she remains incapable of knowing God under her own power. The rest of this excerpt further explains, and then draws out the implications of, this dialectical claim. Note: I adjusted the translation of this sentence because the original translation left out the important word "analogy," obscuring Barth's point. Compare this line from *Church Dogmatics* I/1, rev. ed. (Edinburgh: T&T Clark, 1975), 238, to the German text of Barth's *Kirchliche Dogmatik* I/1, 251.

grace with which God replies to sin, can this possibility revive. But in grace it does revive: not, then, as a natural capacity in man—it is grace after all that comes to sinners, to incapable men—but as a capacity of the incapable, as a miracle that cannot be interpreted anthropologically, nevertheless as a real capacity which is already actualized in faith, regarding whose existence there is no further room for discussion, whose existence can only be stated, since in becoming an event it already showed itself to be a possibility even before any question about it could arise.[6] . . .

As God's Word is spoken to man, it is in him and he is in the Word. The only proof of this mutual indwelling of the Word and man is a reference to the fact that as the Word of God is spoken to some other man it can be in him too, and he in it. The proof of faith consists in the proclamation of faith. The proof of the knowability of the Word consists in confessing it. In faith and confession the Word of God becomes a human thought and a human word, certainly in infinite dissimilarity and inadequacy, yet not in total alienation from its real prototype, but a true copy for all its human and sinful perversion, an unveiling of it even as its veiling. This does not imply an immanent transformation of human thought or human speech. It does not imply even a modest removal of the offense with which the Word is flesh here. Nor does it imply any diminution of the miracle of the mutual indwelling, any supernatural physics trying to make the incomprehensible comprehensible. Again, what must be said here cannot be meant as analysis of a present reality, for as such it evades our grasp and knowledge. In the strict sense it is meant only as recollection of the promise and as expectation of its future fulfillment. But in this sense the mutual indwelling and indeed the union of the divine and human logos in faith cannot be ignored or denied. This mutual indwelling or union is the knowability of the Word of God, the possibility of Church proclamation whether from the preacher's standpoint or the hearer's, and therefore the possibility of dogmatics too.[7] . . .

---

6. In these two paragraphs, Barth moves between both sides of the dialectic he established above in order to express the essential truth they express when held together. He insists that the human recipient of revelation truly exercises faith, which means he makes a real decision to respond to God's revelation in Christ. At the same time, this decision does not stem from the human's natural abilities, nor is it the result of a new capacity possessed by the human. This capacity is strictly a gift from God that comes as God reveals himself to the human and brings him into conformity with his own divine being, will, and action. This event, and the capacity for faith it produces, cannot be examined or explained on creaturely terms. It occurs as a gift of grace. As Barth puts it, in a striking dialectical phrase, it is "a capacity of the incapable."

7. Barth insists that the believer's knowledge of God can be considered true even though it consists of creaturely concepts and words that cannot be identical to the reality of God. The key to this truthfulness is God's actions, and our recognition of this truth takes place as we bear witness to this action. When God reveals himself, he utilizes creaturely words by bringing

If it is true that man really believes 1. that the object of faith is present to him and 2. that he himself is assimilated to the object, then we are led in conclusion to the third point that man exists as a believer wholly and utterly by this object. In believing he can think of himself as grounded, not in self but only in this object, as existing indeed only by this object. He has not created his own faith; the Word has created it. He has not come to faith; faith has come to him through the Word. He has not adopted faith; faith has been granted to him through the Word. As a believer he cannot see himself as the acting subject of the work done here. It is his experience and act. He is not at all a block or stone in faith but self-determining man. He does not sink into passive, apathetic contemplation in faith, and even if he did he would still do so as self-determining man. Whatever his state of soul, at least in thinking, willing and feeling he is himself and lives his own life. Nevertheless, the point is that in faith he must regard this in no sense diminished self-determination, himself in his own activity, in the living of his own life, as determined by the Word of God. In his freedom, in the full use of his freedom as a man, he must see himself as another man that he had no power to become, that he still has no power to become, that he is not free to become or to be (though he is free as he becomes and is), in short, that he can be only by being this man. Man acts as he believes, but the fact that he believes as he acts is God's act. Man is the subject of faith. Man believes, not God. But the fact that man is this subject in faith is bracketed as a predicate of the subject God, bracketed in the way that the Creator encloses the creature and the merciful God sinful man, i.e., in such a way that man remains subject, and yet man's I as such derives only from the Thou of the subject God.[8] . . .

The Word of God becomes knowable by making itself known. The application of what has been said to the problem of knowledge consists in stopping at this statement and not going a single step beyond it. The possibility of knowing the Word of God is God's miracle on us just as much as is the Word itself or its being spoken. . . . If we have understood that the knowability of God's Word is really an inalienable affirmation of faith, but that precisely

---

them into correspondence with his divine reality. Humans have no ability to independently verify the nature of this correspondence, but they can bear witness to what God has done. As other people come to know God through the proclamation of these words, the reality of their knowledge demonstrates that these human words correspond to the reality of God.

8. Note how Barth describes the human in this paragraph. His existence is grounded in God, who creates faith within him by coming to him in and through God's Word. The human's faith is active, involving real self-determination, thinking, and action. And yet the human does all of these things within the context of God's determination to speak to him. The human thus is enclosed within the context of God's decision to be his God, and at no moment can he consider himself or his relationship with God apart from this divine determination.

as such it denotes the miracle of faith, the miracle that we can only recollect and hope for, then as a final necessity we must also understand that man must be set aside and God Himself presented as the original subject, as the primary power, as the creator of the possibility of the knowledge of God's Word. Christ does not remain outside. And it is true enough that man must open the door (Rev. 3:20). But the fact that this takes place is—with respect to the act itself *and* with respect to its possibility—the work of Christ who stands outside. Hence it is also unconditionally true that the risen Christ passes through closed doors (John 20:19).

14

The Doctrine of the Trinity

Introduction

Barth's doctrine of the Trinity is widely considered one of his central contributions to dogmatics. His description of the doctrine is understood best when it is interpreted in light of the function he intends it to perform within his theology. Barth's earlier description of the relationship between revelation and faith requires an explanation of how God unites himself to the human recipient of his revelation. As Barth turns toward this task, he begins with a presupposition: God does not deceive humans when he comes to them, but instead God's encounters them as the one true God. This divine consistency means that God's revelation is always a *self*-revelation. When God unites himself to the human knower, he does so in a manner that corresponds to his eternal being.

Barth appeals to the doctrine of the Trinity to explain how this divine self-consistency works. He reads the biblical material in a traditional manner by arguing that the church had to go beyond the letter of Scripture in order to explain the identity of the Father, Son, and Spirit revealed in Scripture. He largely avoids the tradition's use of the word "person" for the Father, Son, and Spirit, however, because he thinks it is likely to be misunderstood by modern interpreters. Instead, he describes God as "one God in three modes of being." He explains that God lives his eternal life in a "threefold repetition" and that God is fully himself in each of these repetitions. He then connects this idea to revelation. In the event of God's self-revelation, the one God is at the same time the *revealer*, the *revelation*, and the *effect* of this revelation in the recipient of it. This threefold form of revelation enables him to explain how the knowledge of God imparted into the human through the Spirit—the knowledge that comes from revelation of the Son who reveals the hidden Father—corresponds to the eternal triune being of God.

Barth's claims about the Trinity are central to his theology. For years, Barth struggled with the question of how humans can know God without shaping this knowledge according to the confines of human subjectivity. The doctrine of the Trinity provides him with the resources finally to answer this question. It is the culmination of years of careful thought, and it serves as the basis for every claim Barth makes about God in his *Church Dogmatics*.

Church Dogmatics I/1[1]

According to Scripture God's revelation is God's own direct speech which is not to be distinguished from the act of speaking and therefore is not to be distinguished from God Himself, from the divine I which confronts man in this act in which it says Thou to him. Revelation is God speaking in person.

From the standpoint of the comprehensive concept of God's Word it must be said that here in God's revelation God's Word is identical with God Himself. Among the three forms of the Word of God this can be said unconditionally and with strictest propriety only of revelation. It can be said of Holy Scripture and Church proclamation as well, but not so unconditionally and directly. For if the same can and must be said of them too, we must certainly add that their identity with God is an indirect one. Without wanting to deny or even limit their character as God's Word we must bear in mind that the Word of God is mediated here, first through the human persons of the prophets and apostles who receive it and pass it on, and then through the human persons of its expositors and preachers, so that Holy Scripture and proclamation must always become God's Word in order to be it. If the Word of God is God Himself even in Holy Scripture and Church proclamation, it is because this is so in the revelation to which they bear witness. In understanding God's Word as the Word preached and written, we certainly do not understand it as God's Word to a lesser degree. But we understand the same Word of God in its relation to revelation. On the other hand, when we understand it as

1. Karl Barth, *Church Dogmatics* I/1, rev. ed. (Edinburgh: T&T Clark, 1975), 304–5, 307–8, 312, 375–76, 379–83.

revealed, we understand it apart from such relations, or rather as the basis of the relations in which it is also the Word of God. We thus understand it as indistinguishable from the event in virtue of which it is the one Word of God in those relations, and therefore as indistinguishable from God's direct speech and hence from God Himself. It is this that—we do not say distinguishes, since there is no question of higher rank or value—but rather characterizes revelation in comparison with Holy Scripture and Church proclamation.[2]

According to Holy Scripture God's revelation is a ground which has no higher or deeper ground above or below it but is an absolute ground in itself, and therefore for man a court from which there can be no possible appeal to a higher court. Its reality and its truth do not rest on a superior reality and truth. They do not have to be actualized or validated as reality from this or any other point. They are not measured by the reality and truth found at this other point. They are not to be compared with any such nor judged and understood as reality and truth by reference to such. On the contrary, God's revelation has its reality and truth wholly and in every respect—both ontically and noetically—within itself. Only if one denies it can one ascribe to it another higher or deeper ground or try to understand and accept or reject it from the standpoint of this higher or deeper ground. Obviously even the acceptance of revelation from the standpoint of this different and supposedly higher ground, e.g., an acceptance of revelation in which man first sets his own conscience over it as judge, can only entail the denial of revelation. Revelation is not made real and true by anything else, whether in itself or for us. Both in itself and for us it is real and true through itself.[3] This differentiates it even from the witness which the prophets and apostles and the witness which the expositors and preachers of Scripture bear to it, at any rate to the extent that this witness is considered in itself. If we can also say that the witness both in itself and for us is grounded through itself, this is in virtue of the fact that this witness does not merely seek to relate itself to revelation but does actually relate itself to it, because revelation has become an event in it. This can happen. And it must happen if Scripture and proclamation are to be God's Word.[4] . . .

2. This paragraph summarizes Barth's account of the threefold Word of God (see chap. 12). Important elements include the distinction between direct and indirect revelation, the concept of mediation, and the unity-in-difference of the three forms of the Word of God.

3. Barth's point is that the reality and truthfulness of God's revelation cannot be determined on the basis of a criterion other than the event of revelation itself. For example, we cannot say, "God's revelation is true because it can be historically verified." Such an approach would ground the reality of God's revelation on the human's ability to locate and then verify it. The inevitable result of such an approach would be a magnification of human under the guise of "revelation."

4. While God's revelation is real and true on its own terms, Scripture and proclamation are real and true inasmuch as they stem from, and correspond to, God's revelation. Barth employs

According to the Bible, God's being with us is the event of revelation. The statement, understood thus, that God reveals Himself as the Lord, or what this statement is meant to describe, and therefore revelation itself as attested by Scripture, we call the root of the doctrine of the Trinity.

Generally and provisionally we mean by the doctrine of the Trinity the proposition that He whom the Christian Church calls God and proclaims as God, the God who has revealed Himself according to the witness of Scripture, is the same in unimpaired unity and yet also the same thrice in different ways in unimpaired distinction. Or, in the phraseology of the Church's dogma of the Trinity, the Father, the Son and the Holy Spirit in the biblical witness to revelation are the one God in the unity of their essence, and the one God in the biblical witness to revelation is the Father, the Son and the Holy Spirit in the distinction of His persons. . . .

What we are saying is that revelation is the basis of the doctrine of the Trinity; the doctrine of the Trinity has no other basis apart from this. We arrive at the doctrine of the Trinity by no other way than that of an analysis of the concept of revelation. Conversely, if revelation is to be interpreted aright, it must be interpreted as the basis of the doctrine of the Trinity. The crucial question for the concept of revelation, that of the God who reveals Himself, cannot be answered apart from the answer to this question given in the doctrine of the Trinity. The doctrine of the Trinity is itself the answer that must be given here. When we say, then, that the doctrine of the Trinity is the interpretation of revelation or that revelation is the basis of the doctrine of the Trinity, we find revelation itself attested in Holy Scripture in such a way that in relation to this witness our understanding of revelation, or of the God who reveals Himself, must be the doctrine of the Trinity.[5] . . .

By the doctrine of the Trinity we understand the Church doctrine of the unity of God in the three modes of being of Father, Son and Holy Ghost, or of the threefold otherness of the one God in the three modes of being of Father, Son and Holy Ghost.[6] All that had and has to be expounded here in detail

---

this distinction in order to maintain that God's action is the sole basis for revelation even when this revelation occurs through creaturely mediums.

5. Barth thinks the basis of the doctrine of the Trinity is the reality of God's presence with humans in the event of his revelation. The doctrine of the Trinity is the church's reflection on this divine presence. It offers the church's answer to a key question: In light of the particular way God has been present with humans in history, what must be true about God's eternal being?

6. The distinguishing mark of Barth's trinitarian theology is his claim that there is "one God in three modes of being." He prefers the phrase "modes of being" because he worries that the typical word "person" leads to the erroneous notion that the Trinity is the union of three distinct individuals. His central argument is that that the names Father, Son, and Spirit express the reality that the one God exists in a "threefold repetition" in eternity and that God is fully

could and can expound only the unity in trinity and the trinity in unity. This doctrine as such does not stand in the texts of the Old and New Testament witness to God's revelation. It did not arise out of the historical situations to which these texts belong. It is exegesis of these texts in the speech, and this also means in the light of the questions, of a later situation. It belongs to the Church. It is a theologoumenon. It is dogma. We have asked (§8.2) about its root, i.e., the possibility on the basis of which it could be a dogma in a Church which sought to regulate its doctrine by the biblical witness. And we have seen that this possibility lies in the fact that in the Bible revelation means the self-unveiling, imparted to men, of the God who by nature cannot be unveiled to men. According to the biblical witness this matter is of such a nature that in the light of the three elements of God's veiling, unveiling and imparting we have cause to speak of the threefold otherness of the one God who has revealed Himself according to the witness of the Bible. The biblical witness to God's revelation sets us face to face with the possibility of interpreting the one statement that "God reveals Himself as the Lord" three times in different senses. This possibility is the biblical root of the doctrine of the Trinity. But in the Bible it remains on the level of possibility. We are now asking about the meaning of its actualization.[7] With what necessity and right did the Church formulate this dogma? It could do this. Did it have to do it? What insight was it expressing in the dogma and what reason have we, then, to take pains to understand it? . . .

We should start with the fact that the rise of the doctrine of the Trinity, however varied the factors which contributed to it, was at least governed also by the need to clear up a question with which the Church saw itself confronted by Holy Scripture in the delivery of its message. Assuming that the Church

---

himself in each repetition. He explains this claim by examining the pattern of God's revelation. By definition, divine revelation always is God's self-revelation because it involves God's act of giving himself so that humans might know him. For such a self-revelation to occur, God the revealer must be identical to his revelation and to its effect. And this is precisely what takes place in the history of salvation: God's revelation in the Son is God's self-unveiling. At the same time—because it is a revelation of the Son but not the Father—it also is God's self-veiling, and the human's reception of this revelation through the power of the Spirit is simultaneously God's self-impartation to the human. Since this threefold event is a revelation of God—rather than something other than God—it must be that God is himself in each of these three modes even though they are distinct from one another. So the one God is revealed in a threefold repetition, and this self-revelation corresponds to the true reality of God. He is one God in three modes of being. Barth insists that this account of the Trinity not only stands in line with the traditional dogma but also carries several important implications for our knowledge of God. He draws out several of these implications below.

7. The doctrine of the Trinity is not biblical in the sense that it is directly revealed but in the sense that it constitutes a faithful reflection on, and witness to, what God has revealed.

is not only unfaithful by nature, as it has been, of course, in every age, but is also in some degree and sense faithful, so that in its proclamation it has tried to take up the witness of the Old and New Testaments, there can be no cause for surprise that it has come up against the question which found an answer in the doctrine of the Trinity. Nor can there be any cause for surprise that it came up against this particular question in such a relatively early period, nor need we be surprised at the violence of the conflicts into which it was plunged by this question and the inexorability with which it has adhered through the centuries to the broad line achieved at that time. The question which arose for it out of the commitment of its proclamation to Scripture, and which it answered in the doctrine of the Trinity, was in fact a basic and vital question of the first rank for Church preaching and therefore for Church theology too. We thus regard it as right and proper to put discussion of this question at the head of all dogmatics. This is a practical outworking of what many have said theoretically about its significance from the very earliest times.

But the question that is answered by the doctrine of the Trinity is a very specific question regarding the basic concept of the revelation of God or the basic fact of it as attested in Scripture. Even if it be regarded as a mere offshoot of the Logos speculation of later antiquity one must at all events concede that its occasion at least is the manifestation of Jesus Christ understood as the revelation of the Logos. It is trying to discuss the deity of this revealed, incarnate Logos. Its second theme, the concept of the Spirit, points in the same direction. And when it speaks of God the Father it is dealing with the point of origin and relation of these two, the Son and the Spirit.

The specific question about revelation which is answered by the doctrine of the Trinity is, however, the question who it is that reveals Himself, the question of the subject of revelation.[8] One may sum up the meaning of the doctrine of the Trinity briefly and simply by saying that *God* is the One who reveals Himself. But if this meaning is to be fully perspicuous one must also reverse the emphasis and say that God is the One who *reveals* Himself. For the strictness and logic of the answer to the question about the subject of revelation consist in the fact that as we enquire into the interpretation of this answer we find ourselves referred back again to revelation itself. The Church doctrine

8. The last two paragraphs have been building up to this sentence. Barth is explaining why the church was justified in going beyond the content of Scripture when it articulated the doctrine of the Trinity. He argues that the church did so because it was addressing a question that arose directly out of its reading and proclamation of Scripture: Who is the God who speaks his Word to his people as the Father, Son, and Holy Spirit? Because this question arises as a natural response to the content of God's revelation, the church's decision to answer it was an act of faithful obedience rather than unhelpful speculation.

of the Trinity is a self-enclosed circle. Its decisive and controlling concern is to say with exactitude and completeness that *God* is the Revealer. But how can it say this with exactitude and completeness unless it declares that none other than the *Revealer* is God? One might put this more simply by saying that the doctrine of the Trinity states that our God, namely, He who makes Himself ours in His revelation, is really God. And to the question, But who is God? there may then be given the no less simple answer, This God of ours. Is it not true that the main answer and the subsidiary answer are the simple but no less momentous presuppositions of all Christian thought and talk about God? The first and last criterion of Christian proclamation is whether it moves in the circle indicated by these two answers. Christian theology can be only an exercise in this movement.[9] The question of the subject of revelation and therefore of all God's dealings with man, which the Bible itself does not answer but poses in all its sharpness, calls indeed for an answer. Can we not understand the haste with which men felt called to answer it and the undoubtedly extraordinary zeal with which they set about this work? Was this not precisely because it was such a simple and yet such a central matter? And could the question be answered in any other way? Or is this problem not really set in the Bible? Could it be answered otherwise than it has been answered in the doctrine of the Trinity?[10]

The problem which we think we see posed in the Bible and which points towards the Church doctrine of the Trinity consists in the fact that the being and speech and action and therefore the self-revealing of God are described there in the moments of His self-veiling or self-unveiling or self-impartation to men, that His characteristic attributes are holiness, mercy and love, that His characteristic demonstrations are denoted in the New Testament by Good

9. As Barth frames it, the doctrine of the Trinity is answering the question, Who is God? The only way humans can answer this question is if God reveals himself to them. So God must be the revealer, the subject of the revelation. At the same time, this revelation must be an unveiling of God's eternal being and life, or humans would not be able to answer the question. So the *Revealer*—the agent we encounter in the event of revelation—must be the one eternal God if we are to say anything about God at all. This clarifies what the church is saying when it answers the question, Who is God? by formulating the doctrine of the Trinity. It is saying that the being of God is triune because the one eternal God we have encountered in the event of revelation is Father, Son, and Spirit.

10. It is helpful to read this series of questions in light of Barth's argument in *The Epistle to the Romans* that God's revelation places a question mark over the whole of our existence (see chap. 2). Now Barth shows what it looks like to begin to answer this question: it looks like *theology*. The discipline of formulating doctrines like the Trinity is at least part of what a faithful response to God's revelation looks like. This marks a development over the account Barth offered in "The Word of God as the Task of Theology" (see chap. 3). There Barth ended with a picture of an individual whose faithfulness is marked by silence; here he offers a picture of a church which displays faith through the act of speaking.

Friday, Easter and Pentecost, and that His name is correspondingly the name of Father, Son, and Holy Ghost. The Bible does not state expressly that the Father, Son and Holy Ghost are of equal essence and are thus in the same sense God Himself. Nor does it state expressly that thus and only thus, as Father, Son and Holy Ghost, God is God. These two express declarations, which go beyond the witness of the Bible, are the twofold content of the Church doctrine of the Trinity.[11]

The doctrine of the Trinity means on the one side, as a rejection of Subordinationism, the express statement that the three moments do not mean a more and a less in God's being as God.[12] The Father is not to be understood as the true God in distinction from the Son and the Spirit, and the Son and the Spirit are not, in distinction from the Father, favored and glorified creatures, vital forces aroused and set in motion by God, and as such and in this sense revealers. But it is God who reveals Himself equally as the Father in His self-veiling and holiness, as the Son in His self-unveiling and mercy, and as the Spirit in His self-impartation and love. Father, Son and Spirit are the one, single, and equal God. The subject of revelation attested in the Bible, no matter what may be His being, speech and action, is the one Lord, not a demi-god, either descended or ascended. Communion with the One who reveals Himself there always and in all circumstances means for man that this God meets him as a Thou meets an I and unites with him as a Thou unites with an I. Not otherwise! Totally excluded is a communion with this God of the kind that we can have with creatures, namely, of such a kind that the Thou can be changed by an I into an It or He over which or whom the I gains control. Also and particularly as Son and Spirit, the One who reveals Himself according to the witness of Scripture does not become an It or He, but remains Thou. And in remaining Thou He remains the Lord. The subject of revelation is the subject that remains indissolubly subject. One cannot get behind this subject. It cannot become object. All Subordinationism rests on the intention of making the One who reveals Himself there the kind of subject we ourselves are, a creature whose Thouness has limits we can survey, grasp and master, which can be objectified, in face of which the I can assert itself. Note well that according to Subordinationist teaching even the Father, who

11. This paragraph sets up the rest of Barth's argument. In what follows, he will explain how the three moments of God's self-veiling, self-unveiling, and self-impartation—which display the three divine attributes of holiness, mercy, and love in connection to events of Good Friday, Easter, Pentecost—are the basis of the church's doctrine of the Trinity. This doctrine serves two purposes for the church: (1) it affirms that the Father, Son, and Spirit are fully God (against subordinationism); and (2) that God is Father, Son, and Spirit (against modalism).

12. Subordinationism implies that the Son and the Spirit are distinct from the Father in being and thus are not divine but merely glorified creatures.

is supposedly thought of as the Creator, is in fact dragged into the creaturely sphere. According to this view His relation to Son and Spirit is that of idea to manifestation. Standing in this comprehensible relation, He shows Himself to be an entity that can be projected and dominated by the I. Subordination-ism finally means the denial of revelation, the drawing of divine subjectivity into human subjectivity, and by way of polytheism the isolation of man with himself in his own world in which there is finally no Thou and therefore no Lord. It was against this possibility that the Church was striking when it rejected Arianism and every form of Subordinationism. We ask whether it did well in this regard or not.[13]

The doctrine of the Trinity means on the other side, as the rejection of Modalism, the express declaration that the three moments are not alien to God's being as God. The position is not that we have to seek the true God beyond these three moments in a higher being in which He is not Father, Son and Spirit. The revelation of God and therefore His being as Father, Son and Spirit is not an economy which is foreign to His essence and which is bounded as it were above and within, so that we have to ask about the hidden Fourth if we are really to ask about God. On the contrary, when we ask about God, we can only ask about the One who reveals Himself. The One who according to the witness of Scripture is and speaks and acts as Father, Son and Spirit, in self-veiling, self-unveiling and self-imparting, in holiness, mercy and love, this and no other is God.[14] For man community with God means strictly and exclusively communion with the One who reveals Himself and who is subject, and indeed indissolubly subject, in His revelation. The indissolubility of His being as subject is guaranteed by the knowledge of the ultimate reality of the three modes of being in the essence of God above and behind which there is nothing higher. Totally excluded here is all communion that means evading His revelation or transcending the reality in which He shows and gives Himself. God is precisely the One He is in showing and giving Himself. If we hasten past the One who according to the biblical witness addresses us in threefold

13. Barth's description of the motivation behind subordinationism is striking: it signifies the human attempt to encounter the Son and the Spirit as fellow creatures, and thus as equals, in order to possess and control not only them but the Father. It thus reflects the human bent toward idolatry, an identification of the God with the creaturely. The similarity between Barth's description of this error and the problems he has been battling since writing *The Epistle to the Romans* is not accidental.

14. Modalism implies that the Father, Son, and Spirit are merely three distinct manifestations of the one God in created history. It is problematic because it implies that the Father, Son, and Spirit are contingent ways that the one person of God appears in history rather than a revelation of God. The true God remains hidden as a "fourth" being behind these three manifestations, and humans are left to seek the truth about this hidden God on their own.

approach as a Thou we can only rush into the void. Modalism finally entails a denial of God. Our God and only our God, namely, the God who makes Himself ours in His revelation, is God.[15] The relativizing of this God which takes place in the doctrine of a real God beyond the revealed God implies a relativizing, i.e., a denying, of the one true God. Here, too, there is no Thou, no Lord. Here, too, man clearly wants to get behind God, namely, behind God as He really shows and gives Himself, and therefore behind what He is, for the two are one and the same. Here, too, we have an objectifying of God. Here, too, the divine subjectivity is sucked up into the human subjectivity which enquires about a God that does not exist. Here too, but this time by way of mysticism, man finally finds himself alone with himself in his own world. This possibility, which in its root and crown is the same as the first, is what the Church wanted to guard against when it rejected Sabellianism and every form of Modalism. And again we ask whether it did well in this regard or not.[16]

The doctrine of the Trinity tells us—this is the positive thing which it was defending on the polemical fronts—how far the One who reveals Himself according to the witness of Scripture can in fact be our *God* and how far He can in fact be *our* God.[17] He can be our God because in all His modes of being He is equal to Himself, one and the same Lord. In terms of the doctrine of the Trinity knowledge of revelation as it may arise from the witness of Scripture means in all three moments of the event knowledge of the Lord as the One who meets us and unites Himself to us. And this Lord can be our God, He can meet us and unite Himself to us, because He is God in His three modes of being as Father, Son and Spirit, because creation, reconciliation and redemption, the whole being, speech and action in which He wills to be our God, have their basis and prototype in His own essence, in His own being as

15. It is important to distinguish modalism from Barth's account of the one God in three modes of being. Modalism implies that the one God appears in three different modes while remaining undifferentiated in being, such that God's appearance in history as Father, Son, and Spirit is distinct from the reality of his divine being. The true nature of God thus is something other than what the three persons reveal, and humans are left to look for God in "the void" that exists beyond them. For Barth, in contrast, God is one with himself in all three modes of his being. So when God reveals himself as Father, Son, and Spirit in salvation history, he is simply being the one true God that he is. To encounter and know the Father, Son, and Spirit is to encounter and know the real God.

16. Barth's account of the motivation behind modalism is similar to the one he provided for subordinationism: it is an attempt to deny and then evade the reality of God's revelation in and through the Son and the Spirit. Whereas the subordinationist identifies them as creatures and seeks to know them on creaturely terms, the modalist denies that they reveal God and instead engages in his own search for God. But the result of either heresy is the same: an idolatrous, creaturely picture of God shaped and determined by human ideals.

17. Put differently, the doctrine of the Trinity shows us that the one true God is the God who has come to us in Christ and the Spirit.

God. As Father, Son and Spirit God is, so to speak, ours in advance. Thus the doctrine of the Trinity tells us that the God who reveals Himself according to Scripture is both to be feared and also to be loved, to be feared because He can be God and to be loved because He can be our God.[18] That He *is* these two things the doctrine of the Trinity as such cannot tell us. No dogma and no theology as such can. The doctrine of the Trinity as such is not the Word of God which might tell us. But if there is a ministry to this Word of God, a proclamation which can become the Word of God, and a ministry to this ministry, dogmatics as critical reflection on the proper content of proclamation, then the question as to the subject of revelation, to which the doctrine of the Trinity is an answer, must be the first step in this reflection. Scripture, in which the problem of the doctrine of the Trinity is posed, is always the measure and judge of the solution to this problem. It stands above the dogma of the Church and therefore above the critical reflection to which we let ourselves be led by the dogma of the Church. But all things considered we venture to think that, pending better instruction, this leading is an appropriate one.[19]

18. This is a claim about God's self-consistency. When God unites himself to humans in the event of his self-revelation as Father, Son, and Spirit, God is simply being himself. Humans can be confident that they know the truth about God when they reflect on the actions of the Father, Son, and Spirit as revealed in Scripture because these actions correspond to God's divine nature. This knowledge assists worship because it enables humans to have the right posture before God. We know that God is the one whom we should fear because we know that he is God; and yet we know this same God is a God to be loved because God has united himself to us in love.

19. These closing remarks indicate the specific role that doctrines like the Trinity play in the life of the church: they help the church understand both the content and the implications of God's revelation. In this way, although they can never replace or stand alongside this revelation, they can bear faithful witness to it.

CHAPTER 15

The Missions of the Son and the Spirit

Introduction

The doctrine of the Trinity gave Barth the resources to explain how God's revelation to humans corresponds to God's eternal being. In this excerpt, Barth considers the same reality from the perspective of the human knower—namely, how God's objective revelation can become subjectively appropriated by the human recipient of it. Barth answers this question by appealing to the doctrines of Christology and pneumatology. In this excerpt, his goal is to explain how the incarnate life of Jesus Christ and the indwelling power of the Holy Spirit enable humans to know the truth about God's eternal being.

Two points stand out in Barth's treatment of the incarnation. First, Barth emphasizes that because the Son of God is the active subject of the life of Jesus Christ, an encounter with Jesus is an encounter with God in human flesh. God does not hold back when he comes in Jesus, as if he keeps some truth about his divine being and life in "reserve" behind what Christ reveals. No, Jesus reveals the truth about God and God's relationship with humanity. Second, Barth insists that Christ reveals the truth about God's will for sinful humanity. When Jesus bears the consequences of human sin on the cross, he shows that God intends to overcome sin on behalf of humanity so that they might be reconciled to him. It is in this precise sense that Jesus Christ is the objective revelation of God.

Two points also stand out with respect to Barth's treatment of the work of the Holy Spirit. First, he emphasizes that, as the third mode of the one God's eternal being, the Spirit does not add anything new or distinct to God's self-revelation in Jesus Christ. Instead, the Spirit is the agent who imparts Christ's objective revelation into the human knower so that it becomes a subjective reality. Second, the Spirit gives the human an ability that transcends the human's natural capacities. The Spirit is the one who makes the reception of God's revelation possible for the human, and the Spirit creates this possibility *without* violating the human's integrity as a creature. This account of the saving missions of Christ and the Spirit allows Barth to draw a connection between God's eternal life and the biblical history of salvation. It also secures the idea that any knowledge of God must begin with, and remain centered on, this same history.

─── *Church Dogmatics* I/2[1] ───

The doctrine of God's three-in-oneness gives the answer to the question about the subject of the revelation attested in Holy Scripture. This answer may be summarized by saying that the revelation attested in Holy Scripture is the revelation of the God who, as the Lord, is the Father from whom it proceeds, the Son who fulfills it objectively (for us), and the Holy Spirit who fulfills it subjectively (in us). He is the One God in each of these modes of being and action, which are quite distinct and never to be identified with each other. God is the constant Subject of revelation. Neither in His Son in whom He becomes manifest to us, nor in His Holy Spirit in whom He is manifest to us, does He become the predicate or object of our existence or action. He becomes and He is manifest to us. But this very becoming and being is and remains a determination of His existence. It is His act, His work.[2]

It is with this becoming and being, this twofold objective and subjective fulfillment of revelation, that we are concerned now. That means, we have to deal, in the first place, with the incarnation of the Word, with Jesus Christ as God's revelation for us, and after that with the outpouring of the Holy Spirit as God's revelation in us.[3] . . .

1. Karl Barth, *Church Dogmatics* I/2 (Edinburgh: T&T Clark, 1956), 1, 132–34, 147–56, 204, 246–48, 257–58, 265, 269–70.
2. This paragraph summarizes Barth's arguments about divine revelation, faith, and the Trinity developed in chaps. 12–14.
3. The question driving this excerpt is familiar: How can humans know God even though they have no capacity to do so? To address this question, Barth has to establish a connection

"Very God and very Man"—We understand this statement as the answer to the question: Who is Jesus Christ? and we understand it as a description of the central New Testament statement, John 1:14: "The Word was made flesh." . . .

The Word, and therefore the Jesus Christ who is identified with the Word according to John 1:1–18, is "very God." And "very God" means the one, only, true, eternal God. It is not deity in itself and as such that was made flesh. For deity does not exist at all in itself and as such, but only in the modes of existence of the Father, the Son and the Holy Spirit. It is the Son or Word of God that was made flesh. But He was made flesh in the entire fullness of deity, which is also that of the Father and of the Holy Spirit. Here we make contact at once with the mystery of revelation, which is the real object of Christology, namely, the source and root of all the various problems and their solutions which are to engage us from now on.[4] If we wish to state who Jesus Christ is, in every separate statement we must also state, or at least make clear—and inexorably so—that we are speaking of the Lord of heaven and earth, who neither has nor did have any need of heaven or earth or man, who created them out of free love and according to His very own good pleasure, who adopts man, not according to the latter's merit, but according to His own mercy, not in virtue of the latter's capacity, but in virtue of His own miraculous power. He is the Lord who in all His action is always Himself entirely and unalterably, in a manner free of all complications or ties, who in His works in the world and on man never ceases in the very slightest to be God, who does not give His glory to another. In this, as Creator, Reconciler and Redeemer, He is a truly loving, serving God. He is the King of all kings just when He enters into the profoundest hiddenness in "meekness of heart." This has to be said in every statement we make about Jesus Christ.[5] . . .

---

between God—who is the object of human knowledge—and the subjectivity of the human knower. His goal is to demonstrate that this connection is established by God as God unites himself to humanity in the saving work of Christ and the Spirit.

4. To say that Jesus Christ is "very God" is to claim that the incarnate Jesus is the revelation of God. So an encounter with Jesus is an encounter with the one true God in and through human flesh.

5. Barth rejects abstraction when thinking about Christ. The incarnation is not the general uniting of divinity and humanity but the Word made flesh, a real human. And if this human is God, then his life must be a revelation of the truth about God. What does Christ's life reveal? It shows that God has freely decided to relate to humans in love and mercy. So to think concretely about Jesus Christ—that is, to think in light of the objectivity of God's revelation rather than subjective human ideals—is to think about the God who relates to humans in *this* particular

We will begin at once by making a number of affirmations which ought to clarify and establish this prime fact, that the Word which was made flesh is really the eternal Word of the eternal Father.

1. That the Word was made "flesh" means first and generally that He became man, true and real man, participating in the same human essence and existence, the same human nature and form, the same historicity that we have. God's revelation to us takes place in such a way that everything ascribable to man, his creaturely existence as an individually unique unity of body and soul in the time between birth and death, can now be predicated of God's eternal Son as well.[6] According to the witness of the Evangelists and apostles everything miraculous about His being as a man derives its meaning and force from the fact that it concerns the true man Jesus Christ as a man like ourselves. This is true especially of the Easter story, the Gospel of forty days, as the supreme event of revelation. It is true of the sign of His birth of the Virgin at the beginning, and the sign of the empty tomb at the end of His historical existence. It is true of the signs and wonders already manifested between this beginning and end, which proclaim the Kingdom of God in its relation to the event of Easter. What in fact makes revelation revelation and miracle miracle is that the Word of God did actually become a real man and that therefore the life of this real man was the object and theatre of the acts of God, the light of revelation entering the world. . . .

2. That the Word became flesh means, indeed, that He became a man. But we have to be careful about the sense in which alone this can be said. If we ask what the Word became when in His incarnation, without ceasing to be the Word, He nevertheless ceased to be only the Word, and if we allow ourselves to say that He became flesh, we must note that primarily and of itself "flesh" does not imply a man, but human essence and existence, human kind and nature, humanity, *humanitas*, that which makes a man man as opposed to God, angel or animal. . . .

"The Word became flesh" means primarily and of itself, then, that the Word became participant in human nature and existence. Human essence and existence became His. Now since this cannot be real except in the concrete reality of one man, it must at once be said that He became a man. But precisely this concrete reality of a man, this man, is itself the work of the Word, not His presupposition. It is not (in the adoptionist sense) as if first of all there had been a man there, and then the Son of God had become that

---

way. We cannot think rightly about God in any other way because every other way departs from the specific content of God's revelation and falls into speculation.

6. Put differently, the eternal Son of God lives a true human life while remaining fully God. This is why Jesus Christ is the revelation of God.

man.[7] What was there over against the Son of God, and as the presupposition of His work, was simply the potentiality of being in the flesh, being as a man. This is the possibility of every man. And here—for the individuality and uniqueness of human existence belong to the concept of human essence and existence—it is the one specific possibility of the first son of Mary. The Word appropriated this possibility to Himself as His own, and He realized it as such when He became Jesus. In so doing He did not cease to be what He was before, but He became what He was not before, a man, this man. . . .

As the Son of God made His own this one specific possibility of human essence and existence and made it a reality, this Man came into being, and He, the Son of God, became this Man. This Man was thus never a reality by Himself, and therefore, since the Son of God became this Man, He is not another or second being in Jesus Christ alongside of the Son of God. . . . "Jesus Christ very God and very Man" does not mean that in Jesus Christ God and a man were really side by side, but it means that Jesus Christ, the Son of God and thus Himself true God, is also a true Man.[8] But this Man exists inasmuch as the Son of God is this Man—not otherwise. He exists because the Son of God appropriated and actualized His special possibility as a Man. The appropriation of human essence and existence in this special possibility by the Son of God, or the adoption and assumption of this special possibility of human essence and existence as that of the Son of God and the actualization of it by Him and in Him—this is the creation and preservation, this is the sole ground of existence, of this Man, and therefore of Christ's flesh. . . .

Thus the reality of Jesus Christ is that God Himself in person is actively present in the flesh. God Himself in person is the Subject of a real human being and acting. And just because God is the Subject of it, this being and acting are real. They are a genuinely and truly human being and acting. Jesus

7. The adoptionism Barth has in mind stems from the heresy of Nestorianism. Proponents of Nestorianism hold that the incarnation is the result of the moral union of two distinct subjects, the eternal Son and the human Jesus of Nazareth. Adoptionists work from the basis of this Nestorian account. They argue that, as divine, Jesus Christ is the Son of God by nature; and as human, he is the Son of God by adoption. The problem with this approach is that the human Jesus is not the revelation of God but merely the revelation of the human who has been adopted by God. The being of God remains hidden somewhere behind Jesus, and we are left to search for God by looking somewhere other than Jesus. In contrast, Barth asserts that the eternal Son personally unites himself to human flesh in Jesus Christ so that he participates in the fullness of human life as God. This is the basis of the claim that Jesus is the revelation of God and the center of God's relationship with us.

8. Barth again is pushing against Nestorian tendencies in Christology. God is not behind or alongside the incarnate Jesus Christ, as if Jesus shows us one thing but humans have to discover truth about God by looking elsewhere. Rather, because the Son of God is incarnate in Jesus Christ, his human life is the revelation of God.

Christ is not a demigod. He is not an angel. Nor is He an ideal man. He is a man as we are, equal to us as a creature, as a human individual, but also equal to us in the state and condition into which our disobedience has brought us. And in being what we are He is God's Word. Thus as one of us, yet the one of us who is Himself God's Word in person. He represents God to us and He represents us to God. In this way He is God's revelation to us and our reconciliation with God.[9]

3. So far we have looked upon "flesh" as a description of neutral human nature. This fact, too, that the Word became flesh, we have had to establish in its generality. But what the New Testament calls "flesh" includes not only the concept of man in general but also, assuming and including this general concept, the narrower concept of the man who is liable to the judgment and verdict of God, who having become incapable of knowing and loving God must incur the wrath of God, whose existence has become one exposed to death because he has sinned against God. Flesh is the concrete form of human nature marked by Adam's fall, the concrete form of that entire world which, when seen in the light of Christ's death on the cross, must be regarded as the old world already past and gone, the form of the destroyed nature and existence of man as they have to be reconciled with God.[10] . . .

The Word is not only the eternal Word of God but "flesh" as well, i.e., all that we are and exactly like us even in our opposition to Him. It is because of this that He makes contact with us and is accessible for us. In this way, and only in this way, is He God's revelation to us. He would not be revelation if He were not man. And He would not be man if He were not "flesh" in this definite sense. That the Word became "flesh" in this definite sense, this consummation of God's condescension, this inconceivability which is greater than the inconceivability of the divine majesty and the inconceivability of human darkness put together: this is the revelation of the Word of God.[11] . . .

9. Barth's second point has been building up to this sentence: because the eternal Son of God is the subject of the life of the incarnate Jesus Christ, he is God's revelation to us; and because Jesus Christ is the eternal Son of God, he is the one who reconciles humans to God. Revelation and reconciliation always go together.

10. Barth insists that any description of the human relationship with God must account for the reality of human sinfulness. An account of God's relationship with humans based on a hypothetical, ideal human—such as those views that describe God's relationship with the human as created, apart from the sin—falls into abstraction (see chaps. 7 and 8).

11. Although Barth began with the Johannine concept of "flesh," he now has Pauline themes in mind. These remarks echo Paul's statement that Christ did not exploit his equality with God but instead emptied himself by "being born in human likeness" and then lives in obedience even to the point of his death on the cross (Phil. 2:7). Also in the background is Paul's claim that the revelation of the crucified Christ is "foolishness" to human wisdom (1 Cor. 1:23–24).

4. In becoming the same as we are, the Son of God is the same in quite a different way from us; in other words, in our human being what we do is omitted, and what we omit is done.[12] This Man would not be God's revelation to us, God's reconciliation with us, if He were not, as true Man, the true, unchangeable, perfect God Himself. He is the true God because and so far as it has pleased the true God to adopt the true being of man. But this is the expression of a claim upon this being, a sanctification and blessing of this being, which excludes sin. In it God Himself is the Subject. How can God sin, deny Himself to Himself, be against Himself as God, want to be a god and so fall away from Himself in the way in which our sin is against Him, in which it happens from the very first and continually in the event of our existence? True, the Word assumes our human existence, assumes flesh, i.e., He exists in the state and position, amid the conditions, under the curse and punishment of sinful man. He exists in the place where we are, in all the remoteness not merely of the creature from the Creator, but of the sinful creature from the Holy Creator. Otherwise His action would not be a revealing, a reconciling action. He would always be for us an alien word. He would not find us or touch us. For we live in that remoteness. But it is He, the Word of God, who assumes our human existence, assumes our flesh, exists in the place where we exist. Otherwise His action would again not be a revealing, a reconciling action. Otherwise He would bring us nothing new. He would not help us. He would leave us in the remoteness.[13] Therefore in our state and condition He does not do what underlies and produces that state and condition, or what we in that state and condition continually do. Our unholy human existence, assumed and adopted by the Word of God, is a hallowed and therefore a sinless human existence; in our unholy human existence the eternal Word draws near to us. In the

12. In other words, Christ remains distinct from us in his humanity because he does not sin but engages in deeds of righteousness.

13. Barth emphasizes that God does not change when he bears humanity's sin in Christ because his account of God's revelation in Christ depends on this point. If this were not the case—if Christ's death on the cross involved some kind of change or alteration in God's being—then Christ's death on the cross would not be a revelation of God but something other than God. Then how could humans know that Christ's death leads to their reconciliation with God? To avoid this problem, Barth insists that, if God is in Christ, then Christ's death for our sins must correspond to God's eternal being and will. And since sin contradicts God's being and will, Christ's death for our sins must reflect God's intent to overcome sin on humanity's behalf so that humans might be reconciled to him. This explains the intrinsic connection between revelation and reconciliation: if Christ reveals God, then God's revelation to humanity—and human knowledge of God—goes hand in hand with humanity's reconciliation to God in Christ. We will not think rightly about God if we start in any other basis than the crucified Christ.

hallowing of our unholy human existence He draws supremely and help-fully near to us.[14] . . .

◇◇◇

From the doctrine of the Trinity we know that to the question of how the state of revealedness is achieved for us men, there can be only one answer: the one true God and Lord Himself, in the "person" of the Holy Spirit, is His own state of revealedness for us. The answer is, therefore, the same as we had also to give to the question of what was the event of revelation, except that then its special content was the indication of the Son or Word.[15] . . . But the imperative question here is this: what is the meaning of revelation as the presence of God Himself, so far as it is not only an event proceeding from God, but also an event that reaches man? To what extent, in the occurrence of revelation, are we men free for God, so that He can be revealed to us? To what extent is there in this occurrence a revealed state of God for man, and to that extent a human receptivity for God's revelation? The object of this question we call "the subjective reality of revelation." By this is meant no less than the answer prescribed in Holy Scripture, namely, the outpouring of the Holy Spirit.[16] . . .

Almost everything that we can say about man from the standpoint of reve-lation speaks against the possibility that God can be revealed to us. But the work of the Holy Spirit is in favor of that possibility. Now we cannot make either statement except from the standpoint of revelation. Therefore we can-not mean the same thing when, on the one side, we say that God cannot, and, on the other, we say that God can. "God cannot" means that He cannot do it

14. The small-print passages related to this section show that Barth has in mind the pat-tern of 2 Cor. 5:21: "For our sake he made him to be sin who knew no sin, so that in him we might become the righteousness of God." Alongside this verse and others like Gal. 3:13 and Isa. 53, Barth places verses that emphasize the sinlessness of Christ (Heb. 4:15; 1 Pet. 2:22). Taken together, these verses indicate that, since Christ bears our sin but does not commit it, his death reveals that God's will is to save us from sin. This corresponds to Paul's claim that God sent his Son "in the likeness of sinful flesh, and to deal with sin, he condemned sin in the flesh" (Rom. 8:3). For Barth, this salvation from sin includes the sanctification of our human nature. He cites Tertullian approvingly on this point: "We confirm that in Christ was that flesh of which the nature was man's sinful nature, and so sin was emptied from it, because in Christ it was held without sin—that nature which in man was not held without sin" (*De carne Christi* 16). Christ's death on the cross for our sin sanctifies human nature because he removes the stain of sin from it. This means that *real* human nature—human nature that truly reflects God's intention for it—is found in Jesus.

15. On this point, see Barth's remarks about the relationship between God's revelation and God's "self-impartation" to humans through the Spirit in chap. 14.

16. Put differently, what does the reality of human knowledge of God through the Spirit tell us about God, God's relationship to humanity, and human nature?

on the basis of a human possibility. "God can" means, of course, that He can do it on the basis of His own possibility. It is the possibility which is proper to God in the work of the Holy Spirit which we now have to consider. Let us see to it that we do not look for it anywhere but in the work of the Holy Spirit Himself. There is no independent standpoint from which we can survey and either approve or disapprove the ways of God (as though we could suggest other ways to God). We can only keep God's actual ways before us. We can only try to understand both the fact and the extent that they are actual ways. In so doing we shall not even dream that we can know what actual ways are except from our consideration of the actual ways of God. We can give only one basic answer to the question how in the freedom of man it is possible for God's revelation to reach him. This is that it is possible, as it is real, only in the outpouring of the Holy Spirit.[17] We have now to develop this statement.

1. By the outpouring of the Holy Spirit, it is possible for God's revelation to reach man in his freedom, because in it the Word of God is brought to his hearing.[18]

In expounding the subjective reality of revelation we everywhere insisted that it is not only strictly bound to its objective reality, but that it is simply the process by which that objective reality becomes subjective. The Holy Spirit is the Spirit of the Father and of the Son, of the Father who reveals Himself in His Son and only in His Son. But that means that He is the Spirit of Jesus Christ. . . . According to Scripture, everything which can be, everything which is either objectively or subjectively possible in relation to revelation, is enclosed in the being and will and action of the triune God. All capacity in this respect is His capacity, and we can read it from His working. Again according to Scripture, His working is the working of His Word, the work of His Son.[19] Everything distinct from that is directly or indirectly our working,

17. Barth is wrestling with the same dialectical relationship he explored in his discussion of faith (see chap. 13). On one side is the reality that humans are incapable of knowing God on their own; on the other side is the reality that God makes himself known to humans. Both realities are true, and together they indicate that God gives humans a capacity that enables them to know that which they are naturally incapable of knowing. This capacity comes in and through the Holy Spirit. If we are to talk rightly about human knowledge of God, then we must focus on the work of the Spirit as attested in Scripture.

18. This sentence is awkward in both the English and the original German. Here is a paraphrase: the Spirit makes it possible for God's revelation to reach humans without violating their integrity as creatures because the Spirit enables them to actually hear the Word of God.

19. Barth is making an important distinction here. The subjective reality of God's revelation does not occur as a second act of revelation that adds new content to the prior, objective revelation. The subjective reality of revelation is simply the impartation of the objective revelation into the human. For divine revelation to be a revelation of *God*, the effect of this revelation—its subjective reality in the human recipient—must be the same as the objective content of the

and it must first receive revelation, it must first be reconciled to God by the divine working and work. Therefore in relation to revelation all capacity is concretely the capacity of the Word, the capacity of Jesus Christ. There is no alternative: when we ask how a man comes to hear the Word of God, to believe in Christ, to be a member of His body and as His brother to be God's child, at once we must turn and point away to the inconceivable, whose conceivability is obviously in question; and we must say that it depends upon the inconceivable itself and as such, that it can become conceivable to men. The Word creates the fact that we hear the Word. Jesus Christ creates the fact that we believe in Jesus Christ. Up there with Him it is possible for it to be possible down here with me. All the other possibilities which I have and of which I may think are perhaps very fine and significant possibilities in another direction. The fact that we have them means, perhaps, that we are free and open and ready in every conceivable direction: but not in this direction. For the thing for which we have to be free and open and ready at this point does not itself derive from our reality. It does not belong to it. It has only assumed our reality. Therefore it confronts us as a new reality. In the whole range of our possibilities there is nothing to correspond to it or to explain it. And if this is true of the thing itself, it is also true of the reality and the possibility of our communion with it. There is such a thing "because the love of God is shed abroad in our hearts by the Holy Ghost which is given unto us" (Rom. 5:5). But if it is possible for it to exist, the possibility is not in our hearts but in the love of God. Similarly, the "through the Holy Ghost which is given unto us" cannot have its possibility except in the love of God. In other words, the work of the Holy Spirit means that there is an adequate basis for our hearing of the Word, since it brings us nothing but the Word for our hearing. It means that there is an adequate basis for our faith in Christ and our communion with Him, because He is no other Spirit than the Spirit of Jesus Christ. It is, therefore, the subjective possibility of revelation because it is the process by which its objective reality is made subjective, namely, the life of the body of Christ, the operation of the prophetic and apostolic testimony, the hearing of preaching, the seeing of that to which the sacraments point.[20] . . .

---

revelation and God the revealer. So the Spirit does not add new or distinct content to what Christ has revealed; he simply imparts this revelation to the believer. This means that the Spirit's work in history can be discerned only by starting with the work of Jesus Christ, since the Spirit's primary work is to make Christ known.

20. Barth's argument in this paragraph corresponds to the claims he has been making since *The Epistle to the Romans*, although now they have been developed in light of Barth's trinitarian theology. While humans may have many important capacities, none of them are sufficient to obtain knowledge of God. Humans are able to know God only because Christ speaks to them, and they can have this knowledge because the Spirit of Christ enables them to hear his voice.

2. By the outpouring of the Holy Spirit it is possible in the freedom of man for God's revelation to meet him, because in it he is explicitly told by God's Word that he possesses one possibility of his own for such a meeting.[21]

The Word of God which is revealed in revelation declares that man is not actually free for God. This is already expressed by the fact that it is actually the Word or the Son of God who is revealed. What happens is not just anything. It is the last and most peculiar thing which could happen from God's side. God comes forward Himself to be man's Savior. This presupposes, and it is already proclaimed as a truth of divine judgment, that man cannot be helped in any other way. It is not merely that man lacks something which he ought to be or to have or to be capable of in relation to God. He lacks everything. . . . We cannot say that to be a man means to be without God. But we can and must say, negatively, that to be a man does not mean to be with God. To be a man can certainly include to be with God, but only when it is overlapped by the definition: in Christ, that is, as a hearer and doer of the Word of God, in the Church. But this is the new thing added to our being as men by revelation. It is not included in our being as such.[22] . . .

3. By the outpouring of the Holy Spirit it becomes possible for man in his freedom to be met by God's revelation, because in it the Word of God becomes unavoidably his master.[23]

From what has been said under points 1 and 2, we are aware that we have to seek the subjective possibility of revelation, our freedom for the Word of God, only in the Word itself, in Jesus Christ. We have not to abstract from this objective factor and seek it in its effects on and in us. Therefore, in so far as it now becomes our freedom, we have to understand it as a miracle, and not in any sense as a natural freedom and capacity. . . .

That freedom exists where the Word of God or Jesus Christ is to man the Master, and unavoidably the Master. Instead of master we might also say teacher, leader or lord. In this context the word "master" is particularly rich in content. Its counterpart may equally well be pupil, scholar, follower or adherent, or servant. And all this is involved in the freedom of man for the

---

21. To paraphrase, the Spirit makes it possible for God's revelation to reach humans without violating their integrity as creatures because the Spirit makes humans realize they have no other way to know God.

22. This paragraph expresses one of Barth's core convictions: God has no relationship with humans apart from Jesus Christ. The only way humans can relate to God is by hearing the Word of Christ through the Spirit and then responding with faith and obedience in community with other believers.

23. To paraphrase, the Spirit makes it possible for God's revelation to reach humans without violating their integrity as creatures because the Spirit enables them to live in free obedience to God.

Word and by the Word, of which we are speaking. But for the sake of clarity, we must at once add to the concept of "master" that of "unavoidable." By the analogy of faith (*analogia fidei*) it will be understood what is now meant by "master." There are indeed many masters and teachers, and leaders and lords. They are all of them distinguished from this Master by the fact that they can be totally or partially avoided either altogether or from some particular point in time. To stand unavoidably under any other master is a sign of sickness. But to stand under this Master is not only the normal thing, it is the only possible thing. The outpouring of the Holy Spirit exalts the Word of God to be the master over men, puts man unavoidably under His mastery. The miracle of the divine revealedness, the power of Christ's resurrection in a man, consists in this event. In it the "God became man" is actualized in us as "man has God." It is a removal of the contradiction between a possibility which obviously is only God's possibility, and the human experience and activity, which only an unredeemed arrogance could claim as a fitting and worthy vessel for such a content. In this event man is a participator in this divine possibility. Through God he is free for God.[24]

---

24. Barth's point is that the Spirit's impartation of Christ's revelation in humans enables them to worship and obey God alone. In this sense, Barth is echoing the *Shema*: "Hear, O Israel: the Lord is our God, the Lord alone" (Deut. 6:4). The distinction is that, in Barth's account, believers know and obey God alone because Christ exercises his lordship over them through his Spirit.

CHAPTER

16

The Knowledge of God

Introduction

This excerpt from the beginning of *Church Dogmatics* II/1 is one of the most important passages in Barth's writings. After nearly two decades of thinking about the human knowledge of God, Barth now offers his most precise description of what this knowledge involves and how it occurs.

He begins by carefully framing the question. Barth insists that theologians cannot ask *if* humans know God or *whether* the knowledge of God is possible, because these questions can be answered only through speculation. Instead, theologians must begin with the reality that God is known and then consider how this knowledge occurs. This approach keeps theologians focused on the particularity of God's revelation rather than on their own abstract ideas.

The first conclusion Barth draws about human knowledge of God is that it is *mediated*. God reveals himself through created realities while remaining distinct from these realities. This distinction means that humans cannot focus on the created reality itself, but instead they must focus on the way God has chosen to use these realities. The implication is that the knowledge of God takes place in an *event* determined by God's act to reveal himself to humans.

Barth then explains that, while God knows himself immediately and directly, humans know God in a mediated and indirect way. This is the distinction between God's primary and secondary objectivity, and it carries three implications. First, even though humans know God through creaturely realities,

God truly is the object of human knowledge. Second, human knowledge of God is bound to the specific creaturely realities God uses in the event of his self-revelation. Third, since humans only know God through creaturely realities, they know God by *faith*.

Put differently, humans know in God's secondary objectivity, which means that they know God as God reveals himself in creature mediums and they respond to this revelation with faith. Barth concludes that, since this knowledge is dependent on God's act of self-revelation, it is characterized by grace, prayer, and obedience. God gives himself to humans through Christ and the Spirit, and humans pray that they may participate in God's self-knowledge through the mediation of Christ and the Spirit. They also respond to God's actions with obedience by bringing their ideas about God into correspondence with the particular way God has revealed himself in created reality and history.

———————— *Church Dogmatics* II/1[1] ————————

In the Church of Jesus Christ men speak about God and men have to hear about God. About God the Father, the Son and the Holy Spirit; about God's grace and truth; about God's thoughts and works; about God's promises, ordinances and commandments; about God's kingdom, and about the state and life of man in the sphere of His lordship. But always and in all circumstances about God Himself, who is the presupposition, meaning and power of everything that is to be said and heard in the Church, the Subject who absolutely, originally and finally moves, produces, establishes and realizes in this matter. In dogmatics it is the doctrine of God which deals with this Subject as such. In the doctrine of God we have to learn what we are saying when we say "God." In the doctrine of God we have to learn to say "God" in the correct sense. If we do not speak rightly of this Subject, how can we speak rightly of His predicates?[2]

But in relation to this Subject, we are at once confronted with the problem of knowledge. All speaking and hearing in the Church of Jesus Christ entirely rests upon and is connected with the fact that God is known in the Church of Jesus Christ; that is to say, that this Subject is objectively present to the speakers and hearers, so that man in the Church really stands before God. If

1. Karl Barth, *Church Dogmatics* II/1 (Edinburgh: T&T Clark, 1957), 3–26, 47–49.
2. This paragraph sets up this excerpt. As Christians speak about God in the church, how can they know what they mean by the word "God"? And how do they obtain this knowledge? Barth's argument in this section is designed to address these two questions.

it were not so, if man did not really stand before God, if God were not the object of his perception, viewing and conception, and if he did not know God—whatever we understand by "know"—then he could not speak and hear about Him. Then everything declared and heard in the Church would have no Subject and would be left in the air like an empty sound. Then the Church, if it lives only by what is said and heard in it, would not be alive; or its life would be merely an apparent life, life in a dream-world with those subjectless images and concepts as the phantasies of its imagination. But if the life of the Church is not just a semblance, the knowledge of God is realized in it. This is the presupposition which we have first of all to explain in the doctrine of God.[3] We have to learn how far we can know God and therefore speak and hear about Him. . . .

We start out from the fact that through His Word God is actually known and will be known again. On principle we have to reject any anxiety about this occurrence as not only superfluous but forbidden. Knowledge of God within the Christian Church is very well aware that it is established in its reality and to that extent also called in question by God's Word, through which alone it can be and have reality, and on the basis of which alone it can be fulfilled. But precisely because the knowledge of God cannot call itself in question in its effort to understand itself, it cannot ask whether it is real from some position outside itself. This question can be put to it only from God's Word. And from the Word of God this question is in fact put to it. And it is also given the answer there. But it will not want to be set under the Word of God just in order to make its own existence problematical.[4] It is made problematical by the Word of God, but thanks to that same Word it need not fear that it will be made problematical anywhere else. For in the Word of God it is decided that the knowledge of God cannot let itself be called in question, or call itself in question, from any other position outside itself. The Word of God will not let it move from its own place into another. And even if it wanted to, there is no other place from which somebody or something

3. When considering human knowledge of God, it is common to start with the question of how humans are able to know God at all. But Barth rules out this question as abstract and non-theological. Because the discipline of dogmatics operates on the basis of divine revelation, it must begin with the presupposition that God already is known. As a result, theologians approach the "how" question differently: they start with the concrete reality that God is an object of human knowledge in the church and then ask how this knowledge has occurred and what this knowledge involves.

4. Barth rules out the question of whether God is known because the discipline of dogmatics presupposes the reality of this knowledge. While many good questions can be raised about the nature and limits of the knowledge of God, the question of the existence of this knowledge is superfluous to dogmatics.

can compete with the Word of God which establishes the knowledge of God: Not because the knowledge of God bestowed upon the Church makes itself absolute; but because it cannot affront the truth, worth and competence of the Word of God. It must refuse to let its reality be debated from any position, and must start out by establishing its own reality. It is another matter that it can do this only in reflection and response to the Word of God which establishes it. But it cannot retreat from its own reality. Therefore we cannot ask whether God is known.

But this also means that the question cannot be whether God is knowable.[5] Where God is known He is also in some way or other knowable. Where the actuality exists there is also the corresponding possibility. The question cannot then be posed in the abstract but only concretely; not *a priori* but only *a posteriori*. The abstract and *a priori* question of the possibility of the knowledge of God obviously presupposes the existence of a place outside the knowledge of God itself from which this knowledge can be judged. It presupposes a place where, no doubt, the possibility of knowledge in general and then of the knowledge of God in particular can be judged and decided in one way or another. It presupposes the existence of a theory of knowledge as a hinterland where consideration of the truth, worth and competence of the Word of God, on which the knowledge of God is grounded, can for a time at least be suspended. But this is the very thing which, from the point of view of its possibility, must not happen. Just as the reality of the Word of God in Jesus Christ bears its possibility within itself, as does also the reality of the Holy Spirit, by whom the Word of God comes to man, so too the possibility of the knowledge of God and therefore the knowability of God cannot be questioned in a vacuum, or by means of a general criterion of knowledge delimiting the knowledge of God from without, but only from within this real knowledge itself. Therefore it is quite impossible to ask whether God is knowable, because this question is already decided by the only legitimate and meaningful questioning which arises in this connection.[6]

5. The question of whether God is known is asking if human knowledge of God exists at all. The question of whether God is knowable is asking if it even is possible for creatures to know *God*.

6. Barth argues that the question of whether God is knowable is illegitimate for dogmatics because it can only be answered from a non-theological starting point. Dogmatics operates strictly on the basis of the Word of God. But this question requires that theologians adopt a neutral vantage point in relation to God and then—on the basis of their human judgment—determine whether God can be known by humans. The problem is that no such vantage point exists. And how could a human determine whether God can be known without having prior knowledge of God? By what criterion would a human offer this judgment? From Barth's perspective, any answer to the question of God's knowability offered from a position of neutrality would be

The only legitimate and meaningful questions in this context are: how far is God known? and how far is God knowable?[7] These questions are legitimate and meaningful because they are genuine questions of Church proclamation, and therefore also genuine questions of dogmatics—genuine objects of its formal and material task. How God is known and is knowable has to be a matter of continual reflection and appraisal for the teaching Church, and it has to be continually said to the hearing Church so that it may be called to new witness. And with the questions put in this way, both the teaching and the hearing Church will walk in the path of the Word of God. Put thus, they are not inquisitive and superfluous questions; much less are they questions that insult the Word of God by suspending its truth, worth and competence. On the contrary, they are both permitted and commanded, as questions about the right understanding and correct elucidation of the Word of God. In this section we will deal first with the former question—that of the how of the knowledge of God in its actual fulfillment.

This fulfillment is taking place. The Church of Jesus Christ lives. It lives, of course, by the grace of the Word. Therefore the Word is not bound to it, or only so far as the Word, in once bestowing itself upon the Church, has bound itself to it as promise for the future. In view of this promise, however, we have to say that the fulfillment of the knowledge of God is taking place, and that we can only ask about its mode. But also, in view of this promise, we can ask about the reality and possibility of the knowledge of God from within the unambiguous, unreserved and unconditional binding of the Church to the Word. This means above all that the question of the object of this knowledge, like the question of its mode, cannot be regarded as open. There can be no reservations about whom or what we have to think when we ask about the knowledge of God. When the knowledge of God is under discussion we are not free perhaps to think of Him who in the Bible is called God and Lord, but perhaps equally well to think of some other entity which can similarly be described and proclaimed as "God," and which has in fact been described and proclaimed as "God" somewhere and at some time. We cannot equally well ask about the knowledge of the World-Ground or the World-Soul, the Supreme Good or Supreme Value, the Thing in itself or the Absolute, Destiny or Being

---

meaningless for dogmatics because it would be based on abstract speculation rather than the concrete reality of God's revelation.

7. These questions begin with the reality of the church's knowledge of God and then ask what this knowledge involves. To what extent does the church know God? In what sense does the church's creaturely knowledge of God correspond to the reality of God? And what does the existence of the church's knowledge of God tell us about the extent to which God is knowable by creatures? Barth thinks these questions are meaningful and legitimate because they begin with the reality of the Word of God and can be addressed on the basis of the Word of God.

or Idea, or even the First Cause as the Unity of Being and Idea, as we can ask about the knowledge of Him who in the Bible is called God and Lord. . . . The knowledge of God with which we are here concerned takes place, not in a free choice, but with a very definite constraint. It stands or falls with its one definite object, which cannot be different, and which cannot be exchanged for or even joined with any other object. Because it is bound to God's Word given to the Church, the knowledge of God with which we are here concerned is bound to the God who in His Word gives Himself to the Church to be known as God. Bound in this way it is the true knowledge of the true God.[8] . . .

That the knowledge of God in its fulfillment by the revelation of the Word of God is bound to its one, determined and uniquely distinct object, and that it is knowledge of this object and not of another—knowledge of the God who gives Himself to be known in His Word—means further that, without any prejudice to its certainty, but in this very certainty, it is mediated knowledge.[9] That is to say, God is and remains its object. If God gives Himself to man to be known in the revelation of His Word through the Holy Spirit, it means that He enters into the relationship of object to man the subject. In His revelation God is considered and conceived by men. Man knows God in that he stands before God. But this always means: in that God becomes, is and remains to him Another, One who is distinct from himself, One who meets him.[10] Nor is this objectivity of God neutralized by the fact that God makes man His own through the Holy Spirit, in order to give Himself to be owned by him. For what else does this mean but that He gives Himself to man in His Word as a real object? He makes man accessible for Himself. He lets Himself be considered and conceived by man. Man cannot and must not know himself apart from God, but together with God as his "opposite."[11] Again, the objectivity

8. Since theologians address questions about the knowledge of God in light of the reality of the Word of God, the answers they give must be determined by this Word. They cannot start with an abstract and general idea of "God" and then bring that idea into relation with God's revelation to the church. Rather, they must start with God's concrete and particular revelation to the church and then draw conclusions about the knowledge of God on the basis of this revelation.

9. This sentence marks an important turn in Barth's argument because it is where he begins offering his own answer to the question of the knowledge of God. We can paraphrase this answer: when theologians talk about the church's knowledge of God on the basis of the reality of God's revelation to the church, the first thing they can say is that this knowledge is *mediated*—i.e., this knowledge occurs as God reveals himself in and through creaturely realities.

10. Immediately after stating that the church's knowledge of God is mediated knowledge, Barth issues four qualifications that govern his discussion of this idea. The first qualification is that God remains totally distinct from the creature even as the creature knows him. The human's knowledge of God does not stem from any merging or blending of the human with the divine.

11. The second qualification is that God remains distinct from the human even as the Spirit imparts God's revelation to the human. The Spirit's presence does not mean that God has united

of God is not restricted by the fact that we have to understand God Himself as the real and primarily acting Subject of all real knowledge of God, so that the self-knowledge of God is the real and primary essence of all knowledge of God. That God is originally and really object to Himself does not alter the fact that in a very different way He is also object to man. And the fact that God knows Himself immediately is not neutralized by the fact that man knows Him on the basis of His revelation and hence mediately, and only mediately, and therefore as an object.[12] The reality of our knowledge of God stands or falls with the fact that in His revelation God is present to man in a medium. He is therefore objectively present in a double sense. In His Word He comes as an object before man the subject. And by the Holy Spirit He makes the human subject accessible to Himself, capable of considering and conceiving Himself as object. The real knowledge of God is concerned with God in His relationship to man, but also in His distinction from him. We therefore separate ourselves from all those ideas of the knowledge of God which understand it as the union of man with God, and which do not regard it as an objective knowledge but leave out the distinction between the knower and the known.[13] . . .

The fact that man stands before the God who gives Himself to be known in His Word, and therefore to be known mediately, definitely means that we have to understand man's knowledge of God as the knowledge of faith. In this consists its reality and necessity, which are not and cannot be attacked from without. And from this follow all determinations of the mode of its fulfillment.[14] We must now discuss the assertion that the knowledge of God is the knowledge of faith.

---

himself to the human such that she now can simply look within herself to know God. Always and at every moment, the human must look to God's objective revelation in order to know God.

12. The third qualification stems from the reality that true knowledge of God is identical to God's self-knowledge. God has this knowledge immediately and directly, and it does not need to be mediated through anything else. This makes God's knowledge of God distinct from human knowledge of God, which is both revealed and mediated. This distinction does not mean that humans do not have real knowledge of God. God is still the object of human knowledge even though God's knowledge of himself is distinct from human knowledge of God. The difference between divine and human knowledge of God is located not in the object of knowledge but in the *way* that this object is known.

13. The fourth qualification is that God personally encounters the human in and through the creaturely medium by which he is known. This does not mean that God merges his divine being with creaturely being in the event of revelation. Rather, it means that God makes himself an object to humans by speaking his Word through a creaturely reality and by enabling creatures to hear this Word through the Spirit. Barth insists that God's objective presence in this "double sense" does not erase the distinction between God and creation for all the reasons he outlined earlier in his theology (see chaps. 12–15).

14. Since humans do not see God directly and immediately but instead know God as he reveals himself through a creaturely medium, their knowledge of God is by faith. This does

In the first instance, it is simply a confirmation of the fact that the knowledge of God is bound to the object set before it by God's Word—and to this object in its irrevocable objectivity.[15] Faith is the total positive relationship of man to the God who gives Himself to be known in His Word. It is man's act of turning to God, of opening up his life to Him and of surrendering to Him. It is the Yes which he pronounces in his heart when confronted by this God, because he knows himself to be bound and fully bound. It is the obligation in which, before God, and in the light of the clarity that God is God and that He is his God, he knows and explains himself as belonging to God. But when we say that, we must at once also say that faith as the positive relationship of man to God comes from God Himself in that it is utterly and entirely grounded in the fact that God encounters man in the Word which demands of him this turning, this Yes, this obligation; becoming an object to him in such a way that in His objectivity He bestows upon him by the Holy Spirit the light of the clarity that He is God and that He is his God, and therefore evoking this turning, this Yes, this obligation on the part of man. It is in this occurrence of faith that there is the knowledge of God; and not only the knowledge of God, but also love towards Him, trust in Him and obedience to Him. But these various determinations of faith are not to be understood as parts or even certain fruits of faith. Each one is the determination of faith in its entirety. If we speak of the knowledge of faith, we do not speak of something which is faith as well as being all sorts of other things, but we speak—even if from a distinct angle—of faith in its entirety. Everything that is to be said of the nature of faith in general will also have to be said of the knowledge of God as the knowledge of faith. And we cannot speak of the knowledge of God except by speaking of the nature of faith in general—even if from a distinct angle.[16] . . .

---

not make their knowledge of God less than real, nor does it mean that this knowledge must be verified in some other manner in order to be counted as true. But it does mean that, as theologians answer questions about how the church's knowledge of God has occurred and what it involves, they must account for the fact that humans know God only by faith.

15. Barth argues that the first and primary implication of the fact that the church knows God by faith is that the church's knowledge of God is bound to the specific creaturely mediums through which God speaks his Word. Before explaining this point more fully, Barth turns to the task of offering a general account of the nature of faith itself.

16. Barth thinks it is important to offer a general description of faith before offering a specific description of the church's knowledge of God by faith, because the two accounts will correspond to one other. His general description of faith matches his earlier accounts of God's revelation, faith, and the role of Christ and the Spirit in human knowledge of God (see chaps. 12–15). He emphasizes that faith does not stand alongside human acts of obedience, trust, and love for God, but rather, these acts are included within the definition of faith. His point is that the knowledge of faith is not merely one of many possible ways that the church knows God but the only way.

Precisely because we understand faith as the knowledge of God, we must go further and say that we are concerned with the knowledge of the God who is the object of faith. Therefore it is not any sort of object; not an object that can give itself to be known and will be known just like any other object; not an object which awakens love, trust and obedience in the same way as other objects. Its objectivity is the particular and utterly unique objectivity of God. And that is tantamount to saying that this knowledge is the particular and utterly unique knowledge of faith.[17]

If God becomes the object of man's knowledge, this necessarily means that He becomes the object of his consideration and conception. On the strength of this it becomes possible and necessary to speak and hear about God.[18] If it were not so, there would be no knowledge of God and no faith in Him. God would simply not be in the picture. We could not hold to Him. We could not pray to Him. To deny the objectivity of God is to deny the life of the Church of Jesus Christ—which lives on the fact that God is spoken of and heard. It is to deny prayer to God, the knowledge of God, and with knowledge faith in God as well.[19] But not every object is God; and so not all our human consideration and conception is knowledge of God. For although God has genuine objectivity just like all other objects, His objectivity is different from theirs, and therefore knowledge of Him—and this is the chief thing to be said about its character as the knowledge of faith—is a particular and utterly unique occurrence in the range of all knowledge. Certainly the same thing happens in faith that happens always and everywhere when man enters into that uniting and distinguishing relationship to an object, when his subjectivity is opened up to an objectivity and he is grounded and determined anew. But in faith the same thing happens quite differently. This difference consists in the difference and uniqueness of God as its object. Knowledge of faith means fundamentally the union of man with the God who is distinct from him as well as from all his other objects. For this very reason this knowledge becomes and is a special knowledge, distinct from the knowledge of all other objects, outstanding in the range of all knowledge. What our consideration and conception mean in this context cannot be determined from a general understanding of man's consideration and conception, but only in particular

17. This qualification rules out the possibility that a general account of human knowing could be used to explain the knowledge of faith.

18. Barth now seeks to explain the nature of God's objectivity, and he does so by ruling out two errors.

19. The first error is to simply deny God's objectivity by asserting that God is so distant from creation that he is unknowable. Since this view is incompatible with the reality that the church knows God, Barth rules it out as a legitimate way for dogmatics.

from God as its particular object. On the strength of the fact that God in His particularity is its object, and as such is also known, it becomes possible and necessary to speak and hear about God.[20] . . .

If we ascribe objectivity to God (as we inevitably do when we speak of the knowledge of God) a distinction becomes unavoidable. As He certainly knows Himself first of all, God is first and foremost objective to Himself. We shall return to this point in the second part of the present section. In His triune life as such, objectivity, and with it knowledge, is divine reality before creaturely objectivity and knowledge exist. We call this the primary objectivity of God, and distinguish from it the secondary, i.e., the objectivity which He has for us too in His revelation, in which He gives Himself to be known by us as He knows Himself. It is distinguished from the primary objectivity, not by a lesser degree of truth, but by its particular form suitable for us, the creature. God is objectively immediate to Himself, but to us He is objectively mediate. That is to say, He is not objective directly but indirectly, not in the naked sense but clothed under the sign and veil of other objects different from Himself. His secondary objectivity is fully true, for it has its correspondence and basis in His primary objectivity.[21] God does not have to be untrue to Himself and deceive us about His real nature in order to become objective to us. For first to Himself, and then in His revelation to us, He is nothing but what He is in Himself. It is here that the door is shut against any "non-objective" knowledge of God. As such, it would not be knowledge of God, for God is objective to Himself. He is immediately objective to Himself—for the Father is object to the Son, and the Son to the Father, without mediation. He is mediately objective to us in His revelation, in which He meets us under the sign and veil of other objects. It is in, with and under the sign and veil of these other objects that we believe in God, and know Him and pray to Him. We believe in Him in His clothed, not in His naked, objectivity. That we know Him in

---

20. The second error is to think that God's objectivity is the same as that of other objects, such that the knowledge of faith works in the same way as every other kind of human knowledge. Since *God* is the object of the knowledge of faith, this knowledge is distinct from every other kind of human knowledge.

21. The distinction between primary and secondary objectivity is one of the most important concepts in Barth's theology because it is the way he explains how God's revelation works. *Primary objectivity* refers to God's self-knowledge: in his triune life, God knows himself as his own object. God's self-knowledge is the ground of the *secondary objectivity* of God, in which God gives himself as an object to be known by humans. God's primary objectivity is not distinct from God's secondary objectivity with respect to the truth of the object, because God is the object of knowledge in both cases. God knows God, and so do humans. The distinction is in the *way* God is known as an object by God and humans: God knows himself immediately and directly, but humans know God through the mediation of creaturely realities and thus only indirectly.

faith has a double significance. We really know Him in His objectivity (even if it is clothed); and we really know Him only in His clothed objectivity.[22] We do not ask first of all why this must be so, but are content to establish the fact that it is so. Man therefore stands before God in the knowledge of faith. He really and truly stands before God. God is object to him—the object from whom he sees himself to be distinct, but with whom he sees himself united; and conversely, the object with whom he sees himself united, but from whom he sees himself to be distinct. But he always stands indirectly before God. He stands directly before another object, one of the series of all other objects. The objectivity of this other object represents the objectivity of God. In the objectivity of this other object he knows God, i.e., between himself and this other object the acts of distinguishing and uniting, uniting and distinguishing, take place. This other object he genuinely perceives, considers and conceives—but in and with this other object, the objectivity of God. This other object is thus the medium by which God gives Himself to be known and in which man knows God.[23]

We must now describe in greater detail the particular, outstanding knowledge of God of which we have already spoken. It is the particular occurrence of an encounter between man and a part of the reality surrounding him which is different from God. In the encounter the reality of this piece of his environment does not cease to be a definite, creaturely reality, and therefore it does not become identical with God, but it represents God. That is to say, it represents God in so far as it is determined, made and used by God as His clothing, temple, or sign; in so far as it is peculiarly a work of God, which above and beyond its own existence (which is also God's work, of course) may and must serve to attest the objectivity of God and therefore to make the knowledge of God possible and necessary. Thus, to the particularity of this event which, in contrast to all other objects, is grounded in the nature of God, there corresponds the particularity of one such object which, in the sphere of creaturely reality, points to the nature of God, a uniqueness which does not belong to this object in itself and as such, but which falls to its lot in this event in which it is now effective. But it is effective, not on account of its own ability, but in virtue of its institution to the service which this object has

22. Note how this account of faith is more concrete than Barth's earlier definitions (see chap. 13). To know God in faith is to know God under the veil of his clothed objectivity. Or, put differently, we know God in faith when we know him in and through the creaturely realities he uses to reveal himself to us.

23. To summarize: in the event of God's revelation, humans stand before God in the sense that God is the object of their knowledge. Yet they stand before God only indirectly, because their personal encounter with God takes place through a creaturely medium.

to perform at this point. In other words, it is effective in virtue of the special work to which God has at this point determined and engaged it, because it has become the instrument of this work and has been marked off and is used as such. For now it is not only what it is to and in itself. Of course it is always that. But over and above its own self it is now this special work of God, God's sign, the garment of His objectivity, the means by which He gives Himself to be known to man and by which man knows Him—man, who as creature cannot stand directly before God but only before other objects.[24] Here too we have a necessary condition. At bottom, knowledge of God in faith is always this indirect knowledge of God, knowledge of God in His works, and in these particular works—in the determining and using of certain creaturely realities to bear witness to the divine objectivity. What distinguishes faith from unbelief, erroneous faith and superstition is that it is content with this indirect knowledge of God. It does not think that the knowledge of God in His works is insufficient. On the contrary, it is grateful really to know the real God in His works. It really lets itself be shown the objectivity of God by their objectivity. But it also holds fast to the particularity of these works. It does not arbitrarily choose objects to set up as signs, in that way inventing a knowledge of God at its own good-pleasure. It knows God by means of the objects chosen by God Himself. It recognizes and acknowledges God's choice and sanctification in the operation of this knowledge. And, for its part, it uses these special works of God as they ought to be used—as means of the knowledge of God. It lets their objectivity become a witness—yet only a witness—to the objectivity of God. Where the worship of God is made possible and necessary by God Himself, it does not establish an idol worship.[25] Faith, and therefore the knowledge of God, stands or falls with all these determinations of the clothed objectivity of God. It is under these determinations that God is spoken about and heard in the Church of Jesus Christ. Not a single one of them can be set aside or altered without radically injuring the life of the Church. . . .

24. Barth offers a dialectical explanation for how a creaturely reality can serve as the medium of God's self-revelation. On the one hand, he insists that the reality remains creaturely. It does not become divine or acquire new internal qualities as God uses it in the event of revelation. On the other hand, this reality carries a special significance because God has decided to use it in this way. It is not merely just another object, but it is a unique object because of God's relationship to it. Both sides of this explanation must be held together in order to understand the role of these creaturely mediums without overvaluing or undervaluing their role.

25. Because particular creaturely realities are distinguished by God's decision to use them as instruments of his self-revelation, human knowledge of God is bound to these realities. Humans cannot know or worship God without focusing on the particular instruments through which God has revealed himself. At the same time, since these creaturely realities are mere mediums for God's revelation, they cannot replace God as the primary object of knowledge.

But we have not yet come to the end. As knowledge of faith the knowledge of God is just like any other knowledge in that it also has an object. We have seen that thereby the primary objectivity of God is to be distinguished—but not separated—from the secondary. But as knowledge of faith the knowledge of God is unlike all other knowledge in that its object is the living Lord of the knowing man: his Creator, from whom he comes even before he knows Him; his Reconciler, who through Jesus Christ in the Holy Ghost makes knowledge of Himself real and possible; his Redeemer, who is Himself the future truth of all present knowledge of Himself. He and none other is the object of the knowledge of faith. Its difference from all other knowledge—a difference based on its object—is that the position of the knowing man in relation to this object is the position of a fundamentally and irrevocably determined sub-sequence, of a subsequence which can in no way be changed or reinterpreted into a precedence of man. It is the position of grace. Knowledge of God as knowledge of faith either occurs in this position or it does not take place at all.[26] But this means that knowledge of this object can in no case and in no sense mean that we have this object at our disposal. Certainly we have God as an object, but not in the same way as we have other objects. This is true of God both in His primary and also in His secondary objectivity, and therefore in the whole extent of the sphere which it marks out. . . . Knowledge of God is thus not the relationship of an already existing subject to an object that enters into his sphere and is therefore obedient to the laws of this sphere. On the contrary, this knowledge first of all creates the subject of its knowledge by coming into the picture. There cannot be allowed here any precedence of man which can entitle his subsequence—in which God has become the aim of his direction, the object of his knowledge—to ascribe to itself a right of disposal over the object, to make use of a power of disposal over it—as man does continually and obviously in regard to all other objects, whatever the theory of knowledge that he may hold. The precedence which alone comes into consideration here, and which never ceases as such to come into consideration, is the precedence of this object. Only because God posits Himself as the object is man posited as the knower of God. And so man can only have God as the self-posited object. It is and remains God's free grace when he is object for us in His primary and secondary objectivity. He always gives Himself to be known so as to be known by us in this giving, which is always a bestowal, always a free action.[27] How would it be His objectivity if this were

26. Note how Barth frames the knowledge of faith as an event: God acts to reveal himself to the human, and the human responds to God's action in faith.

27. These familiar themes in this section show that many of the convictions that defined Barth's early account of the knowledge of God remain intact in his mature theology.

not so? How could He be our Creator, Reconciler and Redeemer, how could He be the living Lord, if it were not so, and if His being for us were ever to be separated from His activity, so that a direction of man to God's being could exist that was grounded in something other than his being directed by God's activity? Faith stands or falls with the fact of man being directed by God's action, by the action of His being as the living Lord. Man's being directed is his direction to God and thus of necessity his direction to the living Lord; not to any other sort of being, but to the actual being of God. The knowledge of God by faith is therefore concerned with Him and with Him alone. It cannot draw conclusions from the fact that its object creates its own precedence. It cannot withdraw before the actuality of its object into any sort of a safe place from which it can contemplate His being in the abstract, as if it corresponded to a pre-arranged being of the contemplating man himself. For its part it can perform only the act of that being of man which is created and set up by the act of the divine being. It can only perform this act in the way that it has to be carried out on the basis of this creation and setting up: for on the basis of this creation and setting up, man's being is quite incapable of any other act; but this act is absolutely necessary to his being. Therefore it cannot—as it would if man were directed from anywhere else—be directed to anywhere else than to the living Lord. It will in no way be able to precede this act of God, but will only be able to succeed it.[28] It is therefore of decisive practical importance for the content of the knowledge of God (i.e., for the final question, whether it is false or true knowledge of God) whether a man knows or not that he must of necessity pray for its fulfillment as real knowledge of God, that God may give Himself to be known. The position of grace cannot be taken up and held in any other way than by asking and praying for it. The prayer that has to be made here is that God will set Himself as our object and ourselves as knowers of Him.[29] For this will not take place except as His free gift, in the act of His grace—and this in spite of the fact that He is in fact object in Himself and in secondary objectivity in His revelation, in Jesus Christ, in the witness of the Scriptures, in the visibility of the Church, in the audibility of preaching, in the operation of the sacraments, in the whole world of His work and sign. His primary and His secondary objectivity is objectivity for

28. Barth continues to push against the idea that we can know God on the basis of an always-existing "analogy of being" (*analogia entis*) between God and creatures (see chaps. 7 and 8). Barth worries that this kind of knowledge would be determined by creaturely concepts, and so he insists that humans know God only in the particular and unique event of God's self-disclosure in Christ.

29. Barth's appeal to prayer as the characteristic theological activity presents a striking alternative to approaches that depict the knowledge of God as accessible through human-centered activities such as historical investigation, logical demonstration, or mysticism.

us, since He Himself makes Himself into object for us and us into knowers of Him. We understand His work and sign very badly if we want to understand it as an object like other objects, and therefore to use it as a sort of atlas of revelation from which we can read the being of God without God Himself speaking to us through it all in His act as the living Lord, according to His free grace. We understand His work and sign very badly if we think that with their help we can survey and master God from some sort of humanly logical, ethical, or religious precedence. The whole world of His work and sign is then at once changed into a world of dead gods or all too living demons. Necessarily, it is all up with the truth of God's work and sign if we cease to adore its grace. For just as certainly as grace is truth, so certainly can truth only be had as grace. . . .

Knowledge of God is obedience to God. Observe that we do not say that knowledge of God may also be obedience, or that of necessity it has obedience attached to it, or that it is followed by obedience. No; knowledge of God as knowledge of faith is in itself and of essential necessity obedience. It is an act of human decision corresponding to the act of divine decision; corresponding to the act of the divine being as the living Lord; corresponding to the act of grace in which faith is grounded and continually grounded again in God. In this act God posits Himself as our object and ourselves as those who know Him. But the fact that He does so means that our knowing God can consist only in our following this act, in ourselves becoming a correspondence of this act, in ourselves and our whole existence and therefore our considering and conceiving becoming the human act corresponding to the divine act. This is obedience, the obedience of faith. Precisely—and only—as this act of obedience, is the knowledge of God knowledge of faith and therefore real knowledge of God.[30] . . . The being of God is either known by grace or it is not known at all. If, however, it is known by grace, then we are already displaced from that secure position and put in a position where the consideration of God can consist and be fulfilled only in the act of our own decision of obedience. The object of this consideration is God in His almighty and active will. But if it is consideration of God in His almighty and active will, how can it fail to lead at once to decision? Either the consideration will become a flight before

30. These remarks about the relationship between knowledge and obedience build on Barth's earlier claim that faith involves the totality of human actions. He insists that the knowledge of God takes place only within the context of the human's entire life with God. This life is determined by God's act to reveal himself to humans in Christ and enable their response to Christ through the power of his Spirit. Note that Barth describes this revelation and response in terms of the correspondence of divine and human action. This concept will become increasingly important in Barth's theology.

what is considered, and therefore disobedience, and therefore meaningless, thus ceasing to be the knowledge of God; or the consideration will become that correspondence, and therefore obedience, and as such real knowledge of the real God.[31] . . .

Therefore He is the Lord in a way which makes flight or evasion quite impossible. For not even conceptually can flight or evasion ever bring us to a sphere in which He is not the Lord, this Lord. As this Lord He stands before us, gives Himself to be known and is known—or else He is not known at all.[32]

But the inner truth of the lordship of God as the one supreme and true lordship revealed and operative in His proclamation and action—the inner truth and therefore also the inner strength of His self-demonstration as the Lord, as this Lord, consists in the fact that He is in Himself from eternity to eternity the triune God, God the Father, the Son and the Holy Spirit. The fact that, according to that self-demonstration, man is indebted to Him for everything and owes Him everything is grounded in God's own eternal Fatherhood, of which any other fatherhood can be only an image and likeness, however much we may owe to it, however much we may be indebted to it. And that self-demonstration constrains us to gratitude and indebtedness and therefore to the knowledge of God the Father as our Lord, because in eternity God is the Father of His own eternal Son and with Him the source of the Holy Spirit. Further, the fact that according to that self-demonstration God Himself is and does everything for the man who still owes Him everything is grounded in the fact that God is in Himself eternally the Son of the Father, eternally equal to the Father and therefore eternally loved by Him, although and because He is the Son. And that self-demonstration constrains us to adoration of His faithfulness and grace and therefore to the knowledge of God the Son as our Lord, because in eternity God is the only Son, begotten of the Father, and with the Father, and along with Him the source of the Holy Spirit. And finally, the fact that according to that self-demonstration God is the One from whom we have to expect everything is grounded in the fact that God is Himself eternally the Holy Spirit, proceeding from the Father and the Son, and of one

31. Barth frames the decision posed by God's revelation as a stark choice: the human either will reject God's revelation in disobedience and fall into idolatry *or* she will correspond to this revelation by responding in obedience. He leaves no room for a middle option of knowing the truth about God without living in obedience to God. Barth rejects the idea that the knowledge of God can be a purely academic or intellectual enterprise. Rather, knowledge of God always occurs in the context of the church and involves the practices of Christian discipleship.

32. Flight from God's revelation would mean rejecting it as false. Evasion of God's revelation would involve accepting it as merely one of several sources for the knowledge of God. Even this latter option is a dead end, Barth thinks, because God is known in the particularity of his self-revelation or not at all.

essence with them both. And that self-demonstration constrains us to hope, and therefore to the knowledge of the Holy Spirit, because in eternity God is also the Holy Spirit proceeding from the Father and the Son, and their unity in love. In this way the self-demonstration, and in this way the proclamation and action of God through His Word in the covenant concluded with man, is grounded in God Himself. In this way and on this ground it has its compelling force. Because God is in Himself the triune God, both in His Word and in the work of creation, reconciliation and redemption, we have to do with Himself.[33] It is therefore impossible for us to postpone the decision—which means the encounter with Him—on the grounds that He is perhaps quite different from the One who proclaims Himself and acts in this way. And because God is in Himself the triune God, in this His Word we have to do with the final revelation of God which can never be rivaled or surpassed. It is, therefore, quite impossible to ask about other lords alongside and above this Lord. In the life of God as the life of the triune God things are so ordered and necessary that the work of God in His Word is the one supreme and true lordship in which He gives Himself to be known and is known. When God speaks about Himself, He speaks about the fact that He is the Father, the Son and the Holy Spirit. And therefore everything else that He has to say to us, all truth and reality, all enlightenment and salvation, depends on the fact that primarily and comprehensively He is speaking about Himself.

But in the light of this the problem of the knowledge of God must be restated in a new way. If it is true that God stands before man, that He gives Himself to be known and is known by man, it is true only because and in the fact that God is the triune God, God the Father, the Son and the Holy Spirit. First of all, and in the heart of the truth in which He stands before us, God stands before Himself; the Father before the Son, the Son before the Father. And first of all and in the heart of the truth in which we know God, God knows Himself; the Father knows the Son and the Son the Father in the unity of the Holy Spirit. This occurrence in God Himself is the essence and strength of our knowledge of God. It is not an occurrence unknown to us; rather it is made known to us through His Word; but it is certainly a hidden occurrence. That is to say, it is an occurrence in which man as such is not a participant, but in which He becomes a participant through God's revelation and thus in a way inconceivable to himself. It is not self-evident that we become

33. Barth's point in this section is that the God whom humans know in the church is the one true God. The knowledge of faith is real knowledge of God because the event that prompts this faith—God's self-revelation in the Word and Spirit—corresponds to God's eternal triune being. God comes to the church as the one true God that he is, and this revelation evokes a response of adoration, worship, and hope by the church.

participants in it, that our knowledge of God acquires truth as the external expression of that inner truth. It does, in fact, acquire truth only as the external expression of that inner truth; that is to say, on the strength of the fact that God is the triune God who knows Himself. If we laud and magnify God on the strength of our own knowledge, bestowed upon us by His revelation, it must always mean that we laud and magnify Him in the hiddenness of His self-knowledge, on the strength of which alone the knowledge of God can ever become real. Our knowledge of God is derived and secondary. It is effected by grace in the creaturely sphere in consequence of the fact that first of all, in itself and without us, it is actual in the divine sphere—in the sphere of God as the sphere of His own truth, of the inner truth even of our knowledge of God, who is always inaccessible to us as such.[34] We stand here before the root of the necessity to fear God because we may love Him, to revere Him in His mystery because He has made Himself so clear and certain to us. The love, clarity and certainty have reference to the fact that God does actually reveal Himself to us as the One who He is. The fear and the mystery have reference to the fact that He reveals Himself to us as the One who He actually is, as the One who first knows Himself in that inner truth of our knowledge of God without which it would be only an empty and evanescent appearance.

34. Barth's striking remarks in this paragraph stand at the heart of his doctrine of the knowledge of God. His claim is that, in and through Christ and the Spirit, humans become participants in God's knowledge of himself. This participation is the basis of the claim that the church's knowledge of God in faith is true. Barth grounds this idea of participation on the doctrine of the triune God. In the eternal triune life, God knows himself: the Father knows the Son, and the Son knows the Father in the Spirit. When God the Father sends the Son into history to unite himself to humans by the power of the Spirit, God determines to make the human recipients of his revelation participants in his own self-knowledge. Specifically, humans know God because they are given a share in the knowledge that Christ himself has as the Spirit unites them to Christ and equips them to live together with Christ. In this sense, as Barth puts it later, God allows us "to take part in the history of the inner life of his Godhead, in the movement in which from all and to all eternity he is Father, Son, and Holy Spirit, and therefore one God." *Church Dogmatics* IV/1 (Edinburgh: T&T Clark, 1956), 215. This human participation in God's self-knowledge is by grace rather than nature; and because this participation takes place through creaturely mediation, the knowledge of God that humans gain is indirect. As they are made participants in God's knowledge of himself through the Word and Spirit, humans never overstep their creaturely bounds; even so, they can be fully confident that they know the one true God. They also can be sure that if their speech about God corresponds to what God has revealed in Christ, then they are speaking correctly about God. These claims constitute Barth's answers to the questions with which this section started.

CHAPTER

17

The Reality of God

Introduction

In this excerpt from *Church Dogmatics* II/1, Barth considers the eternal being of God. His central claim is that God has revealed himself to be the God who loves in freedom. As he develops and explains this claim, Barth insists that the concepts of love and freedom must be defined concretely. Instead of seeing them from the perspective of creaturely ideals, we must define the concepts on the basis of God's revelation in Jesus Christ.

Christ reveals that God's love is self-giving because it involves God's decision to unite himself to humans so they can live in fellowship with him. Christ also shows that God's love is unconditional in the sense that it does not depend on the qualities humans possess or the actions they perform. This love is revelatory because it perfectly corresponds to God's eternal being. God's love for humanity is not a contingent expression of God's nature, as if real truth about God's relationship with humanity might be something different. Rather, the love that God displays in Christ is a true and faithful expression of his being and character. Finally, Christ reveals that God's love is free because it reflects God's self-determination rather than any internal or external obligation. In this sense, God's love is purely gratuitous and given strictly for the benefit of his creatures.

Barth defines freedom in a dialectical manner. On the one hand, he emphasizes that God's freedom reflects his self-sufficiency. God does not need anything outside of himself in order to be God, and God does not realize any potentiality as he relates to the created world. On the other hand, Barth also insists that God's freedom must be defined in light of the particular way God exercises his freedom. God is not free in the sense that he could cease to love creation, nor is the love he displays in Christ merely one part of his eternal being. Rather, Jesus Christ shows us precisely how God lives his freedom as God. Simply put, there is no other God than the God who has freely determined to live his eternal life in relation to humans by giving himself to them in love. Any talk about God's freedom or divine being in distinction from this determination falls into abstraction.

Church Dogmatics II/1[1]

If, then, we now take the decisive turn, directing our attention to the definition and content of the divine being as it confronts us in God's revelation, and if as our first step we take up the concept of love, it is not because we think that somehow we already know generally what love is as the content of an action which is genuinely good, and that on the basis of this knowledge we can equate God with this content. The proper procedure is very different. By the reality of the divine act we are summoned to give an account of the essence of this act, and thereby of the essence of God Himself. And led by Holy Scripture itself, we may and must venture to bring the concept of love (the peculiar and final meaning of which we admit we do not know in what is otherwise a tempting application) into the service of our present task, the declaration of the act and therefore of the being of God.[2] We must recognize quite frankly the possibility that in this use "love" may take on a meaning which is fulfilled in a way which breaks up and reforms its meaning in the tempting application. Intentionally we have not begun with a definition of love, but with the resolve to let the act of God visible in His revelation speak for itself—God is in His act the One who seeks and creates fellowship with us. If we define this action of His as the love of God, and therefore God as the One who loves, and (in the proper sense) as love, our gaze must always be directed strictly on the fact, i.e., on God's act, and must not be allowed to wander under the influence of a concomitant and supposititious general idea of love. If we say with 1 John 4 that God is love, the converse that love is God

1. Karl Barth, *Church Dogmatics* II/1 (Edinburgh: T&T Clark, 1957), 275–81, 301–3.

2. With an account of human knowledge of God in hand, Barth now turns to the question of what the being of God is like. He begins by exploring the love of God. Rather than beginning with the general concept of love, he proceeds according to the method he has just developed (see chap. 16). Knowledge of God's love is based strictly on God's self-revelation to the church, which responds to this revelation in faith. Both the church's definition of God's love and any use the church makes of it stand in line with the account of God's love in Scripture.

is forbidden until it is mediated and clarified from God's being and therefore from God's act what the love is which can and must be legitimately identified with God.[3] The elucidation of this love is our present task.

1. God's loving is concerned with a seeking and creation of fellowship for its own sake. It is the fellowship of the One who loves with the loved himself, and therefore that which the One who loves has to impart to the loved and the loved has to receive from the One who loves. God is not, therefore, the *Good* first, and then the One who loves, because He does not keep this *Good* to Himself but communicates it to others. God is the One who loves, and as such the *Good* and the sum of all good things. God is good in the fact that He is Father, Son and Holy Spirit, that as such He is our Creator, Mediator and Redeemer, and that as such He takes us up into His fellowship, i.e., the fellowship which He has and is in Himself, and beyond which as such there is no greater *Good* which has still to be communicated to us through His fellowship with us. Loving us, God does not give us something, but Himself; and giving us Himself, giving us His only Son, He gives us everything. The love of God has only to be His love to be everything for us.[4] . . .

2. God's loving is concerned with a seeking and creation of fellowship without any reference to an existing aptitude or worthiness on the part of the loved. God's love is not merely not conditioned by any reciprocity of love. It is also not conditioned by any worthiness to be loved on the part of the loved, by any existing capacity for union or fellowship on his side. If he has such a thing, it is itself the prior creation of the love of God. It is not and does not become the condition of that love. It is the object of the divine pleasure which follows the preceding love. The object of the love of God as such is another which in itself is not, or is not yet, worthy of this His pleasure. The love of God always throws a bridge over a crevasse. It is always the light shining out of darkness. In His revelation it seeks and creates fellowship where there is no fellowship and no capacity for it, where the situation concerns a being which is quite different from God, a creature and therefore alien, a sinful creature and therefore hostile. It is this alien and hostile other that God loves. Fellowship with him as such is the fellowship which He seeks and creates. This does not mean that we can call the love of God a blind love. But what He sees when

---

3. These remarks reflect Barth's account of theological language in general. In the same way that God's revelation clarifies the meaning of every word used to describe God and ourselves in relation to God, the revelation of God's love challenges and clarifies every general human idea of love. Barth explains the specific nature of this clarification in the four points that follow.

4. First, God's love is *self-giving*. Talk of God's love refers not to a third thing between God and the human but to God's act to give himself to the human so that she might participate in the eternal love that God himself is.

He loves is that which is altogether distinct from Himself, and as such lost in itself, and without Him abandoned to death. That He throws a bridge out from Himself to this abandoned one, that He is light in the darkness, is the miracle of the almighty love of God.[5] . . .

3. God's loving is an end in itself. All the purposes that are willed and achieved in Him are contained and explained in this end, and therefore in this loving in itself and as such. For this loving is itself the blessing that it communicates to the loved, and it is its own ground as against the loved. Certainly in loving us God wills His own glory and our salvation. But He does not love us because He wills this. He wills it for the sake of His love. God loves in realizing these purposes. But God loves because He loves; because this act is His being, His essence and His nature. He loves without and before realizing these purposes. He loves to eternity. Even in realizing them, He loves because He loves. And the point of this realization is not grounded in itself, but in His love as such, in the love of the Father, the Son and the Holy Spirit. And as we believe in God, and return His love, it is not to be understood from itself, but only from His loving as such.[6] . . .

4. God's loving is necessary, for it is the being, the essence and the nature of God. But for this very reason it is also free from every necessity in respect of its object. God loves us, and loves the world, in accordance with His revelation. But He loves us and the world as He who would still be One who loves without us and without the world; as He, therefore, who needs no other to form the prior ground of His existence as the One who loves and as God. Certainly He is who He is wholly in His revelation, in His loving-kindness, and therefore in His love for us. He has not withheld Himself from us, but given us Himself. Therefore His love for us is His *eternal* love, and our being loved by Him is our being taken up into the fellowship of His eternal love, in which He is Himself for ever and ever. All the same it is a "being taken up." It is not part of God's being and action that as love it must have an object in another who is different from Him. God is sufficient in Himself as object and therefore as object of His love. He is no less the One who loves if He loves no object different from Himself. In the fact that He determines to love such another, His love overflows. But it is not exhausted in it nor confined or conditioned by it. On the contrary,

5. Second, God's love is *unconditional*. Here Barth develops the traditional Reformed claim that God's relationship with humans does not depend on their internal qualities or actions. This emphasizes the purely gratuitous nature of God's love. God does not love us because Christ saves us from our sin; Christ saves us from our sin because God loves us.

6. Third, God's love for humans is *revelatory* because it is a perfect expression of God's nature. God does not love humans accidentally, as a means to an end, or in order to gain or acquire something for himself. No, God loves simply because God is love. So when God comes to humans in love, God is simply being himself.

this overflowing is conditioned by the fact that although it could satisfy itself, it has no satisfaction in this self-satisfaction, but as love for another it can and will be more than that which could satisfy itself. While God is everything for Himself, He wills again not to be everything merely for Himself, but for this other. While He could be everything only for Himself (and His life would not on that account be pointless, motionless and unmotivated, nor would it be any less majestic or any less the life of love), He wills—and this is for us the ever-wonderful twofold dynamic of His love—to have it not only for Himself, but also for us. It does not belong to us to have being, and when we have it it does not belong to us in this being of ours to be the objects of the love of God. We might not be at all, and we might be without being the objects of His love. God does not owe us either our being, or in our being His love. If we are, and if we are objects of the love of God, that means that we on our side are debtors to God, without God owing anything to us. If He loves us, if He has preferred our being to our not-being, our lovableness to our unlovableness, that is for us the ever-wonderful dynamic of His love. It is grace and not nature. For it takes place in the whole intervention of the divine action and being.[7] We cannot go back behind this event. We should not seek and think of God anywhere else than in this act, or as any other than as the One who is at this point and in this way. Just because we must hold fast to this, it must be clear that the fact that we can actually hold on to this rests on the overflowing of the divine love. The eternal correlation between God and us, as shown in God's revelation, is grounded in God alone, and not partly in God and partly in us. It means that we are tied to God, but not God to us. So in the highest and last degree (and this is true of what has been said about the goodness, the basis and the purpose of the divine love) the concept of God's love surpasses and oversteps the common concept of love that we ourselves can produce and presuppose. Here especially the common concept must be interpreted according to the particularity of this object. In this connection especially, we must beware of an unreflecting inversion and therefore of a definition of the divine love on the basis of a common concept of love. If we are not careful at this point we shall inevitably rob God of His deity.[8] . . .

---

7. Fourth, God's love is *free*. Barth's claims here are rooted in God's self-sufficiency. God has no internal or external obligation to love his creatures. He does not love them because he needs them in any way, nor does God love them because they deserve this love. Rather, God's love flows to the creature freely, and it comes purely for the benefit of the creature.

8. We "go back behind" God's love whenever we try to explain *why* God loves humans, say that God's love reveals only *part* of his eternal being, or argue that this love is *contingent* on some creaturely action or characteristic. Rather, because God's love is free, the revelation of this love reflects the truth about God's being and character. Since this kind of love is so distinct from creaturely love, Barth thinks that it is precisely here that we are likely to misunderstand it.

God's being as He who lives and loves is being in freedom.[9] In this way, freely, He lives and loves. And in this way, and in the fact that He lives and loves in freedom, He is God, and distinguishes Himself from everything else that lives and loves. In this way, as the free person, He is distinguished from other persons. He is the one, original and authentic person through whose creative power and will alone all other persons are and are sustained. With the idea of freedom we simply affirm what we would be affirming if we were to characterize God as the Lord. But His lordship is in all circumstances the lordship of His living and loving. Our present question is that of the mode of His lordship and therefore of His living and loving—of the divine characteristics by which, as He who lives and loves, He manifests His sovereignty. This mode is characterized by the fact that it is absolutely God's own, in no sense dictated to Him from outside and conditioned by no higher necessity than that of His own choosing and deciding, willing and doing. If we enquire how, according to His revelation in Jesus Christ, God's lordship differs in its divinity from other types of rule, then we must answer that it is lordship in freedom. It would be senseless to ascribe this characteristic to other kinds of sovereignty, or to any other living and loving but that of God. There are other sovereignties, but freedom is the prerogative of divine sovereignty. Freedom is, of course, more than the absence of limits, restrictions, or conditions. This is only its negative and to that extent improper aspect—improper to the extent that from this point of view it requires another, at least in so far as its freedom lies in its independence of this other. But freedom in its positive and proper qualities means to be grounded in one's own being, to be determined and moved by oneself. This is the freedom of the divine life and love.[10] In this positive freedom of His, God is also unlimited, unrestricted and unconditioned from without. He is the free Creator, the free Reconciler, the free Redeemer. But His divinity is not exhausted in the fact that in His revelation it consists throughout in this freedom from external compulsion: in free utterance and action, free beginning and ending, free judgment and

9. This claim stands at the heart of Barth's argument in this excerpt. He develops it more fully in the paragraphs below by offering a dialectical account of God's freedom.

10. This is Barth's dialectical account of God's freedom. On the one hand, to talk about God's freedom is to talk about the fact that God is absolutely unconditioned by any other being. God needs nothing outside of himself in order to be himself, and the being of every other thing is determined by his lordship. On the other hand, any talk of God's freedom also must reflect the specific way that God has exercised his lordship in his relation to his creatures. In other words, God's freedom cannot be defined solely in terms of his distinction from creation but also must be defined in light of the particular and concrete way that God actually *lives* in his freedom as Lord. We will not understand the meaning of divine freedom unless we understand it in light of God's absolute freedom from creation *and* God's free relationship with creation (see chap. 10).

blessing, free power and spirit. On the contrary, it is only manifest in all this. For He has it in Himself quite apart from His relation to another from whom He is free. He in Himself is power, truth and right. Within the sphere of His own being He can live and love in absolute plenitude and power, as we see Him live and love in His revelation. . . .

Our emphasis in defining the concept must not in any circumstances fall upon this negative aspect. To be sure, this negative side is extremely significant not only for God's relation to the world, but also for His being in itself. We cannot possibly grasp and expound the idea of divine creation and providence, nor even the ideas of divine omnipotence, omnipresence and eternity, without constantly referring to this negative aspect of His freedom. But we shall be able to do so properly only when we do so against the background of our realization that God's freedom constitutes the essential positive quality, not only of His action towards what is outside Himself, but also of His own inner being. The biblical witness to God sees His transcendence of all that is distinct from Himself, not only in the distinction as such, which is supremely and decisively characterized as His freedom from all conditioning by that which is distinct from Himself, but furthermore and supremely in the fact that without sacrificing His distinction and freedom, but in the exercise of them, He enters into and faithfully maintains communion with this reality other than Himself in His activity as Creator, Reconciler and Redeemer. According to the biblical testimony, God has the prerogative to be free without being limited by His freedom from external conditioning, free also with regard to His freedom, free not to surrender Himself to it, but to use it to give Himself to this communion and to practice this faithfulness in it, in this way being really free, free in Himself. God must not only be unconditioned but, in the absoluteness in which He sets up this fellowship, He can and will also be conditioned. He who can and does do this is the God of Holy Scripture, the triune God known to us in His revelation. This ability, proved and manifested to us in His action, constitutes His freedom.[11]

11. Now Barth puts his dialectical account of divine freedom to work. God's freedom could be taken to mean that God is free from creation in the sense that he is free not to love it. But the problem is that this account of freedom emphasizes only one aspect of what must be affirmed, one side of the dialectic. The result is an abstract picture of God's relationship to creation that undermines the content of God's revelation in Christ. If God shows us that he loves us in Christ—but God really is free not to love us—then how can Christ be a true revelation of the being of God? The entire basis of the church's faith is undermined. But when we consider both sides of the dialectic by also describing God's freedom in light of the concrete and particular way God actually lives his freedom, the picture changes. Now we recognize that, even though God did not need to relate to creation, God freely chose to do so by giving himself to humans in love. Barth argues that *this* is the God who has been revealed in Scripture. The God who has come to the church is the God who loves in freedom by giving himself unconditionally in love—and there is no God other than *this* God.

CHAPTER 18

The Doctrine of Election

Introduction

In this excerpt from the opening pages of *Church Dogmatics* II/2, Barth argues that a proper doctrine of God accounts for the reality that God has freely decided to live in fellowship with humanity in and through the man Jesus Christ. This claim stands at the center of Barth's doctrine of the election. His description of this doctrine challenges nearly every prior approach and sets the trajectory for the rest of his theological career.

A distinguishing characteristic of Barth's doctrine of election is his rejection of the idea that God makes a twofold decision by electing some for salvation and then rejecting, or passing over, others. Even though this kind of approach is prominent within Barth's own Reformed tradition, he worries that it is speculative and abstract. The problem with this approach is that Christ reveals only *part* of the truth about God's relationship with humanity because the *real* truth about this relationship remains hidden behind Christ in the secret will of God. Christ no longer stands at the center of God's plan for humanity because he is merely an instrument through which God's decree of salvation is executed. Humans thus are left to speculate about the real nature of God's relationship to them in distinction from what Christ reveals.

In contrast to this approach, Barth insists that Jesus Christ is the revelation of God's singular decision for humanity. He depicts this decision as an election of grace. Barth argues that, instead of electing individuals or groups, God elects to unite himself to the man Jesus of Nazareth. This decision involves God's self-determination: God determines to live his own eternal life in union with his creatures in Jesus Christ. As the representative of humanity, Christ reveals that God has decided to bear the consequences of sin for the sake of humanity's salvation.

Christ also reveals God's will for the lives of his creatures. Because he is the one who unveils God's saving will for humanity, Jesus Christ is the true human. He represents the people of Israel and the church before God, and he represents God to them. He shows them that God's love for and faithfulness to his own Son also involves his love for and faithfulness to them.

Church Dogmatics II/2[1]

Theology must begin with Jesus Christ, and not with general principles, however better, or, at any rate, more relevant and illuminating, they may appear to be: as though He were a continuation of the knowledge and Word of God, and not its root and origin, not indeed the very Word of God itself. Theology must also end with Him, and not with supposedly self-evident general conclusions from what is particularly enclosed and disclosed in Him: as though the fruits could be shaken from this tree; as though in the things of God there were anything general which we could know and designate in addition to and even independently of this particular. The obscurities and ambiguities of our way were illuminated in the measure that we held fast to that name and in the measure that we let Him be the first and the last, according to the testimony of Holy Scripture. Against all the imaginations and errors in which we seem to be so hopelessly entangled when we try to speak of God, God will indeed maintain Himself if we will only allow the name of Jesus Christ to be maintained in our thinking as the beginning and the end of all our thoughts. . . .

This is the decisive result of all our previous discussion. This is the sum and substance of the whole doctrine of the knowledge and reality of God.[2] But that means that the Christian doctrine of God cannot end with the matter which we have treated so far. In a Christian doctrine of God our concern is to define and expound the Subject of all that the Christian Church receives and proclaims. If it is true, then, that this Subject is disclosed only in the name of Jesus Christ, that it is wholly and entirely enclosed in Him, then we cannot

1. Karl Barth, *Church Dogmatics* II/2 (Edinburgh: T&T Clark, 1957), 4–11, 13–14, 25–27, 53–54.

2. See Barth's discussion of these topics in chaps. 16 and 17.

stop at this point, defining and expounding the Subject only in and for itself. We tried to do that on the earlier part of our way. But we should be overlooking and suppressing something essential, and a serious gap would be left in our reflection on the Word of God as the norm of Christian proclamation, if we now tried to proceed without treating of what the Church must receive and proclaim as the work of this Subject, the activity of God as Creator, Reconciler and Redeemer. We should still not have learned to say "God" correctly (i.e., as understood in the Christian Church on the basis of Holy Scripture) if we thought it enough simply to say "God." However well-grounded or critical our utterance, if it has a logical exclusiveness, if it is only "God," it will not suffice. For if it is true that in Jesus Christ there dwells the fullness of the Godhead bodily (Col. 2:9), then in all the perfection with which it is differentiated from everything that is not God, and thus exists for itself, the Subject God still cannot, as it were, be envisaged, established and described only in and for itself. We must not be so exact, so clever, so literal, that our doctrine of God remains only a doctrine of God. We must demonstrate its Christian character by avoiding such abstraction. In virtue of the truth of its specific content it must burst through the frame which apparently—but only apparently—surrounds it. Otherwise the highest reality can, and inevitably will, be reduced to the flattest unreality. All that we have previously said concerning this Subject will be enveloped again in darkness. From the very outset a new obscurity will, in fact, extend over all that we have still to say concerning the work of this Subject. To be truly Christian, the doctrine of God must carry forward and complete the definition and exposition of the Subject God. It must do this in such a way that quite apart from what must be said about the knowledge and the reality of God as such, it makes the Subject known as One which in virtue of its innermost being, willing and nature does not stand outside all relationships, but stands in a definite relationship with another outside himself.[3] It is not as though the object of this relationship, the other, constitutes a part of the reality of God outside of God. It is not as though it is in any other way comparable with God. It is not as though God is forced into this relationship. It is not as though He is in any way constrained or compelled by this other. As we have often enough

3. Barth's central claim in these opening paragraphs is that we know God rightly only when our account of God includes his relationship with humans in Jesus Christ. This claim is grounded on an assertion Barth has spent his entire career defending: theology begins and ends with God's revelation in Christ. Barth now insists that, if this claim is true, then we have to pay attention to the full measure of what the history of Christ's life reveals. Christ shows us that God has decided to live his own divine life together with humans. A dogmatics that fails to account for this divine decision and this relationship remains abstract and false because it strays from its true object of knowledge (see chap. 10).

seen and asserted, there can be no question of any such compulsion coming upon God from without. God is love. But He is also perfect freedom. Even if there were no such relationship, even if there were no other outside of Him, He would still be love. But positively, in the free decision of His love, God is God in the very fact, and in such a way, that He does stand in this relation, in a definite relationship with the other. We cannot go back on this decision if we would know God and speak accurately of God. If we did, we should be betrayed into a false abstraction which sought to speak only of God, not recognizing that, when we speak of God, then in consideration of His freedom, and of His free decision, we must speak also of this relationship.[4] . . .

For the divine attitude is not a matter of chance. It is not revocable or transitory. God lays upon us the obligation of this attitude because first of all He lays it upon Himself. In dealing with this attitude, we have to do with His free but definitive decision. We cannot abstract from it without falling into arbitrary speculation. But we cannot ignore it. Once made, it belongs definitively to God Himself, not in His being in and for Himself, but in His being within this relationship. It belongs to the reality of God which is a reality not apart from but in this decision.[5] It is so adjoined to this reality that we must not allow any objectivity of logic to prevent us from introducing the adjunct as an element in our knowledge of God. We cannot speak correctly of God in His being in and for Himself without considering Him always in this attitude, without allowing both our questions and answers to be dictated by it. We cannot speak accurately or confidently of the work of God unless first we see clearly that the attitude which God has taken up, and by which His work is determined, belongs to God Himself, and cannot in any way be isolated from Him. For that reason, the question of this attitude must be raised specifically and independently within the framework of the doctrine of

4. After affirming that dogmatics must account for God's relationship with humanity in Jesus Christ, Barth immediately adds a qualification: this relationship is not necessary to God. God is free, and so no internal or external necessity binds God to this relationship. But Barth insists that we cannot stop there. Christ shows us that, even though God does not have to relate to us, God has freely decided to do so. A correct description of God will include the reality of this divine decision and its implications. These claims reflect Barth's earlier discussion about the freedom and love of God (see chap. 17).

5. Barth's argument about the "obligation" that God lays on himself stems from his account of the reality of God's perfect being and knowledge. God always acts in a manner consistent with his own divine being, and his actions always reflect his perfect knowledge of himself and all things. So God's decision to enter into a relationship with humanity in Jesus Christ is not haphazard, as if takes place accidentally, spontaneously, or randomly. Rather, this decision reflects God's perfect wisdom and is a faithful expression of his divine being and character. This is why, even though this decision is absolutely free, it also is definitive. If God were to revoke this decision, his wisdom and consistency of character could be called into question.

God. In a Christian doctrine of God, if God is to be exhaustively described and represented as the Subject who governs and determines everything else, there must be an advance beyond the immediate logical sense of the concept to the actual relationship in which God has placed Himself; a relationship outside of which God no longer wills to be and no longer is God, and within which alone He can be truly honored and worshipped as God. If it is true that it pleased the fullness of God to dwell in Jesus Christ (Col. 1:19), then in a Christian doctrine of God this further step is unavoidable. And it is immediately apparent in which direction the step must be taken.[6]

Jesus Christ is indeed God in His movement towards man, or, more exactly, in His movement towards the people represented in the one man Jesus of Nazareth, in His covenant with this people, in His being and activity amongst and towards this people.[7] Jesus Christ is the decision of God in favor of this attitude or relation. He is Himself the relation. It is a relation outside himself, undoubtedly; for both the man and the people represented in Him are creatures and not God. But it is a relation which is irrevocable, so that once God has willed to enter into it, and has in fact entered into it, He could not be God without it. It is a relation in which God is self-determined, so that the determination belongs no less to Him than all that He is in and for Himself. Without the Son sitting at the right hand of the Father, God would not be God. But the Son is not only very God. He is also called Jesus of Nazareth. He is also very man, and as such He is the Representative of the people which in Him and through Him is united as He is with God, being with Him the object of the divine movement. That we know God and have God only in Jesus Christ means that we can know Him and have Him only with the man Jesus of Nazareth and with the people which He represents. Apart from this man and apart from this people God would be a different, an alien God. According to the Christian perception He would not be God at

6. This argument echoes Barth's earlier claims about the nature of dogmatics (see chaps. 11–12). Christians know God because God is a living subject who makes himself an object of human knowledge in the event of his self-revelation. If God is the subject who determines the human knowledge of God through this action—and if God reveals that he has decided to place himself in a permanent relationship with the man Jesus Christ and the people he represents—then dogmatics has no choice but to account for the content of this revelation in its description of God. A theologian who refuses to listen to God's revelation on this point effectively avoids Christ, seizes control of the knowledge of God from God, and becomes the subject who establishes this knowledge. For Barth, the inevitable results of such a move are abstraction and idolatry.

7. Barth describes God's movement as a movement not toward humanity in general but toward the man Jesus of Nazareth and the people represented by him. This distinction serves an important purpose. Now Barth can talk about God's election of humanity in light of the particularity of the biblical narrative—namely, the story of Israel and its fulfillment in Christ—rather than by means of general concepts of divinity and humanity.

all. According to the Christian perception the true God is what He is only in this movement, in the movement towards this man, and in Him and through Him towards other men in their unity as His people.[8]

That other to which God stands in relationship, in an actuality which can neither be suspended nor dissolved, is not simply and directly the created world as such. There is, too, a relationship of God to the world. There is a work of God towards it and with it. There is a history between God and the world. But this history has no independent signification. It takes place in the interests of the primal history which is played out between God and this one man and His people. It is the sphere in which this primal history is played out. It attains its goal as this primal history attains its goal.[9] And the same is true both of man as such and also of the human race as a whole. The partner of God which cannot now be thought away is neither "man" as an idea, nor "humanity," nor indeed a large or small total of individual men. It is the one man Jesus and the people represented in Him. Only secondarily, and for His sake, is it "man," and "humanity" and the whole remaining cosmos. Even human nature and human history in general have no independent signification. They point to the primal history played out within them between God and the one man, and all other men as His people. The general (the world or man) exists for the sake of the particular. In the particular the general has its meaning and fulfillment.[10] The particular is that other over against God

8. Barth draws out the implications of God's decision to live in relationship with humanity by linking it to the concept of self-determination. The basis of this idea is christological: when God decides to unite himself to human flesh in Jesus of Nazareth, God determines that he will not be God apart from this human flesh. This self-determination does not change who God is, as if God becomes a different God than he was before. Instead, it reveals that God has freely determined to live his eternal life in a particular way. Barth will develop this claim and its implication in more depth in his discussion of how Jesus Christ is both the object and the subject of election (see chap. 19).

9. Barth draws a distinction between history (*Geschichte*) and the "primal history" (*Urgeschichte*) that reflects God's decision to relate to humanity in Jesus Christ. We can describe this as the distinction between natural history and salvation history. The two types of history exist in an ordered relationship: natural history exists for the sake of salvation history because it is the space and the place in which God enacts his plan to live in relationship with the human Jesus and his people. So the very existence of natural history—and of the natural world itself—is based on the way God plans to use it to fulfill his decision to relate to humanity in Christ. This means that God's general relation to natural history—such as his providential oversight over it—provides no information about God that is distinct from what we know of God in and through Christ (see chap. 21).

10. In the same way that natural history is determined by primal history, human nature is determined by the reality of the human Jesus. God does not relate to humanity in general but to the man Jesus and then to humanity in and through him. Jesus's life unveils the true meaning and purpose of human nature because he is the one who brings it to its fulfillment in relationship to God.

which cannot be thought away, which is outside of God, which is the object of the divine movement, which is so adjoined now to the reality of God that we cannot and should not say the word "God" without at once thinking of it. We must think at once, then, of Jesus of Nazareth and of His people. The attitude or relation for which God has once and for all decided, to which He has committed us and wills to be committed by us, is the relation or attitude to Jesus Christ. In the person of His eternal Son He has united Himself with the man Jesus of Nazareth, and in Him and through Him with this people. He is the Father of Jesus Christ. He is not only the Father of the eternal Son, but as such He is the eternal Father of this temporal man. He is, then, the eternal Father, the Possessor, the Lord and the Savior of the people which this man represents as King and Head.[11] In this determination, as carried through by His own decision, God is, therefore, the Subject of everything that is to be received and proclaimed in the Christian Church. All His work takes place according to this plan and under this sign. As such it has, of course, a wider reach. The other towards which God moves in this wider sphere is, of course, the created world as a whole. It is, of course, "man" and "humanity." But everything which comes from God takes place according to this plan and under this sign. Everything is from this beginning and to this end. Everything is in this order and has this meaning. Everything happens according to this basic and determinative pattern, model and system. Everything which comes from God takes place "in Jesus Christ," i.e., in the establishment of the covenant which, in the union of His Son with Jesus of Nazareth, God has instituted and maintains and directs between Himself and His people, the people consisting of those who belong to Him, who have become His in this One. The primal history which underlies and is the goal of the whole history of His relationship outside himself, with the creation and man in general, is the history of this covenant. The primal history, and with it the covenant, are, then, the attitude and relation in which by virtue of the decision of His free love God wills to be and is God. And this relation cannot be separated from the Christian conception of God as such. The two must go together if this conception is to be truly Christian. For that reason, this relation must form the subject of a second part of our doctrine of God.[12]

11. Just as human nature cannot be defined in distinction from the human Jesus, neither can the being of God. We cannot think rightly about the triune being of God without thinking about the fact that the eternal Son has united himself to human flesh in Jesus of Nazareth. Nor can we think about the triune God apart from the people represented by Christ.

12. The emphasis on the word *everything* is hard to miss here. Barth's point is that the entirety of created being and history—including our lives—is determined in its depths by God's decision to live together with humanity in Jesus Christ. This decision is the basis and goal of all created history: "from him and through him and to him are all things" (Rom. 11:36).

But as we approach this particular subject, two aspects of the one truth must be considered and two spheres of investigation are disclosed.[13]

It is at once apparent that in the decision by which He institutes, maintains and directs this covenant, in His decision "in Jesus Christ," God on His side does accomplish something quite definite. He executes this decision in His movement towards man, towards the man Jesus Christ and the people which He represents. And this movement is an act of divine sovereignty. To characterize it as such we must select from the fullness of His essential attributes. We must say: This act demonstrates His mercy and righteousness, His constancy and omnipotence. It is as the Lord who lives in the fullness of these perfections that God acts when He institutes and directs this covenant. He constitutes Himself the Lord of the covenant. He is, therefore, its free author. He gives it its content and determines its order. He maintains it. He directs it to its goal. He governs it in every respect. It is His decision that there is a covenant-partner. It is also His decision who this partner is, and what must befall him. It is only as He wills it that the covenant arises at all. The covenant-member is the one whom He ordains. It is what He wills that takes place within the covenant. All that we have to say concerning this aspect of the divine movement may be summed up in the concept which is the title of this chapter: that of the election in the sense of the election of divine grace, the choice which God makes in His grace, thus making this movement, and instituting, maintaining and directing this covenant. In accordance with the theological tradition of the Reformed Churches (and especially the German-speaking), what we have in mind is the election of grace (in translation of ἐκλογὴ χάριτος, Rom. 11:5); and it may be noted how the term reflects the being of God as we have hitherto sought to understand and explain it. It is a question of grace, and that means the love of God. It is a question of election, and that means the freedom of God.[14]

Here, again, we must deal first with grace.[15] The fact that God makes this movement, the institution of the covenant, the primal decision "in Jesus

13. As Barth begins to explore the implications of God's decision to relate to humanity in Christ, he wants to connect this decision to the biblical concepts of election and covenant. To make this connection, he draws on his twofold account of God as the one who loves in freedom (see chap. 17).

14. Barth describes God's decision in Christ as an *election of grace*. His use of the word "election" reflects its biblical background as well as Barth's Reformed tradition. Both sources connect election to the covenant, God's partnership with humanity that proceeds according to God's particular goal for it. This partnership is not an equal one because God is the Lord who determines not only the covenant's existence but also both the identity of the partner and the nature of the partnership.

15. Barth now offers a definition of each of the terms in the phrase "election of grace." He begins with "grace" because it is the key to our knowledge of God.

Christ," which is the basis and goal of all His works—that is grace. Speaking generally, it is the demonstration, the overflowing of the love which is the being of God, that He who is entirely self-sufficient, who even within Himself cannot know isolation, willed even in all His divine glory to share His life with another, and to have that other as the witness of His glory. This love of God is His grace. It is love in the form of the deepest condescension. It occurs even where there is no question of claim or merit on the part of the other. It is love which is overflowing, free, unconstrained, unconditioned. And we must add at once: It is love which is merciful, making this movement, this act of condescension, in such a way that, in taking to itself this other, it identifies itself with its need, and meets its plight by making it its own concern. And we must add at once: It is love which is patient, not consuming this other, but giving it place, willing its existence for its own sake and for the sake of the goal appointed for it.[16] For the moment, however, it is important to stop at the first concept, the concept of grace. God's decision in Jesus Christ is a gracious decision. In making it, God stoops down from above. In it He does something which He has no need to do, which He is not constrained to do. He does something which He alone can constrain Himself, and has in fact constrained Himself, to do. In entering into this covenant, He freely makes Himself both benefactor and benefit. It will be seen that the whole sovereignty of this act is contained already in the concept of grace. Because grace is here the Alpha and Omega, it cannot be otherwise than that, in the total manner already indicated, God should be the Lord "in Jesus Christ." But with this concept the other aspect forces itself to the forefront, and must there remain—that "in Jesus Christ" we have to do with a divine benefit or favor. It is a matter of God's love. If in His majesty He establishes fellowship with the other which does not partake of His majesty, but in its otherness stands in the very depths over against Him, that means favor. In showing His grace, God proves Himself both Savior and Helper. He does so freely as the Lord. But this exercise of lordship is kind as well as good, communicating and sharing its goods. The doctrine of the divine election of grace is the sum of the Gospel. It is the content of the good news which is Jesus Christ.[17]

16. Barth offers a twofold definition of "grace" in this paragraph. First, Barth identifies God's grace as a form of God's love. Drawing from his earlier argument (see chap. 17), he depicts God's love as self-giving, unconditional, revelatory, and free. Yet here he adds further insights. The love that is God's grace is *merciful* because it involves God's act of identifying with sinful humanity in their need and addressing that need. It also is *patient* because this love does not override but upholds the human's integrity as a creature.

17. The second part of Barth's definition of "grace" in this paragraph relates to election. He emphasizes that, while God does not have to show grace to sinful humans, he freely decides

The other part of the concept cannot and should not alter this fact in the least. Election should serve at once to emphasize and explain what we have already said in the word *grace*. God in His love elects another to fellowship with Himself. First and foremost this means that God makes a self-election in favor of this other. He ordains that He should not be entirely self-sufficient as He might be. He determines for Himself that overflowing, that movement, that condescension. He constitutes Himself as benefit or favor. And in so doing He elects another as the object of His love. He draws it upwards to Himself, so as never again to be without it, but to be who He is in covenant with it. In this concept of election there is reflected more clearly, of course, the other element in the being of God: the freedom in which He is the One who eternally loves. The concept of election means that grace is truly grace. It means that God owes His grace to no one, and that no one can deserve it. It means that grace cannot be the subject of a claim or a right on the part of the one upon whom it is directed. It means that it is the determination and decision of the will of God. Again, God elects that He shall be the covenant-God.[18] He does so in order not to be alone in His divine glory, but to let heaven and earth, and between them man, be the witnesses of His glory. He elects the way in which His love shall be shown and the witness to His glory established. He elects creation, man, the human race, as the sphere in which He wills to be gracious. But the existence of creation and of the human race does not constrain Him in the future exercise of grace. He elects even within this sphere. He elects the man of Nazareth, that He should be essentially one with Himself in His Son. Through Him and in Him He elects His people, thus electing the whole basis and meaning of all His works. He elects, i.e., He is free, and He remains free, both in what He does and in what He permits. He does what He does, but without any claim arising that He must do it, or that He must do it in this or that way. Over against Him no claim can ever arise. Nothing can precede His grace, whether in eternity or time, whether from the beginning or in the process of development. In all its manifestations, in all its activity, His grace is free grace. It is the Lord who is the Savior and Helper. His taking to Himself of that other is an act of unconditioned

---

to do so by joining himself to them in Jesus Christ. This election is *gracious* because it involves the giving of God's unmerited favor to fallen humanity in Christ.

18. As he does with grace, Barth offers a twofold account of election. First, election involves God's "self-election," his self-determination to be the covenant-God who gives himself to fallen humanity in Jesus Christ. Since this decision is made freely out of love, it is an election of grace. Barth will develop this point with more concreteness in his discussion of the election of Jesus Christ, where he will claim that Christ himself is the subject of election (see chap. 19).

sovereignty.[19] This is what the word "election" tells us as the second component of the concept "election of grace." It cannot possibly mean any restriction of the evangelical character of the concept. It reminds us emphatically, however, that the good news summarized in this concept is good news only because it proclaims to us the salvation which is the will of the real Lord both of our life and of all life. . . .

The election of grace is the sum of the Gospel—we must put it as pointedly as that. But more, the election of grace is the whole of the Gospel, the Gospel *in nuce*. It is the very essence of all good news.[20] It is as such that it must be understood and evaluated in the Christian Church. God is God in His being as the One who loves in freedom. This is revealed as a benefit conferred upon us in the fact which corresponds to the truth of God's being, the fact that God elects in His grace, that He moves towards man, in his dealings within this covenant with the one man Jesus, and the people represented by Him. All the joy and the benefit of His whole work as Creator, Reconciler and Redeemer, all the blessings which are divine and therefore real blessings, all the promise of the Gospel which has been declared: all these are grounded and determined in the fact that God is the God of the eternal election of His grace. In the light of this election the whole of the Gospel is light. Yes is said here, and all the promises of God are Yea and Amen (2 Cor. 1:20). Confirmation and comfort and help are promised us at this point, and they are promised us at every point. Whatever problems or contradictions we may encounter elsewhere, they all cease to be such, they become the very opposite, when we see them in their connection with the real truth which we must receive and proclaim here. On the other hand, if it is the shadow which really predominates, if we must still fear, or if we can only half rejoice and half fear, if we have no truth at all to receive or proclaim but only the neutral elucidation of a neutral subject, then it is quite certain that we can never again receive or proclaim as such the Gospel previously declared.[21]

19. Second, election involves God's determination of creatures. He elects the natural world to be the place for this covenant and humanity to be the object of his concern. God also elects to unite himself in the Son to the man Jesus and those represented by him. God remains free even as he makes these decisions to relate his creatures because he is the Lord who determines them in their depths.

20. The content of the gospel is an account of the life of Jesus Christ (2 Tim. 2:8). The content of Barth's doctrine of election also is an account of the life of Jesus. Since the content of both is identical, it is right to say that election summarizes the gospel.

21. Barth is responding to the often terrifying ways that the doctrine of election has been used in the history of the church. In some traditions, God's election evokes fear because it involves a mixed message of both salvation and damnation. Barth rejects the notion that election can

We must not seek the ground of this election anywhere but in the love of God, in His free love—otherwise it would not be His—but still in His love. If we seek it elsewhere, then we are no longer talking about this election. We are no longer talking about the decision of the divine will which was fulfilled in Jesus Christ. We are looking beyond these to a supposedly greater depth in God (and that undoubtedly means nothingness, or rather the depth of Satan).[22] What takes place in this election is always that God is for us; for us, and therefore for the world which was created by Him, which is distinct from Him, but which is yet maintained by Him. The election is made with a view to the sending of His Son. And this means always that in Him and through Him God moves towards the world. It means not merely that He creates and sustains the world, but that He works on it and in it by (miracle of all miracles) giving Himself to it. It means that the will for fellowship, which is His very being and to which the world owes its existence, is actively demonstrated to the world in a way which surpasses anything that could be expected or claimed. If we describe this movement as election, then it is only because we would thereby emphasize that it is the active demonstration of His love. Would it be love—the love of the personal God, and as such real love—if it were not an electing? As electing love it can never be hatred or indifference, but always love. And the active demonstration of that love is this: "God so loved the world, that he gave his only begotten Son, that whosoever believes in him should not perish, but have everlasting life" (John 3:16). Whatever may be the inner link in God's election between that giving of His only-begotten Son and the faith in Him by which the intended salvation is effected, this much is certain: that in this election (in giving Himself to this work, and in electing as the object of this work the man Jesus from among the world of men, and in Him the whole race) God loved the world. It is certain that this election is a work in which God meets the world neither in indifference nor in enmity, but in which at the very highest and lowest levels (in the giving of

---

have a twofold meaning. He insists that God's election is God's "Yes" to sinful humanity, his embrace of them in Christ. While Barth acknowledges that there is a negative aspect to this "Yes"—because a "No" to humanity also is spoken—he insists that God says this "No" strictly for the sake of his "Yes." In the end, then, election is solely a decision of grace.

22. Barth's target here is any doctrine of election that splits God's decision into two, as if God decides to save some but also decides to pass over or condemn others. The problem is that this "double" election is derived not from God's revelation in Christ but from some *other* truth about God that exists behind Christ. It makes God's revelation in Christ merely a half-truth since Christ reveals only one part of God's relationship with humanity. It also raises the question: Where and how did the human knower acquire this other "truth" about God? Barth argues that, since it did not come from God's revelation, it must stem from a projection of human ideals arising from human reflection on created realities. The inevitable result of such reflection is a false picture of God.

His only-begotten Son) He is for this man Jesus, and in Him for the whole race, and therefore for the world.[23]

That God wills neither to be without the world nor against it can never be stated more clearly or forcibly than when we speak of His election. At bottom, then, to speak of the election means necessarily to speak of the Gospel. In our teaching concerning the election we must always bring in the fact, definitely and basically and as the meaning and substance of all our assertions, that of and from Himself God has decided for this loftiest and most radical movement towards His creation, ordaining and constituting Himself its Friend and Benefactor. It is in this way, in the form of this election, that God has made His decision. And the tidings of the divine decision in this form are glad tidings. It is as such and in such a sense that they must be delivered: without any concealment of the fact that God does elect (for what need is there of concealment?); without any transmutation of God's way of loving the world into some other way, a general "loving" which involves no election and which is not really love; without any suppression or obfuscation of the fact that in this way and in the form of this election God has truly loved the world. In this form and this form alone the tidings of the divine decision made in Jesus Christ are glad tidings directed to all men, directed indeed to the whole world. It is also true that in the world there is opposition to the love of God, indeed that this opposition constitutes the being of the world as such. The text itself points indirectly but quite definitely to this fact when it says: "Whosoever believes in him should not perish." But the will and the power of God smash this opposition. Where the opposition does not break down in faith in the Son given, even the love of God must itself be destructive. To an opposing world the election must of the same force and necessity become non-election, or rejection. And it is for this reason, and to this extent, that there does exist a definite sphere of damnation ordained and determined by God as the negation of the divine affirmation, the work of the almighty non-willing which accompanies God's willing. But the divine affirmation, the divine willing as such, is salvation and not damnation. The divine election as such does not negate creation but affirms it. The message of God's election means always the message of the Yes determined and pronounced by God.[24] Another message

---

23. In contrast to a false, twofold doctrine of election, Barth lays out the content of a true doctrine of election. It will testify to the fact that God is unequivocally for humanity and for the world. It will describe God in light of his decision to send his Son into the world—and thus give himself to it—so that he might have fellowship with it. It also will emphasize that God's desire for this fellowship is the very basis of the world's existence and that this desire stems from God's free love for the world.

24. Barth insists that, even though opposition to God exists, the existence of this opposition does not change the content of God's election to be God for the world in Jesus Christ. This

can, of course, be given apart from that of God's election, e.g., the message of the blind election of fate, or of the supposedly most enlightened election of our own judgment. Here we shall be told something quite different from the divine affirmation. But we cannot hear of God's election without also hearing God's Yes. If we truly hear, then in face of this election and its meaning it is not possible for us not to be able to hear or obey that Yes, not to will to be amongst those who are affirmed by God. This is not a possibility but an impossibility. It is a turning of the sense of that election into nonsense. It is a descent into the abyss of the divine non-willing and the divine non-electing. Even in such a descent the creature cannot escape God. Even in this abyss it is still in the hands of God, the object of His decision. Yet that does not mean that it has been flung, or even allowed to fall, into the abyss by God Himself. God is and God remains the One who has decided for the creature and not against it. It is by love itself that the creature is confounded. Even there, in the midst of hell, when it thinks of God and His election it can think only of the love and grace of God. The resolve and power of our opposition cannot put any limit to the power and resolve of God. Even in our opposition there comes upon us that which God has foreordained for us. But that means that what comes upon us cannot alter in the slightest the nature and character of the foreordination which is God's decree. In that decree as such we find only the decree of His love. In the proclaiming and teaching of His election we can hear only the proclaiming of the Gospel.[25] . . .

We may look closer and ask: Who and what is the God who is to be known at the point upon which Holy Scripture concentrates our attention and thoughts? Who and what is the God who rules and feeds His people, creating and maintaining the whole world for its benefit, and guiding it according to His own good-pleasure—according to the good-pleasure of His will as it is directed towards this people? If in this way we ask further concerning the one point upon which, according to Scripture, our attention and thoughts should and must be concentrated, then from first to last the Bible directs us to the name of Jesus Christ. It is in this name that we discern the divine decision in favor of the movement towards this people, the self-determination of God as Lord and Shepherd of this people, and the

---

"sphere of damnation" must be seen as the negation of God's election rather than a revelation of it.

25. Again, Barth insists that the doctrine of election is not a twofold decision, a mixed message of both salvation and damnation. Jesus Christ reveals that, in God's free love, God has decided to be for the world by giving himself to the world in his Son. This is the one reality that God wills, and it is the basis of creation itself. Those who reject this determination and fall into the abyss do so in opposition to God's will. Their existence thus does nothing to undermine the reality that the singular content of election is grace.

determination of this people as "his people, and the sheep of his pasture" (Ps. 100:3). And in this name we may now discern the divine decision as an event in human history and therefore as the substance of all the preceding history of Israel and the hope of all the succeeding history of the Church.[26] What happened was this, that under this name God Himself became man, that He became this particular man, and as such the Representative of the whole people that hastens towards this man and derives from Him. What happened was this, that under this name God Himself realized in time, and therefore as an object of human perception, the self-giving of Himself as the Covenant-partner of the people determined by Him from and to all eternity. What happened was this, that it became a true fact that under this name God Himself possesses this people: possesses it no less than He does Himself; swears towards it the same fidelity as He exercises with Himself; directs upon it a love no less than that with which in the person of the Son He loves Himself; fulfilling His will upon earth as in the eternal decree which precedes everything temporal it is already fulfilled in heaven. What happened was this, that under this name God Himself established and equipped the people which bears the name to be "a light of the Gentiles," the hope, the promise, the invitation and the summoning of all peoples, and at the same time, of course, the question, the demand and the judgment set over the whole of humanity and every individual man. As all these things happened under this name, the will of God was done. And according to God's self-revelation attested in Scripture, it is wholly and utterly in these happenings that we are to know what really is the good-pleasure of His will, what is, therefore, His being, and the purpose and orientation of His work, as Creator of the world and Controller of history. There is no greater depth in God's being and work than that revealed in these happenings and under this name. For in these happenings and under this name He has revealed Himself. According to Scripture the One who bears this name is the One who in His own "I" introduces the concept of sovereignty and every perfection. When

---

26. Because God's determination of history is unveiled in the life of the man Jesus, he is the key to understanding the history of salvation that begins with Israel and continues in the church. What does Christ reveal about the content of this salvation history? In this paragraph, Barth lists four things: (1) Christ represents the people of Israel and the church before God. (2) Christ reveals and represents God to both the people of Israel and the church. (3) Christ reveals that God has united himself to his people so that their situation now belongs to him as well. God has determined to be *their* God. Faithfulness to himself now involves fidelity to them; love for himself now involves love for them; and the exercise of his divine will now includes bringing their lives to their fulfillment, the goal for which they were created. (4) Christ shows us that God accomplishes his will for the whole of history through the people of Israel, who serve as representative for all other nations.

the bearer of this name becomes the object of our attention and thoughts, when they are directed to Jesus Christ, then we see God, and our thoughts are fixed on Him.[27]

As we have to do with Jesus Christ, we have to do with the electing God. For election is obviously the first and basic and decisive thing which we have always to say concerning this revelation, this activity, this presence of God in the world, and therefore concerning the eternal decree and the eternal self-determination of God which bursts through and is manifested at this point. Already this self-determination, as a confirmation of the free love of God, is itself the election or choice of God. It is God's choice that He wills to be God in this determination and not otherwise. It is God's choice that He moves towards man, that He wills to be and is the Covenant-partner of man. It is God's choice that under the name of Jesus Christ He wills to give life to the substance of His people's history and to that people itself, constituting Himself its Lord and Shepherd. It is God's choice that in this specific form, in one age, in the very midst of that people's history, He acts on behalf of all ages, thus giving to all created time, becoming indeed, its meaning and content. It is God's choice that for the sake of the Head whose name it bears He has created and established this particular body, this people, to be the sign of blessing and judgment, the instrument of His love and the sacrament of His movement towards men and each individual man. It is God's choice that at every stage in its history He deals with this people with that purpose in view. It is in the utter particularity of His activity, and therefore of His volition, and to that extent of His self-determined being, that He is the electing God. He is so at that one point upon which Scripture concentrates our attention and thoughts. He is so in that He is the Lord and Shepherd of His people. He is so in Jesus Christ, in His only-begotten Son, and therefore from all eternity in Himself. To put it the other way round: If we would know who God is, and what is the meaning and purpose of His election, and in what respect He is the electing God, then we must look away from all others, and excluding all side-glances or secondary thoughts, we must look only upon and to the name of Jesus Christ, and the existence and history of the people of God enclosed within Him.[28]

---

27. Barth culminates his four-part discussion of history by claiming that if God is to be known at all, then he must be known in light of the way he has revealed himself within the history that runs from Israel through the church—and Jesus Christ stands at the center of his history.

28. This paragraph brings Barth back to the claims with which he started. He closes the door to any description of God that does not begin with God's decision to relate to the human Jesus Christ and the people united to him.

CHAPTER
19

The Election of Jesus Christ

Introduction

As Barth works out the implications of his doctrine of election in *Church Dogmatics* II/2, he focuses his argument around the claim that Jesus Christ is both the electing God and the elected man. One way to interpret this idea is to read Barth's explanation of it alongside the text of Ephesians 1:3–14, which opens with the claim that God "chose us in Christ before the foundation of the world" (v. 4). This excerpt in particular can be read as Barth's attempt to explain the realities described by this biblical claim.

Barth positions his argument against the traditional Reformed *decretum absolutum*, or absolute decree. This approach sees divine election as a two-fold decision leading to salvation for some and reprobation for others. Barth criticizes it for viewing Christ as only the object of election, as if he is merely God's chosen instrument to execute his saving decree. The problem is that if Christ is just the object of election, then he reveals only one part of God's twofold decision. This contradicts Scripture's claims that Christ reveals the truth about God. How can the church be confident that Christ brings salvation if the real truth about God's saving decision is something other than what Christ reveals?

Barth's reading of Scripture compels him to pose a bold alternative: Jesus Christ is *both* the subject and the object of election. Barth bases this claim, in part, on John's statement that the Word who became flesh was with God "in the beginning" (John 1:1–2). He argues that Jesus Christ, who is truly God and truly human, is with God in the beginning because the human Jesus is united to the eternal Son in an anticipatory, pre-temporal realization of the union that will take place in time. In this primal history "before the foundation of the world," Jesus Christ elects to live his own eternal life for the salvation of humans by taking on human flesh in time.

These claims are the basis of Barth's argument that Jesus Christ reveals the singular content of God's decision for humanity: God has elected to be *for* humanity. There is no other truth about God's being or will hidden behind Christ, and because this decision involves God's own self-determination, it is neither arbitrary nor contingent. The church can be confident that God's decision to live in union with the man Jesus perfectly expresses his divine being and his saving will for humanity.

Church Dogmatics II/2[1]

In the beginning, before time and space as we know them, before creation, before there was any reality distinct from God which could be the object of the love of God or the setting for His acts of freedom, God anticipated and determined within Himself (in the power of His love and freedom, of His knowing and willing) that the goal and meaning of all His dealings with the as yet non-existent universe should be the fact that in His Son He would be gracious towards man, uniting Himself with him. In the beginning it was the choice of the Father Himself to establish this covenant with man by giving up His Son for him, that He Himself might become man in the fulfillment of His grace. In the beginning it was the choice of the Son to be obedient to grace, and therefore to offer up Himself and to become man in order that this covenant might be made a reality. In the beginning it was the resolve of the Holy Spirit that the unity of God, of Father and Son, should not be disturbed or rent by this covenant with man, but that it should be made the more glorious, the deity of God, the divinity of His love and freedom, being confirmed and demonstrated by this offering of the Father and this self-offering of the Son.[2] This choice was in the beginning. As the subject and object of this choice,

1. Karl Barth, *Church Dogmatics* II/2 (Edinburgh: T&T Clark, 1957), 101–17.
2. Barth is working out the implications of God's decision to unite himself to humanity in Jesus Christ with respect to the divine will. Because God is triune, the operation of his will occurs in a threefold order. It proceeds *from* the Father as he elects his Son to become human for the sake of the world; it is enacted *through* the Son, who elects to be obedient by becoming human and enacting a covenant of grace for humanity; and it is completed *by* the Spirit, who

Jesus Christ was at the beginning. He was not at the beginning of God, for God has indeed no beginning. But He was at the beginning of all things, at the beginning of God's dealings with the reality which is distinct from Himself. Jesus Christ was the choice or election of God in respect of this reality. He was the election of God's grace as directed towards man. He was the election of God's covenant with man.[3] . . .

In its simplest and most comprehensive form the dogma of predestination consists, then, in the assertion that the divine predestination is the election of Jesus Christ. But the concept of election has a double reference—to the elector and to the elected. And so, too, the name of Jesus Christ has within itself the double reference: the One called by this name is both very God and very man. Thus the simplest form of the dogma may be divided at once into the two assertions that Jesus Christ is the electing God, and that He is also elected man.[4]

In so far as He is the electing God, we must obviously—and above all—ascribe to Him the active determination of electing. It is not that He does not also elect as man, i.e., elect God in faith. But this election can only follow His prior election, and that means that it follows the divine electing which is the basic and proper determination of His existence.

In so far as He is man, the passive determination of election is also and necessarily proper to Him. It is true, of course, that even as God He is elected; the Elected of His Father. But because as the Son of the Father He has no need of any special election, we must add at once that He is the Son of God elected in His oneness with man, and in fulfillment of God's covenant with man. Primarily, then, electing is the divine determination of the existence of Jesus Christ, and election (being elected) the human.[5]

Jesus Christ is the electing God. We must begin with this assertion because by its content it has the character and dignity of a basic principle, and because

---

determines that the unity between the Father and Son is not broken by this covenant even as it involves the Son's obedience unto death on the cross.

3. Barth now turns to the doctrine of the incarnation to add one more claim to his account: Jesus Christ, who is fully God *and* fully human, was at the beginning of God's relationship with the world. Jesus Christ is the ground and goal of the world because God created the world in order to relate to humanity in his flesh. Barth now turns to the task of explaining this claim.

4. This paragraph articulates the thesis at heart of Barth's doctrine of election: the incarnate Jesus Christ is both the subject and the object of election, the electing God and the elected man.

5. Jesus Christ is the electing God in the person of the Son, who elects to be for humanity by assuming human flesh. When the Son elects himself, he also elects the man Jesus. As this Son in human flesh, the man Jesus Christ is the elected one who determines to live in correspondence to this decision. These two acts exist in an order, with the divine election preceding the human determination that corresponds to it.

the other assertion, that Jesus Christ is elected man, can be understood only in the light of it.

We may notice at once the critical significance of this first assertion in its relation to the traditional understanding of the doctrine. In particular, it crowds out and replaces the idea of an absolute decree (*decretum absolutum*).[6] That idea does, of course, give us an answer to the question about the electing God. It speaks of a good-pleasure of God which in basis and direction is unknown to man and to all beings outside God Himself. This good-pleasure is omnipotent and incontrovertible in its decisions. If we are asked concerning its nature, then ultimately no more can be said than that it is divine, and therefore absolutely supreme and authoritative. But now in the place of this blank, this unknown quantity, we are to put the name of Jesus Christ. According to the witness of the Bible, when we are called upon to define and name the first and decisive decision which transcends and includes all others, it is definitely not in order to answer with a mysterious shrug of the shoulders. How can the doctrine of predestination be anything but "dark" and obscure if in its very first tenet, the tenet which determines all the rest, it can speak only of an absolute decree? In trying to understand Jesus Christ as the electing God we abandon this tradition, but we hold fast by John 1:1–2.[7]

Jesus Christ was in the beginning with God. He was so not merely in the sense that in view of God's eternal knowing and willing all things may be said to have been in the beginning with God, in His plan and decree. For these are two separate things: the Son of God in His oneness with the Son of Man, as foreordained from all eternity; and the universe which was created, and universal history which was willed for the sake of this oneness, in their communion with God, as foreordained from all eternity.[8] On the one hand,

6. When Barth refers to the *decretum absolutum*, or "absolute decree," he has John Calvin and the Reformed tradition in mind. They took "election in Christ" to mean that the incarnate Christ serves as the instrument of election, the mediator who executes God's decision. This is grounded in God's eternal decree to save some people in Christ and leave others in their sin. Barth's concern with this view is that it locates the truth about God's relationship with humanity in this "absolute decree" rather than in Christ, such that Christ reveals only one part of God's will to us. The remaining truth about God remains hidden, and humans are left to speculate about it in distinction from God's revelation in Christ. While Barth expressed general worries about this kind of approach in his initial remarks about election (see chap. 18), he develops them more directly here.

7. Barth's alternative to the absolute decree is to claim that Jesus Christ himself is the subject of election and thus the revelation of its content. He bases this claim on the opening verses of John: "In the beginning was the Word, and the Word was with God, and the Word was God. He was in the beginning with God" (John 1:1–2).

8. Barth makes an important distinction here. Jesus Christ, as truly God and truly human, is not present in the beginning with God merely in the sense that he is anticipated in the foreknowledge of God or in the sense that God plans to become incarnate at some time in the

there is the Word of God by which all things were made, and, on the other, the things fashioned by that Word. On the one hand, there is God's eternal election of grace, and, on the other, God's creation, reconciliation and redemption grounded in that election and ordained with reference to it. On the one hand, there is the eternal election which as it concerns man God made within Himself in His pre-temporal eternity, and, on the other, the covenant of grace between God and man whose establishment and fulfillment in time were determined by that election. We can and must say that Jesus Christ was in the beginning with God in the sense that all creation and its history was in God's plan and decree with God. But He was so not merely in that way. He was also in the beginning with God as "the first-born of every creature" (Col. 1:15), Himself the plan and decree of God, Himself the divine decision with respect to all creation and its history whose content is already determined. All that is embraced and signified in God's election of grace as His movement towards man, all that results from that election and all that is presupposed in such results—all these are determined and conditioned by the fact that that election is the divine decision whose content is already determined, that Jesus Christ is the divine election of grace.[9]

Thus Jesus Christ is not merely one object of the divine good-pleasure side by side with others. On the contrary, He is the sole object of this good-pleasure, for in the first instance He Himself is this good-pleasure, the will of God in action. He is not merely the standard or instrument of the divine freedom. He is Himself primarily and properly the divine freedom itself in its operation to that which is outside of God. He is not merely the revelation of the mystery of God. He is the thing concealed within this mystery, and the revelation of it is the revelation of Himself and not of something else. He is not merely the Reconciler between God and man. First, He is Himself the reconciliation between them. And so He is not only the Elected. He is also Himself the Elector, and in the first instance His election must be understood

---

future. While the created world is anticipated in this way, things are different with the human Jesus: he is present with God *before* anything was created. He was with God in the beginning as "the Son of God in His oneness with the Son of Man."

9. Barth's claim is this: in eternity, the Son of God elects to unite himself to the human Jesus, and in so doing, he also elects the human Jesus to live in union with himself. Jesus Christ is the name of this eternal Son who has elected to take on human flesh in time. In the election of Jesus Christ, the human Jesus is assumed into a unity with the Son of God in a real anticipation of his future life in time. He is really present in the beginning with God as the one he will become in time. This is why he is "the firstborn of all creation," the one in whom and through whom and for whom all things are created, the one who is "before all things" (Col. 1:15–17). As a result of the election of Jesus Christ, the Son of God will become in time what he already is by anticipation in eternity, and his human life will affirm and correspond to the decision made in eternity.

as active.[10] It is true that as the Son of God given by the Father to be one with man, and to take to Himself the form of man, He is elected. It is also true that He does not elect alone, but in company with the electing of the Father and the Holy Spirit. But He does elect. The obedience which He renders as the Son of God is, as genuine obedience, His own decision and electing, a decision and electing no less divinely free than the electing and decision of the Father and the Holy Spirit. Even the fact that He is elected corresponds as closely as possible to His own electing. In the harmony of the triune God He is no less the original Subject of this electing than He is its original object. And only in this harmony can He really be its object, i.e., completely fulfill not His own will but the will of the Father, and thus confirm and to some extent repeat as elected man the election of God. This all rests on the fact that from the very first He participates in the divine election; that this election is also His election; that it is He Himself who posits this beginning of all things; that it is He Himself who executes the decision which issues in the establishment of the covenant between God and man; that He too, with the Father and the Holy Spirit, is the electing God.[11] If this is not the case, then in respect of the election, in respect of this primal and basic decision of God, we shall have to pass by Jesus Christ, asking of God the Father, or perhaps of the Holy Spirit, how there can be any disclosure of this decision at all. For where can it ever be disclosed to us except where it is executed? The result will be, of course, that we shall be driven to speculating about an absolute decree instead of grasping and affirming in God's electing the manifest grace of God. And that means that we shall not know into whose hands we are committing ourselves when we believe in the divine predestination.[12]

10. Barth's description of Jesus Christ in this paragraph is directed against the traditional Reformed doctrine of absolute decree. In this doctrine, the human Jesus is merely the object of election and the instrument God uses to execute the hidden decree that takes place before and behind Jesus. Barth rejects this view because it undermines both revelation and salvation. He insists that the human Jesus is the subject of election, the one who freely wills himself to be the object of election. As such, he does not reveal only part of God's will but is the singular revelation of the will of God. He also is not merely the instrument of salvation, but rather, he is salvation itself.

11. Here Barth is continuing to work out the implications of the claim that Jesus Christ is the electing God. With the Father and Spirit, the Son of God elects to unite himself to sinful humans in the flesh of Jesus. This decision occurred "before the foundation of the world" (Eph. 1:4). As a result, the human Jesus is present to the eternal Son in an anticipatory, pre-temporal realization of the union that will take place in time when he is conceived in the womb of Mary by the Spirit. Jesus Christ's presence in the beginning is not a pre-temporal incarnation, but rather, it is an advance realization of what will take place in time as a result of God's decision.

12. Barth's persistent worries about the prospect of abstract speculation—and especially the human subjectivity that governs such speculation—are foregrounded here. He argues that, if Jesus Christ is merely the instrument through which God executes his election but is not the

So much depends upon our acknowledgment of the Son, of the Son of God, as the Subject of this predestination, because it is only in the Son that it is revealed to us as the predestination of God, and therefore of the Father and the Holy Spirit, because it is only as we believe in the Son that we can also believe in the Father and the Holy Spirit, and therefore in the one divine election. If Jesus Christ is only elected, and not also and primarily the Elector, what shall we really know at all of a divine electing and our election? But of Jesus Christ we know nothing more surely and definitely than this—that in free obedience to His Father He elected to be man, and as man, to do the will of God. If God elects us too, then it is in and with this election of Jesus Christ, in and with this free act of obedience on the part of His Son. It is He who is manifestly the concrete and manifest form of the divine decision—the decision of Father, Son and Holy Spirit—in favor of the covenant to be established between Him and us. It is in Him that the eternal election becomes immediately and directly the promise of our own election as it is enacted in time, our calling, our summoning to faith, our assent to the divine intervention on our behalf, the revelation of ourselves as the sons of God and of God as our Father, the communication of the Holy Spirit who is none other than the Spirit of this act of obedience, the Spirit of obedience itself, and for us the Spirit of adoption. When we ask concerning the reality of the divine election, what can we do but look at the One who performs this act of obedience, who is Himself this act of obedience, who is Himself in the first instance the Subject of this election.[13] . . .

The election of Jesus Christ is the eternal choice and decision of God. And our first assertion tells us that Jesus Christ is the electing God. We must not ask concerning any other but Him. In no depth of the Godhead shall we encounter any other but Him. There is no such thing as Godhead in itself. Godhead is always the Godhead of the Father, the Son and the Holy Spirit. But the Father is the Father of Jesus Christ and the Holy Spirit is the Spirit

---

God who elects, then it is impossible to say that Jesus Christ reveals the truth about God or salvation. Humans are left to seek this truth elsewhere if they want to know God and the nature of their relationship with him. When it comes to election, this leaves the human in the position of vainly searching the depths of God's mysterious decree instead of receiving God's grace.

13. Barth's argument in this paragraph reflects his doctrine of the Trinity—and specifically his account of the one God in three modes of being (see chap. 14). A key part of that doctrine is the idea that God the revealer must be identical to both the revelation and the impartation of this revelation to the human. If these three are not identical, then humans have no basis from which to say that God's revelation gives them the truth about God. Now Barth is simply applying this argument to the doctrine of election: If Jesus Christ is merely the object but not also the subject of election, then how can humans ever know where they stand in relation to God's electing will?

of the Father and the Spirit of Jesus Christ. There is no such thing as an absolute decree. There is no such thing as a will of God apart from the will of Jesus Christ. Thus Jesus Christ is not simply the manifestation and mirror of our predestination. And He is not a mirror in the sense that our election can be known to us and contemplated by us only through His election, as if our election—with His own election and in the same manner as His own election—is executed (or perhaps not executed!) by a secret and hidden will of God.[14] On the contrary, Jesus Christ reveals to us our election as an election which is made by Him, by His will which is also the will of God. He tells us that He Himself is the One who elects us. In the very foreground of our existence in history we can and should cleave wholly and with full assurance to Him because in the eternal background of history, in the beginning with God, the only decree which was passed, the only Word which was spoken and which prevails, was the decision which was executed by Him. As we believe in Him and hear His Word and hold fast by His decision, we can know with a certainty which nothing can ever shake that we are the elect of God.[15]

Jesus Christ is elected man. In making this second assertion we are again at one with the traditional teaching. But the christological assertion of tradition tells us no more than that in His humanity Jesus Christ was one of the elect. It was in virtue of His divinity that He was ordained and appointed Lord and Head of all others, the organ and instrument of the whole election of God and the revelation and reflection of the election of those who were elected with Him.

Now without our first assertion we cannot maintain such a position. For where can Jesus Christ derive the authority and power to be Lord and Head of all others, and how can these others be elected "in Him," and how can they see their election in Him the first of the elect, and how can they find in His election the assurance of their own, if He is only the object of election and not Himself its Subject, if He is only an elect creature and not primarily and supremely the electing Creator? Obviously in a strict and serious sense we can never say of any creature that other creatures are elect "in it," that

14. I adjusted the English translation of this sentence by adding the referent to the pronouns and rearranging the wording.

15. Note the pastoral tone that Barth's argument takes here. As complex as his theology can be, at the end of the day, Barth is the former pastor from Safenwil writing a *church* dogmatics, and he is concerned with the church's confidence. How can the church be sure that the gospel it proclaims is true? How can the church be sure that a life of discipleship to Jesus corresponds to the truth about God and humans? Barth worries that much of the church's doctrine—especially the teaching about the secret decree of God in election—undermines the ability of the church to answer either of these questions. The remedy is for the church to cleave to Jesus Christ and to allow all its thinking about God to be governed strictly by their faith in him.

it is their Lord and Head, and that in its election they can and should have assurance of their own. How can a mere creature ever come to the point of standing in this way before God, above and on behalf of others? If the testimony of Holy Scripture concerning the man Jesus Christ is true, that this man does stand before God above and on behalf of others, then this man is no mere creature but He is also the Creator, and His own electing as Creator must have preceded His election as creature. In one and the same person He must be both elected man and the electing God. Thus the second assertion rests on the first, and for the sake of the second the first ought never to be denied or passed over.[16]

Because of this interconnection we must now formulate the second statement with rather more precision. It tells us that before all created reality, before all being and becoming in time, before time itself, in the pre-temporal eternity of God, the eternal divine decision as such has as its object and content the existence of this one created being, the man Jesus of Nazareth, and the work of this man in His life and death, His humiliation and exaltation, His obedience and merit. It tells us further that in and with the existence of this man the eternal divine decision has as its object and content the execution of the divine covenant with man, the salvation of all men. In this function this man is the object of the eternal divine decision and foreordination.[17] Jesus Christ, then, is not merely one of the elect but *the* elect of God. From the very beginning (from eternity itself), as elected man He does not stand alongside the rest of the elect, but before and above them as the One who is originally and properly the Elect. From the very beginning (from eternity itself), there are no other elect together with or apart from Him, but, as Ephesians 1:4 tells us, only "in" Him. "In Him" does not simply mean with Him, together with Him, in His company. Nor does it mean only through Him, by means of that which He as elected man can be and do for them. "In Him" means in His person, in His will, in His own divine choice, in the basic decision of God which He fulfills over against every man. What singles Him out from the rest of the elect, and yet also, and for the first time, unites Him with them, is the

16. These remarks stem from Paul's claim that salvation occurs because humans have been chosen "in Christ," who serves as their representative "Head." Barth notes that the traditional doctrine affirms that the incarnate Jesus Christ is only the object of election and that he is elect in his humanity rather than his divinity. But how can salvation be rooted strictly "in" the humanity of Jesus? Salvation is found in *God*. This means that our election "in him" must reference both Christ's humanity and his divinity. The object of election is the God-Man, Jesus Christ—and this means that God must have elected *himself* to be the God-Man, the Son united to human flesh, for the salvation of humans.

17. Barth links Jesus's identity as the elected one directly and irrevocably to the saving work he performs. Jesus Christ is elected for *salvation*.

fact that as elected man He is also the electing God, electing them in His own humanity. In that He (as God) wills Himself (as man), He also wills them. And so they are elect "in Him," in and with His own election.[18] And so, too, His election must be distinguished from theirs. It must not be distinguished from theirs merely as the example and type, the revelation and reflection of their election. All this can, of course, be said quite truly of the election of Jesus Christ. But it must be said further that His election is the original and all-inclusive election; the election which is absolutely unique, but which in this very uniqueness is universally meaningful and efficacious, because it is the election of Him who Himself elects. Of none other of the elect can it be said that his election carries in it and with it the election of the rest. But that is what we must say of Jesus Christ when we think of Him in relation to the rest. And for this reason, as elected man, He is the Lord and Head of all the elect, the revelation and reflection of their election, and the organ and instrument of all divine electing. For this reason His election is indeed the type of all election. For this reason we must now learn really to recognize in Him not only the electing God but also elected man.

18. This insight leads to a powerful conclusion: if God elects himself to take on human flesh in order to save us, then God is *for humanity*. The election of Jesus Christ is revelatory, not merely of a divine decision but also of God's entire posture toward sinful humans. God's decision to save sinners is not arbitrary or fleeting. It expresses the true nature of God's being and character.

CHAPTER

20

God's Decision for the World

Introduction

For centuries, Reformed theologians have debated the logical order of God's decrees of election and reprobation in relation to his decrees to create the world and permit the fall. Supralapsarianism is the view that God's decrees of election and reprobation logically precede his decree to permit the fall. This approach implies that God ordains the fall so that the degrees of election and reprobation will be fulfilled.

Barth embraces supralapsarianism but rejects a twofold absolute decree in favor of a single decree. His central claim is that, out of his own free love, God elects to unite himself to human flesh in Jesus Christ for the salvation of sinful humanity. But where does the fall fit into this account of God's election of grace? Barth's task in this excerpt is to answer this question by offering his own "purified" version of supralapsarianism.

Five claims stand out in this short passage. First, Barth frames this account in terms of God's purpose and goal for the covenant of grace. This passage is as close as Barth comes to explaining why God decides to relate to humanity in and through the election of Jesus Christ. Second, the distinction Barth draws between God's *immediate* "Yes" and "No" and humanity's *historical* "Yes" and "No" is illuminating. This argument explains why God's election of grace in Jesus Christ takes place as a history rather than a simple decision. Third, Barth's nuanced and careful account of God's "Yes" and "No" reframes the ideas of a twofold divine decree. Barth is able to account for what God rejects without making it something that God actively wills. Fourth, Barth's account of the existence of sin and the fall makes it clear that even though the fall is part of God's eternal plan in Jesus Christ, God does not will sin and evil. God permits the fall precisely in order to overcome it in Jesus Christ. Fifth, this excerpt shows clearly why Jesus Christ is the single representative of every human and the key to humanity's salvation.

This passage provides a big-picture overview of Barth's theology that enables interpreters to better understand many of the specific arguments Barth makes throughout his *Church Dogmatics*. It also draws clear and helpful connections between Barth's doctrines of election, creation, theological anthropology, and reconciliation. For these reasons among others, this passage calls for careful reading and study.

Church Dogmatics II/2[1]

Let us try for a moment to think of the supralapsarian doctrine as detached from this background and freed from all the influences which affected it there. Our goal is to understand the work happening in and to the world, to men and for men, and thus the origin, purpose, and meaning of the world and men in terms of the eternal decision of the God who in his love is sovereign.

God's primal and basic purpose in relation to His creation is to impart and reveal Himself and also His glory—because He is the very essence of all glory. And because all things are His creation, because He is the Lord of all things, this primal and basic will is the beginning of all things, the eternal reality in which everything future is already determined and comprehended. And in his primal and basic will that is the beginning of all things, God does not will at random. God wills *man*—not the idea of man, not humanity, not human individuals in their multiplicity and diversity; or rather all of these, but concretely rather than abstractly. God wills *the* man, *His* man, His *elected* man, man predestined as the witness of His glory and the object of His love. God wills humanity *in him*, both every individual man and what we may describe as the idea of humanity—but only *in him*, and therefore, first and foremost and immediately in *him*, this man, his man, the man elected by him.[2]

1. Karl Barth, *Church Dogmatics* II/2 (Edinburgh: T&T Clark, 1957), 140–42. The translation has been adjusted to correct errors and incorporate Barth's original emphasis.
2. These remarks reflect Barth's account of the election of Jesus Christ (see chap. 19). God relates to creation in order to give himself to it in the elected man, Jesus. The existence of every

God's will is that this elect man, as a witness to His glory, should reveal, confirm and verify both positively what God *is* and *wills* and negatively what God is *not* and does *not* will. The latter negative is not a positive claim, but a marking off, a separating, a setting aside; it is not a second divine Yes but a divine No in the sense that it corresponds to the divine Yes, and in this correspondence and opposition, forms the necessary boundary of the divine Yes; so assuredly is God *God* and not *not* God; so assuredly does He live in eternal self-differentiation from everything that He is not and does not will. Because in this sense God is and is not, wills and does not will, he intends and ordains that the object of His love and the witness to His glory in the world created by Him should testify in a twofold manner: he should testify to His Yes and to what He wills, and he also should testify to His No and to what He does not will, so that he would truly exist and live in covenant with him and the fullness of the divine glory would be revealed to him.[3] It is not God's will that this elected man should fall and sin. But it is God's will that sin—that which God does not will—should be repudiated and rejected and excluded by him. It is God's will that this elected man should repudiate what He repudiates, and that thereby the Yes of God should be revealed and proclaimed. God does not will and affirm evil and the fall and an act of sin on the part of this man (it will never come to that, so assuredly is he elected man!), but for the sake of the fullness of His glory, for the sake of the completeness of His covenant with the man, for the sake of the perfection of His love, God wills and affirms this man as sinful—i.e., as one burdened with sins, afflicted by their curse and misery—and He wills and affirms this man as one who stands like Himself in contrast to sin, as his own companion in the necessity of saying No to sin, as the one foreordained to speak the same No and thus corroborate the divine Yes.[4] For this reason, however, it was necessary that this man should really be confronted with what God Himself repudiates, even as God Himself is confronted with it in his self-differentiation, in that disavowal of what He is not and does not will. And it is inevitable that this confrontation with what

---

human is determined by this election and thus by Jesus himself. This determination of human beings by Jesus enables Barth to speak in a double sense throughout this passage: he is simultaneously describing both the man Jesus *and* the humans who exist "in him."

3. God does not have a twofold will, as in the absolute decree. Rather, when God says "Yes" to what he wills, that which he does *not* will is marked off with a "No." God does not will this "No." It can be identified because what God does *not* want is marked off when God wills what he *does* want. God's plan is for the human Jesus to bear witness to God by affirming that which God wills and thereby rejecting that which God does not will. In this way, his human life will correspond to the eternal life of God.

4. Barth is careful to indicate that the elected man Jesus bears the burden of sin without himself committing sin.

God repudiates, with evil, means that for this man—who is certainly not God and therefore not almighty—evil confronts him as a *power*, a power which is, furthermore, *superior* to him as a man. In his case, then, the defeat of this evil power cannot be so self-evident as it was in God's case. It must for him become an event, the content of a *history*: the history of an obstacle and its removing; the history of a death and a resurrection; the history of a judgment and a pardon; the history of a defeat and a victory. In God Himself there is a simple and immediate triumph of light over darkness, with the issue never for one moment in doubt. But in the creaturely sphere—and therefore for men, since God willed men to testify to his glory—this victory must take on historical form in time by becoming an *event*.[5]

In willing man, His man, the elected man, God wills that *this* should be the case: He wills the confrontation of man by the power of evil. He wills man as the one assailed by this power. He wills him as the one who, as man and not God, is himself not equal to this power but is subjected to it. God wills Himself as the One who must and will come to the help of man in this subjection, who indeed is the only one who can and will give men victory in this subjection. God wills Himself as the One by whose *grace* this man should live, and he wills him to be utterly dependent on his grace. He does so in order that this man should proclaim His glory as the one who is freed by Him from the dominion of sin, as the one who is saved by Him from death as the consequence of sin, as the one for whom He Himself must and will and does commit himself should this man really go that way of death. God wills fallible man, not in order that he may fall, but in order that when he has fallen he may testify to the fullness of God's glory.[6] And His willing and election of this fallible man—not for the fall but for his exaltation and resurrection from the fall by His own power, the demonstration in time, in the creaturely sphere, of His eternal self-determination—precisely this predestination of his elect man is God's eternal election of grace, the very essence of all the benefits which God decided and intended to give to man, to humanity, to every individual man and to the whole of creation from eternity, before he began the work of creation. The existence of this man, the predestined as the bearer and representative of the divine Yes and therefore also the divine No, foreordained

---

5. Barth makes it clear: God does not directly will the fall or sin. Rather, God's will is for the human Jesus to affirm that which God affirms and reject that which God rejects. For the rejection to occur, Jesus must be confronted by that which God rejects—namely, evil—so that he can reject it. But evil confronts the human Jesus, who has taken upon himself the full burden of sin, as a hostile and superior power. So the human Jesus's rejection of evil must involve a divine act to overcome this power on his behalf.

6. The human Jesus is "fallen" only in that he bears the consequences of the fall for the sake of humanity.

to victory over sin and death but also to the bearing of the divine judgment, is the divine promise, the divine Word, in whom from eternity the electing God confronts all humanity and every single person, in whom His electing will encounters us and through whom He Himself has dealings with us.[7]

Such, then, is the supralapsarian doctrine as detached and purified from the doubtful presuppositions of the older theology.[8]

7. God wills that the human Jesus be confronted, assailed, and subjected to the power of evil. Although Jesus never sins, he bears the burden of sin and its consequence of death. God wills the subjection of the human Jesus in order to save him by raising him from the dead. Now the risen Jesus can testify to God's "Yes" for creation while also rejecting the "No." God's will for his elect human has now been realized, and the risen Jesus now displays God's glorious triumph over evil by proclaiming God's election of grace to the world.

8. This is Barth's answer to the question about the fall: God assumes the consequences of the fall in Jesus Christ so that he can overcome them for the sake of humanity's salvation.

Covenant and Creation

Introduction

Barth explores the doctrine of creation in this excerpt from *Church Dogmatics* III/1. He begins with the presupposition that theologians cannot talk solely about God's saving work, because God also is the Creator. Any description of God's relationship with humanity must account for the uniqueness of God's act of creation and the qualities that define the reality of created order.

Barth worries, however, that many dogmatic accounts of creation expand the scope of the doctrine beyond its proper limits. He insists that God's act of creation does not reveal the full truth about God's relationship with humanity, and creatures cannot be defined on the basis of their created nature alone. Rather, God's revelation in Jesus Christ unveils something new that goes beyond what creation itself reveals. This insight leads him to the core principle shaping his argument in this excerpt: God's act of creation always must be seen in relation to saving action in Jesus Christ.

The key to understand the relationship between creation and salvation is to see them in their proper order. Barth's central claim is that God's decision to save precedes his decision to create. The covenant is the internal basis of creation because God created the world to serve as the space and the place to execute his saving plan in Jesus Christ. This is what it means to affirm the biblical claim that all things have been created *for* Christ (Col. 1:16). The entire created order—and every particular thing within it—is defined and determined by his life and work.

Barth emphasizes that this description of creation does not undermine the integrity of creation but instead maintains its proper dignity and role. He explains that the created order serves as the external basis of the covenant, because it is the "theater" in which the drama of God's saving work in Christ takes place. This explains why any dogmatic description of God as Reconciler and Redeemer must affirm that God also is the Creator. All three actions are essential to a proper description of God's relationship with humanity.

Church Dogmatics III/1[1]

When the Bible and the Church's confession speak of creation they mean by it a specific work, or a specific element in the one divine work, in which, by reason of His own inner will and determination, God turns outside himself. Creation as such is not reconciliation or redemption, although both reconciliation and redemption have their presupposition in creation, and to that extent already begin with it. To say that the whole revelation of His glory, willed and determined by God, already becomes an event in creation, does not mean that we reverse the statement and say that it is limited to creation, or that all the further content of this revelation can be understood only as a continuation and unfolding of creation. On the other hand, it is not as if creation had only a temporary and dependent meaning alongside the other works, or alongside the other elements of the one divine work, and were thus not equally worthy of independent consideration. God's Word and work, attested by Holy Scripture and the confession of the Church, is articulated and demands to be heard and considered with special attention in each of its articles, and therefore here too, as the self-revelation of God the Creator.[2]

The distinctive element in creation consists in the fact that it comes first among God's works. The Bible begins with it and so does the creed. All the things distinct from God begin with it. If the eternal and determinate will of God is the source of their inner beginning, creation is the source of their external beginning. And herein lies the peculiar dignity of the creation, that

1. Karl Barth, *Church Dogmatics* III/1 (Edinburgh: T&T Clark, 1958), 42–51.
2. Barth opens this excerpt with a twofold caution. On the one hand, we cannot think that God's act of creation reveals the full nature of God's relationship with humanity. Christ reveals something new about the human relationship with God that creation itself does not. On the other hand, salvation in Christ is not the only topic in theology. God's act of creation is unique, significant, and deserves close attention.

as the external beginning of all things it stands in certain respects in direct confrontation with its inner beginning, its eternal source in God's decision and plan. It has no external presupposition; it follows immediately the eternal will of God. Beyond it we can think only of God's triune being in all its perfections, of the depth of the holiness and grace of His decree. It is emphatically the work of God's freedom, and therefore also emphatically God's miracle. If everything is free and glorious in God's other works, it is because in them too God acts and is revealed as Creator. Creation as such is the immediate correlate and realization of the divine purpose to begin with the revelation of His glory. It begins with the fact that the recipient, the scene and the handiwork of this revelation receive existence through Himself. When this takes place, everything commences—everything, that is, which is not the eternal God Himself and His purpose. Excluding God Himself and His purpose, anything prior to this beginning, to the putting into operation of the divine purpose whose goal was this beginning, cannot even be imagined. In all space outside God, creation is the first thing; everything comes from it, is maintained and conditioned, determined and shaped by it. Only God Himself is and remains the First prior to this first. Only God Himself is and remains free and glorious in relation to it. Only God Himself can and will preserve and condition, determine and shape all things in the course of His works otherwise than in the work of creation. But even God Himself, and especially God Himself, will act in such a way in the continuation of His creation, in each new miracle of His freedom, that He remains faithful to this first work of His. He will transform the reality of the creature, in a transformation which includes death, dissolution and new creation, but He will not destroy it; He will not take it away again. He will never be alone again as He was before creation. Nor will the creature be again as it was prior to creation. In all that He will do, God will not cease to be the One who has done this first thing.[3]

But as God's first work, again according to the witness of Scripture and the confession, creation stands in a series, in an indissolubly real connection, with God's further works. And these works, excluding for the moment the work of redemption and consummation, have in view the institution, preservation and execution of the covenant of grace, for partnership in which He has predestined and called man. The history of these divine works which follow creation is itself the execution of the eternal decision of God's will

3. The order of things is always important to Barth, and here he locates the dignity of creation in the fact that it is the first of God's works. This makes creation the presupposition of every creature: we cannot consider any creaturely thing without also thinking of God's act of creation. Nor can we consider God in distinction from this act. Even as we know God through salvation history, God is and always will be the God who freely created the world.

and decree to which it corresponds. But in view of the biblical economy and emphasis, it has to be said at once that the history of this covenant of grace, though its actualization follows creation, has in God's intention and purpose a dignity which, although different from that of creation, is not inferior but equal. It follows creation, but does not derive from it. Even as it follows it, it constitutes the scope of creation. It would be truer to say that creation follows the covenant of grace since it is its indispensable basis and presupposition.[4] As God's first work, it is in the nature of a pattern or veil of the second, and therefore in outline already the form of the second. Creation sets the stage for the story of the covenant of grace. The story requires a stage corresponding to it; the existence of man and his whole world. Creation provides this. If, according to Romans 11:36, all things are "through God" (this is the content of God's deeds for the institution, preservation and execution of the covenant of grace), and finally and lastly (in redemption and consummation) "for God," then, to begin with, all must be "from God." How could things be, and in this existence be "through God" and "for God," if they had not received their specific existence for this purpose "from God"? That this be given to them is in the totality of God's works the function of creation.[5]

Creation must not be separated from this context. It is for this reason that the concept of creation is not in any sense identical with the general concept of a first cause or the final contingency of all things.[6] Of course it includes this concept also. Where else can we look for the first cause or the final contingency of all things if not in creation? But in the Christian concept of the creation of all things the question is concretely one of man and his whole universe as the theatre of the history of the covenant of grace; of the totality of earthly and heavenly things as they are to be comprehended in Christ (Eph. 1:10). On the Christian view nothing has come into being or exists in itself and as

4. While creation is the first of God's works, it is related to all the works that follow after it. The thread connecting them is the covenant determined by God's election of Jesus Christ. Because God's decision to establish the covenant in Christ took place "in the beginning" before creation, it serves as the internal basis of creation. Creation exists for the sake of the covenant.

5. Creation exists to serve as the space for God to execute his decision to take on human flesh in Christ for the sake of humanity. In this sense, creation is the external basis of the covenant: it serves as the theater in which the drama of salvation takes place.

6. To see creation in light of *causality* is to view God's act of creation as the first in a series of ordered causes, such that every event occurring in creation can be traced back to this initial act. This approach distinguishes the act of creation from every other creaturely act: while every act in creation can be traced back to a creaturely cause, the act of creation itself can be traced back only to God. To see creation in terms of *contingency* is to view it in terms of its non-necessity, such that creation has a possible rather than a necessary existence. This also distinguishes the act of creation from every other creaturely act because the actuality of creation cannot be traced to any source other than God.

such, but only in this way and for this purpose. On this view there is no such thing as a self-existent first cause or final contingency of all things. To say that they are "of God" is to say at once, and conclusively, that they were called into being and exist in this concrete connection, that they are of the God who is Lord and Ruler of this history. On the other hand, the absolute authority and power of the divine lordship and rule in this history rest on the fact that it does not take place on soil that is originally foreign to it, but in a sphere ordained and prepared for it and for it alone from the very beginning; in the humanity and universe which are God's creation and therefore His property, and as such the object, scene and instrument of His acts.[7] . . .

When the Christian doctrine of creation speaks of God as the sum total of the first cause and the final contingency of all things, it does so in recognition of the God who is the Father of the Son and who, together with the Son, is the source of the Holy Spirit, and who, as such, is the divinely free and loving person—the Almighty. It tells us that God's first work, the positing of the distinct reality of man and his world, is indelibly marked off from every other source or beginning by the fact that it precedes and prepares for the second work, God's gracious dealing within the sphere of this reality. It tells us that the world and man are real only as they proceed from the hand of God and are kept by Him; only as they are bound and pledged and committed to the God who, as Father, Son and Holy Spirit, wills to manifest in them the glory of His grace within the context of all His works. It tells us that the creature as such is predestined to participate in the history which has its ground and direction in the will of God; that while it *is* and is *what* it is, it is from the very first the bearer of the promise that is unveiled in this history. Conversely, it tells us that the grace of God toward His creature as seen in this history is no less highly and deeply and firmly founded than the ground of its own existence. It shifts God's covenant, and man's part in this covenant, and the destiny of the world, to the point where this covenant is to be concluded, preserved and executed, viz. from the sphere of contingency to the beginning of all things. It forbids us to think meanly of Jesus Christ, His kingdom and His Church, as if the work of our salvation and redemption were a kind of afterthought which we might ignore in view of creation as God's first and principal work.

7. Barth's worries that views that approach creation in terms of causality or contingency fall into the same error: they describe the act of creation in relation to God but not in relation to God's other actions in history, including his saving act in Jesus Christ. Barth thinks this is problematic because it conflicts with the biblical idea that God elected Jesus "in the beginning" and then created the world in order to execute this decision. On these terms, creation cannot be defined merely in terms of its relation to God but must also be defined in relation to the events that God predestined to take place within it.

It is precisely in view of creation that we cannot possibly ignore Jesus Christ. And the Christian doctrine of creation tells us all this in the full certainty of the knowledge that God the Father, Son and Holy Spirit is One, and that this One cannot be untrue but is true to Himself.[8] . . .

The decisive anchorage of the recognition that creation and covenant belong to each other is the recognition that God the Creator is the triune God, Father, Son and Holy Spirit. Where this is and remains clear, the idea of creation will itself receive the necessary concretely Christian form and meaning. It will show itself inflexible in the face of all reinterpretations as a common concept of origin and dependence. By proving itself as its presupposition and backbone, it will also prevent the isolation and therefore the enervation of the idea of reconciliation. But it will also remain within its limits. It will not expand into the sum total of the divine works, nor give occasion for a legalistic or idealistic interpretation of the notion of the covenant. The recognition of the unity of the divine being and its particularity as Father, Son and Holy Spirit will prove effective in all these directions for the recognition not only of the interconnections but also of the variations in the relation between creation and covenant.[9]

8. In this paragraph, Barth lists six insights that a proper doctrine of creation will affirm: (1) God's act of creation is distinct from God's act of reconciliation because creation makes reconciliation possible. (2) Since all created things exist in relation to the God who has freely decided to save humans in Christ, their existence is defined by this decision. (3) Every creaturely thing has been created in order to participate in its own way in God's eternal plan. (4) The covenant is not a contingent event that occurs within a creation that would be the same without it; rather, the covenant is the internal basis of creation. (5) The reality that God's act in Christ, salvation, and the life of the church all take place within creation does not make them less significant than God's initial act of creation. (6) God's acts of creation and salvation correspond to his eternal being and faithfully express his one divine will for creaturely existence.

9. This paragraph contains further characteristics of a proper doctrine of creation: (1) Creation will be described in light of the particularity of God's revelation rather than abstract concepts of causality. (2) The reality of creation will be described in relation to God's reconciliation of sinful humanity. (3) Creation cannot be the primary category by which creatures are described, nor can it serve as the preexisting template into which God's saving work in Christ fits. Rather, because the covenant is the internal basis of creation, God's saving work in Christ defines the being and purpose of creation. (4) The triune God's revelation in history will serve as the basis from which both the relationship and the distinction between creation and covenant are described.

22

The Covenant Partner of God

Introduction

In this excerpt from *Church Dogmatics* III/2, Barth addresses the identity of humans and their existence in the image of God. He argues that humans cannot be defined on their own terms, as if they could simply look at themselves and know what and who they are. This approach leads to an abstraction because it presumes that humans are self-contained and self-defined. In contrast, Barth insists that humans exist in and through their relationships with God and other creatures. A human is a being-in-relation, and the relationship that defines human being above all is the one God establishes with humanity in and through the man Jesus of Nazareth.

With these claims in mind, Barth argues that Jesus Christ is the true human because he is the one who unveils the basis and destiny of human nature. Because Christ stands in the center of God's eternal plan for created history, every other human realizes his or her humanity through their relationship with him. This relationship is mediated through the Word of God as Christ speaks to humans in order to evoke a response of faith and obedience from them.

Barth describes this response as an act of correspondence: it is the primary way that humans partner with God in the covenant of grace. This partnership has a specific form and goal. Through his Word, God calls humans to live for others in the same way that Christ lives for them. He develops this idea by arguing that an analogy of relation (*analogia relationis*) exists between

God and humans. He explains that the relationship between eternal Father and eternal Son is analogous to the relationship between God and the human Jesus, which itself is analogous to the relationship between the human Jesus and other humans. As each person responds to the Word of Christ and lives for the sake of others, their relationship with others is analogous to Christ's relationship with humanity as well as Christ's relationship with God.

These analogous relationships are the key to understanding humanity's existence in the image of God. Humans image God when they live for others just as Christ lived for them. Image bearing thus is a form of witness: as humans give themselves in love for the sake of their neighbors, they testify to the self-giving love of God revealed in the life of Jesus.

Church Dogmatics III/2[1]

Real man lives with God as His covenant-partner. For God has created him to participate in the history in which God is at work with him and he with God; to be His partner in this common history of the covenant. He created him as His covenant-partner. Thus real man does not live a godless life—without God. A godless explanation of man, which overlooks the fact that he belongs to God, is from the very outset one which cannot explain real man, man himself. Indeed, it cannot even speak of him. It gropes past him into the void. It grasps only the sin in which he breaks the covenant with God and denies and obscures his true reality.[2] Nor can it really explain or speak of his sin. For to do so it would obviously have to see him first in the light of the fact that he belongs to God, in his determination by the God who created him, and in the grace against which he sins. Real man does not act godlessly, but in the history of the covenant in which he is God's partner by God's election and calling. He thanks God for His grace by knowing Him as God, by obeying Him, by calling on Him as God, by enjoying freedom from Him and to Him. He is responsible before God, i.e., He gives to the Word of God the corresponding answer.[3] That this is the case, that the man determined by God for life with

1. Karl Barth, *Church Dogmatics* III/2 (Edinburgh: T&T Clark, 1960), 203–4, 207–9, 212–20.
2. Barth's use of the word "reality" (*Wirklichkeit*) is significant because it reflects his conviction that we cannot think about God and humanity by starting with ourselves. For Barth, theologians begin with God's self-revelation to us and then draw conclusions on the basis of this revelation. Only then will our thoughts reflect reality. Humans pose no exception. We know what it means to be human only by reflecting God's revelation to us in the human Jesus.
3. Note that the relationship between God and the human involves an encounter: God personally relates to humans in and through his Word, and humans respond to this Word by

God is real man, is decided by the existence of the man Jesus. Apart from anything else, this is the standard of what his reality is and what it is not. It reveals originally and definitively why God has created man. The man Jesus is man for God. As the Son of God He is this in a unique way. But as He is for God, the reality of each and every other man is decided. God has created man for Himself. And so real man is for God and not the reverse. He is the covenant-partner of God. He is determined by God for life with God. This is the distinctive feature of his being in the cosmos.[4]

But this real man is actually in the cosmos. He is on earth and under heaven, a cosmic being. He belongs to God, but he is still a creature and not God. The one thing does not contradict the other, but explains it. If we are to understand man as the creature of God, we must see first and supremely why God has created him. We must thus regard him from above, from God. We must try to see him as God's covenant-partner, and therein as real man. This is what we have done in the preceding section. But if we are to understand him as God's covenant-partner—which is our present task—we must return to the fact that God has created him and how He has done so, regarding him as a cosmic being, as this particular cosmic being. It is in this distinction from God, in his humanity, that he is ordained to be God's covenant-partner. In this continuation of theological anthropology we now address ourselves to all the problems which might be summed up under the title "The Humanity of Man." Our presupposition is that he is the being determined by God for life with God and existing in the history of the covenant which God has established with him. Only in this way—and we shall not allow ourselves to be jostled off the path which we have found—is he real man, in this being which consists in a specific history.[5] But we must now see and understand this real man as a being distinct from God, as the creature of God, and to that extent as a being here below. It is as he is not divine but cosmic, and therefore from God's standpoint below (with the earth on which and the heaven under which he is), that he is determined by God for life with God. The creation of God, and therefore His positing of a reality distinct from Himself, is the external basis and possibility of the covenant. And the covenant itself is the internal basis and possibility of creation, and therefore of the existence of a reality distinct from God. We must now ask concerning

---

acting in correspondence to it. This idea is fundamental for Barth's account of human being. Humans exist not strictly in and of themselves but only in the context of their ongoing encounters with God and others.

4. To understand the basis of these claims, see Barth's account of the election of Jesus Christ and its implications in chaps. 19 and 20.

5. Note Barth's underlying presupposition: humans are created to relate to God as participants in the covenant established in and through God's election of Jesus Christ. For Barth's explanation of this presupposition, see his doctrine of election in chap. 18.

man, the covenant-partner of God, from the cosmic standpoint, in his life here below, in distinction from God, and to that extent in his humanity.[6] . . .

But what is the right way to this mystery? Everything depends upon our finding the right way at this critical point in our investigation, and therefore in this transitional question. And here, as in theology generally, the right way cannot be one which is selected at random, however illuminating. The arbitrarily selected way would be one of natural knowledge inevitably leading into an impasse. We must be shown the right way. And the way which we are shown can only be the one way. We must continue to base our anthropology on Christology. We must ask concerning the humanity of the man Jesus, and only on this basis extend our inquiry to the form and nature of humanity generally.[7]

That Jesus, who is true man, is also true God, and real man only in this unity (the unity of the Son with the Father), does not destroy the difference between divinity and humanity even in Him. And if in respect of this unity we have to speak of a divinity, i.e., a divine determination of his humanity too, it is not lacking in genuine humanity. There is a divinity of the man Jesus. It consists in the fact that God exists immediately and directly in and with Him, this creature. It consists in the fact that He is the divine Savior in person, that the glory of God triumphs in Him, that He alone and exclusively is man as the living Word of God, that He is in the activity of the grace of God. It consists, in short, in the fact that He is man for God. But there is a humanity of the man Jesus as well as a divinity. That He is one with God, Himself God, does not mean that Godhead has taken the place of His manhood, that His manhood is as it were swallowed up or extinguished by Godhead, that His human form is a mere appearance, as the Roman Catholic doctrine of transubstantiation maintains of the host supposedly changed into the body of Christ. That he is true God and also in full differentiation true man is the mystery of Jesus Christ. But if He is true man, He has the true creaturely form of a man, and there is thus a humanity of the man Jesus. Therefore, as we turn to the problem of humanity, we do not need to look for any other basis of anthropology than the christological. On the contrary, we have to realize that the existence of the man Jesus is quite instructive enough in this aspect of the question of man in general.[8]

6. This is the key question that Barth is addressing in this excerpt: What does it mean to be a human who exists in relation to the God of the covenant?

7. Barth's method for answering the question about human being is the same as ever: he will start with God's revelation in Christ and then offer an account of what it means to be human in light of this revelation.

8. Barth anticipates that questions might be raised about his starting point for describing human being. How can he offer an account of human being by starting with Jesus Christ, given the fact that he also is the Son of God? Barth affirms that Christ's divinity makes him distinct

This time we can state the result of our investigation at the very outset. If the divinity of the man Jesus is to be described comprehensively in the statement that He is man for God, His humanity can and must be described no less succinctly in the proposition that He is man for man, for other men, His fellows.[9] We are now considering Jesus here below, within the cosmos. Here He is the Son of God. Here He is distinguished as a man by His divinity. But here He is human, Himself a cosmic being, one creature among others. And what distinguishes Him as a cosmic being, as a creature, as a true and natural man, is that in His existence He is referred to man, to other men, His fellows, and this not merely partially, incidentally or subsequently, but originally, exclusively and totally. When we think of the humanity of Jesus, humanity is to be described unequivocally as fellow-humanity. In the light of the man Jesus, man is the cosmic being which exists absolutely for its fellows.

We must first return to some earlier statements. The man Jesus *is* as there is enacted a definite history in which God resolves and acts and He Himself, this man, fulfills a definite office, accomplishing the work of salvation. He does this in the place of God and for His glory. He does it as the One who is sent for this purpose. The Word and grace of God are exclusively at work in Him and by Him. He does it for God. This is again His divinity.[10] But the humanity in which He does that for which He is sent is that He is there in the same totality for man, for other men. In no sense, therefore, is He there for Himself first and then for man, nor for a cause first—for the control and penetration of nature by culture, or the progressive triumph of spirit over matter, or the higher development of man or the cosmos. For all this, for any interest either in His own person or intrinsically possible ideals of this kind, we can find no support whatever in the humanity of Jesus. What interests Him, and does so exclusively, is man, other men as such, who need Him and are referred to Him for help and deliverance. Other men are the object of the saving work in the accomplishment of which He Himself exists. It is for their sake that He takes the place of God in the cosmos. Their deliverance is the defense of the divine glory for which He comes. It is to them that the Word and grace of God apply, and therefore His mission, which is not laid upon Him, or added to His human reality, but to which He exclusively owes

---

from humans, but he does not believe this distinction negates Christ's full identity with humans. Jesus is truly divine *and* truly human. In addition, since he is "the firstborn of all creation" who was there with God in the beginning, he serves as the template for human being—the key to understanding it.

9. This is Barth's thesis in this excerpt: Jesus Christ shows us that real human being is a being-for-others. He explains and defends this idea in the paragraphs below.

10. Barth's claims on this point reflect his earlier arguments and the election of Jesus Christ (see chap. 19).

His human reality as He breathes and lives—the will of God which it is His meat to do.[11] From the very first, in the fact that He is a man, Jesus is not without His fellow-men, but to them and with them and for them. He is sent and ordained by God to be their Deliverer. Nothing else? No, really nothing else. For whatever else the humanity of Jesus may be, can be reduced to this denominator and find here its key and explanation. To His divinity there corresponds exactly this form of His humanity—His being as it is directed to His fellows.[12] . . .

He does not merely help His fellows from without, standing alongside, making a contribution and then withdrawing again and leaving them to themselves until further help is perhaps required. This would not be the saving work in the fulfillment of which He has His life. Nor would it serve the glory and right of God, nor help to their right the fellows for whom He is there. For it would not alter their state and fate as sinners fallen victim to death. It would not deal with the root of their misery. The menacing of the cosmos by chaos and the assault on man by the devil are far too serious and basic to be met by external aid, however powerful. And so the being of Jesus for His fellows really means much more. It means that He interposes Himself for them, that He gives Himself to them, that He puts Himself in their place, that He makes their state and fate His own cause, so that it is no longer theirs but His, conducted by Him in His own name and on His own responsibility. And in this respect we have to remember that so long as the cause of men was in their own hands it was a lost cause. Their judgment was just and destruction inevitable, so that anyone taking their place had necessarily to fall under this judgment and suffer this destruction. In His interposition for them the man Jesus had thus to sacrifice Himself in this cause of others. It was not merely a matter of His turning to them with some great gift, but of His giving Himself, His life, for them. It was a matter of dying for them. And if the cause of His fellows was really to be saved and carried through to success, if they were really to be helped, an unparalleled new beginning was demanded, a genuine creation out of nothing, so that the One taking their place had to have the will and the power not merely to improve and alleviate their old life

---

11. Barth is referring here to Jesus's statement in John 4:34: "My food is to do the will of him who sent me and to complete his work."

12. The key to Barth's argument in this paragraph is the idea of *correspondence*. His claim is that the human Jesus freely lives for the sake of humanity and in this way lives in perfect correspondence to God's life. In the background is Barth's argument about the God who loves in freedom (see chap. 17). God does not relate to creation for his own sake or because he is bound to some external principle. Rather, God freely chooses to relate to creation by giving himself to it in love. When the Son of God unites himself to human flesh, he lives in this same way: he never acts for his own sake or for some other end, but instead he gives himself to others in love.

but to help them to a basically new one. Interposing Himself for them, the man Jesus had thus to conquer in this alien cause. He could not merely relieve His fellows of their sin and bear for them its punishment, as though it were enough to set them in this neutral state and wipe the slate clean. He had also to give them the freedom not to sin any more but to be obedient where they had previously been disobedient. To be their Deliverer He had thus to rise again for them to a new life. This is the saving work by which the devilish onslaught on man is repulsed, the menacing of cosmos by chaos overcome and the divine creation inaugurated in a new form in which the glory and right of God are no longer bounded and can no longer be called in question by any adversary. The humanity of Jesus implies that in the execution of His mission as the incarnate Son of God He is for men in this comprehensive and radical sense. It implies that all other men can confidently keep to the fact that this sacrifice was offered once and for all for them, that this victory was won once and for all for them, that the man Jesus died and rose again once and for all for them.[13] . . .

This is the humanity of the man Jesus—the concrete form of His humanity. And the following implications are to be noted.

There is implied first that Jesus has to let His being, Himself, be prescribed and dictated and determined by an alien human being (that of His more near and distant fellows), and by the need and infinite peril of this being. He is not of Himself. He does not live in an original humanity in which He can be far more glorious perhaps in virtue of His divine determination. No, the glory of His humanity is simply to be so fully claimed and clamped by His fellows, by their state and fate, by their lowliness and misery; to have no other cause but that of the fatal Adam whom He now allows to be really the first, giving him the precedence, ranging Himself wholly with him for his salvation as the second Adam.[14] If there is indeed a powerful I of Jesus, it is only from this Thou, from fallen Adam, from the race which springs from him, from Israel and the sequence of its generations, from a succession of rebels, from a history which is the history of its unfaithfulness. He is pleased to have His life

13. Barth insists that Jesus lives for humans in that he meets them in the midst of their concrete situation. He does not merely enable the forgiveness of their sin or perform a transaction on their behalf on the cross. No, the concrete reality of human existence is that humans are subjected to the power of sin and death. So Christ meets them in that reality. He does so by bearing the burden of sin and dying for them so that he can be raised to new life for their sake. In this way, death is defeated and humanity re-created.

14. Barth draws out two implications of the reality that Jesus exists for others in the paragraphs below. The first implication is that Jesus lives in identity with fallen humanity by subjecting himself to the power of sin and death. Although he never sins, he comes "in the likeness of sinful flesh" in order to bear the burden of their sin alongside them (Rom. 8:3).

only from His apostles, His community, those whom He called His own and who constantly forsook and forsake Him. He is pleased to be called by them to His own life, to be given the meaning of His life by them. He is pleased to be nothing but the One who is supremely compromised by all these, the Representative and Bearer of all the alien guilt and punishment transferred from them to Him.[15]

There is also implied that His being is wholly with a view to this alien being; that He is active only in the fact that He makes its deliverance His exclusive task. He moves towards the Thou from which He comes. Disposed by it, He disposes Himself wholly and utterly towards it, in utter disregard of the possibility that another task and activity might better correspond to His divine determination and be more worthy of it. After all, what are these fellow-men? What are to Him all these representatives of the human race, the more pious and noble and the less? Why should He not choose and adopt an original work, completely ignoring these pitiable figures in its execution? Well, He does not do so. He finds it worth His while to live and work for His fellows and their salvation.[16] He does not hold aloof from them. He does not refuse to be like them and with them and in that comprehensive sense for them. He gives Himself freely to them. He has only one goal: to maintain the cause of these men in death and the conquest of death; to offer up His life for them that they may live and be happy. He therefore serves them, without prospect of reward or repayment, without expecting to receive anything from them which He cannot have far better and more richly without them. He therefore interposes Himself for Adam, for the race, for Israel, for His disciples and community. . . .

We could hardly see the man Jesus as attested in the New Testament if we closed our eyes to the twofold fact that His being is both from and to His fellows, so that He is with them, and in this way man in His distinctive sovereignty. If we see Him alone, we do not see Him at all. If we see Him, we see with and around Him in ever-widening circles His disciples, the people, His enemies and the countless millions who have not yet heard His name. We see Him as theirs, determined by them and for them, belonging to each and every one of them. It is thus that He is Master, Messiah, King and Lord. "Selfless" is hardly the word to describe this humanity. Jesus is not "selfless." For in this way He is supremely Himself.[17] The theme of the New Testament

15. Note Barth's emphasis on substitution here: Jesus takes the burden of sin for humanity by living in the place of humanity, on their behalf, so that they might be freed from sin's power.

16. The second implication of Christ's being-for-others is that Jesus lives for the salvation of sinners. Although he confronts and rejects their sin, Christ is not against but *for* sinners.

17. Barth's claim here is that we cannot understand Jesus Christ rightly unless we see him in his relationship with sinful humans. This is similar to the claim he issued in his doctrine of

witness is a kind of incomparable picture of human life and character. What emerges in it is a supreme I wholly determined by and to the Thou. With this twofold definition Jesus is human.

And there is obviously no distance, alienation or neutrality, let alone opposition, between this human definition and the divine. His humanity is not, of course, His divinity. In His divinity He is from and to God. In His humanity He is from and to the cosmos. And God is not the cosmos, nor the cosmos God. But His humanity is in the closest correspondence with His divinity. It mirrors and reflects it. Conversely, His divinity has its correspondence and image in the humanity in which it is mirrored. At this point, therefore, there is similarity. Each is to be recognized in the other. Thus even the life of the man Jesus stands under a twofold determination. But there is harmony between the two. As he is for God, so He is for man; and as He is for man, so He is for God. There is here a basis for comparison which includes His being for God as well as His being for man, since the will of God is the basis and man the object of the work in which this man is engaged.[18] . . .

We must now take a further step, for it is not only by way of His utter obedience to God, but because and in the course of it, that He so fully serves His fellows. The saving work in which He serves His fellows is not a matter of His own choice or caprice but the task which He is given by God. Its execution has nothing to do, therefore, either with the fulfillment of a duty or the exercise of a virtue. For He exists and lives in His saving work. He would not be the One He is if He lived in the execution of another work or in any sense for Himself or a cause alien to this work. He cannot be at all, and therefore for God, without being for men. Hence it is the glory of the One who has commissioned and sent Him, of God, which is revealed and proclaimed in the fact that He is for men. In this there is disclosed the choice and will of God Himself. God first and not the man Jesus is for men. It is He, God, who from all eternity has established the covenant of grace between Himself and man, and has pitied and received Him, pitying and receiving this particularly threatened and needy creature within the threatened cosmos of His creatures and for its deliverance and preservation. The whole witness and revelation of the man Jesus in time, the whole point of His life and existence, is that within

---

election: we cannot formulate a doctrine of God without considering the reality that God has decided to live in relationship with humanity in Jesus Christ (see chap. 18). He now is applying this same insight to the doctrine of Christology.

18. Barth emphasizes that the human Jesus's life for sinners perfectly corresponds to his divine life as the Son of God. It is not as if the human Jesus lives in one way but the truth about God is something different. The human Jesus is the revelation of God, and his life-for-others is the unveiling of God's eternal being and character in time.

the cosmos there should be declared as good news and operative as saving power the fact that God Himself is for man and is his Covenant-partner. God interposes Himself for him, sharing his plight and making Himself responsible for his life and joy and glory. God Himself is his Deliverer. He wills a free man in a free cosmos—freed from the threat to which man has culpably exposed himself and which he is powerless to avert. The God who willed and resolved this, and acted in this way in His incarnate Son, is the basis of the saving work of the man Jesus which has man—His fellow-men exactly as they are—as its object. It is not by accident, then, that Jesus is for man as He is for God. Between His divinity and His humanity there is an inner material connection as well as a formal parallelism. He could not be for God if He were not on that account for man. The correspondence and similarity between His divinity and humanity is not merely a fact, therefore, but has a material basis. The man Jesus is necessarily for His fellows as He is for God. For God first, as the One who gives Him His commission, as the Father of this Son, is for man. This excludes any possibility of the man Jesus not being for man as He is for God.[19] . . .

And now we must take a last and supreme step. There is freedom in God, but no caprice. And the fact that from all eternity God pitied and received man, the grounding of the fellow-humanity of Jesus in the eternal covenant executed in time in His being for man, rests on the freedom of God in which there is nothing arbitrary or accidental but in which God is true to Himself.[20] God for man, participating in and making Himself responsible for him, securing for him fellowship with Himself and therefore His saving help—this whole mystery of the man Jesus is rooted in the mystery of God Himself, which is no mere fact or riddle, but full of meaning and wisdom. And as the mystery of the man Jesus is disclosed to us, we cannot say of the even higher mystery of God Himself that it is simply hidden from us and its meaning and wisdom are unattainable. If "God for man" is the eternal covenant revealed and effective in time in the humanity of Jesus, in this decision of the Creator for the creature there arises a relationship which is not alien to the Creator, to God as God, but we might almost say appropriate and natural to Him. God repeats in

19. Barth closes the door to any view of Christ's saving work that sees this work in distinction from the will of God. Christ is not acting on his own apart from God. Nor is Christ fulfilling a duty in the sense that he is obeying some external obligation or instruction. He also is not simply exercising some internal quality or characteristic and in this sense using humanity to achieve his own goals. Rather, when Jesus Christ acts for the salvation of sinners, he is expressing and revealing God's one will for the salvation of humanity. Jesus lives for sinners because *God* is for sinners.

20. One of Barth's core convictions is that God never acts randomly: his decisions and actions always stand in line with his divine being and character.

this relationship outside himself a relationship proper to Himself in His inner divine essence. Entering into this relationship, He makes a copy of Himself.[21] Even in His inner divine being there is relationship. To be sure, God is One in Himself. But He is not alone. There is in Him a co-existence, co-inherence and reciprocity. God in Himself is not just simple, but in the simplicity of His essence He is threefold—the Father, the Son and the Holy Ghost. He posits Himself, is posited by Himself, and confirms Himself in both respects, as His own origin and also as His own goal. He is in Himself the One who loves eternally, the One who is eternally loved, and eternal love; and in this triunity He is the original and source of every I and Thou, of the I which is eternally from and to the Thou and therefore supremely I. And it is this relationship in the inner divine being which is repeated and reflected in God's eternal covenant with man as revealed and operative in time in the humanity of Jesus.[22]

We now stand before the true and original correspondence and similarity of which we have to take note in this respect. We have seen that there is a factual, a materially necessary, and supremely, as the origin of the factual and materially necessary, an inner divine correspondence and similarity between the being of the man Jesus for God and His being for His fellows. This correspondence and similarity consists in the fact that the man Jesus in His being for man repeats and reflects the inner being or essence of God and this confirms His being for God. We obviously have to do here with the final and decisive basis indicated when we spoke of the ontological character, the reality and the radical nature of the being of Jesus for His fellow-men. It is from this context that these derive their truth and power. The humanity of Jesus is not merely the repetition and reflection of His divinity, or of God's controlling will; it is the repetition and reflection of God Himself, no more and no less. It is the image of God, the *imago Dei*.[23]

The "image"—we must not forget the limitation implicit in this term. If the humanity of Jesus is the image of God, this means that it is only indirectly and

21. The claim that God makes a "copy" of himself stems from Barth's account of the doctrines of the Trinity and election. His central claim is that God remains true to his divine being when he acts in created history because the revealer is one and the same as the revelation. So God does not give humans a false picture when he comes to them; nor does he hold himself back by giving them merely a partial truth. Instead, God reveals himself to humans as the one true God that he is. This means that when the Son of God takes on flesh in Jesus Christ, the human Jesus's relation to God in time is a "copy" of the eternal relation between Father and the Son.

22. This is the heart of the matter for Barth: Jesus Christ's self-giving love for sinners is the actualization and revelation of the eternal self-giving love of God in time.

23. With the preceding claims in hand, Barth is now in position to define the biblical concept "image of God" concretely. He does so by appealing to the notion that an "image" is both similar and dissimilar to its subject matter.

not directly identical with God. It belongs intrinsically to the creaturely world, to the cosmos. Hence it does not belong to the inner sphere of the essence, but to the outer sphere of the work of God. It does not present God in Himself and in His relation to Himself, but in His relation to the reality distinct from Himself. In it we have to do with God and man rather than God and God. There is a real difference in this respect.[24] We cannot, therefore, expect more than correspondence and similarity. We cannot maintain identity. Between God and God, the Father and the Son and the Son and the Father, there is unity of essence, the perfect satisfaction of self-grounded reality, and a blessedness eternally self-originated and self-renewed. But there can be no question of this between God and man, and it cannot therefore find expression in the humanity of Jesus, in His fellow-humanity as the image of God. In this case we have a complete disparity between the two aspects. There is total sovereignty and grace on the part of God, but total dependence and need on that of man. Life and blessedness may be had by man wholly in God and only in fellowship with Him, in whom they are to be sought and found. On God's side, therefore, we have a Savior and Deliverer. And He does not enter into alliance with a second God in His eternal covenant with man as revealed in Jesus Christ. Nor does man become a second God when He takes part in this covenant and is delivered by this Deliverer. The one who enters into this covenant is always the creature, man, who would be absolutely threatened without this help and lost if thrown back upon his own resources. It is in the humanity, the saving work of Jesus Christ, that the connection between God and man is brought before us. It is in this alone that it takes place and is realized. Hence there is disparity between the relationship of God and man and the prior relationship of the Father to the Son and the Son to the Father, of God to Himself.[25]

But for all the disparity—and this is the positive sense of the term "image"— there is a correspondence and similarity between the two relationships.[26] This is not a correspondence and similarity of being, an *analogia entis*. The being

24. Note Barth's use of the word "indirect," which reflects his earlier distinction between direct and indirect knowledge of God (see chap. 16). While the human Jesus is a true revelation of God, this revelation is indirect because the flesh of Jesus is the creaturely medium through which God makes himself known.

25. The first thing that must be said about the image of God (*imago Dei*) in light of the human Jesus is that it reflects the difference between God and humanity. The eternal relationship between the Father and the Son is dissimilar in important ways to the relationship between God and the human Jesus.

26. The second thing that must be said about the *imago Dei* in light of Jesus is that the relationship between the God and the human Jesus corresponds to—and thus is similar to—the eternal relationship between the Father and Son. Since this similarity occurs within a greater dissimilarity, these relationships are *analogous* to one another.

of God cannot be compared with that of man. But it is not a question of this twofold being. It is a question of the relationship within the being of God on the one side and between the being of God and that of man on the other. Between these two relationships as such—and it is in this sense that the second is the image of the first—there is correspondence and similarity. There is an analogy of relation, an *analogia relationis*.[27] The correspondence and similarity of the two relationships consists in the fact that the freedom in which God posits Himself as the Father, is posited by Himself as the Son and confirms Himself as the Holy Ghost, is the same freedom as that in which He is the Creator of man, in which man may be His creature, and in which the Creator-creature relationship is established by the Creator. We can also put it in this way. The correspondence and similarity of the two relationships consists in the fact that the eternal love in which God as the Father loves the Son, and as the Son loves the Father, and in which God as the Father is loved by the Son and as the Son by the Father, is also the love which is addressed by God to man. The humanity of Jesus, His fellow-humanity, His being for man as the direct correlative of His being for God, indicates, attests and reveals this correspondence and similarity. It is not orientated and constituted as it is in a purely factual and perhaps accidental parallelism, or on the basis of a capricious divine resolve, but it follows the essence, the inner being of God. It is this inner being which takes this form outside himself in the humanity of Jesus, and in this form, for all the disparity of sphere and object, remains true to itself and therefore reflects itself.[28] Hence the factuality, the material necessity of the being of the man Jesus for His fellows, does not really rest on the mystery of an accident or caprice, but on the mystery of the purpose and meaning of God, who can maintain and demonstrate His essence even in His work, and in His relation to this work.

27. Barth depicts the correspondence that exists between the human Jesus and God as an analogy of relation (*analogia relationis*) rather than analogy of being (*analogia entis*). The two analogies are distinct because they compare different things. In an analogy of *being*, the *being* of God and the *being* of the human are compared to one another for their similarity and dissimilarity. The two parties in the analogy are God and the human. In an analogy of *relation*, the *relation* between the eternal Father and the eternal Son is compared to the *relation* between God and the human Jesus. The two parties in the analogy are the relationships.

28. Barth uses his analogy of relation to make the point that the relationship of the eternal Father and the eternal Son is similar to the relationship between God and the human Jesus. It is in this precise sense that the human Jesus's relation to other humans serves as a creaturely reflection or "image" of God. The human Jesus's relationship to other humans corresponds to God's relationship with him, which itself corresponds to the eternal relationship between the Father and the Son. The existence of this correspondence means that Jesus's life for others is a revelation of God. It also reveals God's will for humans: we image God in our humanity as we live for others in the same way Jesus did.

CHAPTER 23

God and Nothingness

Introduction

Barth describes that which opposes God's will for creation as *das Nichtige* or "nothingness." The word carries the sense of something that is void, futile, and empty. Barth depicts nothingness as a hostile enemy that opposes humans by undermining and undoing God's good will for their lives.

Barth defines nothingness carefully. He argues that it cannot be described on the basis of a general idea of evil or our own human experience because these starting points lead to an abstraction. He makes it clear that nothingness is neither the "shadow side" of creation nor a necessary by-product of God's good will. It also is not directly identical to *nothing*, as in the lack of something. Rather, nothingness is that which God rejects as he enacts his covenant of grace. It becomes visible in creation whenever something that God wills crosses the boundary into that which God does *not* will.

On the basis of this definition, Barth argues that nothingness can be understood rightly only from the perspective of God's revelation in Jesus Christ. Only when we see God's "Yes" do we also see that to which God says "No." We see the power of nothingness over humans whenever humans sin or in the event of their death. However, this power becomes most clearly visible only in Christ's death for human sins on the cross. But this event also marks the undoing of nothingness. When God raises Christ from the dead, he reveals that nothingness has been defeated once and for all. Even though this victory continues to be worked out in history, humans live with the certain knowledge that the power of nothingness will not prevail against them.

Barth has no interest in offering a theodicy that explains how evil fits into God's plan for creation because he insists that it does *not* fit into God's eternal plan. God opposes nothingness at every turn, and he does not use it to accomplish his good will even as he works to overcome it in Christ. This brings Barth to an important pastoral insight: God's wrath against human sin and evil does not change the reality that God is *for* the creature. God opposes sin, but he does not oppose sinners. Instead, God seeks to reconcile and restore sinners from the power of nothingness. He does so at his own expense by bearing the burden of sin on their behalf in Christ. This sacrifice testifies both to the depth of God's opposition to nothingness and to the depth of God's love.

Church Dogmatics III/3 [1]

There is opposition and resistance to God's world-dominion. There is in world-occurrence an element, indeed an entire sinister system of elements, which is not comprehended by God's providence in the sense thus far described, and which is not therefore preserved, accompanied, nor ruled by the almighty action of God like creaturely occurrence. It is an element to which God denies the benefit of His preservation, concurrence and rule, of His fatherly lordship, and which is itself opposed to being preserved, accompanied and ruled in any sense, fatherly or otherwise. There is amongst the objects of God's providence an alien factor. It cannot escape God's providence but is comprehended by it. The manner, however, in which this is done is highly peculiar in accordance with the particular nature of this factor. It is distinct from that in which God's providence rules the creature and creaturely occurrence. The result is that the alien factor can never be considered or mentioned together in the same context as other objects of God's providence. Thus the whole doctrine of God's providence must be investigated afresh. This opposition and resistance, this stubborn element and alien factor, may be provisionally defined as nothingness. . . .

How do we know that nothingness really exists, and does so in such a way, in such radical superiority, that it cannot be legitimately incorporated into any philosophical system, that we must not try to treat it as one element in

1. Karl Barth, *Church Dogmatics* III/3 (Edinburgh: T&T Clark, 1961), 289, 303–5, 310–12, 363.

the world among others? We know all this clearly, directly and certainly from
the source of all Christian knowledge, the knowledge of Jesus Christ.[2] It must
be clearly grasped that the incarnation of the Word of God was obviously
not necessary merely to reveal the goodness of God's creation in its twofold
form. To be sure, it gives us this revelation too. When God Himself became
a creature in Jesus Christ, He confirmed His creation in its totality as an act
of His wisdom and mercy, as His good creation without blemish or blame.
Yet much more than this was involved.[3] It is written that "the Word became
flesh," i.e., that it became not only a creature, but a creature in mortal peril,
a creature threatened and actually corrupted, a creature which in face and in
spite of its goodness, and in disruption and destruction of its imparted goodness, was subject not to an internal but to an external attack which it could
neither contain nor counter. The Word became a creature which had fallen
under the sway of a possessive and domineering alien, and was therefore itself
alienated from its Creator and itself, unable to recover or retrace its way home.
The Word became a creature to which it was of no avail to be the creature
of God, or to receive confirmation of its creation by Him, or to remember
the wisdom and mercy in which it was created, because it was betrayed and
haphazardly subjected to a determination inimical to its creation in wisdom
and mercy. That the Word became flesh means that the Word became a creature of this kind, a lost creature. That God's Word, God's Son, God Himself,
became flesh means no other than that God saw a challenge to Himself in
this assault on His creature, in this invading alien, in this other determination
of His creature, in its capture and self-surrender. It means that God took to
heart the attack on His creature because He saw in it an attack on His own
cause and therefore on Himself, seeing His own enemy in this domineering
alien, intruder, usurper and tyrant. God therefore arose, and in His Son gave
and humbled Himself, Himself becoming flesh, this ruined and lost human
creature, setting Himself wholly in the place of His work and possession. To
be sure, He did this in confirmation of His goodness as Creator and of that
of His creature. But for this reason He did so in His own most proper cause,

2. Barth's claim about the starting point for our knowledge of nothingness corresponds to
his method: dogmatics begins with God's revelation in Jesus Christ rather than with our own
observations. It also reflects Barth's conviction about nothingness itself. Nothingness is not
identical to nothing, the absence of something. Rather, nothingness is that which contradicts
God's will in his election of grace. It is that to which God says "No," a hostile power that stands
in opposition to the "Yes" that God proclaims to creation in Jesus Christ. As such, nothingness
can only be known in the light of Christ.

3. Barth's description of this additional information corresponds to his account of the
election of Jesus Christ and the place of the fall in the execution of this decision (see chaps. 19
and 20).

repelling an injury and insult offered to Himself. He did so in necessary and righteous wrath, not against His creature but against its temptation and destruction, against its deviation, defection and consequent degeneration. He did so as a Judge asserting His own right and therefore restoring that of His creature. And therefore in His Son He exposed Himself with it to this assault, to this alien, to this hostile determination, yielding to this adversary in solidarity with His creature, and in this way routing it, achieving what the creature, who was and is only secondary in this matter, could not accomplish but yet required for its deliverance.[4]

Our present interest in all this is that it is obviously the decisive ground of our knowledge of the whole problem with which we are concerned. Here we can see what nothingness is. Here we can see its true nature and reality. Here we can see that it is an antithesis not only to God's whole creation but to the Creator Himself. What challenged Him and provoked His wrath, what made Him come forth as the Judge, what made Him yield to nothingness in order to overcome it, was obviously nothing that He Himself had chosen, willed or done. It was nothing that He would or could previously have affirmed. It was nothing—day or night—that He as Creator had declared to be very good. It was nothing that could be considered the end and aim of His creation. That which rendered necessary the birth of His Son in the stable of Bethlehem and His death upon the cross of Calvary, that which by this birth and death He smote, defeated and destroyed, is that which primarily opposes and resists God Himself, and therefore all creation. It is obvious that this neither can nor may be understood as something which He Himself has posited or decreed, and that it cannot be subsumed under any synthesis. It thus demands on our part a wholly different seriousness from that imposed by life and the world— the seriousness of a radical fear and loathing founded on hope in the God who is primarily affected but who is omnipotent and supreme and therefore our only hope.[5] What is nothingness, the real nothingness which is not to

4. Note how positively Barth frames God's relationship to his creature here. God stands in solidarity with his creature who is good but under oppression. He so closely identifies with his creature that he sees an attack on it as a personal attack. He responds to this attack with wrath, *not* against the creature but against the prospect of its destruction. He comes as a righteous Judge, *not* to condemn the creature but to set things right for it. And God accomplishes these things by assuming the creature's plight and then defeating the power that subjects it on the creature's behalf. Barth's emphasis at every turn is that God is *for* his creature. The existence of evil and sin does nothing to change this posture.

5. Barth rejects any theodicy that explains the existence of evil by incorporating it into an account of God's sovereign plan for the world. He makes it clear: there is no relationship between God and evil other than absolute opposition. God does not will the existence of evil in any respect, nor does he use evil in the service of his eternal plan. Always and every moment, God opposes evil and works to overcome it for the sake of the creature.

be confounded with the negative side of God's good creation behind which it seeks to shelter for greater strength? What is nothingness unmasked and deprived of that camouflage by which it seeks to deceive us, and we ourselves? In plain and precise terms, the answer is that nothingness is the "reality" on whose account (i.e., against which) God Himself willed to become a creature in the creaturely world, yielding and subjecting Himself to it in Jesus Christ in order to overcome it. Nothingness is thus the "reality" which opposes and resists God, which is itself subjected to and overcome by His opposition and resistance, and which in this twofold determination as the reality that negates and is negated by Him, is totally distinct from Him. The true nothingness is that which brought Jesus Christ to the cross, and that which He defeated there. Only from the standpoint of Jesus Christ, His birth, death and resurrection, do we see it in reality and truth, without the temptation to treat it as something inclusive or relative, or to conceive it dialectically and thus render it innocuous. From this standpoint we see it with fear and trembling as the adversary with whom God and God alone can cope. But it is to be noted that in this we see it where our one real hope against it is grounded and established. If there is confusion concerning it, we obviously do not see it from the standpoint of Jesus Christ.[6] . . .

We have called sin the concrete form of nothingness because in sin it becomes man's own act, achievement and guilt. Yet nothingness is not exhausted in sin. It is also something under which we suffer in a connection with sin which is sometimes palpable but sometimes we can only sense and sometimes is closely hidden. In Holy Scripture, while man's full responsibility for its commission is maintained, even sin itself is described as his surrender to the alien power of an adversary.[7] Contrary to his will and expectation, the sin of man is not beneficial to him but detrimental. He is led astray and harms himself, or rather lets himself be harmed. He is not merely a thief but one

6. God does not create nothingness, nor is it a necessary by-product of creation or the shadow side of creation. Nothingness is that which God does *not* will in his election of grace, that to which God says "No" in Jesus Christ. The reality of its existence is the divine *non*-willing. Since God's will is the source and criterion of all good in creation, nothingness is intrinsically evil. It meets humans as a hostile power that stands against the reality God has established. Its form becomes visible within the world as God opposes it in Jesus Christ, particularly in his death and resurrection. At these key places—at the cross and the empty tomb—the outline of God's enemy becomes the most apparent.

7. While nothingness has no intrinsic reality and is not visible in and of itself, it is not identical to nothing. Nothingness is that which God does *not* will in his election of grace. It thus is real only in its opposition to God's will and action in creation. It takes a concrete form only when the creature—whose existence *is* willed by God—crosses into that which God does *not* will. This action is sin. Yet nothingness is not identical to the act of sin since it precedes this act and opposes the totality of the human's existence even as the human colludes with it.

who has himself fallen among thieves. Sin as such is not only an offense to God; it also disturbs, injures and destroys the creature and its nature. And although there can be no doubt that it is committed by man, it is obviously attended and followed by suffering, i.e., the suffering of evil and death. It is not merely attended and followed by the ills which are inseparably bound up with creaturely existence in virtue of the negative aspect of creation, but by the suffering of evil as something wholly anomalous which threatens and imperils this existence and is no less inconsistent with it than sin itself, as the preliminary experience of an absolutely alien factor which is radically opposed to the sense and purpose of creation and therefore to the Creator Himself. Nor is it a mere matter of dying as the natural termination of life, but of death itself as the intolerable, life-destroying thing to which all suffering hastens as its goal, as the ultimate irruption and triumph of that alien power which annihilates creaturely existence and thus discredits and disclaims the Creator. There is real evil and real death as well as real sin. In another connection it will be indicated that there is also a real devil with his legions, and a real hell. But here it will suffice to recognize real evil and real death. "Real" again means in opposition to the totality of God's creation. That nothingness has the form of evil and death as well as sin shows us that it is what it is not only morally but physically and totally. It is the comprehensive negation of the creature and its nature. And as such it is a power which, though unsolicited and uninvited, is superior, like evil and death, to all the forces which the creature can oppose to it. As negation nothingness has its own dynamic, the dynamic of damage and destruction with which the creature cannot cope. Knowledge of these important features is attained when it is seen in these forms, i.e., the forms of evil and death. Evil and death may be distinguished from sin in so far as they primarily and immediately attack the creature but indirectly and properly the Creator, whereas sin primarily and immediately attacks God and only indirectly the creature. Yet both attack the creature no less than God. And it is also a common feature that they are necessarily incomprehensible and inexplicable to us as creatures. It is absolutely essential that nothingness should be seen in all these forms and aspects if we are to understand what is at issue and to what we refer.[8]

But in this totality, in the form in which it is not merely evil but the supreme adversary and assailant, in the mode in which it must be suffered by

---

8. Evil and death also are concrete forms of nothingness because they mark the negation of God's will for the creature. They directly oppose the creature because they negate the creature's existence. This makes them different from sin, which directly opposes God by rejecting his will. For the background behind Barth's claims in this paragraph, see his account of God's decision for the world in chap. 20.

the creature, nothingness is to be known only at the heart of the Gospel, i.e., in Jesus Christ.[9] In the incarnation God exposed Himself to nothingness even as this enemy and assailant. He did so in order to repel and defeat it. He did so in order to destroy the destroyer. The Gospel records of the miracles and acts of Jesus are not just formal proofs of His Messiahship, of His divine mission, authority and power, but as such they are objective manifestations of His character as the Conqueror not only of sin but also of evil and death, as the Destroyer of the destroyer, as the Savior in the most inclusive sense. He not only forgives the sins of men; He also removes the source of their suffering. He resists the whole assault. To its power He opposes His own power, the transcendent power of God. He shows Himself to be the total Victor. He works as the perfect Comforter. This emphasis is unmistakeable in the New Testament, and if for any reason we erase it we necessarily annul its testimony and silence the voice of Him to whom it testifies.[10] For here there not only speaks but acts the One who has come to hurl Himself against the opposition and resistance of nothingness in its form as hostile and aggressive power. Here there speaks and acts the One who for the salvation of the creature and the glory of God has routed nothingness as the total principle of enmity, physical as well as moral. He is not only the way and the truth; He is also the life, the resurrection and the life. If He were not the Savior in this total sense, He would not be the Savior at all in the New Testament sense. It is a serious matter that all the Western as opposed to the Eastern Church has invariably succeeded in minimizing and devaluating, and still does so today, this New Testament emphasis. And Protestantism especially has always been far too moralistic and spiritualistic, and has thus been blind to this aspect of the Gospel. In this respect we have every cause to pay more attention rather than less. We certainly cannot afford to make arbitrary demarcations, and therefore not to see, or not to want to see, the total Savior of the New Testament. According to the New Testament, the last and true form in which Jesus exposed Himself to this total enemy is that of His crucifixion. He did it by suffering death, this death, the death of condemnation. The New Testament says that He suffered death for the forgiveness of the sins of many, but it also

9. If nothingness becomes visible only as God's creation crosses the frontier into that which God does not will—and if the human life of Jesus is the reason God created the world and the center of his divine will for the world—then it makes sense that nothingness becomes most fully visible in the death of Jesus Christ. The cross is the moment when the full measure of that which God opposes becomes clear.

10. It is interesting how Barth incorporates the ministry of Jesus as recorded in the Gospels into his account. When we see Jesus healing the sick, raising the dead, forgiving sins, and declaring the reality of God's kingdom, we are seeing Christ actively confront the power of nothingness.

says, and the two statements must not be dissociated, that He did so in order
to take away the power of death, real death, death as the condemnation and
destruction of the creature, death as the offender against God and the last
enemy. In His resurrection from the dead God reveals that He has done this.
His resurrection sums up the whole process of revelation. It is the manifestation of the divine act which according to the New Testament was effected in
His work, the work of His person. According to this witness, it shows that
His death is God's own reconciling and liberating act against nothingness,
in all its scope and dimensions.[11] But since this may be affirmed only of Him,
only of the divine act which, according to the witness of the New Testament,
was effected and revealed in Jesus Christ, from this standpoint too the only
knowledge which includes a knowledge of true nothingness is that of Jesus
Christ. In Him, i.e., in contradistinction to Him, nothingness is exposed in
its entirety as the adversary which can destroy both body and soul in hell, as
the evil one which is also the destructive factor of evil and death that stands
in sinister conflict against the creature and its Creator, not merely as an idea
which man may conceive and to which he can and does give allegiance but as
the power which invades and subjugates and carries him away captive, so that
he is wholly and utterly lost in face of it. In the incarnation Jesus Christ, God
Himself, has exposed Himself to this real nothingness. And He has proved
Himself to be its Victor. In so doing He has disclosed and revealed its true
nature and threat, its impotence against the creature, and its utter impotence
against the Creator. This being the case, we have every reason to adhere to
the truth that Jesus Christ Himself is the objective ground of our knowledge
even of nothingness. . . .

What is nothingness? In the knowledge and confession of the Christian
faith, i.e., looking retrospectively to the resurrection of Jesus Christ and pro-
spectively to His coming again, there is only one possible answer. Nothingness
is the past, the ancient menace, danger and destruction, the ancient non-being
which obscured and defaced the divine creation of God but which is consigned
to the past in Jesus Christ, in whose death it has received its deserts, being
destroyed with this consummation of the positive will of God which is as such
the end of His non-willing. Because Jesus is Victor, nothingness is routed and
extirpated. It is that which in this One who was both very God and very man

11. Barth insists that—despite the tendency among some Protestants to emphasize the cross
at the expense of the empty tomb—Jesus's death and resurrection must be held together and
emphasized equally. Christ's death marks his subjection to the power of nothingness and thus
is its chief visible form; his resurrection marks God's victory over this enemy for the sake of the
human Jesus and those united to him. Together they reveal God's overcoming of nothingness
on behalf of the people subjected to it.

has been absolutely set behind, not only by God, but in unity with Him by man and therefore the creature. It is that from whose influence, dominion and power the relationship between Creator and creature was absolutely set free in Jesus Christ, so that it is no longer involved in their relationship as a third factor. This is what has happened to nothingness once and for all in Jesus Christ. This is its status and appearance now that God has made His own and carried through the conflict with it in His Son. It is no longer to be feared. It can no longer "nihilate."[12] But obviously we may make these undoubtedly audacious statements only on the ground of one single presupposition. The aspect of creaturely activity both as a whole and in detail, our consciousness both of the world and of self, certainly do not bear them out. But what do we really know of it as taught by this consciousness? How can this teach us the truth that it is really past and done with? The only valid presupposition is a backward look to the resurrection of Jesus Christ and a forward look to His coming in glory, i.e., the look of Christian faith as rooted in and constantly nourished by the Word of God.[13]

12. The death and resurrection of Jesus Christ expose nothingness in its real form: it is both the power that opposes God and the totality of creaturely life *and* the power that has been defeated by God in Jesus Christ for the sake of his creatures. Both affirmations must be made in their fullness if we are to speak rightly of nothingness.

13. Barth issues a final caution. The claim about the defeat of nothingness is not the result of optimism, a belief in the kindness of God, or a weakened sense of the power of evil. This claim is based solely on God's revelation in Jesus Christ and the victory won in him. The proper response to this claim, and thus to nothingness itself, is faith and hope.

24

God with Us

Introduction

This selection introduces several themes Barth will develop at length in his doctrine of reconciliation in *Church Dogmatics* IV/1–4. It is one of the most clarifying sections in Barth's dogmatics because it applies several key ideas Barth developed in earlier volumes directly to Christ's saving work. This passage is the moment at which the reader begins to see the goals toward which Barth's theology has been moving all along. For this reason, much of the material in this section might seem familiar. Several of the claims Barth makes here had been a part of his theology for decades prior, including his claim that God's relationship with humanity takes place in and through the saving work of Jesus Christ. But with the content of the earlier volumes working behind and alongside him, Barth's claims now possess a new depth and power.

He argues that Jesus Christ reveals that God has freely decided to live his eternal life in union with humanity. God and humans will live together in a "common history," a covenantal partnership ordered around the saving work of Christ and the Spirit. At the center of this work is Christ's descent into the depths to bear the burden of human sin as humanity's representative. This substitutionary act means that God's relationship with humanity is not a general relationship between divinity and humanity but a particular one centered on Christ's death for the sins of humanity.

Barth emphasizes that Christ's saving work corresponds to God's plan from the beginning. God did not create humans and then later decide to save them; rather, God decided to save humanity in Christ and then created them. This means that human life has to be approached from an eschatological perspective. The truth about human beings is not located in their created being, nor does God save humans merely to return them to their original state. Humans were created to be what they will become in and through Christ.

Barth explains this idea by appealing to the concept of participation: Jesus Christ takes on human flesh so that humans can participate in the being of God. He cautions that this participation does not mean that humans are absorbed into the divine life. Instead, they live in union with Christ as they respond to his Word with gratitude and obedience by serving others. The distinguishing act of this service is their testimony in the world and their lives marked by the qualities of faith, hope, and love.

———————————————— *Church Dogmatics* IV/1[1] ————————————————

1. Our starting-point is that this "God with us" at the heart of the Christian message is the description of an act of God, or better, of God Himself in this act of His. It is a report, not therefore a statement of fact on the basis of general observation or consideration. God with us, or what is meant by these three words, is not an object of investigation or speculation. It is not a state, but an event. God *is*, of course, and that in the strictest sense originally and properly, so that everything else which is, in a way which cannot be compared at all with His being, can be so only through Him, only in relation to Him, only from Him and to Him. Now even when He is "with us," He is what He is, and in the way that He is; and all the power and truth of His being "with us" is the power and truth of His incomparable being which is proper to Him and to Him alone, His being as God. He is both in His life in eternity in Himself, and also in His life as Creator in the time of the world created by Him; by and in Himself, and also above and in this world, and therefore according to the heart of the Christian message with us men. And He is who He is, and lives as what He is, in that He does what He does. How can we know God if His being is unknown or obscure or indifferent? But how can we know God if we do not find the truth and power of His being in His life, and of His life in His act? We know about God only if we are witnesses—however distantly and modestly—of His act. And we speak about God only as we can

1. Karl Barth, *Church Dogmatics* IV/1 (Edinburgh: T&T Clark, 1956), 6–16.

do so—however deficiently—as those who proclaim His act. "God with us" as it occurs at the heart of the Christian message is the attestation and report of the life and act of God as the One who is.[2]

But if it means that God is with us—and the message of the Christian community certainly implies that it does really apply to us men—then that presupposes that we men, in our own very different way, which cannot be compared with the being of God, but which on the basis of the divine being and life and act is a very real way, that we also *are*, and that we are in that we live in our time, and that we live in that we ourselves act in our own act. If the fact that God is with us is a report about the being and life and act of God, then from the very outset it stands in a relationship to our own being and life and acts. A report about ourselves is included in that report about God. We cannot therefore take cognizance of it, be more or less impressed by it, and then leave it as the report of something which has taken place in a quite different sphere in which we ourselves have no place. It tells us that we ourselves are in the sphere of God. It applies to us by telling us of a history which God wills to share with us and therefore of an invasion of our history—indeed, of the real truth about our history as a history which is by Him and from Him and to Him.[3] The divine being and life and act takes place with ours, and it is only as the divine takes place that ours takes place. To put it in the simplest way, what unites God and us men is that He does not will to be God without us, that He creates us rather to share with us and therefore with our being and life and act His own incomparable being and life and act, that He does not allow His history to be His and ours ours, but causes them to take place as a common history. That is the special truth which the Christian message has to proclaim at its very heart.[4]

2. Even as Barth affirms that God is "with us," he still does not believe we can know God on our terms. He maintains his conviction that God's distinction from creation means that humans are unable to know God under their own power. Humans are able to know God only as God personally reveals himself to them in an event of revelation. The good news is that this revelation enables humans to know the real God, even if only indirectly and through creaturely mediation, because the revelation is identical to the revealer.

3. The idea that God's revelation unveils the "real truth" about creaturely history goes back to Barth's commentary *The Epistle to the Romans*. In light of his theological development, however, Barth's description of the content of this true history is much more concrete than it was in that volume.

4. These striking claims stem from Barth's doctrines of election and theological anthropology (see chaps. 18–19 and 22). God's self-revelation in Jesus Christ reveals that God has decided to live his own eternal life together with humans in the midst of a "common history," a covenant of grace. Jesus stands at the center of covenant because—as the Son of God in human flesh—he is the one who fulfills its promises on both the divine and human side. So the message "God with us" brings news about both God and humanity: God has determined that humans will be his people because he has decided to be their God in Jesus Christ. Human life is determined by God and for God.

2. We have just said, and this is what is meant in the Christian message, that we have to do with an event, with an act of God. The whole being and life of God is an activity, both in eternity and in worldly time, both in Himself as Father, Son and Holy Spirit, and in His relation to man and all creation. But what God does in Himself and as the Creator and Governor of man is all aimed at the particular act in which it has its centre and meaning. And everything that He wills has its ground and origin in what is revealed as His will in this one act. Thus it is not merely one amongst others of His works as Creator and Governor. Of course, it can and must be understood in this way, in accordance with the general will and work of God. But within this outer circle it forms an inner. The one God wills and works all things, but here He wills and works a particular thing: not one with others, but one for the sake of which He wills and works all others. As one with others this act is also the goal of all the acts of God; of the eternal activity in which He is both in Himself and in the history of His acts in the world created by Him. It is of this that the "God with us" speaks.

Therefore even from the standpoint of us men the "God with us" does not refer to the existence of man generally as the creaturely object of the will and work of His Lord. It does refer to it. It includes it. The being, life and act of man is always quite simply his history in relation to the being, life and act of his Creator. We can say the same of all creatures. But it is far more than this. For within and beyond this general activity, God Himself in His being, life and act as Creator wills and works a special act. All His activity has its heart and end in a single act. Within and out of the general history, which with all creatures man can have in common with God in His being, life and act, there arises this act of God and that which corresponds to it in the being, life and activity of man, as a qualified history, his true history. And if the "God with us" at the heart of the Christian message speaks of the unifying factor between God and man, it speaks of a specific conjoining of the two, not always and everywhere but in a single and particular event which has a definite importance for all time and space but which takes place once and for all in a definite here and now.[5]

3. From the standpoint of its meaning the particularity of this event consists in the fact that it has to do with the salvation of man, that in it the general

5. Barth is emphasizing the need for particularity and concreteness in our account of God's life with us. God does not relate to humans in a general way, as if he creates us so that we are simply "with" him in some sense. God's will is specific: he has decided to live with humans in and through the flesh of Jesus Christ. Any account of God's relationship with humanity must begin with the particular reality of Jesus and what he reveals about the content of God's decision for created history and humanity.

history which is common to God and man, to God and all creation, becomes at its very heart and end a redemptive history. Salvation is more than being. Salvation is fulfillment, the supreme, sufficient, definitive and indestructible fulfillment of being. Salvation is the perfect being which is not proper to created being as such but is still future. Created being as such needs salvation, but does not have it: it can only look forward to it. To that extent salvation is its *eschaton*. Salvation, fulfillment, perfect being means—and this is what created being does not have in itself—being which has a part in the being of God, from which and to which it is: not a divinized being but a being which is hidden in God, and in that sense (distinct from God and secondary) eternal being. Since salvation is not proper to created being as such, it can only come to it, and since it consists in participation in the being of God it can come only from God.[6] The coming of this salvation is the grace of God—using the word in its narrower and most proper sense. In the wider sense the creation, preservation and over-ruling of the world and man are already grace. For if this is not proper to created being as such, it can only come to it. Only from God as the One who is originally and properly can it come about that it also has being, that it is, and not that it is not. And by that very fact there is always held out to it the opportunity of salvation: the expectation of being in perfection in participation in the divine being. But the "God with us" at the heart of the Christian message does not mean this general grace. It means the redemptive grace of God. It is this which constitutes, factually, the singularity of the event. It is this which marks out the event within the whole history of the togetherness of God and man. Not merely the creating, preserving and over-ruling of created being, not merely the creating of an opportunity for salvation, but the fact that it actually comes, that God gives it. God gives to created being what can only be given to it and what can be given only by Him. And He does really give it: Take what is mine—this final, supreme, unsurpassable gift; take it, it is meant for you. It is because it has to do with this that the activity of God indicated by the "God with us" is singular and unique. And so, too, is the invasion of the history of our own human being, life and activity described by this "God with us." And so, too, is the whole circle of God in which we find ourselves according to this center

6. Barth's description of salvation is bold: it is a participation in the being of God. This idea has to be defined with care. This participation is by grace rather than nature, and so it is something that happens *to* humans rather than the natural fulfillment of their being. It takes place strictly because the Son of God has assumed human flesh so that humans can live "in him" by the power of the Spirit. Barth also emphasizes human participation in God in Christ does not involve the merging of humanity and divinity, as if humans cease to be creatures. Rather, this participation takes the form of a distinct relationship, one that occurs as Christ relates to the human as Lord and the human responds in faith and obedience.

of the Christian message.[7] The general grace of God in creation, preservation and over-ruling still remains. That is already grace. We recognize it distinctly as such only when we see God and ourselves in the inner and special circle of His will and work, in the light of this one, particular, redemptive act of God. It is only from this standpoint that the general grace of being and the opportunity which it offers can and do become a subject for genuine gratitude and a source of serious dedication. For here it is provided that that opportunity is not offered in vain, that it is actually taken, taken by God Himself. What concerns us here is the redemptive grace of God, and to that extent something that is more and greater.[8]

4. In the light of this we must now try to outline this particular event with rather greater precision. According to the Christian message "God with us" means God with the man for whom salvation is intended and or-dained as such, as the one who is created, preserved and over-ruled by God as man. It is not as though the expectation belonged to his created being. It is not as though he had any kind of claim to it. God cannot be forced to give us a part in His divine being. The matter might have ended quite well with that general grace of being—which even in itself is great enough. But where God is not bound and man has no claim, even more compelling is the will and plan and promise of God. It goes beyond, or rather it precedes His will and work as Creator. Therefore it has to be distinguished from it, as something prior, which precedes it. The ordaining of salvation for man and of man for salvation is the original and basic will of God, the ground and purpose of His will as Creator. It is not that He first wills and works the being of the world and man, and then ordains it to salvation. But God creates, preserves and over-rules man for this prior end and with this prior purpose, that there may be a being distinct from Himself ordained for salvation, for perfect being, for participation in His own being, because as the One who loves in freedom He has determined to exercise redemptive grace—and that there may be an object of this His redemptive grace, a

7. Grace can be described in different ways. There is the grace of creation in which God gives creatures being, preserves them in their existence, and oversees their lives in accordance with his sovereign will and plan. This kind of grace is distinct from saving grace, which breaks into creation as a new and unique event when God reconciles sinners in and through Jesus Christ. Barth insists that God's relationship with us is determined solely by saving grace. As a result, he argues that we know what it means to say "God with us" only by looking at God's relationship to us in Christ rather than God's relationship to us in his act of creation.

8. Barth extends his argument a bit further: since we understand God's relationship with us only through God's saving grace in Jesus Christ, this grace also is necessary to understand how God relates to us in his act of creation and his providential oversight. We will know the truth about creaturely being and history only when we see them in light of Jesus (see chap. 21).

partner to receive it.[9] A further point which we must now make in describing the event indicated by the "God with us" is this. The "God with us" has nothing to do with chance. As a redemptive happening it means the revelation and confirmation of the most primitive relationship between God and man, that which was freely determined in eternity by God Himself before there was any created being. In the very fact that man is, and that he is man, he is as such chosen by God for salvation; that *eschaton* is given him by God. Not because God owes it to him. Not in virtue of any quality or capacity of his own being. Completely without claim. What takes place between God and man in that particular redemptive history is fulfillment to this extent too, that in it God—the eternal will of God with man—is justified, the eternal righteousness of His grace is active and revealed, in and with the divine right, and so too the right which He has freely given and ascribed to man by determining this concerning him. It belongs to the character of this event and its particularity that with the end it reveals the basis and beginning of all things—the glory of God, which is that of His free love, and with it—well below, but eternally grounded upon it—the dignity of man, that dignity with which He willed to invest man although it is not proper to him.[10]

5. But again we must go further. "God with us" in the sense of the Christian message means God with us men who have forfeited the predetermined salvation, forfeited it with a supreme and final jeopardizing even of our creaturely existence. As the way from that beginning in God to the end of man with God is revealed in this particular event, its line is not a straight one, but one which is radically and—if God Himself were not there as hope—hopelessly broken. The situation of man in this event is this. He occupies a position quite different from that which he ought to occupy according to the divine intention. He does not conduct himself as the partner God has given Himself to receive His redemptive grace. He has opposed his ordination to salvation. He

9. Barth now turns to the task of offering a concrete account of human being. We will know what it means to be human when we see humanity not in light of God's act of creation but in light of God's purpose for creation. After all, God did not create humans first and then later decide to save them; he created them after he already had decided to save them in Jesus Christ. When God created humanity, he had the life of the human Jesus in mind, and so Jesus's life reveals God's purpose for humans: they are destined to participate in the life of God in and through him.

10. Barth emphasizes that God's decision to save humans in Christ is not random but purposeful. This decision reflects God's perfect will, and it is enacted in a way that corresponds to God's freedom and love. This divine purpose also establishes and upholds human worth: as God reconciles humanity, they are able to live as his covenant partners and fulfill the purpose for which they were created.

has turned his back on the salvation which actually comes to him. He does not find the fulfillment of his being in participation in the being of God by the gift of God. Instead, he aims at another salvation which is to be found in the sphere of his creaturely being and attained by his own effort. His belief is that he can and should find self-fulfillment. He has himself become an *eschaton*. This is the man with whom God is dealing in this particular redemptive history: the man who has made himself quite impossible in relation to the redemptive grace of God; and in so doing, the man who has made himself quite impossible in his created being as man, who has cut the ground from under his feet, who has lost his whole reason for existence.[11] What place has he before God when he has shown himself to be so utterly unworthy of that for which he was created by God, so utterly inept, so utterly unsuitable? when he has eliminated himself? What place is there for his being, his being as man, when he has denied his goal, and therefore his beginning and meaning, and when he confronts God in this negation? Despising the dignity with which God invested him, he has obviously forfeited the right which God gave and ascribed to him as the creature of God. But it is with this lost son in a far country, with man as he has fallen and now exists in this sorry plight, that God has to do in this redeeming event.[12] And this is what reveals the gulf. This is what shows us how it stands between God and man. This is where we see the inadequacy of the partner, the point where the relationship breaks down. At a pinch this can be overlooked if we do not think of the redeeming event as the heart and end of their interconnection, if we conceive it abstractly as the interconnection of Creator and creature. We may take this antithesis very seriously, but we shall always have good grounds to think of it as an antithesis which can be bridged. As such it does not contain any breach, any gulf, any enmity, either on the one side or on the other, any judgment and punishment on the part of God or suffering on the part of man. But this cannot possibly be overlooked in the redeeming event referred to in the "God with us." On the

11. A striking aspect of Barth's discussion of sin is his idea that to live in sin is to live an impossible existence. This claim makes sense within the context of Barth's doctrine of election. If God's election of Jesus Christ is the basis of the created world and human being, then this decision defines reality. A *real* human is one who corresponds to God's decision by living as the covenant partner of God in the world. To reject God's will and break from the covenant is to cross into that which God does *not* will for his creation, the nothingness that God rejects. It is to move from reality into unreality by seeking to be human in an impossible way—a way other than the one true possibility God has established for human life (see chap. 23).

12. Barth is comparing sinful humans to the prodigal son from Jesus's parable in Luke 15:11–32. This comparison is significant because Barth will use it as a template for his account of reconciliation: God saves his prodigal children by sending Jesus Christ into the far country to make their plight God's own (see chap. 25).

contrary, what constitutes the particularity of this event is that as a redeeming event, as the fulfillment of the gracious will of God, as the reaffirmation of His right and ours, it can be conceived only in the form of a Yet and a Nevertheless, which means that it cannot be conceived at all. If man has forfeited his salvation, what do we have to grasp in this event but the inconceivable fact that all the same it is given to him? If in so doing man has lost his creaturely being, what do we have to grasp but again the inconceivable fact that all the same he will not be lost? Is it not the case that only here, in the light of the antithesis which is here revealed and overcome, is grace really known as grace, that is, as free grace, as mercy pure and simple, as pure fact, having its basis only in itself, in the fact that it is posited by God? For who really knows what grace is until he has seen it at work here: as the grace which is *for* man when, because man is wholly and utterly a sinner before God, it can only be against him, and when in fact, even while it is for him, it is also a plaintiff and judge against him, showing him to be incapable of satisfying either God or himself?[13] And looking back once again, it is the grace of God as mercy pure and simple, as a sheer Yet and Nevertheless, which reveals, and by which we have to measure, how it stands with the man to whom it is granted. It is not independent reflection on the part of man, or an abstract law, but grace which shows incontrovertibly that man has forfeited his salvation and in so doing fatally jeopardized his creaturely being—which reveals his sin and the misery which is its consequence. From the redemption which takes place here we can gather from what it is that man is redeemed; from the pure fact of the salvation which comes to man without and in spite of his own deserts we may know the brute fact which he for his part dares to set against God. Because the "God with us" at the heart of the Christian message has to do with that pure fact of the divine mercy, we must not fail to recognize but acknowledge without reserve that we, and those for whom God is according to this message, are those who have nothing to bring Him but a confession of this brute fact: "Father, I have sinned."[14]

6. But if the Christian "God with us" does nevertheless speak, not of a renunciation, but of the fulfillment of the redemptive will of God in that event,

13. Barth insists that the truth about God's relationship with humanity cannot be known on the basis of God's act of creation alone because creation does not reveal the true nature of this relationship. The gulf between God and humanity does not merely reflect the distinction between Creator and creature, but it also reflects the reality of human sin against God. Any true account of God's relationship with humans must account for human fallenness as well as their finitude, and this means that this relationship must be described in light of God's saving grace in Jesus Christ. For an early form of this argument, see chap. 7.

14. Barth argues that humans can recognize the depth of their sin only in light of what Jesus Christ does to overcome it at the cross and the empty tomb.

then no matter how inconceivable may be that which we have to grasp in this connection, it refers to something quite different from the blind paradox of an arbitrary act of the divine omnipotence of grace. We are confronted here by the determination of that event which reveals unequivocally its uniqueness amongst the acts of God, that it declares an absolutely unique being and attitude and activity on the part of God. "God with us" means more than God over or side by side with us, before or behind us. It means more than His divine being in even the most intimate active connection with our human being otherwise peculiar to Him. At this point, at the heart of the Christian message and in relation to the event of which it speaks, it means that God has made Himself the One who fulfills His redemptive will. It means that He Himself in His own person—at His own cost but also on His own initiative—has become the inconceivable Yet and Nevertheless of this event, and so its clear and well-founded and legitimate, its true and holy and righteous Therefore. It means that God has become man in order as such, but in divine sovereignty, to take up our case. What takes place in this work of inconceivable mercy is, therefore, the free over-ruling of God, but it is not an arbitrary overlooking and ignoring, not an artificial bridging, covering-over or hiding, but a real closing of the breach, gulf and abyss between God and us for which we are responsible. At the very point where we refuse and fail, offending and provoking God, making ourselves impossible before Him and in that way missing our destiny, treading under foot our dignity, forfeiting our right, losing our salvation and hopelessly compromising our creaturely being—at that very point God Himself intervenes as man.[15] Because He is God He is able not only to be God but also to be this man. Because He is God it is necessary that He should be man in quite a different way from all other men; that He should do what we do not do and not do what we do. Because He is God He puts forth His omnipotence to be this other man, to be man quite differently, in our place and for our sake. Because He is God He has and exercises the power as this man to suffer for us the consequence of our transgression, the wrath and penalty which necessarily fall on us, and in that way to satisfy

---

15. Barth is drawing an important distinction here. The fact that God's relationship with creation is determined by the election of grace does not mean that God establishes a *general* relationship of grace with humans in creation. Grace is not a principle or a constantly available feature of human existence. Rather, God's covenant of grace establishes a *particular* relationship of grace with humans in the flesh of Jesus Christ. As the Son of God in human flesh, he meets humanity in their concrete need and makes it his own. He bears the burden of sin and its consequences on their behalf, and he does this at his own expense even to the point of death. In this sense, Jesus Christ himself is the relationship that God establishes with humanity. The election of grace is not the establishment of a general principle but God's decision to give himself in the person of the incarnate Jesus.

Himself in our regard. And again because He is God, He has and exercises the power as this man to be His own partner in our place, the One who in free obedience accepts the ordination of man to salvation which we resist, and in that way satisfies us, i.e., achieves that which can positively satisfy us.[16] That is the absolutely unique being, attitude and activity of God to which the "God with us" at the heart of the Christian message refers. It speaks of the peace which God Himself in this man has made between Himself and us.

We see the seriousness and force of the divine redemptive will in the fact that it is not too little and not too much for Him to make peace between Himself and us. To that end He gives Himself. He, the Creator, does not scorn to become a creature, a man like us, in order that as such He may bear and do what must be borne and done for our salvation. On the contrary, He finds and defends and vindicates His glory in doing it. Again, we see our own perversion and corruption, we see what is our offense and plight, in the fact that God (who never does anything unnecessary) can obviously be satisfied only by this supreme act, that only His own coming as man is sufficient to make good the evil which has been done. So dark is our situation that God Himself must enter and occupy it in order that it may be light. We cannot fully understand the Christian "God with us" without the greatest astonishment at the glory of the divine grace and the greatest horror at our own plight.

But even when we understand the entry of God for us in becoming man as the making of peace between Himself and us, we have still not said the decisive thing about this action. What He effects and does and reveals by becoming man—for us—is much more than the restoration of the situation as it previously had been—the obviating of the loss caused by our own transgression and our restoration to the place of promise and expectation of the salvation ordained for us. God makes Himself the means of His own redemptive will, but He is obviously more than this means. And in making peace by Himself He obviously gives us more than this peace, i.e., more than a restoration to wholeness, more than the preserving and assuring to us of our creaturely being and this as our opportunity for salvation. For when God makes Himself the means of His redemptive will to us, this will and we ourselves attain our goal. What is, at first only God's gracious answer to our failure, God's gracious

---

16. Barth's emphasis on substitution will play a major role throughout his doctrine of reconciliation. Here Barth emphasizes that Christ's partnership with humans involves standing in their place as their substitute and representative. From this position, Christ accomplishes two things simultaneously: he bears the burden of human sin so they can relate to God *and* he maintains the consistency of God's perfect being and will in his relationship with humans. That Christ can accomplish both things stems from his identity as the eternal Son in human flesh, the one who is truly God and truly human.

help in our plight, and even as such great and wonderful enough, is—when God Himself is the help and answer—His participation in our being, life and activity and therefore obviously our participation in His; and therefore it is nothing more nor less than the coming of salvation itself, the presence of the *eschaton* in all its fullness. The man in whom God Himself intervenes for us, suffers and acts for us, closes the gap between Himself and us as our representative, in our name and on our behalf, this man is not merely the confirmation and guarantee of our salvation, but because He is God He is salvation, our salvation. He is not merely the redeemer of our being but as such the giver and Himself the gift of its fulfillment and therefore the goal and end of the way of God—and all that as the peacemaker and savior.[17] It is when this great thing takes place that there takes place the even greater. This great thing is included in the "God with us" of the Christian message in so far as this speaks of God's intervening and becoming man, but in this great thing there is also included the even greater, indeed the greatest of all.

7. From all this it is surely obvious that the "God with us" carries with it in all seriousness a "We with God": the fact that we ourselves are there in our being, life and activity.

This does not seem to be apparent at a first glance. For who are we? We have seen already that we are (1) those whose history is absorbed into the history of the acts of God, and (2) made to participate in that event which is the center and end of all the divine acts, and (3) given a share in the grace with which God actually brings salvation to man, and (4) that we are such as those whom God has thereto ordained from all eternity, but unfortunately (5) we are those who have refused His salvation and in that way denied their own destiny and perverted and wasted and hopelessly compromised their own being, life and activity, who inevitably therefore find themselves disqualified and set aside as participants in that event, and cannot be considered in relation to it. Yet beyond that and in a sense conclusively (6) we are those whose place has been taken by another, who lives and suffers and acts for them, who for them makes good that which they have spoiled, who—for them, but also without them and even against them—is their salvation. That is what we are. And what is left to us? What place is there for us when we are like that? In what sense is the history of the acts of God at this center and end our history? Are

17. Barth argues that the more "decisive" or significant implication of God's decision to unite human flesh in Jesus Christ is that it reveals the purpose for which humans were created. Salvation does not involve returning humans to their original created state. It involves God's participation in human being in Christ and humanity's participation in the life of God through Christ. God's true purpose for humanity lies in the future, and the union of God and humanity in Christ is the moment when this future breaks into the present.

we not without history? Have we not become mere objects? Have we not lost all responsibility? Are we not reduced to mere spectators? Is not our being deprived of all life or activity? Or does it not lack all significance as our life and activity? "God with us"—that is something which we can easily understand even in these circumstances. But how is it to include within it a "We with God"? And if it does not, how can it really be understood as a "God with us"?

The answer is that we ourselves are directly summoned, that we are lifted up, that we are awakened to our own truest being as life and act, that we are set in motion by the fact that in that one man God has made Himself our peacemaker and the giver and gift of our salvation. By it we are made free for Him. By it we are put in the place which comes to us where our salvation (really ours) can come to us from Him (really from Him). This actualization of His redemptive will by Himself opens up to us the one true possibility of our own being. Indeed, what remains to us of life and activity in the face of this actualization of His redemptive will by Himself can only be one thing. This one thing does not mean the extinguishing of our humanity, but its establishment.[18] It is not a small thing, but the greatest of all. It is not for us a passive presence as spectators, but our true and highest activation—the magnifying of His grace which has its highest and most profound greatness in the fact that God has made Himself man with us, to make our cause His own, and as His own to save it from disaster and to carry it through to success. The genuine being of man as life and activity, the "We with God," is to affirm this, to admit that God is right, to be thankful for it, to accept the promise and the command which it contains, to exist as the community, and responsibly in the community, of those who know that this is all that remains to us, but that it does remain to us and that for all men everything depends upon its coming to pass. And it is this "We with God" that is meant by the Christian message in its central "God with us," when it proclaims that God Himself has taken our place, that He Himself has made peace between Himself and us, that by Himself He has accomplished our salvation, i.e., our participation in His being.[19]

18. Humans were not created simply to be creatures. They were created to be what they will become in and through the saving work of Jesus Christ. Christ's saving work thus does not negate or undermine the reality of human existence, as if the current state of human existence sets the standard. Christ brings human nature to its fulfillment by making them participants in the life of God.

19. God created the world in order to give himself to humans in Jesus Christ so they can live as participants in his own divine being and life. This involves not their absorption into God but their establishment as distinct beings who live in correspondence to God. They live in gratitude, obedience, and responsibility to God as they give themselves to others as God has given himself to them in Christ.

This "We with God" enclosed in the "God with us" is Christian faith, Christian love and Christian hope. These are the magnifying of the grace of God which still remain to us—and remain to us as something specifically human, as the greatest thing of all, as action in the truest sense of the word. We do not forget that it is a matter of magnifying God out of the depths. Our magnifying of God can only be that of the transgressors and rebels that we are, those who have missed their destiny, and perverted and wasted their being, life and activity. Therefore our magnifying of God cannot seek and find and have its truth and power in itself, but only in God, and therefore in that one Man in whom God is for us, who is our peace and salvation. Our faith, therefore, can only be faith in Him, and cannot live except from Him as its object. Our love can only be by Him, and can only be strong from Him as its basis. Our hope can only be hope directed upon Him, and can only be certain hope in Him as its content. Our faith, love and hope and we ourselves—however strong may be our faith, love and hope—live only by that which we cannot create, posit, awaken or deserve. And although our believing, loving and hoping themselves and as such are in us, they are not of us, but of their object, basis and content, of God, who in that one man not only answers for us with Him but answers for Himself with us, who gives it to us in freedom that we may believe, love and hope: open eyes, ears and hearts for Himself and His work, knowledge to the foolish, obedience to the wayward, freedom to the bound, life to the victims of death; and all in such a way that the glory of our own being, life and activity is still His, and can be valued, and exalted and respected by us only as His; but all in such a way that in and with His glory we too are really exalted, because in the depths where we can only give Him the glory, we find our true and proper place. It is in this way and in this sense that the Christian community proclaims "We with God" when it proclaims "God with us."[20]

20. Barth describes human relationship to God as taking concrete form in the acts of faith, hope, and love. They begin by acknowledging the nature of their relationship with God: they are sinners who relate to God because God sought them out to reconcile them to himself. They live by *faith* because their entire lives are centered on God and his action; they live in *love* as they receive the love of God and correspond to it; and they live in *hope* for their future life with God. Since these actions occur as a response to God's action, their lives testify to God's relationship with them and thus glorify God.

25

The Obedience of the Son of God

Introduction

This excerpt from *Church Dogmatics* IV/1 features Barth's treatment of the doctrine of the atonement. This doctrine addresses the question of how Jesus Christ's death on the cross deals with the problem of human sin. Barth begins his answer to this question by arguing that the atonement is not a theory but a *person*. The church should not think primarily about its own explanation of what Christ's death accomplishes, but instead it should focus on what Christ's self-sacrificial death reveals about God's being and character. Only then will the truth about what Christ's death achieves become apparent.

Barth's argument on this point is shaped by a key presupposition: the Son of God does not change or cease to be God when he bears the burden of sin in the flesh of Jesus Christ. How could Christ's death on the cross bring salvation if he is something other than truly God at that moment? Barth emphasizes this point strongly and repeatedly: the fullness of deity is present in Christ when he dies on the cross. Barth then concludes that, if Christ is fully God at the cross, then his death is a revelation of God.

The revelation challenges our ideas about God because the humility and obedience Christ displays on the cross run against the grain of human expectations about the nature of deity. Barth argues that theologians face a stark choice at this precise point. On the one hand, they can define the being of God in terms of the "supreme attributes" that stand in contradiction to qualities like humility and obedience. When Christ displays these attributes on the cross, they then must posit the existence of a "contradiction or rift" in the being of God and conclude that Christ is something other than fully God at this moment. Or, on the other hand, they can base their account of God's being strictly upon what God reveals about his being in Jesus Christ. This means that when Christ displays humility and obedience on the cross, they respond not by rejecting this revelation but by reformulating their prior ideas about the nature of deity in light of what Christ reveals. Barth adopts this latter approach because he thinks the former approach falls into abstraction.

Barth then draws out the implications of Christ's revelation on the cross for the triune life of God. He arrives at a bold and provocative conclusion: if the humility and obedience that Jesus Christ displays on the cross are proper to the eternal being of God, then God must be a God who both commands and obeys within his own triune life. His explanation of this idea makes this one of the most powerful and contested passages in Barth's *Church Dogmatics*.

———————————— *Church Dogmatics* IV/1[1] ————————————

The atonement is history. To know it, we must know it as such. To think of it, we must think of it as such. To speak of it, we must tell it as history. To try to grasp it as supra-historical or non-historical truth is not to grasp it at all. It is indeed truth, but truth actualized in a history and revealed in this history as such—revealed, therefore, as history.[2]

But the atonement is the very special history of God with man, the very special history of man with God. As such it has a particular character and demands particular attention. As such it underlies and includes, not only in principle and virtually but also actually, the most basic history of every man. It is the first and most inward presupposition of his existence, and it reveals itself as such. First of all, there took place and does take place the history of God with man and man with God, and then and for that reason and definitely on that basis man exists, and he can be called to knowledge and his own fully responsible decision and in that way have an actual part in that happening. The atonement takes precedence of all other history. It proves itself in fully

1. Karl Barth, *Church Dogmatics* IV/1 (Edinburgh: T&T Clark, 1956), 158–59, 177, 179–80, 183–84, 186–88, 192–93, 197–204.
2. The atonement refers to the reconciliation of God and humanity that occurs as a result of Jesus Christ's death on the cross. Barth emphasizes its historicity to push against generality. The atonement is not a doctrine, a principle, or a general truth. It is a divine act that takes place in and through Jesus.

responsible attitudes. It cannot be revealed and grasped and known without this proof. But when it is revealed and grasped and known, it is so in its priority, its precedence, its superiority to all other histories, to the existence of all the men who take part in it. In this sense everyone who knows it as truth knows in it the truth of his own existence.[3]

The atonement is, noetically, the history about Jesus Christ, and ontically, Jesus Christ's own history.[4] To say atonement is to say Jesus Christ. To speak of it is to speak of His history. If we do not simply speak of it, but know it as we speak of it, if we take part in it as we know it, if we decide with full responsibility as a result of it, we decide in relation to Jesus Christ. For He is the history of God with man and the history of man with God. What takes place in this history—the accusation and conviction of man as a lost sinner, his restoration, the founding and maintaining and sending of the community of God in the world, the new obedience of man—is all decided and ordained by Him as the One who primarily acts and speaks in it. It is His work which is done. He Himself accomplishes and guarantees it, for in Him it comes to pass that God is the reconciling God and man is reconciled man.[5] He is Himself this God and this man, and therefore the presupposition, the author, in whom all human existence has its first and basic truth in relation to that of God. It is in His self-offering to death that God has again found man and man God. It is in His resurrection from the dead that this twofold rediscovery is applied and proclaimed to us. It is in His Holy Spirit that it is present and an event for us. In all its different aspects the doctrine of reconciliation must always begin by looking at Him, not in order to leave Him behind in its later developments, but to fix the point from which there can and must be these later developments.

3. Barth thinks the atonement "takes precedence" over all histories because it unveils their true meaning. This idea stems from God's election of Jesus Christ to bear the burden of sin for the sake of human salvation. The world was created to be the space and place in which God executes this decision, and the atonement is the preeminent moment when the content of this decision is unveiled (see chaps. 18–22).

4. Barth draws an important distinction here. With respect to human knowledge (noetic), the atonement is the history of Jesus Christ's death on the cross for our sins. With respect to reality (ontic), the atonement is an event in the history of Jesus Christ's eternal life as the Son of God. Specifically, it is the moment when he bears the full consequences of sin in obedience to his election by God.

5. One of Barth's purposes for drawing the distinction between the knowledge and reality of the atonement is that he wants to make sure it is seen as an act of God. The atonement is not primarily a doctrine that can be objectified and analyzed. It is the preeminent event in which God unveils the truth about his eternal being in Jesus Christ. And like any other revelation of God, this event demands a response of obedience on the part of the human. This obedience includes bringing the human's knowledge of God into correspondence with the reality of God.

The first aspect under which we shall try to consider the doctrine of reconciliation in this chapter is that of the condescension active and known in it, that condescension in which God interests Himself in man in Jesus Christ. We might put it in this way: the aspect of the grace of God in Jesus Christ in which it comes to man as the (sinful) creature of God freely, without any merit or deserving, and therefore from outside, from above—which is to say, from God's standpoint, the aspect of His grace in which He does something unnecessary and extravagant, binding and limiting and compromising and offering Himself in relation to man by having dealings with him and making Himself his God.[6] In the fact that God is gracious to man, all the limitations of man are God's limitations, all his weaknesses, and more, all his perversities are His. In being gracious to man in Jesus Christ, God acknowledges man; He accepts responsibility for his being and nature. He remains Himself. He does not cease to be God. But He does not hold aloof. In being gracious to man in Jesus Christ, He also goes into the far country, into the evil society of this being which is not God and against God. He does not shrink from him. He does not pass him by as did the priest and the Levite the man who had fallen among thieves. He does not leave him to his own devices. He makes his situation His own. He does not forfeit anything by doing this. In being neighbor to man, in order to deal with him and act towards him as such, He does not need to fear for His Godhead. On the contrary. We will mention at once the thought which will be decisive and basic in this section, that God shows Himself to be the great and true God in the fact that He can and will let His grace bear this cost, that He is capable and willing and ready for this condescension, this act of extravagance, this far journey. What marks out God above all false gods is that they are not capable and ready for this. In their otherworldliness and supernaturalness and otherness, etc., the gods are a reflection of the human pride which will not unbend, which will not stoop to that which is beneath it. God is not proud. In His high majesty He is humble. It is in this high humility that He speaks and acts as the God who reconciles the world to Himself. It is under this aspect first that we must consider the history of the atonement.[7] . . .

6. Barth looks first at the "outer moment" of God's act to bear the consequences of sin in the flesh of Jesus Christ. He then will consider this action in light of God's eternal being.

7. This paragraph expresses the claim governing Barth's entire argument: "He remains himself." Barth affirms that God is immutable. He does not change or somehow cease to be God when he bears the burden of sin in Jesus Christ. Rather, when God condescends in Jesus to make the lowly human situation his own, he remains God. In this sense, despite our expectations, the humble and lowly act of bearing human sin reveals the reality of God's eternal being and will.

That God as God is able and willing and ready to condescend, to humble Himself in this way is the mystery of the "deity of Christ"—although frequently it is not recognized in this concreteness. This deity is not the deity of a divine being furnished with all kinds of supreme attributes. The understanding of this decisive christological statement has been made unnecessarily difficult (or easy), and the statement itself ineffective, by overlooking its concrete definition, by omitting to fill out the New Testament concept "deity" in definite connexion with the Old Testament, i.e., in relation to Jesus Christ Himself. The meaning of His deity—the only true deity in the New Testament sense—cannot be gathered from any notion of supreme, absolute, non-worldly being. It can be learned only from what took place in Christ. Otherwise its mystery would be an arbitrary mystery of our own imagining, a false mystery. It would not be the mystery given by the Word and revelation of God in its biblical attestation, the mystery which is alone relevant in Church dogmatics. Who the one true God is, and what He is, i.e., what is His being as God, and therefore His deity, His "divine nature," which is also the divine nature of Jesus Christ if He is very God—all this we have to discover from the fact that as such He is very man and a partaker of human nature, from His becoming man, from His incarnation and from what He has done and suffered in the flesh. For, to put it more pointedly, the mirror in which it can be known (and is known) that He is God, and of the divine nature, is His becoming flesh and His existence in the flesh.[8] . . .

The Christian theological tradition has always been in agreement that the statement "The Word was made flesh" is not to be thought of as describing an event which overtook Him, and therefore overtook God Himself, but rather a free divine activity, a sovereign act of divine lordship, an act of mercy which was necessary only by virtue of the will of God Himself. The statement cannot be reversed as though it indicated an appropriation and overpowering of the eternal Word by the flesh. God is always God even in His humiliation. The divine being does not suffer any change, any diminution, any transformation into something else, any admixture with something else, let alone any

8. How should God's "deity" be described? Barth draws a stark contrast between two approaches to this question. The first approach describes God on the basis of his distinction from creation. Every creaturely quality is negated in order to arrive at a description of God's being: creatures are contingent, weak, ignorant, sinful, and lowly, and so by contrast, God must be eternal, omnipotent, omniscient, holy, and glorious. The result is a God of "supreme attributes" who is absolutely other than his creatures. Barth rejects this approach because it is abstract and speculative. He takes the second approach: our definition of deity must be defined in light of God's revelation in Jesus Christ. We must pay attention to the concrete and particular content of God's revelation in Jesus of Nazareth because his flesh is the mirror in which we see the truth about God's deity.

cessation. The deity of Christ is the one unaltered because unalterable deity of God. Any subtraction or weakening of it would at once throw doubt upon the atonement made in Him. He humbled Himself, but He did not do it by ceasing to be who He is. He went into a strange land, but even there, and especially there, He never became a stranger to Himself. . . .

But it is not enough simply to follow the great line of theological tradition and to reject all thought of an alterability or alteration of God in His presence and action in the man Jesus. What depends on this rejection is clear. If God is not truly and altogether in Christ, what sense can there be in talking about the reconciliation of the world with God in Him?[9] But it is something very bold and profoundly astonishing to presume to say without reservation or subtraction that God was truly and altogether in Christ, to speak of His identity with this true man, which means this man who was born like all of us in time, who lived and thought and spoke, who could be tempted and suffer and die and who was in fact tempted, and suffered and died. The statement of this identity cannot be merely a postulate. If with the witnesses of the New Testament we derive it from what took place in this man, if it only confirms that the reconciliation of the world with God has actually taken place in the existence of this man, if it can only indicate the mystery and the miracle of this event, we must still know what we are presuming to say in this statement. It aims very high. In calling this man the Son or the eternal Word of God, in ascribing to this man in His unity with God a divine being and nature, it is not speaking only or even primarily of Him but of God. It tells us that God for His part is God in His unity with this creature, this man, in His human and creaturely nature—and this without ceasing to be God, without any alteration or diminution of His divine nature. But this statement concerning God is so bold that we dare not make it unless we consider seriously in what sense we can do so.[10] . . .

We begin with the insight that God is "not a God of confusion, but of peace" (1 Cor. 14:33). In Him there is no paradox, no antinomy, no division, no inconsistency, not even the possibility of it. He is the Father of lights with whom there is no variableness nor interplay of light and darkness (James 1:17). What He is and does He is and does in full unity with Himself. It is in full unity with Himself that He is also—and especially and above all—in Christ,

9. This question hovers in the background of Barth's argument. To put it differently: How can Jesus Christ save humanity from sin if he is something other than truly God in this act? After all, God alone can forgive sins (Mark 2:7). If the fullness of deity does not dwell in Jesus when he bears our sin on the cross, then how can this death save us?

10. Barth gives an unequivocal answer to the question he posed: God is fully in Christ when he bears sin on the cross, and he is so without ceasing to be God. Barth acknowledges that the implications of this reality challenge human ideals about the nature of deity, but he insists that this is what must be affirmed if we believe that Christ's death brings salvation.

that He becomes a creature, man, flesh, that He enters into our being in contradiction, that He takes upon Himself its consequences. If we think that this is impossible it is because our concept of God is too narrow, too arbitrary, too human—far too human. Who God is and what it is to be divine is something we have to learn where God has revealed Himself and His nature, the essence of the divine. And if He has revealed Himself in Jesus Christ as the God who does this, it is not for us to be wiser than He and to say that it is in contradiction with the divine essence. We have to be ready to be taught by Him that we have been too small and perverted in our thinking about Him within the framework of a false idea of God. It is not for us to speak of a contradiction and rift in the being of God, but to learn to correct our notions of the being of God, to reconstitute them in the light of the fact that He does this.[11] We may believe that God can and must only be absolute in contrast to all that is relative, exalted in contrast to all that is lowly, active in contrast to all suffering, inviolable in contrast to all temptation, transcendent in contrast to all immanence, and therefore divine in contrast to everything human, in short that He can and must be only the "Wholly Other."[12] But such beliefs are shown to be quite untenable, and corrupt and pagan, by the fact that God does in fact be and do this in Jesus Christ. We cannot make them the standard by which to measure what God can or cannot do, or the basis of the judgment that in doing this He brings Himself into self-contradiction. By doing this God proves to us that He can do it, that to do it is within His nature. And He shows Himself to be more great and rich and sovereign than we had ever imagined. And our ideas of His nature must be guided by this, and not *vice versa*.

We have to think something after the following fashion. As God was in Christ, far from being against Himself, or at disunity with Himself, He has

11. The key to this section is the remark about those who posit a "contradiction and rift in the being of God" with respect to God's revelation in Christ. They might say something like this: "God is *God*, the supreme Lord whose attributes make him wholly other and distinct from creation. So when Christ acts in humility and obedience, he is not acting in his divinity but only his humanity, because such actions contradict the qualities intrinsic to God's divine being." Barth rejects this approach because it makes a critical mistake: the being of God is defined before and apart from God's revelation in Jesus Christ. So when Christ comes in humility and obedience, his revelation is rendered impossible because it contradicts preexisting notions of God. Barth insists that an account of God's being must work in the opposite direction: we begin with God's revelation in Christ and then figure out what God's eternal being must be like in light of what Christ reveals. If Christ's revelation contradicts our ideas about God, then these ideas must be reformulated.

12. This remark is striking because Barth's target is *himself*—at least his earlier self who emphasized the idea that God is the "Wholly Other" at the expense of his relationship with humanity in Christ. Barth sees his own theological journey as a living example of the kind of intellectual reformation he is advocating (see chap. 10).

put into effect the freedom of His divine love, the love in which He is divinely free. He has therefore done and revealed that which corresponds to His divine nature. His immutability does not stand in the way of this. It must not be denied, but this possibility is included in His unalterable being.[13] He is absolute, infinite, exalted, active, impassible, transcendent, but in all this He is the One who loves in freedom, the One who is free in His love, and therefore not His own prisoner. He is all this as the Lord, and in such a way that He embraces the opposites of these concepts even while He is superior to them. He is all this as the Creator, who has created the world as the reality distinct from Himself but willed and affirmed by Him and therefore as His world, as the world which belongs to Him, in relation to which He can be God and act as God in an absolute way and also a relative, in an infinite and also a finite, in an exalted and also a lowly, in an active and also a passive, in a transcendent and also an immanent, and finally, in a divine and also a human—indeed, in relation to which He Himself can become worldly, making His own both its form, the form of a servant, and also its cause; and all without giving up His own form, the form of God, and His own glory, but adopting the form and cause of man into the most perfect communion with His own, accepting solidarity with the world. God can do this.[14] And no limit is set to His ability to do it by the contradiction of the creature against Him. It does not escape Him by turning to that which is not and losing itself in it, for, although He is not the Creator of that which is not, He is its sovereign Lord. It corresponds to and is grounded in His divine nature that in free grace He should be faithful to the unfaithful creature who has not deserved it and who would inevitably perish without it, that in relation to it He should establish that communion between His own form and cause and that of the creature, that He should make His own its being in contradiction and under the consequences of that contradiction, that He should maintain His covenant in relation to sinful man (not surrendering His deity, for how could that help? but giving up and sacrificing Himself), and in that way supremely asserting Himself and His deity.[15] His particular, and highly particularized, presence in grace, in which

13. Put differently, God is simply being *God* when he comes in Jesus Christ. The humility and obedience that Christ displays in his death on the cross does not contradict but reveals God's being.

14. In these sentences Barth emphasizes God's freedom by making God the agent. His point is that God does not take the form of a servant and live in solidarity with sinners out of obligation or need. He does so because he has freely decided to do so. And like all of God's decisions, this particular decision corresponds to his eternal being as the God who loves in freedom.

15. The reality that sin contradicts God's will does not inhibit God's freedom to bear it on behalf of humanity, nor does it undermine God's integrity. God's bearing of sin displays God's faithfulness: he does not turn away when humans are unfaithful to God and themselves

the eternal Word descended to the lowest parts of the earth (Eph. 4:9) and tabernacled in the man Jesus (John 1:14), dwelling in this one man in the fullness of His Godhead (Col. 2:9), is itself the demonstration and exercise of His omnipresence, i.e., of the perfection in which He has His own place which is superior to all the places created by Him, not excluding but including all other places. His omnipotence is that of a divine plenitude of power in the fact that (as opposed to any abstract omnipotence) it can assume the form of weakness and impotence and do so as omnipotence, triumphing in this form. The eternity in which He Himself is true time and the Creator of all time is revealed in the fact that, although our time is that of sin and death, He can enter it and Himself be temporal in it, yet without ceasing to be eternal, able rather to be the Eternal in time. His wisdom does not deny itself, but proclaims itself in what necessarily appears folly to the world; His righteousness in ranging Himself with the unrighteous as One who is accused with them, as the first, and properly the only One to come under accusation; His holiness in having mercy on man, in taking his misery to heart, in willing to share it with him in order to take it away from him. God does not have to dishonor Himself when He goes into the far country, and conceals His glory. For He is truly honored in this concealment. This concealment, and therefore His condescension as such, is the image and reflection in which we see Him as He is. His glory is the freedom of the love which He exercises and reveals in all this. In this respect it differs from the unfree and loveless glory of all the gods imagined by man.[16] Everything depends on our seeing it, and in it the true and majestic nature of God: not trying to construct it arbitrarily; but deducing it from its revelation in the divine nature of Jesus Christ. From this we learn that the form of God consists in the grace in which God Himself assumes and makes His own the form of the servant. We have to hold fast to this without being disturbed or confused by any pictures of false gods. It is this that we have to see and honor and worship as the mystery of the deity of

---

but remains the same God he always has been. This consistency is the basis of salvation. A God who dealt with sin by becoming something other than God, or a God who lost himself in relation to sin by being overcome by it, would be of little help. How could a being other than or less than God reconcile humans to God?

16. Here Barth is showing what it looks like to reconfigure the "supreme attributes" in light of God's revelation in Christ. Jesus shows that God is omnipresent in the sense that he can be fully present as God in a particular place, even one that contradicts him in sin. God displays his omnipotence by triumphing in and through weakness, and he shows his eternal nature by entering into a temporal world without being constrained by it. God's wisdom is demonstrated by what seems like foolishness; his righteousness by accepting the blame for sin in order to justify sinners; his holiness through his mercy; and his glory in the humility and lowliness he manifests as Christ seeks and saves the lost.

Christ—not an ontic and inward divine paradox, the postulate of which has its basis only in our own very real contradiction against God and the false ideas of God which correspond to it.[17] . . .

The way of the Son of God into the far country is the way of obedience. This is the first and inner moment of the mystery of the deity of Christ. Now that we have dealt with the second and outer moment, it is to this [inner mystery] that we must turn.[18]

We have seen already that if in faith in Jesus Christ we are ready to learn, to be told, what Godhead, or the divine nature, is, we are confronted with the revelation of what is and always will be to all other ways of looking and thinking a mystery, and indeed a mystery which offends. The mystery reveals to us that for God it is just as natural to be lowly as it is to be high, to be near as it is to be far, to be little as it is to be great, to be abroad as to be at home. Thus, when in the presence and action of Jesus Christ in the world both created by Him and characterized as evil through the sin of man God chooses to go into the far country, to conceal His form of lordship in the form of this world and therefore in the form of a servant, He is not untrue to Himself but genuinely true to Himself, to the freedom which is that of His love.[19] He does not have to choose and do this. He is free in relation to it. We are therefore dealing with the genuine article when He does choose and do this. Even in the form of a servant, which is the form of His presence and action in Jesus Christ, we have to do with God Himself in His true deity. The humility in which He dwells and acts in Jesus Christ is not alien to Him, but proper to Him. His humility is a new mystery for us in whose favor He executes it when He makes use of His freedom for it, when He shows His love even to His enemies and His life even in death, thus revealing them in a way which is quite contrary to all our false ideas of God. But for Him this humility is no

17. Barth returns to the relationship between the noetic and the ontic, and he frames their relationship as a stark choice: our account of God will be defined either by the reality of God's revelation in Jesus Christ or by our own ideas. And since God is fully in Christ, any conflict between the reality of revelation and our own ideas indicates that we need to reformulate our ideas rather than deny the truthfulness of revelation.

18. After examining the "outer moment" of God's saving work in Christ, Barth now turns to the "inner mystery" of God's triune being. This turn is grounded on Barth's conviction that *revelation* is identical to the *revealer*. God does not give information about himself while remaining at a distance. Nor does God give humans only a partial revelation, as if the real truth about his being remains hidden behind what he displays. Rather, God's revelation is always a *self*-revelation involving his personal encounter with humans to make himself knowable by them. Since all God's actions are grounded in God's eternal being and life, we can draw conclusions about God's inner being on the basis of his act of self-revelation in Christ.

19. For the sake of clarity, I have adjusted the translation of this sentence and added the referent for the pronoun.

new mystery. It is His sovereign grace that He wills to be and is amongst us in humility, our God, God for us. But He shows us this grace, He is amongst us in humility, our God, God for us, as that which He is in Himself, in the most inward depth of His Godhead. He does not become another God. In the condescension in which He gives Himself to us in Jesus Christ He exists and speaks and acts as the One He was from all eternity and will be to all eternity. The truth and actuality of our atonement depends on this being the case. The One who reconciles the world with God is necessarily the one God Himself in His true Godhead. Otherwise the world would not be reconciled with God. Otherwise it is still the world which is not reconciled with God.[20]

But we must dig deeper if we are to understand the free love of God established in the event of atonement. If the humility of Christ is not simply an attitude of the man Jesus of Nazareth, if it is the attitude of this man because, according to what takes place in the atonement made in this man (according to the revelation of God in Him), there is a humility grounded in the being of God, then something else is grounded in the being of God Himself. For, according to the New Testament, it is the case that the humility of this man is an act of obedience, not a capricious choice of lowliness, suffering and dying, not an autonomous decision this way, not an accidental swing of the pendulum in this direction, but a free choice made in recognition of an appointed order, in execution of a will which imposed itself authoritatively upon Him, which was intended to be obeyed. If, then, God is in Christ, if what the man Jesus does is God's own work, this aspect of the self-emptying and self-humbling of Jesus Christ as an act of obedience cannot be alien to God. But in this case we have to see here the other and inner side of the mystery of the divine nature of Christ and therefore of the nature of the one true God—that He Himself is also able and free to render obedience.[21] . . .

Let us first review the three presuppositions which, at all costs, we must accept and affirm.

20. This paragraph captures the crux of the matter for Barth. When God comes in Christ to bear the sin of those who have made themselves his enemies (Rom. 5:10), he comes as the one true God that he is. God does not change when he comes in Christ, nor does he hide himself or act falsely. This means that the humility Jesus displays in his incarnate life is not alien but proper to God's being. While this humility is surprising given the human tendency to imagine a God of supreme attributes, it does not come as a surprise to God. God is humble, and he is simply being himself when he comes in Christ. Indeed, his immutability is the key to our salvation because, if *God* is not the one who bears the cost of human sin in Jesus Christ's death on the cross, then humans are still lost in sin.

21. Barth extends his argument further: if Jesus shows us not only humility but also obedience, then obedience itself must be grounded in the being of God. This insight leads Barth into the inner mystery of the Trinity.

It is a matter (1) of determining the acting subject of the reconciliation of the world with God. According to the witness of the New Testament, when we have to do with Jesus Christ we are dealing with the author and finisher of this work, with the Mediator between God and man, with the One who makes peace between the two, with no other and no less than the One who has taken upon Himself and away from the world the enmity of the world against God and the curse which rests upon it, with the One who (we shall treat of this in the second part of the section) accomplishes the ineluctable judgment of the world in such a way that He Himself bears it in order to bear it away. We have to do with the One who has the competence and power for this work. In relation to the fact that He is the One who does this, the New Testament witness to His deity has to be understood and taken seriously as expressed in the different titles under which it speaks of Him. Everything depends upon our seeing and understanding as the New Testament does that He is the acting subject in this work. If we grant that we are at one with the New Testament in this, we must also follow it in seeing the true God at work in Him. In matters of the atonement of the world with God the world itself cannot act—for it is the world which is at enmity with God, which stands in need of reconciliation with Him. It cannot act even in the form of a supreme and best being produced by it and belonging to it. Anyone other or less than the true God is not a legitimate subject competent to act in this matter. At this point the subordinationist interpretation is evasive.[22] And it has to be rejected as unsatisfactory. When we have to do with Jesus Christ we have to do with God. What He does is a work which can only be God's own work, and not the work of another.[23]

But (2) it is a matter of the subject of the atonement as an event which takes place not only to the world but in the world, which not only touches the world from without but affects it from within to convert it to God, which is itself an event in the world. According to the witness of the New Testament, the world is not abandoned and left to its own devices. God takes it to Himself, entering into the sphere of it as the true God, causing His kingdom to come on earth as in heaven, becoming Himself truly ours, man, flesh, in order to overcome sin where it has its dominion, in the flesh, to take away in His own person the ensuing curse where it is operative, in the creaturely world, in the reality which is distinct from Himself. It is in relation to the fact

22. A subordinationist view holds that Jesus Christ is not truly divine but merely similar to God in some respect. It drives a wedge between the historical life of Christ and the eternal being of God.

23. The first presupposition that must be affirmed is this: because God is the subject of the life of Jesus Christ, his saving work is the work of God.

that what He does in the atonement He does in this way, in the power of His own presence and action, that we have to take seriously the New Testament witness to the being of the one true God in Jesus Christ; the realistic and not the nominalistic sense in which it accords these titles to Jesus Christ, whatever they are and however their formulation may be taken.[24] Again everything depends on our accepting and following out in all its realism the New Testament presupposition "God was in Christ." If we grant this—as the *credo* of Christian confession assumes—we have to follow the New Testament in understanding the presence and action of God in Jesus Christ as the most proper and direct and immediate presence and action of the one true God in the sphere of human and world history. If this is not so, then as the subject of the act of atonement He can only touch the world from without, not affect it from within, not truly convert it to Himself. It would not, therefore, be a real reconciliation of the world with Him. At this point the modalistic interpretation of the deity of Christ is evasive.[25] And for that reason it must be regarded as unsatisfactory and rejected. When we have to do with Jesus Christ we do have to do with an "economy" but not with the kind of economy in which His true and proper being remains behind an improper being, a being "as if." We have to do with an economy in which God is truly Himself and Himself acts and intervenes in the world. Otherwise the atonement made in this economy is not a true atonement.[26]

It is a matter (3)—and this is the connecting point—of the one true God being Himself the subject of the act of atonement in such a way that His presence and action as the Reconciler of the world coincide and are indeed identical with the existence of the humiliated and lowly and obedient man Jesus of Nazareth. He acts as the Reconciler in that—as the true God identical with this man—He humbles Himself and becomes lowly and obedient. He becomes and is this without being in contradiction to His divine nature (He is not therefore exposed to the postulate that He can become and be this only as a creature), but in contradiction to all human ideas about the divine nature. He becomes and is this without encroaching on Himself (He is not subject to the postulate that He can become and be this only improperly, in an appearance which is alien to His own being), but as a saving approach to

24. To assign the title "God" and "Lord" to Jesus in a nominalistic manner would be to apply these titles with no sense that they connect to an underlying reality. Barth rejects such a view. These titles are applied to Jesus realistically because they correspond to his true being.

25. A modalist view holds that Jesus Christ is merely a way that God appears within creation but that this "mode of appearance" does not reflect the reality of God's being. It again drives a wedge between the historical life of Jesus and the eternal being of God.

26. The second presupposition that must be affirmed is this: God really enters into the creaturely realm in Jesus Christ and assumes the burden of sin for the sake of human salvation.

us, an encroachment upon us which is authoritative and demands our conversion.[27] According to the New Testament witness we have the presence and
action not only of the man Jesus, but in the existence of that man the action
and presence which is supremely proper to God Himself as the Reconciler of
the world. God chooses condescension. He chooses humiliation, lowliness and
obedience. In this way He illuminates the darkness, opening up that which is
closed. In this way He brings help where there is no other help. In this way He
accepts solidarity with the creature, with man, in order to reconcile man and
the world with Himself, in order to convert man and the world to Himself.
The God of the New Testament witness is the God who makes this choice,
who in agreement with Himself and His divine nature, but in what is for us
the revelation of a new mystery, humbles Himself and is lowly and obedient
amongst us.[28] In this respect, too, the New Testament witness has to be taken
seriously. Everything depends on our accepting this presupposition, on our
seeing and understanding what the New Testament witnesses obviously saw
and understood, the proper being of the one true God in Jesus Christ the Crucified. Granted that we do see and understand this, we cannot refuse to accept
the humiliation and lowliness and supremely the obedience of Christ as the
dominating moment in our conception of God. Therefore we must determine
to seek and find the key to the whole difficult and heavily freighted concept of
the "divine nature" at the point where it appears to be quite impossible—except
for those whose thinking is orientated on Him in this matter—the fact that
Jesus Christ was obedient unto death, even the death of the cross. It is from
this point, and this point alone, that the concept is legitimately possible.[29] . . .

Is it a fact that in relation to Jesus Christ we can speak of an obedience
of the one true God Himself in His proper being? From the three inalienable

27. To phrase these two sentences differently: in Jesus Christ, God humbles himself in obedience without contradicting or violating his divine nature. Rather, this revelation of divine humility and obedience contradicts our false ideas about God and compels us to reformulate them.

28. Barth's emphasis on God's *choice* indicates that God does not come in humility and
obedience out of some internal need or external necessity. God comes in this manner because he
freely decided to address the need of the humans he loves. This decision also does not indicate
that God has determined to be something other than what he eternally is in this event. God's
decisions always correspond to his perfect being and will, and he never acts in contradiction
to his character. Finally, the fact that this decision involves the Son of God's taking on human
flesh also does not indicate a change on God's part. The Son does not change *into* flesh but
unites it to himself so that he remains truly God even as he also is truly human. So when the
Son takes on this flesh—and lives with humility and obedience within it—he is still living his
one eternal divine life as God.

29. The third presupposition that must be affirmed is this: in Jesus Christ—and particularly
in his death for the sins of humanity—God reveals that both humility and obedience are proper
to his divine nature.

presuppositions just expounded it is plain that we not only can do so but have to do so, that we cannot avoid doing so either on the one side or on the other. We have not only not to deny but actually to affirm and understand as essential to the being of God the offensive fact that there is in God Himself an above and a below, a before and an after, a superiority and a subordination. And our present concern is with what is apparently the most offensive fact of all, that there is a below, an after, a subordination, that it belongs to the inner life of God that there should take place within it obedience.[30]

We have to reckon with such an event even in the being and life of God Himself. It cannot be explained away either as an event in some higher or supreme creaturely sphere or as a mere appearance of God. Therefore we have to state firmly that, far from preventing this possibility, His divine unity consists in the fact that in Himself He is both One who is obeyed and Another who obeys. . . .

As we look at Jesus Christ we cannot avoid the astounding conclusion of a divine obedience. Therefore we have to draw the no less astounding deduction that in equal Godhead the one God is, in fact, the One and also Another, that He is indeed a First and a Second, One who rules and commands in majesty and One who obeys in humility. The one God is both the one and the other. And, we continue, He is the one and the other without any cleft or differentiation but in perfect unity and equality because in the same perfect unity and equality He is also a Third, the One who affirms the one and equal Godhead through and by and in the two modes of being, the One who makes possible and maintains His fellowship with Himself as the one and the other. In virtue of this third mode of being He is in the other two without division or contradiction, the whole God in each. But again in virtue of this third mode of being He is in neither for itself and apart from the other, but in each in its relationship to the other, and therefore, in fact, in the totality, the connection, the interplay, the history of these relationships. And because all division and contradiction is excluded, there is also excluded any striving to identify the two modes of being, or any possibility of the one being absorbed by the other, or both in their common deity. God is God in these two modes of being which cannot be separated, which cannot be autonomous, but which cannot cease to be different.[31] He is God in their concrete relationships the one to the

30. Barth's three essential presuppositions lead him to the conclusion that obedience is proper to God. But obedience implies the existence of one who is *below* another, *after* another, and *subordinate* to another. How can these things be true of the inner being of the triune God? Barth now turns to this question.

31. Barth's argument is this: if Jesus Christ is God—and if his acts of obedience are in accordance with the being of God—then the one God must be the God who commands *and* the

other, in the history which takes place between them. He is God only in these relationships and therefore not in a Godhead which does not take part in this history, in the relationships of its modes of being, which is neutral towards them. This neutral Godhead, this pure and empty Godhead, and its claim to be true divinity, is the illusion of an abstract "monotheism" which usually fools men most successfully at the high-water mark of the development of heathen religions and mythologies and philosophies. The true and living God is the One whose Godhead consists in this history, who is in these three modes of being the One God, the Eternal, the Almighty, the Holy, the Merciful, the One who loves in His freedom and is free in His love.[32]

And His speaking and activity and work outside Himself consist in the fact that He gives to the world created by Him, to man, a part in the history in which He is God, that there is primarily in the work of creation a reflection, in the antithesis of Creator and creature an image and likeness, and in the twofoldness of the existence of man a reflection of this likeness of the inner life of God Himself.[33] And then supremely and finally (at the goal and

---

God who obeys. Barth explains this idea by appealing to his account of the Trinity as one God in three modes of being (see chap. 14). God is fully God in each of his three modes of being. This means that any talk of *command* and *obedience* in God cannot imply a breach or distinction in God's being, as if the Father, Son, and Spirit have distinct levels of being or act as different subjects with distinct wills. No, Barth insists that God has one being and one will. But he also affirms that there is an order to the relationships between the Father, Son, and Spirit in the unity of their being and will. This is where Barth locates the command and obedience. He argues that God's oneness includes the Father's begetting of the Son and the Son's obeying of the Father. The Son's obedience to the Father does not compromise the Son's unity and equality with the Father because this obedience *is what it means* to be begotten of the Father. The Spirit affirms the perfect unity and equality of the Father and the Son in their relationship of command and obedience as he exists in the Father and Son. This unity means that we cannot distinguish the Father over against the Son or the Son in opposition to the Father. They are what they are in their shared, ordered relationship with one another through the Spirit. The only thing we can say is that the *triune God* is the one who both commands and obeys. This explains why the humility and obedience of Jesus Christ does not contradict but corresponds to the eternal being of God. The eternal Son is the one who, in and through his own divine obedience, lives in perfect unity with the Father by the Spirit. So when the Son of God unites himself to human flesh in Jesus, he is simply enacting the pattern of his eternal life in time.

32. Barth's reference to the "history" of the triune relationships should not be identified with creaturely history. He means the eternal history lived by the Father, Son, and Spirit in their relationality and differentiation. This history is infinitely distinct from creaturely history. It reflects the reality that God is the *living* God, and the God whose oneness of being includes "interplay" of the above and below, commanding and obeying, that exists between the Father and the Son who live in the unity of the Spirit. This eternal history is the basis of the covenant history where this same triune relationality and differentiation is displayed in time.

33. To be given "a part" in the eternal history of God is to be made a participant in the being of God. So in and through Christ and the Spirit, believers participate in the interplay of relationships of the triune God.

end of His whole activity as established at its beginning) they consist in the fact that God Himself becomes a man amongst men in His mode of being as the One who is obedient in humility. In the work of the reconciliation of the world with God the inward divine relationship between the One who rules and commands in majesty and the One who obeys in humility is identical with the very different relationship between God and one of His creatures, a man. God goes into the far country for this to happen. He becomes what He had not previously been. He takes into unity with His divine being a quite different, a creaturely and indeed a sinful being. To do this He empties Himself, He humbles Himself. But, as in His action as Creator, He does not do it apart from its basis in His own being, in His own inner life. He does not do it without any correspondence to, but as the strangely logical final continuation of, the history in which He is God. He does not need to deny, let alone abandon and leave behind or even diminish His Godhead to do this. He does not need to leave the work of the Reconciler in the doubtful hands of a creature. He can enter in Himself, seeing He is in Himself not only the One who rules and commands in majesty, but also in His own divine person, although in a different mode of being, the One who is obedient in humility. It is the free grace of the atonement that He now not only reflects His inner being as God as He did in creation, that He not only represents it in a likeness as He did in the relationship of Creator and creature, but that He causes it to take outward form in itself and as such. In His mode of being as the One who is obedient in humility He wills to be not only the one God but this man, and this man as the one God. He does not owe this to the creaturely world. He does not owe it even to Himself. He owes it just as little and even less than He did the creation. Neither in the one case nor in the other—and even less in this case—can there be any question of the necessary working of an inward divine mechanism, or a mechanism which controls the relationship of God and the world. God gives Himself to the world in coming to the world as its Reconciler. But He can give Himself to it. He is His own master in such a way that He can go into the far country to do it. He does not need to cease to be radically and totally above, the first, in order to become radically and totally below, the second. Even below, as this second, He is one with Himself, equal with Himself as God. He does not change in giving Himself. He simply activates and reveals Himself outside Himself, in the world. He is in and for the world what He is in and for Himself. He is in time what He is in eternity (and what He can be also in time because of His eternal being). He is in our lowliness what He is in His majesty (and what He can be also in our lowliness because His majesty is also lowliness). He is as man, as the man who is obedient in humility, Jesus of Nazareth, what He is as God (and what He can be also as man because He is it as God in this mode of divine being). That is the true deity of Jesus Christ, obedient in humility, in its unity and equality, its *homoousia*, with the deity of the One who sent Him and to whom He is obedient.[34]

34. Barth closes this section by reiterating his central claim: when we see the humility and obedience of the human Jesus Christ, particularly in his death on the cross, we are seeing a revelation of the true God. The eternal life that God's lives as Father, Son, and Spirit is made manifest in time in the historical life of Jesus Christ, the incarnate Son of God, who lives in humility and obedience to the Father by the power of the Spirit.

26

The Exaltation of the Son of Man

Introduction

Barth argues that humans are justified *and* sanctified by grace. In this excerpt from *Church Dogmatics* IV/2, Barth explains the christological basis of this claim by showing how the believer's sanctification results from the ongoing work of the risen Jesus Christ. Barth describes sanctification as a "merciful exchange" between Christ and humanity. While Christ receives humiliation by bearing the burden of humanity's sin, humans receive exaltation as human nature is elevated to the throne of God in the resurrection of Jesus. Since both events take place in the person of Christ, the history of his eternal life is the key to understanding the relationship between his saving work in the past and the effect of that work within the lives of believers in the present.

Barth explains the relationship between Christ's past and present work by emphasizing that God's salvation of humanity is not an end in itself, as if God saves simply in order to save. God saves for a purpose: he wants to create a community that lives and works as his faithful covenant partners. God elects Jesus Christ with this goal in mind. After Jesus bears the consequences of sin on behalf of humanity, God raises him from the dead precisely so that every other human can live a life of covenant faithfulness through their union with him.

Behind this argument is Barth's unique account of the connection between the objective reality of Christ's saving work and the subjective realization of this work in the life of the believer. He insists that Christ does not merely create a possibility that later becomes a reality when it is actualized by the human. Rather, Christ's perfect saving work in the believer includes within itself the believer's realization of that work. In other words, the present-tense sanctification of the believer is the direct result of what Christ already accomplished in the past. In this sense, Barth argues that the whole of human life has been "enclosed" in the life of Jesus Christ, and he will be faithful to complete here and now the good work he began there and then.

These ideas serve as the basis for Barth's claim that Jesus Christ is the representative for all humanity. When God raised Jesus from the dead, he brought human nature to the destiny for which it was created. Everyone united to Christ shares in his exaltation, and to think about human nature in distinction from Christ is to think abstractly. To think concretely is to recognize that, as the risen Christ continues his work to fulfill God's covenant plan, he does so through the people to whom he has united himself. Their covenant faithfulness takes place in and through his own as he completes his saving mission in the world.

Church Dogmatics IV/2[1]

We have to do with the eternal beginning of all the ways and works of God when we have to do with Jesus Christ—even in His true humanity. This is not a "contingent fact of history." It is the historical event in which there took place in time that which was the purpose and resolve and will of God from all eternity and therefore before the being of all creation, before all time and history, that which is, therefore, above all time and history, and will be after them, so that the being of all creatures and their whole history in time follow this one resolve and will, and were and are and will be referred and related to them.[2] The true humanity of Jesus Christ, as the humanity of the Son, was and is and will be the primary content of God's eternal election of grace, i.e., of the divine decision and action which are not preceded by any higher apart from the trinitarian happening of the life of God, but which all other divine decisions and actions follow, and to which they are subordinated. As a history which took place in time, the true humanity of Jesus Christ is, therefore, the

---

1. Karl Barth, *Church Dogmatics* IV/2 (Edinburgh: T&T Clark, 1958), 31–36, 268–74, 280–81.

2. Barth opens this excerpt with themes drawn from his account of the relationship between covenant and creation (see chap. 21).

execution and revelation, not merely of *a* but of *the* purpose of the will of
God, which is not limited or determined by any other, and therefore by any
other happening in the creaturely sphere, but is itself the sum of all divine
purposes, and therefore that which limits and determines all other occurrence.[3]

For God's eternal election of grace is concretely the election of Jesus Christ.
But this means that it is the decision and action in which God in His Son elected
and determined Himself for man, and, as we have now to consider, man for
Himself. It is the decision and action of God in which He took to Himself the
rejection of sinful man with all its consequences and elected this man—our
present theme—to participation in His own holiness and glory: humiliation
for Himself and exaltation for man![4] The secret, the very depth of the secret,
of God's grace is that at the beginning of all His works and ways He acted in
this way and not otherwise, that He elected this so strangely merciful exchange.
It is the election of grace as the election of Jesus Christ. It is in the reconciliation of the world with God as it took place in time in this One that the depth
of this secret, God's eternal election of grace, is manifested as the beginning
of all His works and ways. It is in Him that we see this exchange. For He is
both. As the Son of God He is the One who elects man and therefore His own
humiliation. As the Son of Man He is the One who is elected by God and therefore to His own exaltation. He is God's eternal, twofold predestination, from
which everything else, all God's other purposes and therefore all occurrence,
proceed, and in which all things have their norm and end. For what God willed
and did, and still wills and does, and is to will and do, is—directly in the history of His incarnate Word (and the further history to which it gives rise, and
which is the meaning of this last time), and indirectly in God's fatherly rule
as Creator, Sustainer and Ruler of the cosmos—the execution and revelation
of this twofold predestination, and therefore of the election of Jesus Christ,
the unfolding of that which is enfolded in this eternal divine decree. He, Jesus
Christ, is the One who was and is and will be, of whom and by whom and to
whom are all things, very God and very man.[5]

Very man—this is what particularly interests us from the present standpoint. As we have seen, at the beginning of all the ways and works of God it

3. Barth identifies the humanity of Jesus Christ as both the content of God's election of
grace and the purpose for creation. This claim introduces the major theme of this excerpt.

4. I altered the translation to restore Barth's original punctuation. He adds the exclamation
to emphasize the importance of the exchange between Christ and humanity. This exchange is
the basis of his claims about humanity in this section.

5. Barth's remarks about a "twofold predestination" reflect his doctrine of election. He
rejects the absolute decree in which God decides to elect some for salvation but to pass over
others. Instead, he argues that God elects himself in Jesus Christ with a twofold determination: for humiliation as the Son of God and exaltation as the Son of Man (see chaps. 18–19).

is a matter of the election of grace as made in the election of Jesus Christ, of the one Son of God as electing and the one Son of Man as elected, and therefore of God's predestination as it is directed from and to this One. But this means that we have to do with the eternal resolve and will of God, with His one primal decision, not only in the fellowship of God with man as established by the free grace of God but also in the fellowship of man with God as established by the same free grace; not only in the divine movement from above to below but also in the human movement from below to above; not only in the act of God as such but also in the human history which it sets in train.[6] God was not alone, nor did He work alone, at that beginning of all His works and ways. He was not without man. And that man should be there for God and in His presence, that he should be loved by Him and love Him in return, he did not need first to be created, let alone to become a sinner; to fall a victim to death, let alone to attempt all kinds of counter-movements in this situation. The man who by the grace of God is directed to the grace of God, and therefore exalted and caught up in this homeward movement is not one who comes late on the scene and must later still make his exit and disappear. He does not exist only secondarily. He is there at the point from which all things and he himself (created last) derive in the temporal execution of the will of God. For in the eternal election of God he is with God's Son the first, i.e., the primary object and content of the primal and basic will of God.[7] He is not, of course, a second God. He is not eternal as God is. He is only the creature of God—bound to time, limited in other ways too, unable in his own strength to escape the threat of nothingness.[8] But as this creature—because this is what God sees and wills—he is before all things, even before the dawn of his own time. As the primary object and content of the creative will of God he is in his own way just as really before and with God as God is in His. He, too, has a basic reality in the counsel of God which is the basis of all reality.

6. God's grace is not an end in itself. It is given in order to produce a human act that corresponds to God's action. Barth insists that this human response must be considered in any account of God's will and action in the history of the covenant.

7. When Barth claims that God "was not without man" in the beginning, he is not talking about humanity in general but the human Jesus. This claim is drawn from his account of the election of Jesus Christ (see chap. 19). The center of Barth's account is his claim that the human Jesus is present "in the beginning" with God in an anticipatory realization of the union with the Son that will occur in time. On this basis, Barth argues that Jesus Christ is both the object *and* the subject of God's election of grace. This is why Barth says both that the human Jesus "is there" with God in the beginning *and* that he is "the primary object and content" of God's electing will.

8. Here Barth is talking about Jesus Christ with respect to his humanity. For the context behind these two sentences, see Barth's description of the relationship between God's election of the human Jesus and nothingness in chap. 20.

At no level or time can we have to do with God without having also to do with this man. We cannot conceive ourselves and the world without first conceiving this man with God as the witness of the gracious purpose with which God willed and created ourselves and the world and in which we may exist in it and with it. It is not the world and ourselves, ourselves and the world, who are first elected and willed by God and come into being—and then at a later stage and place this man. But He was and is there first, the One whom God has elected and willed, who is there in being. And we in the world, and our being and existence before Him, can only follow and be subject, as we are elected and willed by God in Him.[9] . . .

The truth is that this human history, "the earthly life of Jesus," belongs with the act of God to that which is revealed. It is manifest with it in time ("in these last days," as 1 Pet. 1:20 puts it), but it is also with it as the content of the eternal decree and will of God. It was foreordained with it before the foundation of the world. There is no divine, eternal, spiritual level at which the Christ-event is not also "worldly" and therefore this human history. The concept of the true humanity of Jesus Christ is therefore primarily and finally basic—an absolutely necessary concept—in exactly the same and not a lesser sense than that of His true deity. The humanity of Jesus Christ is not a secondary moment in the Christ-event. It is not something which happens later, and later again will pass and disappear. It is not merely for the purpose of mediation. Like His deity, it is integral to the whole event.[10]

All that follows depends on this. Reconciled man is not merely a shadow of the reconciling God. The exaltation of God is not to be envisaged only optionally with the humiliation of God. Sanctification is not a mere appendix of justification. The edification of the Christian community is not a mere accompaniment of its gathering. Christian love is not just an incidental

---

9. The order of the relationship between Christ and creation is critically important for Barth. God did not decide to create the world and then decide that the human Jesus would enter into this already-existing creation. No, God decides to unite himself to human flesh in Jesus "before the foundation of the world" (Eph. 1:4), and then he creates the world to serve as the place in which this decision will be executed. In Barth's mind are Paul's statements that all things are created in, through, and for Jesus Christ, who is both "before all things" and the one in whom "all things hold together" (Col. 1:16–17; see chap. 21).

10. Barth's statement that Jesus Christ's humanity is as basic to his identity as his deity is both striking and counterintuitive. When talking about God's decree of salvation, it would seem to make sense for the divinity of the Son to be the primary focus. But Barth rejects such an approach as an abstraction. There is no Son other than the Son who has elected to unite himself to the human Jesus. The flesh of Jesus is not a temporary costume, nor is it merely an instrument the Son uses to reveal himself to creatures. The human flesh of Jesus is the goal toward which the Son of God has determined himself from all eternity. As a result, we cannot consider the Son's relationship to humanity in Jesus Christ apart from this determination or his human flesh.

by-product of Christian faith. All these developments of the second problem of the doctrine of reconciliation are intimately bound up with the first, and for all the differences they are of equal dignity.[11] . . .

It is clear from the very outset that in our consideration of this aspect we must still keep our gaze fixed on Jesus Himself and not allow it to wander in any other direction. The given fact of His existence as the royal man, and His effective power and lordship, cannot be allowed to sink into the background, becoming the content only of a completed christological statement which we have now conveniently left behind to construct a second statement of which Christ is no longer the subject but we ourselves at a certain distance from Him—the Christian as a being which is certainly in relationship to Christ, but has also its own independent existence. We have to reckon quite seriously with the fact that the anthropological sphere is genuinely dominated by the Son of Man as its Lord, and therefore that our knowledge of ourselves is included and enclosed in the knowledge of Jesus. Our self-testing can only take place before Him. It is as those who are judged by the *Lord* (1 Cor. 11:32) that we can go out from the judgment into which we must always enter with ourselves. He Himself is the answer even to the question of the discerning knowledge and use and living out of the freedom which we are granted in Him. He in whom the decision has been taken concerning us is not only the living, creative source of the change which it means for us, but also its measure and criterion. He determines its meaning and extent and depth. As the One who is with us and for us He decides what we can and should and must become and be in Him and through Him and with Him.[12] He in whom the old is already past

11. Barth's point is that we cannot forget that God elects Jesus Christ for the sake of human salvation. And this salvation is not primarily about God's action even though God is the primary actor. God saves in order to establish a community of humans who live as God's faithful covenant partners through their participation in Christ. Behind this claim is Paul's statement that God "chose us in Christ before the foundation of the world to be holy and blameless before him in love" (Eph. 1:4). Barth believes that God's choice can never be separated from the human holiness and love produced by it.

12. This paragraph introduces a theme central to Barth's argument in this section. It concerns the relationship between Christ's *objective* work of salvation and the *subjective* realization of that work in the life of the human. Barth insists that this relationship should be seen as a single, differentiated act rather than a two-stage process that begins with Christ's act and then is followed by a second human act. Or, to put it more concretely, Barth rejects the idea that Christ's death on the cross creates the *possibility* for salvation that becomes an *actuality* only when the human acts to accept it. The problem with this two-stage approach is that it makes the human's act decisive in the realization of salvation. The real action—the act that actually saves—takes place with the human in the present while Jesus's action is left behind as a thing of the past. Barth rejects this approach because he insists that Jesus Christ is the living Lord of the past *and* the present. Christ saves by uniting humans to himself in his death so that he can live in and through them as their risen Lord. This means that Christ's objective saving work

and the new has already come draws the sharp line between the two which we have now to know and observe. It is only as we look at Him, therefore, that we can know and observe this line. . . .

We must begin, therefore, by emphasizing a statement that we could only make implicitly, only announce, as it were, in the earlier stages of this christological basis when in the second sub-section we considered the incarnation of the Son of God, and its eternal foundation and revelation. For what was it that really took place in the event which we then recognized and described as the homecoming of the Son of Man, as His elevation and exaltation to fellowship with God, to the side of God, to participation in His lordship over all things, as the communication of properties and graces and acts?[13] Was it just the isolated history of this one man? This is certainly the case, for what took place and has to be noted as this communication between divine and human being and activity in this One was and is only, as the reconciliation of man with God by God's own incarnation, His own history and not that of any other man. But for all its singularity, as His history it was not and is not a private history, but a representative and therefore a public one. His history in the place of all other men and in accomplishment of their atonement; the history of their Head, in which they all participate. Therefore, in the most concrete sense of the term, the history of this One is world history. When God was in Christ He reconciled the world to Himself (2 Cor. 5:19), and therefore us, each one of us. In this One humanity itself, our human essence, was and is elevated and exalted. It is in perfect likeness with us, as our genuine Brother, that He was and is so unique, so unlike us as the true and royal man. To that in which a man is like all others, and therefore a man, there now belongs brotherhood with this one man, the One who is so utterly unlike him and all other men. To human essence in all its nature and corruption there now belongs the fact that in the one Jesus Christ, who as the true Son of God

---

includes within itself the subjective realization of that work in the human. He is the decisive agent of both the work in the past *and* the realization of that work in the present. He is decisive in this way because, in both tenses, salvation is determined by the fact that human being is *being in Christ*. As Barth sees it, this account corresponds to Paul's description of his own salvation in Christ: "I have been crucified with Christ; and it is no longer I who live, but it is Christ who lives in me" (Gal. 2:19–20).

13. Barth uses the phrase "communication of properties and graces and acts" (*communicatio idiomatum et gratiarum et operationum*) in line with its usage in the Reformed tradition. The communication of *properties* indicates that the attributes of the eternal Son can be ascribed to the human Jesus, and vice versa, as long as they are attributed to the person rather than the other nature. The communication of *graces* refers to the grace Jesus receives as he grows in knowledge, power, and obedience over the course of his life. The communication of *acts*, or *operations*, indicates that Jesus Christ performs the work of salvation in and through his two distinct natures.

was and is also the true Son of Man, it has now become and is participant in this elevation and exaltation. There is no human life which is not also (and primarily and finally) determined and characterized by the fact that it can take place only in this brotherhood. And therefore there is no self-knowledge which does not also include, which does not necessarily have primarily and finally as its object, the fact that man as such is the brother of this one man.[14] Its true theme and origin can only be a declaration of the Christmas message.

And what is this message? It is not just the supernatural indicative that there was then born an exceptional man who was God Himself, a creature who was also the Creator who rules over all things, and that this remote fact is our salvation if we today will accept it. Nor is it the supernatural imperative that what took place then can and should be repeated today, God Himself being born in us, or in our soul.[15] What it does tell us is that in the union of God with our human existence which then took place uniquely in the existence of this man, prior to our attitude to it, before we are in any position to accept or reject it, with no need for repetition either in our soul or elsewhere, we today, bearing the same human essence and living at a particular point in time and space, *were* taken up (quite irrespective and even in defiance of our own action and merits) into the fellowship with God for which we were ordained but which we ourselves had broken; and that we *are* therefore taken up into this fellowship in Him, this One. The Christmas message speaks of what is objectively real for all men, and therefore for each of us, in this One. Primarily and finally we ourselves *are* what we are in *Him*. But to be in Him is to be like Him, to be His brothers, to have a share in that in which He is quite unlike us, in His fellowship with God, in God's pleasure in Him, but also in His obedience to God, in His movement towards Him. There can be no question of our standing in any sense in this fellowship, or making this obedient movement to God, apart from Him or without Him, in an abstract and subjective selfhood. But there can also be no question of our not being in

14. Barth's key claim in this paragraph is that Jesus Christ's human life is not just his own, but rather, it determines the reality of *every* human life because every human exists in and through him. Jesus is totally distinct from every other human due to his divinity. But Jesus also is the true human, the one elected in the beginning to represent humanity by bearing the burden of sin so that humans might be reconciled to God. His life determines the destiny of every human life because he is the one who brings human being to the "elevated and exalted" end for which it was made. For this reason, there is no way to know the truth about human being without knowing him.

15. Barth rejects two possibilities for seeing the incarnation: It is not a miraculous external event in the past that we must affirm and apply to our lives in the present. Nor is it an internal spiritual reality that becomes realized as we repeat it in the present. The problem in both cases is that the human is placed in the center of the event of salvation.

Him as the elected, called, instituted and revealed Lord and Head of all men, of our not being in His representative existence, as if our own obedience were not anticipated and virtually accomplished in His.[16]

In the self-knowledge whose object and origin is the declaration of the message of the birth of the man Jesus we know ourselves—if we seriously accept it in its direct and in both its primary and secondary content—as those who are His, as Christians. But this means that we know ourselves as men with whom God has fellowship and who have fellowship with God; to whom God has said Yes and who say Yes to God; as "men of goodwill," i.e., as men of the covenant as it is maintained and fulfilled not only on the side of God but also on that of man, so that the Vulgate rendering "of goodwill among men" (*hominibus bonae voluntatis*), although it is incorrect, is not absolutely impossible.[17] For what took place in the history which is the content of the name of Jesus Christ is that the covenant between God and man was maintained and restored on both sides: on both sides perfectly, because in this history the Son of God became also the Son of Man; and for the same reason representatively, i.e., in such a way that the case of all men is advocated and conducted by this One, all men being included in this One in the covenant as it is perfectly maintained and restored on both sides. There is no one, therefore, who does not participate in Him in this turning to God. There is no one who is not himself engaged in this turning. There is no one who is not raised and exalted with Him to true humanity. "Jesus lives, and I with Him."[18]

It is this "and I" which is always the subject of the self-knowledge in which man may seek and find himself in this One. Except in Christ no one can know and confess that he is a Christian. No other self-knowledge, however deep or pious or believing, can lead to this "and I." Unless it begins with the "Jesus lives" it cannot possibly end with the "I." Apart from the one Son of Man whose existence is the act of the Son of God, there is no other man who keeps the covenant, who turns and is obedient to God, who shares the divine

16. The message of the incarnation is that the existence of every human is determined by Jesus Christ. God created the world with the human Jesus in mind, and the life of every human is ordered around and determined by him. Humans *are* what they are in *Christ* because he is their head and representative. As a result, the reality of every human life is not determined by what humans themselves do—particularly in their sin and rebellion against God—but by what Christ does as the true and faithful covenant partner of God.

17. The Vulgate is the Latin translation of the Greek New Testament. Barth is referring to the angels' declaration to the shepherds: "Glory to God in the highest, and on earth peace, good will toward men" (Luke 2:14 KJV). His point is that this phrase, whether translated as "men of goodwill" or "goodwill among men," captures a truth about God's relationship to humanity. God has fulfilled his covenant promises on both the divine and the human sides in Jesus Christ.

18. This is the title of a hymn by the German poet Christian F. Gellert (1715–1769).

goodwill. The audacity of regarding ourselves as men who move and are obedient and are therefore pleasing to God, as Christians, except as we look to this
One, and our being in Him as the One who takes our place and acts for us,
is sheer foolhardiness—a flight of Icarus which, whether we realize it or not,
will meet at once with its merited reward.[19] In an abstract, subjective selfhood,
apart from Jesus Christ, none of us exist as those who move and are obedient
to God, and therefore we cannot really know ourselves as such. It is only in
this One that we genuinely exist ourselves as men like this, as Christians. A
true knowledge of ourselves as such, and therefore of our Christian actuality,
stands or falls for all of us with our knowledge of Jesus Christ. In Him we are
hidden from ourselves. Only in Him can we be revealed. We cannot, therefore,
be revealed to ourselves or know ourselves directly, but only indirectly, in relation to the One who for us too is the Mediator between God and men. We
can boast of ourselves only as we do not boast of ourselves, but of the Lord.

Yet as we boast of the Lord we are undoubtedly invited to boast of ourselves;
of our being as those who keep the covenant, and are turned and obedient to
God, in Jesus Christ; of our true humanity; of our elevation and exaltation.
We, too, are directly elevated and exalted in the elevation and exaltation of
the humiliated Servant of God to be the Lord and King. Apart from Him we
are still below, but in Him we are already above. Without Him we are turned
from God and disobedient, but with Him we are turned to God and obedient.
Outside Christ, looking abstractly and subjectively at ourselves, we are not
Christians. But as we look at Him we are Christians indeed: not presumptuous
Christians but also not frigid; not cocksure but also not despairing or skeptical; not Christians who either rend themselves in a dialectic or falsely deify
themselves; but genuinely happy Christians who can and even should know
and confess that they are such.[20] There is certainly a dialectic in all this, for we
ourselves have used the phrases: "apart from Him" and "in Him"; "without
Him" and "with Him"; "looking at ourselves" and "looking at Him." But
when we hear the Christmas message we are not spectators of ourselves, so
that we do not fall victim to the illusion that it indicates and describes two
scales, or the two sides of a see-saw, which alternately rise and fall, thus
inviting us to understand ourselves alternately or simultaneously in abstract

19. In Greek mythology, Icarus flew so close to the sun that his wax wings melted and he fell
into the sea. Barth uses this reference to emphasize that humans have no ability to relate to God,
or even to know themselves, apart from Jesus Christ. This theme is central to Protestant theology.

20. If humans exist "in Christ," then it is right to say that they share in the benefits that
Christ himself possesses as the resurrected Lord. In Christ, human nature has been exalted,
and we cannot think about what it means to be a human apart from this exaltation. Barth sees
this as an implication of Paul's claim that our lives are "hidden with Christ in God" (Col. 3:3).

subjectivity and concrete objectivity, apart from Christ and in Him, without Him and with Him, looking at ourselves and looking at Him. This dialectic of the scales or see-saw is our own fatal contribution to the matter, and it is a contribution that we must refrain from making, because it has nothing whatever to do with the declaration of the Christmas message. This tells us unequivocally, unilaterally and positively that the "Jesus lives" also includes the "and I"; that the latter cannot be separated from it; that there is, therefore, no place from which man can be his own spectator and question the reality of the fact that he belongs to Jesus. The dialectic of the Christmas message is that of a decision which is being—and has already been—taken: the decision that we are not apart from Christ but in Him; that we are not without Him but with Him; that if we are to see ourselves we must not look at ourselves but look at Him. It tells us that we are those for whom He stands surety as the Son of Man, whose turning from God is superseded by His turning to Him, whose disobedience is already overshadowed and outmoded by His obedience, whose abstract and subjective and therefore corrupt humanity is corrected and rectified by His true humanity. It tells us that we are men whose selfhood He has made His own affair, who can seek and find it, therefore, only in Him. It does not tell us that we are Christians and something else, but simply and unreservedly that we are Christians.[21] Does this mean that we are invited to a false assurance? The only false assurance is when we miss the Christmas message, and therefore think we can and should seek and find and know ourselves otherwise than in the Son of Man who stands surety for us, in Him as our sanctification. And the falsest of all false assurances is when we imagine that in that "otherwise" we can order and please ourselves in a continual uncertainty. As we shall see, the being of man in Jesus Christ, and the knowledge of it, is a strict and bold and stimulating matter. We shall learn to know its incisive consequences, and we shall then be amazed that anyone could be afraid of a false assurance. But first and foremost we have to realize that we are invited and commanded to understand inclusively the message of the Son of God who became one with us, and therefore of the existence of the royal man Jesus. Our existence is enclosed by His, and therefore we ourselves are addressed and claimed as those who are already directed and obedient to God in Him, as those who are already born again and converted, as those who are already Christians. "We have peace with God through our Lord Jesus Christ" (Rom. 5:1). Many serious and penetrating things result

21. Here Barth offers a pastoral application of his argument. Since all human being is in Christ—and since salvation is determined solely by Christ's saving work—humans are relieved of the burden of having to determine whether they are saved on the basis of their own actions or subjective feelings. They need only to look at Christ's objective life and work.

from this peace, as emerges in Romans 5–8. But they result from the fact that we *have* this peace. Only half-serious and superficially penetrating things can result from a lack of peace with God, or from a supposed peace that we have or think we have in some other way than "through our Lord Jesus Christ." The Christmas message is: "Peace on earth to men of (God's) goodwill." And what is meant is the peace with God which is included for all the children of men in the child who was born there and then.[22] . . .

Because this is the case, Jesus Christ is our justification (1 Cor. 1:30). That is, as those who are of like humanity with Him, in Him as our Head and Representative we are righteous and acceptable and pleasing to God even as we are. In and with Him as our Brother, and therefore with the forgiveness of our sins for His sake, we are accepted and loved and blessed as God's dear children. But we must also continue that because this is the case He is also our sanctification. That is, as those who are of like humanity with Him, in Him as our Head and Lord, we are claimed as those who are regenerate and converted, as those who are already engaged in that turning to God, and therefore as Christians. It is only because this is the case, because we are what we are in Jesus Christ before God and therefore in truth, that it can be said of us that we are righteous before God and that we are also holy before God.[23] If it were not so, both statements would be sheer madness. But because it is so, they are unavoidable and we have to risk them; the second no less than the first. And it is the second which is important in the present context. We will not develop it for the moment. But we must look at its basis, which consists in the fact that the elevation and exaltation of the Son of Man, in the person of the One who was the Son of God and in this way and as such the Son of Man, includes in anticipation the elevation and exaltation—or shall we distinguish and say rather more cautiously the setting up—of all those who as men are brothers of this One. It is in the anticipation that takes place in this One that the sanctification of man has its root, and therefore the life of the Christian community, and Christian love. . . .

22. Worries about "false assurance" arise when people might think they are saved when in fact they are not. Barth rejects the legitimacy of these worries if the criterion by which assurance is measured is the human's own subjectivity. Our own ideas or feelings about God cannot serve as the basis of our assurance. Rather, Jesus Christ stands as the surety of salvation, and we either believe the message about him or we do not.

23. Barth is making a classic Reformed point here: believers are justified *and* sanctified by grace. In the context of his particular account of the covenant, however, Barth's version of this "double grace" takes on a different form. Christ sanctifies humans by living as the true covenant partner with God on their behalf, and they participate in his action in and through their own correspondence to his work within the ongoing history of the covenant. Barth will develop this theme in his account of Christ's relationship to the church in the chapters to come.

What is it that we have heard and said? We have maintained that the necessary statement about the being of Jesus Christ no less necessarily includes in it a statement about all human being; the statement which the Christian can and must venture in view of the fact that his confession "Jesus lives" involves also the confession "and I with Him." What the community recognizes in faith in the being of Jesus Christ its Lord is the divine decision which in this One as the Lord of all men has been taken for all men and concerning the being of all men. It is, therefore, their participation in His exaltation. The connection between these two statements is quite unequivocal in the New Testament. The New Testament does not know of a Jesus Christ who is what He is exclusively for Himself. Nor does it know of a self-enclosed human being confronting this man Jesus. We might think of sinful man. But according to the New Testament it was to seek and save sinners that the man Jesus came. Even sinful man is seen together with the man Jesus, which means that in the man Jesus even sinful man is confronted by the One in whom the divine decision has been made concerning him, in whom there is already resolved and accomplished his deliverance from sin, his elevation, his restoration as a true covenant-partner of God. In other words, there is no Jesus existing exclusively for Himself, and there is no sinful man who is not affected and determined with and by His existence.

chapter 27

The Glory of the Mediator

Introduction

Barth describes Jesus Christ's ongoing ministry to the world in *Church Dogmatics* IV/3. After dying for humanity's sins and being raised from the dead in glory, Christ does not rest but remains active. Or, as Barth puts it, Christ "strides through the ages still left to him until his final return in its final form."[1] With his victory over sin and death accomplished, his action takes on a new dimension and form. From his seat at the right hand of the Father, Christ now serves as the Prophet who proclaims the good news of his victory to the world.

In this excerpt, Barth presents several key themes related to Christ's prophetic work. Two themes especially stand out. First, Barth emphasizes that forces of nothingness continue to confront Christ as he reveals himself to the world. To be sure, because Christ already won the decisive victory in and through his death and resurrection, the outcome of his confrontation is certain. But this victory now must be realized in history, and this realization takes place only gradually. It occurs whenever Christ shines a light on falsehood by proclaiming the truth through his Word. It also occurs as Christ confronts the world marked by self-centered disobedience by calling forth a community defined by acts of self-sacrificial love.

Second, and related, Barth emphasizes that God's reconciliation of sinners takes place as a history. Christ's victory over sin and death took place in time

1. Karl Barth, *Church Dogmatics* IV/3.2 (Edinburgh: T&T Clark, 1962), 663.

and space, and so does its realization. Salvation is not a theory but a person, and the benefits of salvation are realized in time as the history of his life is proclaimed and humans realize that their true origin and destiny have been determined by him. For example, when Christ's atoning death for humanity's sin is proclaimed, humans realize they are implicated in this event because this death was for *their* sin. Christ is not merely a historical person but a living Lord whose personal history determines the life of every other person. His ministry to the world inaugurates a "wider and new history," a counterhistory that unveils the world's true order and the purpose for which it was created.

Church Dogmatics IV/3.1[2]

The relationship between God and man denoted by the terms life, covenant and reconciliation does not rest on any necessity immanent in either the existence and nature of God or those of man. God does not owe it to man. And man has no claim to it. From the standpoint of both God and man it seems rather to be excluded and impossible. It exists as it is created and takes place in Jesus Christ. Seen from above, it is actual in the free act of grace for which God determines Himself and upon which He resolves in Jesus Christ. Seen from below, it is actual in the free act of obedience in which man acknowledges the doing of the will of God active in the divine act of grace. In this its actuality as a free act of grace and obedience, it is a new thing between God and man. It is the sphere and character of this new thing, in that the life is also light, the covenant Word and the reconciliation revelation. It is still a matter of Jesus Christ and His activity, but now in His prophetic office and work. Here, too, nothing is self-evident, given or necessary. As the actuality of the relationship takes place, so its truth, i.e., its self-declaration, and therefore the grounding of its recognition, can only take place. Its occurrence is the prophecy of Jesus Christ. That He Himself—and in Him the life, covenant and reconciliation—shine out and are disclosed and made known, is an event, and can only be understood as such. It is a drama which can only be followed, or rather experienced and recounted.[3]

2. Karl Barth, *Church Dogmatics* IV/3.1 (Edinburgh: T&T Clark, 1961), 166–68, 180–82, 211.

3. We can rephrase this paragraph: God's relationship with humans is not a necessity but a free decision. God decides to relate to humanity by electing Jesus Christ to bear their sin on their behalf; and humans are elected to live in obedience to God in and through their participation in Christ's life. Since this relationship results from God's decision to relate to humanity through the human Jesus, it is not a general feature of created existence. Rather, this relationship is

The necessity of a historical understanding of the equation results supremely from the fact that His light, Word and revelation no less than His life, covenant and reconciliation, are challenged by an opposition which encounters them, and His prophetic no less than His high-priestly and kingly service and rule thus consist practically in the overcoming of this opposition and answering of this challenge. They occur in an environment to which they are superior in right and might, but which is either hostile or alien, or at any rate strange. The "world" is this environment: humanity; man in and with the cosmos; man in his creaturely and historical nature.[4] But we do well to think also of the Church and individual Christians in this respect. By this environment the Son of God and Man, Jesus Christ, is Himself challenged and assaulted as He challenges and assaults it by His existence and with His Word. His life is constantly confronted by death, the covenant by unfaithfulness and apostasy, reconciliation by strife. But this is also the situation of His prophetic office and work, ministry and action. His Word is met by the contradiction and His truth by the falsehood of His environment, and they consist in the exposing, resisting and overcoming of the falsehood and contradiction. This does not mean that absolute and final limits are set to Him, but it does mean that He has to contend with limits of relative and provisional seriousness. He is noticeably though not invincibly confined. And as His Word contradicts the contradiction, it seems for its part to subject itself even to a certain bondage and conditioning, and to be spoken with a relative and provisional but unmistakeable restraint. We recall the expression in John 1:5: "The light shines," but it shines "in darkness" (whatever this may signify in detail). Yet we must not forget the continuation: "and the darkness did not overcome it." This light which streams into the world is still the eternal light which cannot be vanquished or extinguished. Nevertheless, this does not alter the previous statement that it shines in a place or environment which is certainly illumined by it, but does not even partially shine itself, not corresponding to its shining with any brightness of its own, but being differentiated from it as darkness, and as such negatively opposing it with its own limited power. In face of this environment it does not yield but makes its way. Yet, in order finally to exclude and destroy it, it must do so step by step and therefore in a history. Or, as we might say, the Word of the covenant is uttered, going out through all lands, to the end of the world, like the voice and sound of Psalm 19:4. Yet is it not something self-evident, given or necessary, but a new and special and

---

realized as an event in time when Christ declares himself as the risen Lord and humans respond to Christ with faith and obedience. The divine-human relationship must be described on these specific historical terms in order to be understood correctly.

4. For the background behind these claims, see Barth's account of nothingness in chap. 23.

wonderful thing both as a whole and in detail, if this does not take place in vain, if the Word achieves its object, if it finds ears which are open or even partially open. Or again, reconciliation is revealed in all its clarity. Yet, as it is itself an event, it can only be an event if in the place where it happens, in the reconciled world of humanity, its revelation is confirmed by the fact that it is perceived in its truth and clarity, and it is thus recognized as the reconciliation of the world of humanity. Comprehensively, the great Prophet Jesus Christ is certainly present and at work, pronouncing authoritatively the first and last and total truth concerning the name and kingdom and will of God.[5] Yet like the prophets before Him, and even in the circle of those who are with Him, He is a lonely Newcomer and Stranger, a Messenger who has something to say to the world which it does not and cannot know of itself, which is closed to it as it arbitrarily or indolently closes itself against it, which it is neither willing nor ready to receive, so that it is something which has to happen, and only can happen, if He does not remain lonely, if His message is not in vain but wins a hearing and obedience, if the seed sown by Him is not scattered to the winds but germinates and brings forth fruit.

Hence we cannot in any sense understand in static terms the relationship between Him and the surrounding world of darkness. It is certainly not dualistic. We do not have the equilibrium of opposing forces, as though darkness had the claim and power finally to maintain itself against light, as though its antithesis, opposition and challenge to light, its restricting of it, rested on an eternal and lasting order. On the other hand, it is not monistic. The power of light is not so overwhelming in relation to that of darkness that darkness has lost its power altogether, as though its antithesis were already removed, its opposition brushed aside, its challenging and restricting of light of no account. The only alternative is to think of it in terms of dynamic teleology, namely, in relation to the power of light, Word and revelation as this is active in great superiority yet has not so far attained its goal but is still wrestling toward it, being opposed by the power of darkness, which even though it yields in its clear inferiority, is still present and even active in its own negative and restrictive way. A history is here taking place; a drama is being enacted; a war waged to a successful conclusion. If from the very first there can be no doubt as to the issue of the action, there can also be no doubt that there is

5. While Jesus Christ won a decisive and objective victory over nothingness in his death and resurrection, this victory is realized in time as the triumphant Christ reveals himself to the world. As he goes about this prophetic work, Christ is challenged by false words and actions that contradict and oppose him. He nevertheless prevails over this opposition step by step by proclaiming his victory to the world in distinct events of self-disclosure to humans.

an action, and that it is taking place, and can thus be described only in the form of narration.[6] . . .

Our concern is with this event of reconciliation as an event of revelation. It is with the life which shines as such, the covenant which speaks for itself, the reality of the fellowship of God and man restored in Jesus Christ as this declares itself to be also truth. It is with Jesus Christ Himself in His prophetic office and work, as He confesses and makes Himself known as the humiliated Son of God and the exalted Son of Man, and therefore as the Mediator between God and man, and therefore as the One who restores fellowship between them and accomplishes the justification and sanctification of man. In this context, therefore, our problem is that of knowing the atonement. How is it that its occurrence is not hidden but may be and actually is perceived? How is it that it does not remain alone, but achieves significance, regard and acknowledgement in the world and among men? How is it that the cosmos reconciled in Jesus Christ realizes how matters stand with it? How is it that men come to see in Jesus Christ their Fellow and Brother? How is it that they are discovered, and discover themselves, as the people who have their own life, and are justified and sanctified, in Him?[7] It is in this connection that the prophetic office and work of Jesus Christ are relevant as an integrating factor in the event of reconciliation. A "prophet" in the biblical sense is one to whom it is given to see and understand the doing of the will of God on earth, and who is also charged to declare, expound and explain, and thus to mediate, his understanding, thus enabling others to participate in what takes place. Jesus Christ is the Prophet who knows and proclaims the will of God which is done in His existence. The Synoptic statement that "the kingdom of God is at hand," materially identical with the Johannine "I am," is the sum and substance of His prophetic message and therefore of the knowledge mediated

6. Barth uses the term "dynamic teleology" to describe the history of God's covenant of grace. This history is *dynamic* because it involves an ongoing conflict between Christ and the power of nothingness. It is not dualistic because Christ is supreme and victorious over this power; yet is not monistic because this victory has yet to be fully realized. Because the reality of this victory is certain, it can be described as *teleological*. The history of the covenant is progressing in a dramatic fashion toward the end that God determined from the beginning as Christ overcomes darkness with his light.

7. Barth believes that Christ's objective saving work includes within itself the subjective realization of that work within the human recipient. It is not as if Christ performs a work of salvation that needs a human response in order to be complete. Rather, the human's response to Christ is enclosed within Christ's saving act (see chap. 27). Given this reality, Barth is now asking an additional question: How does Christ bring about the subjective realization of his saving work within humans? Or, put differently, how do humans realize that they are saved in Christ?

by Him.[8] This is the context in which the historicity of the atonement now calls for particular emphasis.

It can be no more than a question of particular emphasis. Reconciliation as a whole is history which as such can only be recounted. History is the life of all men actualized in Jesus Christ. It is the history of the covenant fulfilled in Him. That the Son of God humiliated Himself to be with us and for us in order that He could uncover the pride of man and positively accomplish his justification, the gathering of His community in the world and the awakening of faith in Him; and again, that the Son of Man should be exalted to fellowship with God in order that He should uncover the sloth of man, and positively accomplish his sanctification, the upbuilding of a community of God on earth, and the awakening of love, all this was worked out on the dramatic way of conflict from Bethlehem to Golgotha, and was and is therefore history. Salvation takes place in this salvation history. There cannot, then, be intended an exclusive but only a special emphasis, to be undertaken as a part for the whole, if we underline the historicity of the atonement specifically in relation to the fact that in its fulfillment this is itself the answer to the problem of its declaration and knowledge, or if we point out that in its prophetic element it has a specifically historical character. All that can be meant is that in our present context, in its prophetic element, its historical character forces itself upon us with a special and direct insistence acquired only at this point, and is thus to be firmly grasped.[9] How far is this really so? How far does the historicity of the atonement particularly impinge upon us at this point, in relation to the prophetic work and office of Jesus Christ, so that it is meaningful to give it particular attention in the present context?

The general answer to this question must be to the effect that, as the event of reconciliation is also that of revelation or prophecy, as the life as such is also light, it emerges from the apparent distance in which it is played out for us men, and comes to affect us directly, so that we are not merely implicated in its occurrence, but realize that this is the case.[10] As it is heard and perceptible as Word, it engages our attention and we men see that the event of reconciliation of which it speaks is an event for us and to us, and that we

8. This is Barth's answer to the questions raised in the previous note: humans subjectively realize the objective reality of their salvation in Christ as Christ proclaims himself to them.

9. Barth's point here is that Jesus Christ's saving work is the *entire history of salvation* rather than a single historical act. So as he emphasizes the event of the atonement in particular, he cautions that this event cannot be seen as *the* moment of salvation. Rather, the atonement is a particular event that enables us to interpret the entire history of salvation rightly.

10. Barth's key claim is that the revelation of the atonement enables humans to realize that *they* are implicated in Christ's death on the cross due to their sin and that his death is a death *for them*.

are implicated in such a way that we can no longer exist at all without being implicated. "We men" means all the men who have not yet perceived, or who have forgotten or denied again. It means all the men who in the first instance think that they are not directly, properly and seriously implicated either in the history of Israel or in that of Jesus Christ as first its intimation and then its enactment. It means all the men who can be and actually are of the opinion that they belong to another sphere than that in which it has taken place that the kingdom of God has drawn near, that God has reconciled the world to Himself, that He has established and maintains and fulfills the covenant between Himself and man, that He makes a reality of true life in fellowship with Himself. No matter what has taken place according to the witness of the Bible, as they see it they themselves are not affected in their own sphere, but are remote from it, being at best only spectators of a rather unusual drama or hearers of rather a strange message, and therefore free either to regard the matter as so much more history or myth, or to turn away from it with a complete lack or disengagement of interest to pursue their own more pressing thoughts and affairs. Are we not all men who think that they can treat the occurrence of reconciliation, the history of salvation, in this way? In the first instance, and continually, does not the story seem to affect us in this way, and therefore not really to affect us, because it does not seem to refer in any sense to ourselves? But in so far as the event of reconciliation is also that of revelation; in so far as the justification and sanctification of man are also his vocation; in so far as Jesus Christ is not only High-priest and King but also Prophet, this appearance is torn aside and this opinion is made untenable. For as reconciliation is also revelation, the life light, the covenant Word and Jesus Christ Prophet, the sphere is burst wide open where we shut ourselves off from Him, the distance which we think that we can and should keep is overcome, the water pours over the dam behind whose shelter we believe that we have solid ground under our feet apart from the being and action of Jesus Christ, and, putting an end to our mere seeing and hearing, to our evaluations in terms of history and myth, and to our unconcerned hastening past Him to very different thoughts and affairs, He brings us right into the picture, namely, into His picture, the dynamic picture of His action. No safeguard, protest or shrugging of the shoulders can help us here. Whatever it may or may not mean for us subjectively; whatever may be its reflection in our consciousness, the fact that reconciliation is also revelation and Jesus Christ lives and works as Prophet means that objectively we can no longer be remote from Him in a private sphere, but that we are drawn into His sphere, into what takes place in Him. This occurrence becomes objectively our own experience. We experience here what takes place there in the supposed but only apparent "there" which in reality encloses our here and in which our here is also there. That man's here (and he himself in his here) is truly there; that the there of that history is here in reality man's own history—this is what is disclosed as reconciliation is also revelation and Jesus Christ acts also as Prophet. In His prophecy He draws the logical conclusions of His own well-founded claim to lordship over the whole world and all men. In His prophecy He comes "unto his own" (John 1:11).[11] . . .

We may conclude that the reconciliation of the world to God is in every respect history. But there is particular reason to emphasize its historicity at this point, in relation to its third form.[12] In this form, in its character as light, Word and truth, it is historical in a distinctive and outstanding way. Generally speaking, this is because, as revelation which is the basis of knowledge, it here bursts from within and in its own strength its apparent restriction and isolation as that which has occurred in a specific time and place, transcending itself and moving into world-occurrence and the occurrence of each individual life, in order that it may there show itself and its occurrence to be the origin, meaning and goal of all occurrence and thus seize all occurrence and refashion it for participation in itself, impressing upon it its own law and giving it its own direction. It is the reconciliation of the whole world, of all men. Yet as such it must, it wills to be understood and grasped by the whole world and all men.[13] It sees to it itself that this should happen in its third form in which its reality is also truth, the act of God in Jesus Christ is also the Word of God, the life is also light. As atonement takes place in this dimension, too, as it is also revelation establishing knowledge, it expresses and asserts what it is for the whole world and for each and every man. It thrusts down its roots and wins for itself form and existence in this outside sphere. It becomes the

---

11. Humans prefer to live in a self-enclosed way by defining their own lives while keeping Jesus in the distance as an isolated figure in the past. But Christ's revelation exposes this self-determination as false. To encounter the history of Christ's death for sins, and to understand it within the context of Israel and all humanity, is to be confronted with the reality that Christ's history is *humanity's* history. Humans do not live in a separate sphere but within the sphere of Jesus Christ. When Christ reveals himself to humans, he confronts them with their true identity: they are sinners who have been saved by him as a result of God's election before the foundation of the world. In this way, Christ's objective work of salvation becomes their own objective experience.

12. By "third form" of reconciliation, Barth means its form as a Word prophetically delivered by Christ as he reveals himself to the world.

13. Barth's claim is that, when the risen Christ proclaims himself as the context of the reconciling work, the "there and then" becomes the "here and now" and vice versa. The events that took place in the past—specifically, Christ's death on the cross for sins—become the present reality of the hearer of Christ's Word; at the same time, this hearer participates in, and is determined by, Christ's death on the cross. Because Christ confronts the human here and now as the one who died there and then, he is the connecting point between the two moments.

beginning of a corresponding wider and new history: of a wider to the extent that it takes place outside in the world and in and among men; and of a new to the extent that its occurrence is something novel and different and strange in relation to other events in this outer sphere.[14]

14. Barth returns to the insight with which he began: because the reality of salvation is realized by humans through Christ's proclamation, it takes place as an event *in* history even as it determines the entire reality *of* history.

28

The Scope of Salvation

Introduction

Barth's rejection of the Reformed absolute decree (*decretum absolutum*) and his own doctrine of election raised concerns among some readers that Barth affirmed an *apokatastasis*, or universal salvation. Barth anticipated these questions and addressed them in *Church Dogmatics* II/2.[1] His answers did not satisfy everyone, however, and he continued to receive similar questions as readers worked through subsequent volumes of the *Church Dogmatics*. If God has elected the man Jesus Christ to be the representative for all human-ity—and if Jesus Christ has dealt with sin once and for all in his death and resurrection—then does that mean every human is saved?

Whenever Barth received this question, he typically responded by reframing it. He worried that discussions about universalism tended toward abstraction. Instead of beginning with God's freedom as displayed in his love, the ques-tion often was framed on the basis of general principles or presuppositions about what "must" be the case. Barth refused to speculate. He also rejected the idea that we can know what must be before actually hearing God's reve-lation in Jesus Christ. As with his treatment of every other subject matter in dogmatics, Barth insisted that the issue of salvation must be addressed strictly in light of God's revelation in Jesus Christ. This selection from *Church*

---

1. See Karl Barth, *Church Dogmatics* II/2 (Edinburgh: T&T Clark, 1957), 417–19.

Dogmatics IV/3.1 gives a sense of where Barth thought a faithful hearing of this revelation would lead the church.

—————————— *Church Dogmatics* IV/3.1[2] ——————————

A final word is demanded concerning the threat under which the perverted human situation stands, in spite of its limitation by the powerful and superior reality of God and man, to the extent that from below it is also continually determined by the falsehood of man in a sinister but very palpable manner. Can we count upon it or not that this threat will not finally be executed, that the sword will not fall, that man's condemnation will not be pronounced, that the sick man and even the sick Christian will not die and be lost rather than be raised and delivered from the dead and live? This question belongs to eschatology, but two delimitations may be apposite in this context.[3]

First, if this is not the case, it can only be a matter of the unexpected work of grace and its revelation on which we cannot count but for which we can only hope as an undeserved and inconceivable overflowing of the significance, operation and outreach of the reality of God and man in Jesus Christ. To the man who persistently tries to change the truth into untruth, God does not owe eternal patience and therefore deliverance any more than He does those provisional manifestations. We should be denying or disarming that evil attempt and our own participation in it if, in relation to ourselves or others or all men, we were to permit ourselves to postulate a withdrawal of that threat and in this sense to expect or maintain an *apokatastasis* or universal reconciliation as the goal and end of all things. No such postulate can be made even though we appeal to the cross and resurrection of Jesus Christ. Even though theological consistency might seem to lead our thoughts and utterances most clearly in this direction, we must not arrogate to ourselves that which can be given and received only as a free gift.[4]

Secondly, there is no good reason why we should forbid ourselves, or be forbidden, openness to the possibility that in the reality of God and man in Jesus Christ there is contained much more than we might expect and therefore the supremely unexpected withdrawal of that final threat, i.e., that in the

---

2. Karl Barth, *Church Dogmatics* IV/3.1 (Edinburgh: T&T Clark, 1961), 477–78.

3. Barth originally intended to write a fifth volume of the *Church Dogmatics* on the doctrine of redemption. He did not live to finish it.

4. Note how Barth frames this first delimitation in terms of God's freedom. Grace can never be a constantly available feature of created existence.

truth of this reality there might be contained the super-abundant promise of the final deliverance of all men.[5] To be more explicit, there is no good reason why we should not be open to this possibility. If for a moment we accept the unfalsified truth of the reality which even now so forcefully limits the perverted human situation, does it not point plainly in the direction of the work of a truly eternal divine patience and deliverance and therefore of an *apokatastasis* or universal reconciliation? If we are certainly forbidden to count on this as though we had a claim to it, as though it were not supremely the work of God to which man can have no possible claim, we are surely commanded the more definitely to hope and pray for it as we may do already on this side of this final possibility, i.e., to hope and pray cautiously and yet distinctly that, in spite of everything which may seem quite conclusively to proclaim the opposite, His compassion should not fail, and that in accordance with His mercy which is "new every morning" He "will not cast off for ever" (Lam. 3:22–23, 31).[6]

5. Barth's argument that there might be "much more" to the reality of Jesus Christ does not mean that God might unveil something *other* than what he already has revealed. This possibility will be a further unveiling of himself and the content of his one eternal plan.

6. Barth's two points work dialectically. On the one hand, we must remember that God is free and that we cannot count on him to save all people as if he is bound to do so. On the other hand, the reality that God's love in Jesus Christ has prevailed against sin and evil leaves us with a command to hope and pray for the salvation of all. Both truths must be affirmed, leaving the theologian in the position of looking to Christ with a cautious yet real hope.

Christian Community

Introduction

In this excerpt from *Church Dogmatics* IV/3.2, Barth explains the origin and
power of the Christian community by showing how its existence relates to
the saving work of Jesus Christ and the Holy Spirit. Barth prefers the word
"community" to "church" because he thinks it more clearly expresses the
New Testament's sense of the "people of God."[1] He begins this passage
by emphasizing the distinction between the Christian community and other
human communities. Even though it exists as a visible reality in the world,
the Christian community cannot be defined on the basis of any quality it
possesses. Nor is its existence determined by the will of its members, as if
their decision to form a community explains its origin and purpose. The
Christian community exists as the result of God's election of Jesus Christ.
His mission includes the task of gathering and equipping a people to live as
God's covenant partners in and through his own divine power. Christ's action
in fulfillment of this divine purpose is the origin and basis of the community.

The community's life takes place together with Christ as he ministers
to the world. Barth describes this relationship carefully so that its proper
order is maintained. Christ is not present and active in the world because
the community exists; rather, the community exists because Christ is present

1. For Barth's remarks on this point, see Karl Barth, *Church Dogmatics* IV/1 (Edinburgh:
T&T Clark, 1956), 651–52.

and active in the world. The Word of God stands at the center of their relationship, and the Holy Spirit is the bond of unity between them. This union does not involve the merging of humanity into divinity but the Spirit's empowerment of a human response to Christ's command. The result is a correspondence of divine and human action that occurs through the power of the Word and Spirit.

Christ gathers and commissions his community by speaking his Word to it, and the Spirit empowers the community to respond to this Word in faith and obedience. These obedient actions are ordered toward the fulfillment of the community's mission. The Christian community does not live for itself, as if it were its own end. Rather, it exists precisely so it can bear witness to Christ. The testimony is the primary way it partners with Christ in the fulfillment of God's eternal plan.

Church Dogmatics IV/3.2[2]

How does the Christian community exist or live or continue within world-occurrence?[3] . . .

In a first general and comprehensive formulation our answer is to the effect that the Christian community exists in virtue of its secret.[4] This means by way of delimitation that it does not exist in virtue of its own controllable power, freedom or capacity. It neither exists of itself nor can understand itself of itself. The power, freedom and capacity in virtue of which it exists cannot be understood as an element in general cosmic being. Or, as we may say more positively, the Christian community exists as it is called into existence, and maintained in existence, by its secret.[5] It exists in this way alone, but in this way truly, indisputably and invincibly. It lives by its secret. Without it, it could only fall. But it cannot fall, for it stands with its secret. Its secret is its ontic and noetic basis, its noetic as its ontic and its ontic as its noetic, and in both cases its clear basis in the sense that it may be indicated and described in terms of

2. Karl Barth, *Church Dogmatics* IV/3.2 (Edinburgh: T&T Clark, 1962), 751–63.

3. This question concerns the basis and reality of Christian community. How does this community come into being? By what power does it live?

4. By "secret" Barth means God's decision to relate to humans in Jesus Christ for the sake of their salvation. This decision is the ground of the world's existence and the purpose of history even as it remains hidden from those who either fail to see it or deny its reality. Because of God's revelation in Christ, however, the church knows the reality of this "secret" and can live confidently in line with the order of the universe (see *Church Dogmatics* IV/3.2, 749–50).

5. Put differently, the community exists not due to its own decision or capacities but as a result of God's decision to be for humanity in Christ.

its efficacy.[6] This basis is identical with the will and work and Word of God. Hence it neither need nor can be established on the part of man, and for this reason and to this extent it cannot be perceived or explained. Yet it is identical with the will and work and Word of God as effectively addressed to the world and specifically to the community, and for this reason and to this extent it may be known in its operation for all its inscrutability and inexplicability. It may thus be indicated, named and described as its ontic and noetic basis. We can thus point to it. In virtue of it, the Christian community is what it is in the world, visible and yet invisible, in the world and yet not of it, dependent and yet free, weak and yet strong. In the light of it, it sees world-occurrence and understands itself. In relation to its effective operation we can point to it and point back to it, denoting, defining and describing.[7] With this reference, then, we can answer our third and final question.

Two exalted names are both indispensable and adequate to denote and describe the basis and secret of the people of God in relation to the efficacy not concealed from it. Both in different ways are identical with the name of the God who has turned to it. Hence neither can be separated from the other, but each is necessary to elucidate the other. They are the names of Jesus Christ and the Holy Spirit. Jesus Christ acts and works and creates in and in relation to the Christian community by the Holy Spirit and therefore again in the mystery of God. The one effective action of God in this twofold form is the basis and secret of the Christian community. In making this reference and therefore in answering our final question, we may thus make two strictly related statements which mutually complement and elucidate one another.[8]

The first is that the Christian community exists as called into existence and maintained in existence by Jesus Christ as the people of His witnesses bound,

6. The word "ontic" has to do with *reality*; "noetic" has to do with the *knowledge*. So Barth is saying that God's decision in Jesus Christ is the basis of the community's reality and knowledge. The community's knowledge is that of its reality in Christ, and its reality in Christ is the basis of its knowledge. Through the reality of God's decision in Christ and the community's knowledge of it, God produces visible effects within the community that correspond to his divine will.

7. Barth's initial answer to the question about the existence of the Christian community is nuanced. He acknowledges that the Christian community exists as a visible reality within the world in the sense that it can be pointed to and described on creaturely terms. Even so, he insists that the community's existence is not based on the qualities inherent to the community itself. Its existence is based on the reality of God's decision in Jesus Christ and on the community's knowledge of this decision as a result of the Word of God.

8. Barth now makes his initial answer about the community's "secret" concrete by identifying the community's existence with the work of Jesus Christ and the Holy Spirit. They do not work separately, as if Christ acts first and then the Spirit. They perform one act of God in a twofold form.

engaged and committed to Him. It exists in virtue of His calling. The power of His calling is the power of the living Word of God spoken in it. And the power of this Word is the power of His Holy Spirit. As this power shines as divine power and is at work in the world, there takes place in the world and its occurrence the new and strange event of the gathering, upbuilding and sending of the Christian community. As Jesus Christ in the power of the Holy Spirit, or the Holy Spirit as His Spirit, creates recognition, establishes knowledge, calls to confession and therefore quickens the dead, the existence of the community begins and endures. Hence its existence is absolutely given, imparted or presented to it by Him as the One who in the power of His enlightening Spirit, the Creator Spirit, is at work on it and in it.[9] In relation to Him it has neither right nor claim to existence, and therefore no control over it. It cannot control its existence and therefore it cannot control itself. It does not exist in virtue of its own ability but only of His. It lives only as He, the living One, has controlled and still controls it. Its power and freedom and ability to be and live and persist in world-occurrence, it can treat only as His property for which it is responsible to Him, by the assignment of which it is set in His service, for the exercise and application of which it must render an account by continuing to be what it is and accepting and discharging its ministry. It exists as it belongs to Him, listens to Him and is obedient to Him. It really does exist, but only in this way, as the Christ community, as the branches in the Vine. "Apart from me you can do nothing" (John 15:5)—indeed, you can be nothing except perhaps a pile of broken and withering branches that can only be burned. He is the secret, the basis, the Creator and Lord, of the existence of His people.[10]

Thus the being of the people of God is grounded only in its God, and the being of the Christian community only in Jesus Christ as its Lord. . . .

We say further that the Christian community exists as He, Jesus Christ, exists. It does not exist merely because He exists, because its existence is established and created by His election, vocation and governance. This is also true. But there is more to it than this. The first point, which includes the second,

9. Barth is offering a fuller description of Christ's relationship to the church here. This description can be summarized in four key claims: (1) Christ calls a community into existence to serve as his witnesses. (2) Christ calls this community by speaking his Word to them through the power of his Spirit. (3) The Spirit empowers the community to respond to Christ's Word in faith and obedience. (4) The community exists strictly because the Spirit's power is at work on it and within it.

10. There are many communities in the world that exist for the sake of a common purpose, but the church is different from them all because its existence is determined by Jesus Christ. It exists as his "property," and he creates it so that it can work with him in his ministry to the world. Apart from this call and ministry, the church has no existence at all.

is that it exists as He exists, as to His being as its Head there belongs its own creaturely, earthly, human, historical and therefore distinct being as His body. It exists as its being is a predicate and dimension of His, and not *vice versa*. The being of Jesus Christ, then, is not, as Schleiermacher in his own brilliant fashion understood and explained, the supreme, decisive and distinctive predicate of His community, the model and historical point of connection for its living piety. To be sure, it exists as it believes in Him, loves Him and hopes in Him. But the fact that it does these things is not the basis of its existence. It does not live by them, i.e., by its own activity, by its faith and love and hope. It does not derive from them. Nor does Jesus Christ for His part exist only as the community is what it is and does what it does. No, the community exists only as He exists. "Because I live, ye shall live also" (John 14:19) is the right order. Hence we can and must venture to say that the being of the community is a predicate or dimension of the being of Jesus Christ Himself.[11] In this full and strict sense it belongs to Him and is His property. This is the source of its life and existence. Hence it has no option but to exist in faith in Him, love for Him and hope in Him. It exists as He exists. For He does not exist without it. He alone is who and what He is. But He is not alone as who and what He is. He is it for Himself, yet not only for Himself, but also with His own, and by anticipation with all who will become His own when His own shall be manifested in accordance with their determination as such. He is it together with them, being not only very God but also very man, and as such representing all men to God and God to all men. As very God alone He is also very man all together, so that His being does not exclude but includes within itself that of His own. In Him it is true and actual that God alone is God, yet that as the only God He is not alone, but that as the Creator, Reconciler and Redeemer of His creature He has ordered and bound Himself to this other which is so wholly distinct from Himself. To this great context belongs our

---

11. Barth draws an important distinction here. He argues that Christ does not exist and work in the world because the community exists—as if Christ would not be present in the world without the church. Rather, he argues that community exists because Christ exists and is working in the world. Apart from Christ's existence, the church would not be present in the world. He identifies Friedrich Schleiermacher (1768–1834) with the former approach. Schleiermacher argued that Christ no longer exercises a personal influence on the disciples after his ascension. Instead, they live with a common spirit and develop their own spontaneous activity in the pattern of Christ's activity during his ministry. In this sense, their activity "prolongs the personal action of Christ" in the world (see Friedrich Schleiermacher, *The Christian Faith*, §122.3; also §§123–25). Barth thinks the relationship works in the opposite direction. The church is not the basis of Christ's activity, but rather, Christ's activity is the basis for the church. As he sees it, this claim stands in line with Paul's description of believers as members of Jesus Christ's own body (Eph. 5:30).

statement that the Christian community exists as Jesus Christ exists, that its being is a predicate, dimension and form of existence of His.[12] . . .

In relation to the people of God existing in worldly form in terrestrial and human history, and therefore in relation to the Christian community, we certainly have to say that the being of Jesus Christ is not restricted to His being in the height and distance and transcendence of God, that it is not exhausted by this first predicate, that it has more than this first dimension and form, that in His being that of God Himself shows itself to be one which is not merely otherworldly, but which also condescends mercifully to this world. In the community it takes place that Jesus Christ Himself, the living Word of God, is present and revealed to certain men together in world-occurrence as the One He is above in the height and hiddenness of God.[13] And it also takes place that by these men together He is acknowledged, recognized, and confessed as this Word from the height, as their heavenly Head, and that He is confessed by them together as the Lord of all humanity. These men in their own time and place here find themselves commonly ruled and determined by the fact that in speech and action He always comes to their time and place. In other words, they find themselves ruled and determined by the common recollection of His accomplished coming and the common expectation of the awaited coming which He has still to fulfill. In the witness commonly entrusted to these men there still shines here and now in world-occurrence the light of Easter Day, and there already shines the light of the last of all days, the one light of His life both behind and before.[14] It is as this light shines that the community exists. It shines to the community and in the community. It shines in the form of the very human life, choices, speech and activity of the men united in it. It shines in their particular human history which as such is also an element in

12. These remarks reflect Barth's doctrine of election where he claims that God freely decides to unite himself to humanity in Jesus Christ (see chap. 18). This means that the Son of God has determined to live his eternal life in union with the flesh of the human Jesus *and* the people he represents. By his free choice, the Son's existence is bound to these people; and by necessity, these people are bound to him.

13. This section began with a question: How does the church exist within the world? The answer is that the church exists as Jesus Christ himself lives in and through it within the world. The risen Lord Jesus Christ does not merely exist beyond the world in the heights of heaven. He also exists within the world as he lives his eternal life in and through his community. He is present to this community through his self-revelation to them in the Word, and he performs his work in the world through them as they respond to this Word with faith and obedience.

14. What does Christ's existence in the world through the church look like? It looks like a community of people who hear his Word and then respond by acknowledging that Christ is the Head of their body and the Lord of the world. It also looks like a community whose lives are determined by the reality that the one who *was* raised from the dead and *will* come again lives and works among them *now* in and through his Word.

human and secular history generally. It shines in movements which are wholly creaturely and indeed, being made by sinful men, both capable and guilty of error. Yet this light shines as these movements, as the life, choices, thought, speech and activity of the men united here, follow the life movement of Jesus Christ as their model, either well or badly imitating, reflecting, illustrating and attesting it.[15] It is precisely as this takes place that His community exists. The community thus exists precisely as He Himself as its model is first present and alive in it, evoking, ordering and guiding its movements by His own; and as He Himself is also secondarily, or in reflection, illustrated and attested by the movements and in the being and activity of His community. We are thus forced to say that the community has its being as a predicate and dimension, and in a distinctive force, of His being. It exists as He alone lives with God, and yet as He who alone lives with God lives also in it, reflecting Himself in it, so that as the primarily active Subject He is not only above but also below, and below as the One He is above, present within it not merely as its recollected and expected but also as its present life. It exists as He does not exist abstractly in heaven, as a Head without a body, but is also with the community on earth, the heavenly Head of this earthly body. It thus exists as it, too, does not exist abstractly as a body existing only in worldly fashion in the world, but as it is His body, the body of this heavenly Head, a predicate or dimension of His being representing the merciful condescension of God to the world, His earthly-historical form of existence. This unity of its being with that of Jesus Christ, the existence of Jesus Christ in His singularity but also His totality, is the basis and secret of its existence.[16] . . .

The Holy Spirit is the power of God proper to the being of Jesus Christ, the one in whose exercise and operation He causes His community to become what it is. It is through the power of His Holy Spirit as the creative power of his summoning Word that the community exists as He, Jesus Christ, exists. As He wields this divine power of His in relation to the community, its existence occurs as *another*, as an earthly-historical predicate, as the second dimension and form of existence of His own being, and He makes it in the strict and intimate sense the people He possesses, the Christ-community.[17]

15. For the sake of clarity, I adjusted the translation of the last few sentences by replacing the pronoun "it" with its referent, the "light" that "shines."

16. Barth now states his key claim with more specificity: the church exists because Christ himself exists in and through it. Christ attests himself to the church in his Word, and the church responds by bearing witness to Christ in the world through its words and deeds. In this sense, Christ's presence in the world is not abstract but concrete because he exists in union with his community. The community's existence likewise is concrete because it exists "in Christ."

17. Barth summarizes the argument he made above, but now he includes an additional element by explaining where the Holy Spirit fits in: the Spirit is the power of God through which

What is this power of God? Our first point in characterization is that this power, and therefore the Holy Spirit, is the power of the grace of God addressed to the whole world in the one Son of God and Son of Man in free, creative action in and on this people. As God is gracious to humanity, He creates, upholds and governs within it this particular people of witnesses, causing it to come to be and to exist as such, to exist as Jesus Christ exists, giving it a share in His being, endowing it with the power, freedom and capacity to do its human work, to bear the witness entrusted to it. If it enjoys and exercises this power, it is not its own, but an alien power addressed and ascribed to it, the power of the free grace of God being great enough—for this is the point of it—to impart, address and ascribe its own power to this people as its witness among other peoples. The event in which this takes place is the work of the Holy Spirit.[18] As it takes place, this people exists, existing as Jesus Christ exists. As it takes place, its being is the predicate, dimension and form of existence of His being. As it takes place, it has the power to become His people and to take up and discharge its ministry of witness. It is thus also the free grace of God that it may exist as witness of this grace to all humanity and serve it with its human action. . . .

This action of the Holy Spirit as the work of the free grace of God in Jesus Christ is the basis and secret of the existence of the Christian community. This is the second statement to be made in answer to our third and final question.[19] We shall now try to shed light on it.

The Holy Spirit is the power, and His action the work, of the coordination of the being of Jesus Christ and that of His community as distinct from and yet enclosed within it. Just as the Holy Spirit—as Himself an eternal divine "person" or mode of being, as the Spirit of the Father and the Son (who proceeds from the Father and the Son)—is the bond of peace between the two, so in the historical work of reconciliation He is the One who constitutes and guarantees the unity of the whole Christ, i.e., of Jesus Christ in

---

Christ establishes and governs his community in the world. I adjusted the translation of this paragraph for the sake of clarity.

18. Barth's first point in regard to the Spirit's power is that it stands in line with God's determination in the covenant of grace. God elected Jesus Christ to bear the burden of human sin so that humanity might exist in him. This existence in Christ takes a corporate form as Christ lives in and through his community. The Spirit is the power that actualizes this community by enabling it to hear and then respond to the Word that Christ speaks to it. This is how the community participates in God's covenant: it bears witness to Christ as Christ bears witness to himself both in the community and in the world.

19. This question is, "What is this power of God?" Or, put differently, "What does it mean to call the Holy Spirit the power of God?" Barth's first answer is that the Spirit is the power of grace. His second answer is that the Spirit is the power that establishes the community in relation to Christ.

the heights and in the depths, in His transcendence and in His immanence. He is the One who constitutes and guarantees the unity of the first and the second predicates, of the primary and the secondary dimensions and forms of existence of His being. He is the One who constitutes and guarantees the unity in which He is at one and the same time the heavenly Head with God and the earthly body with His community.[20] This coordination and unity is the work of the active grace of God. Its freedom, the freedom of God and His action and operation, should not be overlooked nor forgotten for a single moment when we venture, as we must, to see and confess Jesus Christ as the same on both sides, as the Head at the right hand of the Father and as the body in the being of the community in its temporal and spatial present and situation, and therefore as the Lord in His totality. His being in this unity, and therefore the secret and basis of the existence of His community, is not a datum or state. It is a history which takes place as Jesus Christ exercises His power, as this power is operative as the power of His calling Word, and therefore as the gracious power of the Holy Spirit.[21]

The work of the Holy Spirit, however, is to bring and to hold together that which is different and therefore, as it would seem, necessarily and irresistibly disruptive in the relationship of Jesus Christ to His community, namely, the divine working, being and action on the one side and the human on the other, the creative freedom and act on the one side and the creaturely on the other, the eternal reality and possibility on the one side and the temporal on the other. His work is to bring and to hold them together, not to identify, intermingle nor confound them, not to change the one into the other nor to merge the one into the other, but to coordinate them, to make them parallel, to bring them into harmony and therefore to bind them into a true unity.[22] In the work

20. Recall that Barth argued that Christ lives and works in the world in two dimensions: in himself and in the community that exists in him. The Spirit is the bond of unity between these two dimensions because it is the power that coordinates the being and activity of Christ with the being and activity of his human community.

21. To paraphrase: as the one who coordinates the life of Christ with the life of his community, the Spirit is the key to understanding how Christ can be seated at the right hand of the Father *and* present to his community in the midst of time. Christ's life in both dimensions should be described in dynamic rather than static terms. It takes place in the present as the risen and transcendent Christ speaks his Word in and to the community through the power of his Spirit.

22. Having just affirmed that the Spirit is the bond of unity between Christ and the church, Barth now issues two cautions. First, we have to remember that the Spirit is bringing divine action into unity with human action. This necessarily involves disrupting the course of the creaturely and often sinful human action. Second, the Spirit does not unify Christ and the community by erasing the distinction between them, as if humanity is now merged into divinity. Rather, the Spirit works by bringing the human action into correspondence with the divine action while retaining the distinction between them.

of the Holy Spirit there takes place that which is decisive for the calling and therefore the existence both of the individual Christian and of the Christian community, namely, that the light of the crucified and risen and living Jesus Christ does not merely shine objectively, but shines subjectively into fully human eyes and is seen by them; that His Word as the Word of God does not only go out into all lands and even to the ends of the world (Ps. 19:4), but here and now is heard by very human ears and received and understood by very human reason; that God's revelation of His accomplished act of reconciliation has its counterpart here and now in human faith and love and hope and knowledge, its echo in human confession at this specific time and place; that its creative freedom finds an equivalent in real creaturely freedom. In the work of the Holy Spirit it takes place that Jesus Christ is present and received in the life of His community of this or that century, land or place; that He issues recognizable commands and with some degree of perfection or imperfection is also obeyed; that He Himself actively precedes this people; that in its action or refraining from action there is more or less genuine and clear reflection, illustration and attestation of His action, more or less faithful discipleship in the life of this people, and therefore a fulfillment of its commission.[23] . . .

◇◇◇

The community of Jesus Christ is for the world, i.e., for each and every man, for the man of every age and place who finds the totality of earthly creation the setting, object and instrument and yet also the frontier of his life and work.[24] The community of Jesus Christ is itself creature and therefore world. Hence, as it exists for men and the world, it also exists for itself. But it is the human creature which is ordained by nature to exist for the other human creatures distinct from it. It is what it is, and exists for itself, only in fulfillment of this ordination. Even within the world to which it belongs, it does not exist ecstatically or eccentrically with reference to itself, but wholly

23. Barth's point here is that the Spirit brings human action into unity with divine action by enabling the community to hear Christ's word and then respond with faith and obedience. His description of the Spirit's work corresponds to his earlier accounts of revelation and the Trinity (see chaps. 12–14). Christ's speech to the community is a self-revelation in the sense that Christ is making himself an object of human knowledge. The human becomes capable of receiving this knowledge only as the Spirit gives her the capacity to do so in faith. Both this capacity for faith and the obedience that follows it are not natural to the human but come as a gift of the Spirit. The distribution of this gift is how the Spirit coordinates the community's free life with God's free decision in Christ.

24. Barth's claim is an implication of the argument developed above. Because the community exists as Christ exists, it lives in the same way that Christ lives: for the sake of the world. This explains why Christ establishes the community through the power of his Spirit. He does so in order to fulfill the purposes for which he was elected in the beginning.

with reference to them, to the world around. It saves and maintains its own life as it interposes and gives itself for all other human creatures.

In this way it also exists for God, for the Creator and Lord of the world, for the fulfillment of His purpose and will for and to all human creatures. First and supremely it is God who exists for the world. And since the community of Jesus Christ exists first and supremely for God, it has no option but in its own manner and place to exist for the world. How else could it exist for God?[25] The center around which it moves eccentrically is not, then, simply the world as such, but the world for which God is. For God is who He is, not in the abstract nor without relationship, but as God for the world. The community of Jesus Christ is the human creature whose existence as existence for God has the meaning and purpose of being, on behalf of God and in the service and discipleship of His existence, an existence for the world and men.

That it exists for the world because it exists for God follows simply and directly from the fact that it is the community of Jesus Christ and has the basis of its being and nature in Him. He calls, gathers and upbuilds it. He rules it as its Lord and Shepherd. He constitutes it ever afresh in the event of His presence and by the enlightening power of His Holy Spirit. He is the centre around which it moves eccentrically. In Him and by Him it is won for God and claimed for His discipleship and service. For in Him God is not for Himself but for the world.[26] In Him God has given Himself to and for the world to reconcile it to Himself. In Him God, supremely and truly God, has become man. This decides the orientation, meaning and purpose of His community. As the people created by Jesus Christ and obedient to Him, it is not subsequently or incidentally but originally, essentially and by definition summoned and impelled to exist for God and therefore for the world and men. In this way but only in this way, as the human creature thus orientated, can it and will it also exist for itself, in correspondence with the fact that the God who acts and speaks in Jesus Christ expresses His own true divinity precisely in His true humanity.[27]

---

25. Barth's point is that, because the community is a community of Christ, it does not exist for its own sake but for the sake of the people God elected Christ to save.

26. The community does not exist for the world in an abstract sense. It exists for the world specifically because God is for the world in Jesus Christ. This divine self-determination makes the community's commitment to the world concrete. It exists for the world by serving Christ, and this service takes the form of bearing witness to him within the world.

27. The community's existence for the world is not an optional second step in its life. It does not exist in Christ first and then act to exist for the world. Rather, its existence in unity with Christ *is* its being for the world in partnership with Christ.

PART 3

Barth's Political Engagement

Karl Barth's engagement with political matters was shaped by three wars. The outbreak of World War I, and his former teachers' endorsement of the German war policy, prompted Barth's search for a new way of doing theology. The positive reaction of his fellow Christian socialists to the war also made Barth hesitant to trust any political party for the rest of his life. The years leading up to World War II were perhaps the most formative for Barth's political views. In the 1930s, he confronted the Nazi Party and its ideology expressed through their representatives in the German Christian movement. His vocal criticism of this movement eventually brought him into conflict with the Nazi government and led to his dismissal from the University of Bonn. His public opposition to Hitler, his support of the Allied cause in the war, and his intense desire to rebuild German society after the war also shaped his political views. Finally, late in his life, Barth's involvement in politics was shaped by the Cold War. He refused to be drawn into the ideological war between the sides and instead sought to articulate a vision for peace and hope in the midst of fear.

The selections in part 3 focus on the second of these three wars because this is the period in which Barth's political theology reaches its mature form.

This section begins with a previously untranslated text from 1962 where Barth offers his reflections on the forces and events that shaped German society during the 1920s (chap. 30). These remarks set the stage for the powerful Advent sermon that Barth preached in Bonn on December 10, 1933 (chap. 31). He uses Paul's argument in Romans 15 to emphasize the unique role of the Jewish people in the history of Christianity and to draw a stark contrast between a Christ-centered approach to the Jews and the anti-Semitism of the German Christians.

The next chapter contains the Barmen Declaration, which formed the theological basis of the German Confessing Church's resistance to the German Christians and their Nazi supporters (chap. 32). Penned almost entirely by Barth, this text provides the clearest summary of his political theology and served as the lens through which he approached the church's engagement with political matters through the end of his life. Barth's "Letter to American Christians" serves as an example of his approach to politics in the midst of war (chap. 33). It provides an account of Barth's support for the Allied efforts in the war as well as his critique of the church's complicity in the events leading up to the war. The selections conclude with an excerpt from Barth's 1946 lecture on the relationship between the church and state that he delivered in the ruins of the University of Bonn (chap. 34). This lecture attempted to articulate a vision for the church's engagement in political matters that would prevent the kind of mistakes that led to the German Christian movement and the Nazi regime.

30

A Brief Reminiscence of the 1920s

Introduction

In April 1961, the German magazine *Magnum* dedicated an issue to German culture in the 1920s. It featured dozens of photographs of prominent figures, including intellectuals like Jean-Paul Sartre, Martin Heidegger, Karl Jaspers, and Karl Barth. It also contained contributions from several of the subjects in the photos, including this essay by Barth. This essay was reprinted in a newsletter associated with the Swiss Reformed Church the following year, and this is the version translated here.

Three things stand out in this short piece. First, Barth frames this decade as a time of intense personal growth and development. These were the years when Barth transitioned from his pastorate in Safenwil to professorships at the University of Göttingen (1921–1925) and the University of Münster (1925–1930). Barth later recalled that he struggled with challenges that came with his new occupation, and this essay captures that sense of transition and anxiety. Even though he commanded a great deal of attention and published at a high rate, Barth later viewed his theology during this period as a work in progress. Second, Barth's description of the political movements in Germany during this period is significant. As a Swiss citizen, Barth always felt like an outsider to German political life. It is clear from this essay, however, that Barth cared about Germany and the success of the new government after the end of World War I. Although he did not anticipate the rise of Hitler, he clearly recognized that nefarious forces were stirring within German culture. Third, Barth's personal investment in his students is clear in this piece. His teaching posts put him in contact with hundreds of German students who were preparing for service in the German Church. These relationships would add to the intensity of his confrontation with German Church leadership as it embraced the Nazi movement in the years that followed.

"Zwischenzeit"[1]

In consideration of what I was asked to write, what I am able to provide is not a historical-philosophical interpretation of this period; I just don't have it in me to do this. Thus, I will make do by briefly reporting on how I perceived and experienced the twenties.

This decade fell roughly between the thirty-fifth and the forty-fifth years of my life. In the fall of 1921, I moved from Switzerland to Germany, from pastoral work in a parish to an academic post in a university.[2] Everything that I saw and heard around me was very new, especially what I now had to do myself. For all of the next decade, I was focused on adjusting to my new role. Of course, it was not as if I did nothing else; I frequently looked up from my books and notebooks and listened attentively to what was going on.

I saw a Germany that was on the verge of recovering from the lost World War and its consequences—the word "Versailles," said in a North German accent, often sounded in my ears like the crack of a whip—but that obviously was not able to recover.[3] I identified with the efforts of a few sober-minded men: the small, well-intentioned circles who took the "Weimar Republic" and its constitution seriously, who wanted to construct a German social democracy, and who, in a loyal manner, wanted to ensure the country reasonable space in the midst of an environment that was initially still suspicious enough of it to be opposed to this.[4] But I also saw and heard the "German National-ists," as we called them back then, who I remember as the least joyful of God's

----

1. Karl Barth, "Zwischenzeit," in *Kirchenblatt für die reformierte Schweiz* 118 (1962): 38–39; translation by Matthew J. Aragon Bruce.

2. Barth is referring to his move from his pastorate in Safenwil to the University of Göttingen to take up the position of Honorary Professor of Reformed Theology.

3. This is a reference to the Treaty of Versailles, signed on June 28, 1919, which brought an end to World War I. Germans widely held it to be unfair and disgraceful.

4. The Weimar Republic refers to the government of Germany from 1919 to 1933. The name comes from the city of Weimar, where the constitution was composed and adopted in August 1919.

creatures I have ever encountered, who had learned nothing and forgotten nothing, who torpedoed everyone as well as every attempt to achieve the best that was possible on that basis [i.e., on the basis of the Weimar Republic], and who in so doing—along with their diatribes intended to fill the cups of wrath—probably contributed more than anyone else to the outpouring of those cups in the following two decades over the German nation. At that time, I fundamentally erred by not perceiving any danger in National Socialism, which was already beginning to emerge. For to me, its ideas and methods, its leading figures, seemed absurd from the outset. I thought the German people were just too sensible to fall for this possibility.

In the lecture hall and elsewhere, I watched and listened to the students of that time. They are the brightest spot of my recollections. The "Youth-movement" called, and they gave themselves in those years.[5] I credit it to their optimistic outlook that I quickly grew fond of them for their great open-mindedness and intellectual agility in all respects. And for their part, they became for me an often agitating but always stimulating partner, who, with their speeches, objections, and contradictions, greatly facilitated the full development of my theological research and teaching. Not all of them, but many of them, with whom and to whom I then spoke at that time were more or less completely sacrificed to the complete intellectual confusion that erupted in the 1930s. Others knew how to resist it courageously.

From the beautiful literature of those decades (it is however to be distinguished by that fact that, to be precise, it was no longer "beautiful" but rather an honest mirror of the divided situation), I took with me what came my way in my hours of leisure and holidays. These were the books, which later were ostracized by the uncultured barbarians as "corrupting," as "gutter literature" and which were, in large part, burnt.[6] The real and lasting fruitful encounters that I had with this field of literature at that time, I unfortunately, however, no longer recall.

In the German Protestant Church of that time, to which I as a theologian was especially connected and bound, I was never really comfortable. There were two reasons why: [First,] it had, in any case in its leading institutional bodies and circles, an unmistakably drunken list after the black-white-red

5. Barth is referring to a specific movement that took place during the Weimar era. It was shut down and then taken over by the Nazis when they came to power.

6. The phrase "gutter literature" is a translation of *Asphaltliteratur*, a technical term used by the Nazis to designate literature that Nazis judged to contradict traditional German culture. The Nazis idealized traditional rural ways of life; asphalt literature was that which was urban and therefore foreign to proper German-ness. They deemed this literature immoral and often associated it with authors of foreign descent, particularly Jews.

reaction.[7] And [second,] after, for the first time, being placed on its own two feet vis-à-vis the State, it developed a remarkably pompous self-consciousness, which no longer seems to correspond to the content and substance of its proclamation. There were already here and there "bishops," and those who loved bishops, and those who wanted to become bishops themselves. And already there were a number of people who saw, flouting the deceitfulness of that time, the morning-star of an entire "century of the Church" rising on the horizon. I was unable to consider either trend as the appropriate cause of the Church, and so I fought against them as best as I could. When thereafter "German Christianity" became an altogether different sort of event, I was grieved, but it was not surprising because it had already been announced only too clearly in all sorts of signs in the twenties.

In theology, my own field, I perceived the situation to be determined by three different factors. First of all, the predominance of the "liberals"—i.e., the historically and psychologically orientated method of theology, which extended from the modern period of the recent past to the beginning of the century—was in fact already judged to be problematic, but it was by no means broken. Next, by means of several different variants, there was a return to Luther, especially to the so-called early Luther, which of course could later be exchanged with little effort for a new Lutheran Confessionalism.[8] And, finally, the situation was determined by the early stages of a new foundation for theology based on a Kierkegaardian "existential philosophy." Whoever could not choose any of these three paths was thereupon directed—like the confederates who had sworn according to the Rütli-Oath "to take their cattle to winter pasture"—to prepare their own way and only afterwards to announce their reasonable proposal.[9] This was the case with me. Nonetheless, in everything I had produced in the 1920s, I was only in the first stages of the direction in which I really wanted to go. These may not have been my apprenticeship years, but they were after all still my journeyman years.[10]

7. This is an allusion to the decision by leaders in the German Church to side with the alliance of several conservative parties. For example, they sided with the alliance of the German National People's Party with both the Stahlhelm (a paramilitary organization) and the Agricultural League (a political party comprised of landowners who were antidemocratic and nationalist and thus opposed to the Weimar Republic).

8. Barth is referring here to the so-called Lutheran renaissance that occurred during this period.

9. The quote is drawn from the legendary oath of the Old Swiss Confederacy, dated to 1307, taken on the Rütli meadow above Lake Uri, which is near Seelisberg. Barth uses it to emphasize that he had to carve his own way forward.

10. Barth refers to the traditional training of skilled craftsmen that involved moving from the position of an apprentice to that of a journeyman, who was a paid employee. During the 1920s in Germany, France, Switzerland, and other European countries, it was still common for young

Zwischen den Zeiten was the name of a journal, which at this time was founded by a group to which I also belonged, and was published for a short decade.[11] I perceived and experienced the twenties as a time "between the times." In something like a sign of the dark words of Isaiah 21:11–12: "Watchman, what time of the night is it? The watchman says: The morning comes and also the night. If you will inquire, then come again and inquire."

---

men to travel around the country for a period of time on completing their apprenticeship. The Nazis viewed these men as comparable to Gypsies and banned the practice. This is no doubt part of the reason Barth employs the metaphor here. His point is that he was still early in his development during this period.

11. *Zwischen den Zeiten* means "between the times," which accounts for Barth's reference in the next sentence. For Barth's farewell letter marking his departure from this journal, see chap. 9.

31

Sermon on Romans 15:5–13

Introduction

Barth delivered this sermon at an Advent service associated with the University of Bonn on December 10, 1933. It culminated a year of resistance against the German Christian movement and its efforts to reorganize the German Church in line with the ideology and policies of the Nazi government.

Barth vehemently opposed the anti-Semitism at the heart of the movement. This racist ideology is articulated in "The Original Guidelines of the German Christian Faith Movement," written by leader Joachim Hossenfelder in 1932.[1] He argues that the "era of parliamentarianism" is over and that German Christians now must show "the power of [their] faith" by standing "front and center in the battle that will decide the life and death of [their] people." This battle is for the purity of German blood. Racial distinctions reflect the natural order of God's creation, and the Christian faith "does not destroy race, but instead deepens and sanctifies it." The German Church obeys God whenever it preserves racial divisions. On this basis, even the idea that Jews could be converted to Christianity is to be rejected because their conversion marks the "point at which foreign blood enters the body of our people." The

---

1. See Joachim Hossenfelder, "The Original Guidelines of the German Christian Faith Movement" (1932), in *A Church Undone: Documents from the German Christian Faith Movement, 1932–1940*, ed. Mary M. Solberg (Minneapolis: Fortress, 2015), 48–52. The quotations below are drawn from this text.

implication is unspoken but clear: Christian identity is equated with German identity, and anyone with Jewish blood is to be considered an outsider to both the faith and the nation.

When they gained institutional control of the Church, the German Christians enforced this racist ideology by appealing to the "Aryan Paragraph" from the new "Law for the Restoration of the Professional Civil Service." This law required anyone serving in a public office to prove their Aryan heritage and promote the interests of the state in their work. Church leaders utilized the law to remove pastors with Jewish heritage from their positions and dismiss others who officiated mixed-race marriages.

Barth fought against the German Christians in every venue available to him. In the July 1933 issue of *Theological Existence Today!*, he responded to their claims by declaring that the Church "is not determined by blood, therefore, not by race, but by the Holy Spirit and Baptism." He then draws a clear line: any church that excludes Jewish Christians from membership "ceases to be a Christian Church."[2] By the end of the summer, Barth decided to resign from the journal *Zwischen den Zeiten* because he did not want to be linked with supporters of the German Christians. He placed this concern at the center of his public farewell to the journal that October (see chap. 9). At a meeting of other opponents of the German Christians that same month, Barth publicly raised questions about the government's treatment of Jews. After word of these remarks reached Nazi officials, they responded by interrogating him for three hours.[3] Through it all, Barth continued his lectures on dogmatics. During the winter semester of 1933, he focused on the Old Testament's testimony to Jesus Christ and made a point to emphasize the intrinsic "bond between Church and Synagogue."[4]

Given legal restrictions, Barth faced intense pressure not to speak about the government's policies from his academic post. Barth refused to stay silent, however, and insisted that he had every right to criticize the theological presuppositions undergirding the German Christian movement and the policies they supported. This sermon summarizes several key biblical and theological themes Barth used to criticize their position. When it was published in *Theological Existence Today!* a few months later, Barth sent a copy to Adolf Hitler.

2. Karl Barth, *Theological Existence To-day! A Plea for Theological Freedom*, trans. R. Birch Hoyle (London: Hodder & Stoughton, 1933), 52.

3. See Eberhard Busch, *Karl Barth: His Life from Letters and Autobiographical Texts* (Grand Rapids: Eerdmans, 1994), 231.

4. These lectures are collected in the section labeled "A Time of Expectation" in *Church Dogmatics* I/2 (Edinburgh: T&T Clark, 1956), 70–101, citation on 101.

———————————— **"Sermon for Advent 2, 1933"**[5] ————————————

May the God of steadfastness and encouragement grant you to live in harmony
with one another, in accordance with Christ Jesus, so that together you may
with one voice glorify the God and Father of our Lord Jesus Christ. Welcome
one another, therefore, just as Christ has welcomed you, for the glory of God.
For I tell you that Christ has become a servant of the circumcised on behalf
of the truth of God in order that he might confirm the promises given to the
patriarchs, and in order that the Gentiles might glorify God for his mercy. As
it is written, "Therefore I will confess you among the Gentiles, and sing praises
to your name"; and again he says, "Rejoice, O Gentiles, with his people"; and
again, "Praise the Lord, all you Gentiles, and let all the peoples praise him"; and
again Isaiah says, "The root of Jesse shall come, the one who rises to rule the
Gentiles; in him the Gentiles shall hope." May the God of hope fill you with
all joy and peace in believing, so that you may abound in hope by the power
of the Holy Spirit. (Rom. 15:5–13)

Dear friends! The church of Jesus Christ is a crowd, a band, a gathering—
a "community," as the lovely old word *Gemeinde* says, which we must just
learn to understand again completely afresh—a community that is not held
together by common interests nor by the blood we share nor even by opinions
and convictions we hold in common, but surely by the fact that, within it,
there ever again sounds forth, not to be silenced and not to be faked and not
to be confused with any other sound, this voice that we hear at the beginning
and at the end of our text: *"But may the God of patience and consolation*
grant you!" "But may the God of hope fill you!"[6] (Rom 15:5, 13). The voice
that talks to us in this way, so beseeching and, at the same time, bestowing so
much, so serious and also so friendly, is, in the words of the Apostle Paul, the
voice of the divine Word itself, from which the Church of Jesus Christ is born
and from which it must also ever again nourish itself and only can nourish

5. For the critical edition of this sermon, see "Römer 15, 5–13," in *Karl Barth Gesamtaus-*
gabe, vol. 31, *Predigten 1921–1935*, ed. Holger Finze-Michaelsen (Zurich: Theologischer Verlag
Zürich, 1998), 296–305. The English text here is drawn from the translation by John Michael
Owen in "Karl Barth's Sermon for Advent 2, 1933: Introduction and Translation," *Colloquium*
36, no. 2 (2004): 161–80. Some of the information in the notes below has been drawn from the
notes found both in the German critical edition and Owen's translation.

6. Barth begins with a claim typical of his theology: the church is a community of diverse
people held together by God's voice as heard in Scripture. But now Barth goes further by offering a list of specific things that do *not* unify the church: shared interest, blood, or convictions.
This list is significant because these are things that the Nazi Party and their supporters in the
German Church are appealing to as they make their case for a unified Germany. The contrast
Barth draws here is intentional, and it serves his opening point. A true church will listen to the
voice of God rather than the voice of the Führer.

itself.[7] *God* knows who God is, and in his Word he *tells* us: He is the God who gives patience, consolation and hope. *God* knows that we have need of him like nothing else and do not at all have him at our command; and in his Word he *tells* us, pulls our thoughts and wills together and towards himself, that we must beseech him: May *he* grant us! May *he* fill us! And *God* knows how close to us, how ready for us he is; and in his Word he *tells* us, by laying it on our lips as a sigh uttered in the closest proximity, and in the deepest, most confident trust, to him: May he, he *give* us! May he *fill* us! This voice with which God tells us what he knows about himself and us may sound forth from far off—the Apostle Paul is indeed really a long way away from us and the whole Bible is very far away from all the books and newspapers that we otherwise read—but if only that voice does still just ring out with *its* sound, *its* message, *its* claim and encouragement, then the Church of Jesus Christ is there, in which I, too, as I hear this voice, "am and shall ever remain a living member."[8]

But in this season of Advent, we have occasion to think that the fact that there is a Word of God for us and a church of Jesus Christ as the locale of the consolation, patience and hope that come from God is not a matter of course. It is not like the air, always and everywhere real. It is not placed in our hands by nature or by history, so that we could deal with it as something that belonged to us. The fact that there is God's Word in the Church is not established in human spiritual life, nor is it a cultural achievement, nor does it belong to the nature and character of any particular people or race, nor is it grounded in the necessary course of world history. It is much rather a mystery, with which our existence is—not, say, fitted out from within, but clothed from without, which is in no sense founded in us, but wholly in an alien power and force over us.[9] That there are the Church and God's Word is

---

7. Barth's use of the word "voice" in this context recalls the first of the Berne Theses of 1528, one of the guiding documents of the Swiss Reformation: "The holy Christian Church, whose only Head is Christ, is born of the Word of God, and abides in the same, and listens not to the voice of a stranger."

8. Even though Paul is "a long way away," Barth argues that God's voice is heard here and now. Christ gathers his church by encountering them directly in the Word. This is emphasized by the quotation from question 54 of the Heidelberg Catechism: "I believe that the Son of God, through his Spirit and Word, out of the entire human race, from the beginning of the world to its end, gathers, protects, and preserves for himself a community chosen for eternal life and united in true faith. And of this community I am and always will be a living member."

9. This paragraph contains concepts typical of Barth's theology and his critique of Protestant liberalism. The Word of God breaks into history as an unveiled mystery. As such, God's Word is not a general feature of existence or something that humans can possess or objectify. It also cannot be discovered through our own spiritual or cultural practices because it is an "alien power" that breaks into our existence from the outside. But just as in the first paragraph, Barth

true because, and only because, as our text says, *"Christ has welcomed us"* (Rom. 15:7), picked us up like a beggar from the street, taken us up as people who had not at all thought or been able to think of taking him up, but who could really only be taken up. We could also say: *adopted*, as an orphan child is adopted into the family, adopted as something that we are not at all by nature, viz., as his siblings and as children of his Father. We could also say, *included* or *taken in* into the sphere where he, the Son of God, leads, rules, bears the responsibility, and manages things so that no one apart from him may have worry or anxiety. We should never of ourselves have come along and entered into this sphere. But he has taken us in.[10] That is the message of Christmas, which we shall soon be able to celebrate again: Christ has welcomed us! And welcomed us, at that, *"to the praise of God"* (Rom. 15:7): not as if it had to be that way, not in accordance with any law of nature or because God had had need of us, and also not for the sake of our needs and wishes, but because it suited him in his freedom to be great and glorious by his Son's welcoming us, adopting us, including us and taking us in.[11] That is why the angels sang on Christmas Eve: Glory be to God on high and peace on earth among the human beings of good-pleasure (Luke 2:14)—of his, the divine good-pleasure! But now, precisely according to our text, all of that is true in a double sense, which has to be borne in mind.[12]

It certainly means for a start the all-embracing fact that he has taken on being human, viz. taken it on in order as God to be our neighbor and, at the same time, as a human being to be God's neighbor. So that, in him, God's kingdom has drawn near to us human beings (Matt. 4:17); and, in him, we human beings may, on the other hand, stand before God's throne as well-pleasing to God. Because God himself has in Jesus Christ clothed himself with being human, we are clothed with the mystery of the Word and the Church.[13]

But, over and above that, we are here given something special to consider. It is not a matter of course that we belong to Jesus Christ, and he, to us. *"Christ*

---

adds something new to his account: God's revelation does not belong to a particular people or race, nor can it be grounded in the movement of history. Barth's target here is clearly the German Christians and the Nazi Party, with which they are aligned.

10. Note how Barth depicts Christ's act of welcome in terms of his act of taking in, picking up, including, receiving, and adopting his people. This welcome is no mere greeting. Christ welcomes us by assuming us into his life. This act transforms us from homeless orphans to members of God's own family.

11. Barth's emphasis on God's freedom in salvation previews themes he later will develop in *Church Dogmatics* II/1 (see chaps. 17–18).

12. Barth explores the "double sense" of Christ's welcome in the next two paragraphs.

13. The first way Christ welcomes us is by taking on flesh. Barth depicts this "all-embracing" welcome as an exchange: Christ became human so that we can stand before God in him.

has become a servant of the circumcised on behalf of the truth of God in order that he might confirm the promises given to the patriarchs" (Rom. 15:8).[14] What that says is that Christ belonged to the people of Israel. *That* people's blood was, in his veins, the blood of the Son of God. *That* people's character he has accepted by taking on being human, not for the sake of that people or of the superiority of its blood and its race, but for the truth, i.e., for the proof of the truthfulness, the faithfulness, of God.[15] On account of the fact that God had made a covenant with that people and with that people alone, a stiff-necked and wicked people [cf. Exod. 32:9], but with *that* people of all peoples, had bestowed his presence upon it and given it the promise of an incomparable redemption—not in order to reward and distinguish the Jews, but to confirm, to fulfill, that free, gracious promise "given to the Fathers," Jesus Christ has been a *Jew*. He has himself once said of himself: To the lost sheep from the house of Israel and to them alone is he sent (Matt. 15:24; cf. 10:5–6). For us who are not Israel, that means a closed door. If it is now, after all, open, if Christ now after all also belongs to us, and we, to him, that must surely say once again in a special sense: "Christ has welcomed us to the praise of God" (Rom. 15:7). We are reminded that that is the case by the existence of the Jewish people right up to this day. Frederick the Great is supposed once to have asked Zimmermann, his personal physician, whether he could name him a single completely certain proof of the existence of God; and he is supposed to have received the laconic reply, "Your Majesty, the Jews!" The man was right. The Jew reminds us by his existence that we are not Jews and therefore intrinsically "without Christ, alien and outside the citizenry of Israel and strangers to the testaments of promise, without hope and without God in the world" (Eph. 2:12). The Jew reminds us that it is something special, new and wonderful, if we are now, despite all that, "no longer guests and strangers, but fellow citizens with the saints and members of God's household" (Eph. 2:19). We are not that by nature. The Jew, in his so puzzlingly strange, and equally puzzlingly indestructible, existence in the midst of all other peoples, is the living proof that God is free to choose whom he will, that he does not owe it to us to choose us, too, that it is grace, when

14. The second way Christ welcomes us is by including us into the story of Israel. The "us" here are gentiles who made up Barth's audience.

15. Barth's interpretation of Paul's claim that Christ was sent to the people of Israel could hardly be more pointed. His references about Christ's nationality and blood are aimed directly against Nazi propaganda that the identity of the German people is rooted in their Germanic blood and character. He also notes that, unlike the Nazis, Christ did not seek to establish the superiority of his people but pursued faithfulness to God. The effect of Barth's description is striking: Christ is identified directly with the Jewish people currently being persecuted by the German authorities, whose motivations contradict the truth of God.

he does also choose us.[16] It could well be that one is warding off this indeed stringent proof of God, warding off the God of free grace, when one wards the Jews off with all too much passion.[17]

But the special, new, wonderful thing about the way in which Christ—although a "servant of the Circumcision for the sake of God's truth"—has now also welcomed us, consists in the fact that Israel, the people blessed with God's election and grace, has behaved towards this its redeemer in no other way than—all peoples of all times and lands would also have done in its place.[18] It has namely rejected him and nailed him to the cross, not in foolish precipitance, not out of a misunderstanding, but in precise, conscious continuation of the manner in which it had always behaved towards its God. "My people," as God had so often called this people, proved itself once more and now definitively to be "not my people" (Hosea 1:9). But the prophet Hosea had indeed said precisely the opposite; and now it became true in just this way in the crucifixion of Christ! "It shall happen in the place where one has said to them, 'You are not my people,' that one will say to them: 'O you children of the Living God'" (Hosea 1:10). "Father, forgive them, for they do not know what they are doing!" (Luke 23:34)—that was said to this people on Golgotha. Except that that could then no longer only be said to it. By putting itself on a par with the other peoples, Israel also put the other peoples on a par with itself. The closed door opened. Israel itself had to open it. God's covenant and truth were not broken, but came to fulfillment for those in Israel—but now also for those among the Heathen—who now recognized and accepted God's mercy as the work of his covenant and truth. For that was the fulfillment of the Covenant, God's faithfulness precisely in the death of Christ on the Cross: "God imprisoned all in disobedience, so that he might have mercy on *all*" (Rom. 11:32).[19]

16. By highlighting the miraculous existence of the Jewish people, Barth also emphasizes that God chose Israel instead of the gentiles, to whom the door was closed. This makes Christ's act of opening the door an act of pure grace. Gentiles are being welcomed into the life of another people to share in promises that are not their own.

17. Barth's description of the Jewish people as both chosen and indestructible leads him to conclude that a rejection of the Jews is a rejection of *God*. The implication for the Nazi Party and its supporters in the German Church is clear.

18. Barth is aware that the history of the church is replete with anti-Semitic condemnation of the Jewish people for their role in the crucifixion of Jesus. He attempts to undermine this way of thinking by universalizing their rejection of Christ as something that "all peoples of all times and lands" would have done.

19. Barth accomplishes a remarkable reversal here. Israel's rejection of Christ at his crucifixion no longer *distinguishes* them from other peoples, as if they are particularly wicked. Instead, this act is precisely what *unites* them to other peoples because it displays universal traits shared by all humanity. Their disobedience to God at this moment also does not mark them for

That is why it can now go on to say, *"The Heathens praise God on account of mercy"* (Rom. 15:9). Hear that properly: Not because they were better, purer, more upright than the Jews! If there were any advantage, the Jews would still have it today, not because of any good qualities, but because it has pleased God to choose *them*, with *them* to make the covenant that he fulfilled in Christ, in order to keep it with us, as well. So the reason why the Heathen praise God is that God has, in the Christ crucified in the midst of Israel, shown and confirmed upon them, who were not Israel, *his mercy to them, too.* Because the covenant with Israel became manifest for Israel and for the Heathen as a covenant of *grace* for *sinners* who cannot boast of any faith that they have kept, who are only able to live from mercy, but who really are permitted to live from mercy. That is the end of the Jews' advantage and of our disadvantage. That's what a real Jew cannot understand right up to the present day: That precisely the covenant that God certainly concluded with his people, and with his people alone, has become manifest in that people's rejection of Christ as the free, undeserved goodness that God wants to do for everyone.[20] Precisely this covenant!, says Paul, and he allows precisely the book of this one, old and now fulfilled covenant to speak and to witness to the glory of God among the Heathen: *"Therefore I will praise thee among the Heathen and sing to thy name." "Rejoice, you Heathen, with his people!" "Praise the Lord, all Heathen, and praise him, all peoples!" "There will be the root of Jesse, and he will rise up to rule over the Heathen; on him will the peoples hope"* (Rom. 15:9–12). It is *thus* then that Christ has received us to the praise of God. "Salvation comes from the Jews" (John 4:22). Jesus Christ was a Jew. But by his bearing and taking away, in the sin of the Jews, the sin of the whole world and our sin, too (cf. John 1:29), salvation has come from the Jews to us also. We rejoice in this wide opening door, when we rejoice that there is a Word of God for us and so a church of Jesus Christ. How should we not, each time we reflect on that, have to think above all of the Jews? And how should we not, each time that we reflect on the Jews, think above all how "the Heathens praise God on account of *mercy*"?[21]

---

condemnation because it opens a way for salvation for all peoples. So, in effect, Barth takes the incident most often used to reject the Jewish people and uses it as the basis for their acceptance.

20. Barth's exposition of verse 9 undermines the existence of any distinctions between Jews and gentiles with respect to their relationship with God. Neither one has an advantage over the other because Christ reveals that God's goodness is willed "for everyone."

21. Note how Barth reframes the way gentiles should consider the Jewish people. Every time gentiles think about their own salvation, they also should think of the Jewish people; and every time they think of the Jewish people, they also should think about their salvation. In short, the word that should define the relationship between gentile and Jew is not condemnation but mercy.

Now we can understand the other thing that our text has to say to us about the Church of Jesus Christ: As Christ has welcomed us to the praise of God, "*welcome one another*" (Rom. 15:7). That is a law that there is no getting around. That is a command, and a strict, inexorable command, at that. But the Heathen and the Jews, all those welcomed by Christ who praise God on account of mercy, fulfill this command.[22] They welcome one another. "Welcome one another" means mutually to see each other as Christ sees us. He sees us all as covenant-breakers, but also as such with whom God wills, despite that, to maintain his covenant. He sees us in our religious and secular Godlessness, but also as those to whom the Kingdom of God has drawn near. He sees us as such as are utterly dependent on mercy, but also as such as mercy has already befallen. He sees us as Jews in conflict with the true God and as heathens at peace with the false gods, but he also sees us both united as "children of the Living God" (Hosea 1:10).[23] But we are, to be sure, unable of ourselves to see each other in that way. If we see each other of ourselves, then it is regularly the case that we miss both the first thing, that we are covenant-breakers, and the second, that, despite that, God maintains his covenant. We then take both the perfections and the faults that we perceive in each other much too seriously; we then praise each other much too loudly and we then censure each other much too vehemently. Either way, we do not then welcome one another.

22. Barth frames Paul's instruction to "welcome one another" as a law and command, but this command is performed on the basis of mercy. This reflects Barth's distinct approach to the relationship between the gospel and the law. His central claim is that the one Word of God is both gospel and law: "In its content, it is Gospel; in its form and fashion, it is Law." *Church Dogmatics* II/1 (Edinburgh: T&T Clark, 1957), 511. This approach reverses Martin Luther's order of law and gospel, and it also undermines the opposition Luther sees between them. Luther's premise is that the law condemns but the gospel brings salvation. This conviction shapes his political theology. Since the law works punitively, Luther draws a distinction between the state—which enacts and enforces laws—and the church. The state's laws reflect God's will as revealed in the natural order of creation, while the church's work is determined by the gospel of Christ. Barth worries that this approach contains a fatal flaw: the state inevitably determines for itself what God's order of creation means. This leaves room for a Führer to impose his own interpretation onto creation and say that it reflects the will of God. Barth closes the door to such a move. For him, the gospel is the substance of the law, and the single message of both the law and gospel is grace. This means that God's will for the entire order of creation and human life is revealed in Jesus Christ and can be known only through him.

23. We "welcome one another" when we "see each other as Christ sees us"—and this means seeing others as sinners and as those saved by grace. Barth's description of these two categories carries subtle implications for his hearers. While the Jewish people are in conflict with God, the gentiles live comfortably with "false gods." This places the gentiles—with whom Barth's audience would identify—in the position of not knowing God at all. But then even this distinction is erased by the fact that both groups are united in Christ as "children of the living God." So Barth continues to relativize the distinctions between Jew and gentile by placing both groups into a common unity where their differences are no longer operative.

We are then in the market-place and not in the Church. The Word of God is then surely silent.[24] But when it is *not* silent, when we consider that we have been welcomed by Jesus Christ to the praise of God, then we see each other with the eyes of Jesus Christ, and that surely means then that our deep breach of covenant, godlessness and pitifulness are not concealed, but that neither is the faithfulness of God steadfastly holding sway over each one of us, and that, overlooking all perfections and faults, praise and censure—however important they may be in their own place—we can only join hands in order together to praise God's faithfulness to us, the unfaithful Ones. When we see each other in this way, then we welcome one another, then we are in the Church of Jesus Christ. For that is what the Church of Jesus Christ is: the community of those who, listening to the Word of the God of patience, comfort and hope, welcome one another as Christ has welcomed us. That is "the Communion of Saints." The praise of God on account of mercy has brought them together and will hold them together through everything, hold them together in a way that no friendship or common convictions or community of a people, or state can hold human beings together, hold them together in the way that, in the whole world, only the members of the Body of Christ are held together by him, the Head (cf. Col. 2:19).[25]

And now we can close with a brief indication of the things that are prayed for in our text.[26]

It is first of all this, "that you may be of one mind among yourselves in accordance with Jesus Christ, so that you may unanimously with one mouth praise the God and Father of our Lord Jesus *Christ*" (Rom. 15:5–6). That means: From the mutual welcoming of each other as Christ has welcomed us, it would have to follow that, in the Church of Jesus Christ, one thought and one will would be alive and powerful in everyone—not, to be sure, some or other kind of human unity in thought and will, but a unity of perhaps very diverse human thinking and willing in the purpose of now letting the praise of God on account of mercy be heard, of passing it on, of arousing it also in those who do not yet know that mercy has befallen them. That purpose would then of necessity have to be carried out "unanimously with one mouth." But

24. To fail to see one another in light of Christ is to let the creaturely powers that dictate the order of the world—particularly the power of the marketplace—determine our perception.

25. Here we see Barth's description of the true church of Jesus Christ. It is a community in which God's Word is heard, perfections and faults are overlooked, and God's mercy in Christ becomes the lens through which all people are seen. It thus is a community that welcomes others in the pattern of Christ's welcome. As Barth sees it, not even a state can hold people together with this sort of unity; the blood of Christ runs deeper than the blood of any people.

26. That Barth ends with a description of prayer is not a mere formality; it shows that he knows that the kind of welcome he has called for in this sermon takes place only as a divine event.

that means that the Church of Jesus Christ would have to be a community
that together knew the heard Word, in order to confess it together. It would
have to be! Is it? If it is, where are its knowledge and its confession? And if
it is not, why isn't it? Our text tells us simply to pray for the Church that it
may become a church of knowledge and confession.[27] If only we would again
just unanimously pray together for that. What does praying mean? Crying,
calling, reaching out, that what is after all already true once and for all, that
Christ has accepted us, may also be true for us. Church knowledge and Church
confession would surely follow upon such a prayer, if it were serious (cf. James
5:16), as thunder follows lightning.

The other thing is this: That God may "*fill you with all joy and peace
in believing, that you may have full hope through the power of the Holy
Spirit*" (Rom. 15:13). That means: From the mutual acceptance of each
other as Christ has accepted us, it would have to follow that, in the Church
of Jesus Christ, all unhappiness would at least be on the way to joyousness,
all discordance would at least be on the way to peace, all distress of our
own present would somehow finally be swamped by hope for the presence
of the Lord. Are confession and knowledge missing in our church because
there is so much unmoved and immovable unhappiness, discordance and
distress among us? Or is there so much rigid unhappiness, discordance and
distress among us, despite our supposed faith, because our church is lacking
in knowledge and confession? It will surely be the case that a certain connection exists here. And it is therefore understandable that here, too, it is
simply pointed out to us that we have to pray for the Church, to pray that,
in its believing, joy and peace may increase, that we may—not by the power
of our own sentiments, but by the power of the Holy Spirit—share in a full,
an overflowing hope. And indeed our prayer will again have simply to be
that it may after all not remain so hidden from us that Christ has accepted
us to the praise of God.[28] If that does remain hidden from us, then we shall
scarcely accept one another; and, as long as we fail to accept one another,
how are we supposed to have peace, joy and hope? They are certainly waiting at our door. And they will be given us, when we seriously pray for the
one thing for which one must pray.

27. Paul's first prayer is for the church to know and confess the Word so the church can live
as one community under the Word. Since Barth thinks these human acts of knowledge and
confession take place through God's grace, he sees this prayer as a request for the personal
intervention of God.
28. Paul's second prayer is for the church to realize that Christ has embraced them in grace.
Barth emphasizes that this realization originates not from an internal human act but from an
act of God.

The thoughts of many human beings are, at this time, more seriously concerned than previously with the question of what the Church lacks and of what we in the Church lack. Let us note that our text is not speaking of that, but that, where it could speak of it, it simply prays, and also tells us to pray, to the God of patience, comfort and hope, who is the Lord of the Church. If we hear that, and let ourselves be told that we should, may and can simply pray, then it may thereby become clear to us that there is one thing, and the decisive thing, at that, that the Church and we in the Church do not in fact lack today, either: the *Word* out of which it is born. When we hear that there is a *prayer* that can achieve much [cf. James 5:16], then we certainly *have* the Word of God. Let us *keep* it, by doing what we are thus urged by the Word of God to do! Perhaps this present time has come upon our church so that we may learn to pray differently and better than hitherto, and thus to keep what we have [cf. Rev. 3:11].[29]

29. Barth's sermon ends where it began: with a focus on the reality that the Word of God is the sole basis of the church's existence and life.

CHAPTER 32

The Barmen Theological Declaration

Introduction

Along with its enforcement of the "Aryan Paragraph," another key feature of the German Christian movement was its adherence to the "Führer Principle." This principle established that the Führer's word stands above any written law and that the government's policies and practices should reflect this reality. Within the German Church, the principle effectively placed the word of Adolf Hitler alongside the Word of God as a source of authority.

The German Christian leadership defended this idea by advocating a kind of natural theology. For example, in a response to Barth, theologian and Nazi sympathizer Emmanuel Hirsch insisted that divine revelation cannot be limited merely to Scripture. Rather, "by observing the signs of God's presence in the historical reality in and around him, [the Christian] receives faith in the gospel, and in turn, out of his faith in the gospel he hears and understands anew God's presence in the reality of life in and around him."[1] The implication was that the events of history—and more specifically, the particular historical movement led and interpreted by Hitler—should stand alongside Christ and Scripture as a source for the church's understanding of God.

---

1. Emmanuel Hirsch, "What the German Christians Want for the Church: An Assessment of Karl Barth's Attack" (1933), in *A Church Undone: Documents from the German Christian Faith Movement, 1932–1940*, ed. Mary M. Solberg (Minneapolis: Fortress, 2015), 107.

In response to these kinds of arguments, Barth spent the early part of 1934 helping to organize an effective opposition to the German Christians.[2] After his interrogation by Nazi authorities in April, Barth realized that he likely would be dismissed from his teaching position at the University of Bonn. Any contribution he would make would need to happen quickly.

After much discussion, a Confessing Synod of the German Evangelical Church was scheduled for the end of May. To prepare for this event, Barth traveled to Frankfurt on May 16 to meet with Lutheran theologians Thomas Breit and Hans Asmussen. Their goal was to write a series of theses to be discussed at the synod. Barth later recalled that, "fortified by strong coffee and one or two Brazilian cigars," he composed the document while his companions took an afternoon nap. He was particularly pleased that the first thesis directly confronted the church's embrace of the "Führer Principle" and the natural theology that undergirded it.

The theses were presented to a committee of the Confessing Synod on the evening of May 30, 1934, in the Reformed church at Barmen-Gemarke. They suggested a change to one sentence. The following day, the delegates voted unanimously to adopt the declaration as the theological basis for the German Confessing Church.

─────────────── **Barmen Declaration**[3] ───────────────

In view of the errors of the "German Christians" and of the present Reich Church Administration, which are ravaging the Church and at the same time also shattering the unity of the German Evangelical Church, we confess the following evangelical truths:

■ 1. "I am the Way and the Truth and the Life; no one comes to the Father except through me" (John 14:6).

"Truly, truly I say to you, he who does not enter the sheepfold through the door but climbs in somewhere else, he is a thief and a robber. I am the Door; if anyone enters through me, he will be saved" (John 10:1, 9).

2. This historical account is drawn from Eberhard Busch, *Karl Barth: His Life from Letters and Autobiographical Texts* (Grand Rapids: Eerdmans, 1994), 245–48.

3. This translation is from Douglas S. Bax and is drawn from the *Journal of Theology for Southern Africa* 47 (June 1984): 78–82.

Jesus Christ, as he is attested to us in Holy Scripture, is the one Word of God which we have to hear, and which we have to trust and obey in life and in death.[4]

We reject the false doctrine that the Church could and should recognize as a source of its proclamation, beyond and besides this one Word of God, yet other events, powers, historic figures, and truths as God's revelation.[5]

■ 2. "Jesus Christ has been made wisdom and righteousness and sanctification and redemption for us by God" (1 Cor. 1:30).

As Jesus Christ is God's comforting pronouncement of the forgiveness of all our sins, so, and with equal seriousness, he is also God's vigorous announcement of his claim upon our whole life. Through him there comes to us joyful liberation from the godless ties of this world for free, grateful service to his creatures.

We reject the false doctrine that there could be areas of our life in which we would belong not to Jesus Christ but to other lords, areas in which we would not need justification and sanctification through him.[6]

■ 3. "Let us, however, speak the truth in love, and in every respect grow into him who is the head, into Christ, from whom the whole body is joined together" (Eph. 4:15–16).

The Christian Church is the community of brethren in which, in Word and sacrament, through the Holy Spirit, Jesus Christ acts in the present as Lord.

4. This affirmation of the first thesis is foundational for the rest of the document. Its rejection of any authority in the church other than Jesus Christ as revealed in Scripture is emphasized by the citation from John 14:6. The qualification "as attested to us in Holy Scripture" challenges German Christians who appeal to the authority of Christ to actually support their claims about Christ with concrete biblical evidence. The reference to life and death at the end emphasizes the high stakes involved in the question of authority.

5. This negation directly challenges claims made by German Christians. That their teaching is "false" is reinforced by the citation from John 10, which puts them in the position of thieves and robbers. Barth later noted that the clause does not rule out that God can speak in other ways, as if God's speech is limited only to Scripture. It simply prohibits the church from using these other words as the source of its proclamation. See *Church Dogmatics* II/1 (Edinburgh: T&T Clark, 1957), 178.

6. The second thesis affirms that Jesus Christ holds sole authority in the church. The total nature of his rule also implies that the church will need to make political as well as theological judgments. Note that Christ's authority leads to joy, liberation, and grateful service. This stands in stark contrast to totalitarianism.

With both its faith and its obedience, with both its message and its order, it has to testify in the midst of the sinful world, as the Church of pardoned sinners that it belongs to him alone and lives and may live by his comfort and under his direction alone, in expectation of his appearing.

We reject the false doctrine that the Church could have permission to hand over the form of its message and of its order to whatever it itself might wish or to the vicissitudes of the prevailing ideological and political convictions of the day.[7]

■ 4. "You know that the rulers of the Gentiles exercise authority over them and those in high position lord it over them. So shall it not be among you; but if anyone would have authority among you, let him be your servant" (Matt. 20:25–26).

The various offices in the Church do not provide a basis for some to exercise authority over others but for the ministry with which the whole community has been entrusted and charged to be carried out.

We reject the false doctrine that, apart from this ministry, the Church could, and could have permission to be given special leaders [Führer] vested with ruling authority.[8]

■ 5. "Fear God, honor the King!" (1 Pet. 2:17).

Scripture tells us that by divine appointment the State, in this still unredeemed world in which also the Church is situated, has the task of maintaining justice and peace, so far as human discernment and human ability make this possible, by means of the threat and use of force. The Church acknowledges with gratitude and reverence toward God the benefit of this, his appointment. It draws attention to God's Kingdom [Reich], God's commandment and justice, and with these the responsibility of those who rule and those who are ruled. It trusts and obeys the power of the Word, by which God upholds all things.[9]

7. The third thesis applies the claims of the first two theses to the church's order. The presence of the living Christ means that the church has a Lord and cannot give its authority over to any other. The negation emphasizes that the church's faith cannot be merged to contemporary politics.

8. The fourth thesis challenges the abuses of German Church leadership, particularly against nonconforming pastors. The negation emphasizes the autonomy of the church in relation to outside authorities.

9. The fifth thesis is the heart of the Declaration. While the state exists by God's decision, it performs its tasks as far as human discernment and ability allow. This draws a line between the state's activities and God's will. The church gives gratitude to God rather than the state

We reject the false doctrine that beyond its special commission the State should and could become the sole and total order of human life and so fulfill the vocation of the Church as well.[10]

We reject the false doctrine that beyond its special commission the Church should and could take on the nature, tasks and dignity which belong to the State and thus become itself an organ of the State.[11]

■ 6. "See I am with you always, to the end of the age" (Matt. 28:20).

The Church's commission, which is the foundation of its freedom, consists in this: in Christ's stead, and so in the service of his own Word and work, to deliver to all people, through preaching and sacrament, the message of the free grace of God.

We reject the false doctrine that with human vainglory the Church could place the Word and work of the Lord in the service of self-chosen desires, purposes and plans.[12]

The Confessional Synod of the German Evangelical Church declares that it sees in the acknowledgement of these truths and in the rejection of these errors the indispensable theological basis of the German Evangelical Church and a confederation of Confessional Churches. It calls upon all who can stand in solidarity with its Declaration to be mindful of these theological findings in all their decisions concerning Church and State. It appeals to all concerned to return to unity in faith, hope and love.

Verbum Dei manet in aeternum.[13]

---

for its work. The church instructs the state by informing it about the divine appointment to maintain justice and peace, but the church never looks to the state as its final authority. This point is emphasized by the final clause, which references Hebrews' claim that Christ "sustains all things by his powerful word" (Heb. 1:3). This reference draws attention back to the first thesis and carries a clear implication: the church will obey God rather than the state. If the state fails to pursue the tasks of justice and peace, the church will confront the state by drawing attention to its divine appointment.

10. The first negation applies the claims of the first and second theses to the state by emphasizing that the state cannot adopt a religious character.

11. The second negation rejects the notion that the church can serve partisan political interests. Its primary task with relation to the state is to draw attention to the state's divine appointment to maintain justice and peace.

12. The sixth thesis argues that the mission of the church is to serve the gospel rather than any human message.

13. "The Word of the Lord endures forever." This motto of the Reformation is based on 1 Pet. 1:25.

CHAPTER 33

The Role of Christians in Wartime

"A Letter to American Christians"

Introduction

In 1942, American Presbyterian minister and ecumenical theological Samuel McCrea Cavert (1888–1976) met Karl Barth while traveling through Switzerland for meetings related to the World Council of Churches. The war was raging, and Barth asked Cavert how American Christians were approaching the situation. During their conversation, Cavert suggested that Barth write a letter to the Americans similar to the one he had written to the Christians in Great Britain the year before. Barth initially declined because he knew little about the American church and did not want to speak ignorantly. Mutual friends stepped in, however, and encouraged Barth that his remarks would be well-received. Barth agreed to write the letter if Cavert posed specific questions he could answer. Barth received the questions and composed his responses in December 1942. Because of delays caused by the war, it was published in the United States two years later.

This excerpt from that letter provides an illuminating glimpse into how Barth applied his theological convictions to the practical matters of church life in a time of crisis. It also reveals the topics Barth considered to be most important with respect to the relationship between the church and the state. Barth establishes common ground with his audience by appealing to

Americans' beloved concepts of human rights and freedom. Then Barth turns these concepts to his own purposes by using them to set up a challenging argument to his readers. While he leaves no doubt that he supports the war against Hitler's Germany, he also makes it clear that all sides are receiving God's judgment for their sins. The church has played its own part in these failures, and in response it should recommit itself to the task of preaching the gospel of Jesus Christ. The primacy of this task does not mean, however, that the church should withdraw from politics. Jesus Christ is the Lord of the entire world, and faithfulness to him demands clear speech and concrete action related to the most pressing matters in society. While the church never can allow itself to become just another political party, it can and must display its allegiance to its Lord by bearing witness to the spiritual and political realities of his reign.

———————— "A Letter to American Christians"[1] ————————

Dear Friend,

You and several other Christians in the United States have asked me (independently of one another) to write to America a letter of similar content to those which I have directed to France and England during the last few years.[2] The somewhat presumptuous character of letters of this sort, and also the responsibility I take through them, is very obvious. After all, I am not seated in an apostolic chair which would formally bestow upon me the duty or the right to send out such epistles now and again!

Moreover, I have experienced how easy it is to be misunderstood in a milieu for the most part foreign, and in view of the enforced brevity of such utterances. I confess, for instance, that I am somewhat anxious at the thought of certain journalists who habitually pass by the really important content and by preference quote a few all too readily understood catchwords, peddling them about as my message, under the title "Dr. Barth says—" Now the United States in particular is so big, so remote from here—not only geographically, and so little known to me inwardly, that I hesitated more than ever before.

1. Karl Barth, "A Letter to American Christians," in *The Church and the War* (Eugene, OR: Wipf & Stock, 2008), 19–20, 22–25, 28–34.
2. Barth sent two letters to French Protestants, the first before the invasion in December 1939 and the second after the invasion in October 1940. He sent his letter to Great Britain in the midst of the war April 1941. The letters are collected in Karl Barth, *A Letter to Great Britain from Switzerland* (London: SPCK, 1941).

On the other hand, I realize that the need for mutual understanding and strengthening grows more and more urgent, and as my American friends place some confidence in me, I shall try to come up to their expectations. You, dear friend, have come to my aid by laying before me a number of specific questions, answers to which you consider especially important for the Christians of America. I shall try, then, as far and as well as I can, to take a stand in regard to those questions. . . .

Your first question was:

> How can a Christian be, at the same time, a loyal citizen of a national state and a loyal member of the Church Universal, which transcends national interests?

I think that as a Christian one must keep in mind first of all that it is not the essential nature of the State that it should be purely national, i.e., limited to a specific land and people and serving only national interests. That is the concept of the State which won through in the nineteenth century. But it was not the concept of the Middle Ages nor of the Roman Empire and Law, and above all, not that of the Bible. How could God prefer just one—this or that—national state, rather than first and foremost *his own*, the *true* State, within *all* national states?[3]

Is not the function of government within the sovereignty of all nations and races (inclusive of the "state" form which may exist in any independent African tribe, or even in a robber's cave!) essentially the same: *the establishment and maintenance of an order of relationship between common rights and personal freedom*, or rather, *responsibility?*[4] Has there ever been a national state which, through international agreements with other states, could forego placing itself on the level of this common and obviously superior state-concept? That today the state practically exists only in a plurality of national states is only a historical and therefore variable fact, not an intrinsic and unalterable one. For example: once upon a time it was altogether different in Europe and it can again be altogether different,

3. This remark corresponds to the fifth thesis of the Barmen Declaration, which states that the church's task is to draw "attention to God's Kingdom" in its relationship to the state. This divine kingdom supersedes all national boundaries even as it exists within every nation.

4. Three things stand out in this description of governmental function: (1) Barth's appeal to "common rights" carries special significance for his American audience. (2) Barth's rephrasing of "freedom" as "responsibility" pushes against the idea of an absolute human autonomy. (3) Framing the issue in terms of the relationship between inherent rights and responsible action gives priority to the person possessing the rights. While persons who possess rights do not have to prove that they have them, actors need to demonstrate that their actions are responsible.

in Europe and in the rest of the world. Perhaps we must realize from the present war at least the clear insight that in this connection many changes must sooner or later take place.

So long as this has not occurred, the Christian will not fail to recognize and respect in the national state in which he lives, the essential, the internationally valid order of the true state instituted by God in his patience.[5] Between the universal Church and the true state no essential or inevitable antithesis can exist, since after all both have been instituted by God, though with differing purpose. Nor can there be such contradiction between the universal Church and the national State in so far as the latter, in its sphere is in itself that essentially international, God-instituted true State. The Christian, therefore, can very well be, as a matter of principle, a loyal citizen of a National State (for instance: you a good American and I a good Swiss) and a loyal member of the universal Church. In fact, as long as there are only national states, he has no other choice than to direct to his national state the obedience and cooperation which he owes to the righteous state. He would not be giving to God that which is God's if he thought himself too good to give to Caesar (i.e., the National State) that which is Caesar's.[6]

But—he will do the latter, however, in *this* way: He will stand consistently for the universal, all-uniting order of the righteous state, even while giving full recognition to the rightly understood interests of the national state in which he lives. Thereby he will seek and further the best interests of his national state likewise. He will be on the watch for and if necessary protest against and resist everything in his national state which is incompatible with its character as the true state. He will, to the best of his ability, do his part to perfect and keep the national state as a righteous state. He will of course always be found among those who champion the effort to place international relations more and more completely on a basis on which national states can stand together as true states. A totally national state which serves only national interests—and we can see today that at least approximations of such a caricature are possible—would thereby by that very fact cease to be a righteous state. In this unrighteous state the Christian can show his civic loyalty

5. Barth's statements about the distinct historical forms of nation-states challenge the notion that, in and of themselves, states possess inalienable rights. Instead, the rights of the people both precede and transcend the existence of any state. This order reflects God's will, and Barth thinks that a "true state" will correspond to it. Given his audience, it is no accident that these claims correspond to the founding conviction of the United States, which begins with the claim that people are "endowed by their Creator with certain unalienable rights."

6. Put differently, if a state lives in line with God's will by upholding an order in which "common rights" are maintained responsibly, then a Christian can participate fully and freely in the life of the state.

only by resistance and suffering.[7] Let us be thankful, you as an American, I as a Swiss, that this conflict in which our brethren in Germany, for instance, find themselves, has been spared us at least to this extent, that our national states, with all their imperfections, can nevertheless be classed to a fair degree as "righteous" states. Let us use this fact to the utmost advantage! We shall have our hands full.

Your second question:

> Is this war to be conceived as the judgment of God on mankind? And if so, is there no distinction to be made between the more guilty and the less guilty?

Yes, I firmly believe that this war, like every other war, is a particularly visible form of the judgment of God on mankind. In times of peace the exercise of police power and the pronouncement and carrying out of sentence to maintain public order are unavoidable, but, even so, they are an indication of the divine judgment on human society. The same thing holds when two or more national states find no other way of ordering their relations to one another and of adjusting their national interests than through force of arms. The same thing holds even when, as is the case in the present war, the righteous state must be defended by force of arms against the explosion of anarchy and tyranny.[8]

The necessity for the application of the *ultima ratio*, after all, invariably indicates many preceding wrongs and mistakes, and surely they are never all on one side.[9] Human sin, the rebellion of man against his God, has then once more reached a stage where, when the state unsheathes the sword which, according to Romans 13, it does not bear in vain, a terrible sign of the wrath of God must become unmistakably apparent.[10] It will then be wise—even in

7. Barth lays out four responsibilities for Christian citizens: (1) Their primary loyalty should be to God and God's kingdom. (2) They should promote a properly ordered relationship between human rights and personal freedom within their state while protesting any distortion of this relationship. (3) They should promote international peace on the basis of God's all-encompassing reign and God's will that states value the rights God has granted to all people. (4) They should resist any action of a state that promotes its own interests at the expense of other states or the rights common to all people.

8. Barth does not exclude the Allies from God's judgment. Even those fighting against the Nazis stand guilty and responsible before God for their sin.

9. The *ultima ratio* is the "last resort." In a political context, this idea is linked to the decision to bear arms against another.

10. See Rom. 13:1–2: "Let every person be subject to the governing authorities; for there is no authority except from God, and those authorities that exist have been instituted by God. Therefore whoever resists authority resists what God has appointed, and those who resist will incur judgment."

regard to the present war—to admit to oneself that over against this judgment of God there are no degrees of guilt. Who will measure the amount of culpability? . . . I should like therefore to give to the first part of your question the answer that we must give heed to Romans 13:1–7; and to the second part of your question that we must place beside the above words the words of Romans 3:23, and in this relation realize the whole political as well as Christian truth.[11]

Your third question:

> What is the true function of the Church and its ministers in relation to this war? Should church bodies and pastors actively support the prosecution of the war by preaching about the issues involved, by urging the membership of the churches to serve in the armed forces, to buy war bonds, etc.? Or should they confine their activities to the timeless "spiritual" ministries? What are the limits beyond which the Church should not go in identifying itself with any political cause? In what sense is it true that the Church is not at war?

If I understand correctly, you are asking me first of all what the churches, i.e., the church bodies and their ministers, should or should not say and do in the present situation. I should not like to evade the question, but I should like to point out that the first consideration is an entirely inward task of the Church: Is the Church clearly aware that its mission in every, and therefore also in this time, is solely (and this in the fullest sense of the concept!) *to preach the word of God to the mankind of today, according to the Holy Scripture?*[12] Has it accepted the events and problems of our time as an admonition to renew its awareness of the breadth of this mission in all its aspects? In other words, has the Church realized that the world catastrophe which has befallen us has a connection with a catastrophe of the Church, and that to face this fact is far more important and urgent than all the "yeas" and "nays" which the Church must preach to the outside, and that to face it is the prerequisite for every vigorous "yea" and "nay" directed to the outer world?[13]

11. Romans 3:23 affirms that "all have sinned and fallen short of the glory of God."

12. This statement corresponds to the sixth thesis of the Barmen Declaration: "The Church's commission, which is the foundation of its freedom, consists in this: in Christ's stead, and so in the service of his own Word and work, to deliver to all people, through preaching and sacrament, the message of the free grace of God."

13. Barth sees a connection between the war and the failure of the church with respect to its mission. He does not make this connection one of correlation, as if the church's failures led to the war or vice versa. Yet he still discerns a relationship between the church's distorted doctrine and action and the ideology that drove the Nazi government to engage in war. On the basis of this relationship, he concludes that the church cannot address the political situation if it does not first address its own failures.

I should here like to take the liberty of proposing a counter-question: what is being done today in the church bodies, ministerial conferences, theological faculties, but above all in the studies of the individual pastors of all denominations in the United States, to the end that the Church shall again be the Church, understand itself as such and act accordingly? Did not the manifest unsureness of the churches on both sides of the Atlantic in recent years, in the light of the events of our time, stem to some degree from the fact that nothing (or too little), had been done for the inward regeneration of the churches? You cannot gather grapes from thistles. It could not be expected that a club for the furtherance of religious humanism would have the discernment to recognize the National Socialist menace and find the correct warning voice to lift against it. And today we cannot expect that it would give the nations clear guidance in the great difficulties of their wartime problems and sufferings; that it would represent the Kingdom of Christ, and not enter the service of some earthly sovereignty. The narrow way of clean-cut decision and complete freedom is trod only by the Church that is the Church or is about to become the Church once more.[14]

I do not know whether, and to what extent, such a Church again exists in America—we in Europe have scarcely taken more than the first steps in that direction—but if there is something comparable in the United States, I shall be all the better understood if I say that the true function of the Church consists first of all in its own regeneration: in a regeneration no less thorough than the Reformation through which Protestantism began in the sixteenth century. How do matters stand in your country in this respect? In sending this counter-question, I should like to reply as follows to your third question:

1. If the Church is really preaching the Word of God, then this will mean active support of the war effort in so far as it testifies, with a clarity consistent with the Word of God, that the carrying through of this stern police action against Hitler's Nihilism is a necessary task of the righteous state; that therefore the United States has rightly embarked upon this task and that the American Christian is obligated to help his country, within the framework of his vocation and his abilities, in the accomplishment of this task.[15]

Recently we read here in Switzerland a pronouncement by ninety-three leading American Protestants and we were informed that this was a statement

14. Barth's counterquestion strikes a hard blow. What does it look like for the church to be the church? Rather than a community that focuses on itself or on an abstract notion of human rights, the church is a community established by and centered on the Word of God. Barth develops this idea more concretely in what follows.

15. Barth addresses the question of whether the church should confine itself to spiritual rather than political matters by rejecting the distinction. As the church focuses on the Word of God, it will be compelled to support the political and material war against Hitler's Germany.

characteristic of the majority of the American churches. In this statement is the sentence: "We abhor war, but upon the outcome of this war depends the realization of Christian principles to which no Christian can be indifferent." I venture to doubt that this is the unequivocal language, appropriate to God's Word, which should be employed today. If the realization of Christian principles depends upon the outcome of this war, then there is no point in the assurance that war is abhorrent: for it is surely only unnecessary and unjust wars which are condemned as abhorrent, and among this number the present one is not to be classed. If, conversely, war as such is really condemned, then the realization of Christian principles must definitely not be made dependent on its outcome: that would mean the determination to do evil in violation of conscience, in order that good may result. I give this as an example of what I do not consider to be the true exercise of the pastoral function and true preaching in the present situation. The Word of God cannot be rightly preached in such equivocal sentences, and an adequate "active undergirding of the war effort" can likewise not be attained by such phrases.[16]

2. If the Church really proclaims the Word of God according to Holy Scripture, then there can be no reason for its making the war, its causes, problems, tasks and outlook, the theme of its preaching and for its making the obligation to military service and to buy war bonds and the like the contents of its exhortation. Holy Scripture does not demand of the preachers of the Gospel (nor is it needed by the people of today any more than in all other ages) that they proclaim from the pulpit again what is already being sufficiently stated by the newspapers and the propaganda agencies of the State far better than the preachers could state it. Unhappy preachers, and above all, unhappy parishes, where that is the case.

What, then, shall they preach? The Word of the reconciliation of the world with God through Jesus Christ (2 Cor. 5:17–21) and nothing else. But this in its full scope! When they preach about the sole sovereignty of Jesus Christ, His human origin among the people of Israel, His triumph over powers and dominations, about God's mercy and patience revealed in Him; the dual benefaction of Church and State realized in Him; about the impossibility of serving two masters, about freedom, and the service of the children of God conceived in the Holy Spirit, they are inevitably preaching, through a simple, strict interpretation of the biblical texts (and as a rule without naming persons and things specifically) against Hitler, Mussolini and Japan; against anti-Semitism, idolization of the State, oppressive and intimidating methods,

---

16. Barth makes it clear that he considered the Allied war against the Axis powers to be a just war that merits full theological justification.

militarism, against all the lies and the injustice of National Socialism and Fascism in its European and its Asiatic forms, and thus they will naturally (and without "dragging politics into the pulpit") speak on behalf of the righteous state and also for an honestly determined conduct of the war. And this procedure will also admirably take care of the necessary practical exhortation—usually without the need to refer to military service, war loans, and the like. Just at this time the message of Holy Scripture is in itself strong and unequivocal enough to be comprehensible in a very pointed way, even to a child. We must simply make ourselves once more obedient to it, wholeheartedly, and rule out all secondary purposes.[17]

3. When the Church is truly preaching the Word of God to the man of today, there can be no question of confining itself to a "timeless" spiritual service. What exactly is that, anyway? There is a "timeless" religion, a "timeless" standard of morals. The Word of God, however, is never "timeless." The time in which we live is the time accorded to us, through God's patience, between the resurrection of Jesus Christ and His second coming. Therefore it is God's time.[18] Therefore He and His Word have a necessary, innate relation to everything that transpires within this time, and thus to the American man of today who sees himself in one way or another involved in the war against Germany, Italy and Japan.

What kind of sermon and what sort of ministry would it be whose consolation and admonition guided mankind to some timeless vacuum remote from the real conditions of this world with its anxieties and problems, or which led men to a sort of religious-moral "private" life? I wonder if the people in America, who are now, it appears, sponsoring that type of preaching and ministry, are quite aware that they are thereby moving in the wake of a certain type of German Lutheranism which has been preaching for centuries that the Gospel and the Law, the transcendent and the terrestrial, the Church and the State, Christian and political living, may be regarded and treated as two neatly separated realms. Do they realize the extent to which this evil doctrine furthered the German nationalism, *étatisme* and militarism of the nineteenth century and finally the National Socialism of today?[19] If the Church in America has a craving for smoothing the road in that country for the rise of a similar

17. Barth reframes the content of political preaching by arguing that it must be preached in its "full scope." The presupposition here is that the gospel carries political implications and that faithful preaching of Christ requires paying attention to the practical and concrete realities of the lives of those hearing the church's message.

18. These themes arise in connection to Barth's doctrine of election (see chaps. 18–19). He also discusses them in his section "Man in His Time," in *Church Dogmatics* III/2 (Edinburgh: T&T Clark, 1960), 437–640.

19. The French word *étatisme* means "authoritarian control by the state."

secularistic monster, a diligent regimen of "timeless" spiritual ministry is highly to be recommended: no slogan is more pleasing to the devil than this one! If such is not their desire, churchmen must bear in mind that for some reason it pleased the Word of God to become finite and therefore also law-bound, imminent and political in the person of Jesus Christ, not only without detracting from His character as Gospel, as hope of resurrection, as the utterance of the Church, but rather in confirmation and fulfillment thereof.[20]

Leave to the Word its whole independence and dignity by preaching it according to Holy Scripture! But leave to it also, on the other hand, its full strength and scope, by not forgetting for a moment to preach it to the man of today as such and therefore also in its whole finite and political clarity and categorical firmness.

4. Identification of the Church with a political cause? No! Under no circumstances and not even within the most modest limits! That is not the idea at all, that the Church identify itself—even remotely—with any political cause, that of the Allies, for instance, and so provide the religious accompaniment to the terrible sounds which must now travel round the world. By doing so it would betray its Lord and surrender itself without rendering the cause of the Allies the least assistance.[21] A single true man with an ordinary gun in his hand would be more useful to the Allies' cause than the bells and organs of all the churches in the world if they, having betrayed their Master and thereby surrendered themselves, were no longer "true" churches. In complete independence (of the Allied cause as well) they can and should be a light to their members and to the entire world, a light making visible the fact that the terrible calamity of our day is no blind accident, no mere expression of general human benightedness, no senseless free-for-all between different imperialistic systems; that it would not do any good to turn away from it in indignation and divert one's thoughts because it is so "horrible" and to escape from it and leave to others the responsibility for seeing it through.

The churches can and should make it plain that Jesus Christ is now, as always, Lord of the world and all its dominions and that today's world-rending struggle also is being fought (whether mankind realizes and admits it or not) for His sake and in honor of Him, and has His Promise, so that those who

20. For Barth, any preaching that focuses on spiritual truths at the expense of concrete political realities is false because its contradicts the reality of Jesus Christ. When Jesus entered into time and space, he assumed the political as well as spiritual burdens of his people. This aspect of his work is not secondary but central to the gospel.

21. This claim corresponds to the third thesis of the Barmen Declaration: "We reject the false doctrine that the Church could have permission to hand over the form of its message and of its order to whatever it itself might wish or to the vicissitudes of the prevailing ideological and political convictions of the day."

know and love Him must, before all others, take this war seriously.[22] Or is there not some danger that the meaning of this war may be misconstrued, and become simply futile, insane, and abhorrent? How could it be otherwise? Human life is always threatened by this possibility. The noblest cause is not immune from becoming an evil one in our hands, and if this war is a good cause, it is nevertheless a dangerous one, a temptation for all the participating nations, governments, and armies.

Woe betide, if the Church should desecrate itself in this cause instead of seeing to it, on the contrary, that this cause be consecrated through the Church, that the righteousness and necessity of this war for the defense of the righteous state be preserved to the nations, to their governments and armies consciously, thus giving them a clear conscience in the conduct of it but also preserving the moderation necessary to its proper conclusion. This mission, by virtue of which it preaches a righteous peace in the midst of war and thus approves the war only for the sake of the righteous peace (but for its sake does so in wholehearted earnest), is the prophetic mission of the Church in this war. And if it is only Church, and remains Church, it cannot be estimated to what extent it may impose limitation on itself in its realization of this mission. Its spiritual mission in this respect is illimitable. Let the Church take care, however, that it be and remain strictly true to it as to its spiritual mission.[23]

5. The sentence, that the Church is not at war, is *true to the extent* that it may mean: the Church is in no sense one of the instruments of the warring state. In war as in peace it serves its own Lord, pursues its own cause and speaks its own language: the cause and message of the Gospel, which is directed to friend and foe alike and is not dependent on the outcome of the war, whatever it may be. It prays, while admonishing the friendly powers to remain absolutely steadfast, for the Church and for the enemy. It always remains determined and ready to intercede, if necessary, for the rights of the enemy also.

22. Barth's argument on this point follows the pattern he developed from the beginning of his career. Just as God is distinct from creation, the cause of Christ is distinct from every human political party. At the same time—just as God's saving work in Christ reconfigures our understanding of history—the kingdom politics of Jesus Christ redefines our understanding of human politics. The choice is not between Christ or politics but between a false politics—one ordered around strictly human values and aims—and the true politics that corresponds to the reality unveiled by Jesus.

23. Barth outlines three key tasks for the church here: (1) The church should view the politics of the war in light of Christ rather than Christ through the politics of the war. (2) The church should preach peace and thus approve of the war against Hitler for the sake of peace. (3) The church should restrain itself from entering into political allegiances but instead preach the politics of Christ.

The same sentence is *in part not true*, in so far as it can mean that the Church is neutral; that it looks on and takes care not to compromise itself; that it preaches a Gospel which is indifferent to the question of a righteous state; that it is motivated by no clear political decisions and objectives; that it might even disseminate the lie that recognition between left and right, between good and evil in this war is not required; and that it confines its activities to that timeless spiritual service, etc., etc.[24]

That same sentence is *wholly true* in so far as it means that the Church in wartime lives and works—to the very degree that it takes the war seriously—in the deepest peace of the knowledge that He, who makes all things new, is already seated victoriously at the right hand of God, the King, whose sovereignty has no end, who needs no service from us but who has not scorned the enlistment on His behalf of our earnest, determined, persistent service in Church and State.

24. I adjusted the punctuation in this translation for the sake of clarity. Barth make it clear that this entire paragraph is *not* how the church should relate to the war.

34

"The Community of Christians and the Community of Citizens"

Introduction

In August 1945 Barth returned to Germany for the first time since the end of the war to visit friends, preach in German churches, and deliver lectures. He was saddened by what he saw. Germany was devastated materially, politically, and spiritually, and a tremendous rebuilding effort was needed on all fronts. During his visit, friends asked Barth to take up his former position at the University of Bonn so that he could contribute to the reconstruction effort. Barth never seriously considered the possibility. He had already decided to spend the rest of his career at the University of Basel focusing on his *Church Dogmatics*, which he considered his life's work.

Yet Barth cared about the German people and did not want to abandon them in their time of need. Like many others, he worried that they would fall back into the political ideologies and practices that had led to two wars. He was critical of the Allied reconstruction effort for focusing on material rebuilding of Germany while neglecting the ideological reconstruction that also needed to take place. He thought the German people were being given little instruction about how to construct a truly democratic society. In addition, he was concerned that German Christians still were mired in false patterns of thinking regarding the relationship between the church and state.

With these concerns in mind, Barth accepted an invitation to spend the summer semester of 1946 at the University of Bonn. He lived in a small apartment and spent his time delivering lectures, holding seminars, giving radio interviews, and having dozens of conversations with people from all backgrounds. The university buildings lay in ruins, and Barth recalled lecturing to students with "grave faces" while the sound of construction equipment hummed in the background.[1] Given the circumstances, Barth lectured without a manuscript or notes for the first time in his career. He focused on the needs of his audience and sought to address their concerns directly.

This excerpt comes from his lecture "The Community of Christians and the Community of Citizens." Barth later recalled that his former friend turned Nazi sympathizer Friedrich Gogarten sat scowling in the front row, although they never spoke personally. Barth's goal in this lecture is to work out the implications of the fifth thesis of the Barmen Declaration for the church's relationship with the state. Instead of two distinct realms, Barth uses the image of two concentric circles: Jesus Christ stands at the center, with the church as the inner circle and the state as the outer circle. This way of configuring the relationship carries two important implications. First, it rules out the notion that the state's role can be described on the basis of an appeal to natural law. This closes the door to the theological justifications that the German Christians had used to explain their support for Nazi ideology. Second, it compels the church to engage the state without becoming merely another political party within it. The church maintains its commitment to Jesus Christ even as it calls the state to fulfill its God-given tasks.

"The Community of Christians and the Community of Citizens"[2]

However much human error and human tyranny may be involved in it, the State is not a product of sin but one of the constants of the divine Providence and government of the world in its action against human sin: it is therefore an instrument of divine grace. The civil community shares both a common origin and a common center with the Christian community.[3] It is an order of

1. Karl Barth, *Dogmatics in Outline*, trans. G. T. Thompson (New York: Philosophical Library, 1949), 7.

2. Karl Barth, "The Christian Community and the Civil Community," in *Community, State, and Church: Three Essays* (Eugene, OR: Wipf & Stock, 2004), 156–60, 165–67, 171–73. The original German title is better translated "The Community of Christians and the Community of Citizens."

3. To explain the relationship between the church and the state, Barth uses the image of two concentric circles that share a common center. The center is Jesus Christ. The inner circle

divine grace inasmuch as in relation to sinful man as such, in relation to the world that still needs redeeming, the grace of God is always the patience of God. It is the sign that mankind, in its total ignorance and darkness, which is still, or has again become, a prey to sin and therefore subject to the wrath of God, is yet not forsaken but preserved and sustained by God. It serves to protect man from the invasion of chaos and therefore to give him time: time for the preaching of the gospel; time for repentance; time for faith.[4] Since "so far as human discernment and human ability make this possible" and "by means of the threat and use of force," provision is made in the State for the establishment of human law and (in the inevitably external, relative, and provisional sense) for freedom, peace, and humanity, it renders a definite service to the divine Providence and plan of salvation, quite apart from the judgment and individual desires of its members.[5] Its existence is not separate from the Kingdom of Jesus Christ; its foundations and its influence are not autonomous. It is outside the Church but not outside the range of Christ's dominion—it is an exponent of His Kingdom. It is, according to the New Testament, one of the "powers" created through Him and in Him and which subsist in Him (Col. 1:16–17), which cannot separate us from the love of God (Rom. 8:37–39) because they are all given to Him and are at His disposal (Matt. 28:18). The activity of the State is, as the Apostle explicitly stated, a form of divine service (Rom. 13:4–6). As such it can be perverted just as the divine service of the Church itself is not exempt from the possibility of perversion. The State can assume the face and character of Pilate. Even then, however, it still acts in the power which God has given it: "You would have no power over me unless it had been given you from above" (John 19:11). Even in its perversion it cannot escape from God, and His law is the standard by which it is judged. The Christian community therefore acknowledges "with gratitude and reverence toward God the benefit of this, his appointment."

---

is the church, which looks to Jesus and orders its life around him. The outer circle is the state: it does not see Jesus directly but only sees the inner circle that exists within it. As this inner circle, the church's task is to bear witness to the state by proclaiming the reality of Christ and the content of his will to the state. He develops this image throughout this excerpt in order to explain how the state serves as an instrument of God's grace and to describe the church's relationship to the state.

4. God's patience is revealed as he restrains the effects of sin so that humanity might be spared the full implications of it. The government is one of the instruments God uses to this end.

5. These quotations come from the fifth thesis of the Barmen Declaration. It opens with the claim that "the State, in this still unredeemed world in which also the Church is situated, has the task of maintaining justice and peace, so far as human discernment and human ability make this possible, by means of the threat and use of force." Barth's point is that the government's maintenance of justice and peace is a concrete manifestation of God's providence. It is in this sense that the government's actions reflect the authority of Jesus Christ.

The benefaction which it acknowledges consists in the external, relative, and provisional sanctification of the unhallowed world which is brought about by the existence of political power and order.[6] In what concrete attitudes to particular political patterns and realities this Christian acknowledgement will be expressed can remain a completely open question. It makes one thing quite impossible, however: a Christian decision to be indifferent; a non-political Christianity. The Church can in no case be indifferent or neutral towards this manifestation of an order so clearly related to its own mission. Such indifference would be equivalent to the opposition of which it is said in Romans 13:2 that it is a rebellion against the ordinance of God—and rebels secure their own condemnation.[7]

The Church must remain the Church. It must remain the inner circle of the Kingdom of Christ. The Christian community has a task of which the civil community can never relieve it and which it can never pursue in the forms peculiar to the civil community. It would not redound to the welfare of the civil community if the Christian community were to be absorbed by it (as Rothe has suggested that it should) and were therefore to neglect the special task which it has received a categorical order to undertake.[8] It proclaims the rule of Jesus Christ and the hope of the Kingdom of God. This is not the task of the civil community; it has no message to deliver; it is dependent on a message being delivered to it. It is not in a position to appeal to the authority and grace of God; it is dependent on this happening elsewhere. It does not pray; it depends on others praying for it. It is blind to the Whence? and Whither? of human existence; its task is rather to provide for the external and provisional delimitation and protection of human life; it depends on the existence of seeing eyes elsewhere. It cannot call the human pride into

6. Barth again quotes from the fifth thesis of the Barmen Declaration: "The Church acknowledges with gratitude and reverence toward God the benefit of this, his appointment. It draws attention to God's Kingdom, God's commandment and justice, and with these the responsibility of those who rule and those who are ruled." The church reacts in this way because the state's actions occur within the context of Christ's reign and reflect Christ's influence inasmuch as they correspond to God's will.

7. Romans 13:2: "Therefore whoever resists authority resists what God has appointed, and those who resist will incur judgment." Barth identifies indifference to the state directly with resistance against it. This identification makes sense only because the state's action is identified with God's providential order. To be indifferent to the state in this case is to be indifferent to God's will as he executes his saving plan in history.

8. Richard Rothe (1799–1867) was a German Lutheran theologian who argued that as humans develop their spirituality more and more in conformity to Christ, the distinction between their spiritual and political life is erased. Eventually the state will completely replace the church as the highest order of human society. This means that the contemporary decline of the church is something to be embraced rather than feared.

question fundamentally, and it knows of no final defense against the chaos which threatens it from that quarter; in this respect, too, it depends on ultimate words and insights existing elsewhere. The thought and speech of the civil community waver necessarily between a much too childlike optimism and a much too peevish pessimism in regard to man—as a matter of course it expects the best of everybody and suspects the worst! It obviously relies on its own view of man being fundamentally superseded elsewhere. Only an act of supreme disobedience on the part of Christians could bring the special existence of the Christian community to an end. Such a cessation is also impossible because then the voice of what is ultimately the only hope and help which all men need to hear would be silent.[9]

The Christian community shares in the task of the civil community precisely to the extent that it fulfills its own task. By believing in Jesus Christ and preaching Jesus Christ it believes in and preaches Him who is Lord of the world as He is Lord of the Church. And since they belong to the inner circle, the members of the Church are also automatically members of the wider circle. They cannot halt at the boundary where the inner and outer circles meet, though the work of faith, love, and hope which they are under orders to perform will assume different forms on either side of the boundary.[10] In the sphere of the civil community, the Christian community shares common interests with the world and its task is to give resolute practical expression to this community of interest. The Christian community prays for the civil community. It does so all the more since the civil community as such is not in the habit of praying. But by praying for it, it also makes itself responsible for it before God, and it would not be taking this responsibility seriously if it did no more than pray, if it did not also work actively on behalf of the civil community. It also expresses its active support of the civil community by acknowledging that, as an operation of a divine ordinance, the civil power is also binding on Christians and significant and just from the Christian point of view. It expresses its active support of the civil community by "subordinating" itself, in the words of the Apostle (Rom. 13:1), to the cause of the civil

9. In the image of two concentric circles around a common center, the outer circle cannot relate to the center apart from the inner circle. For example, it cannot appeal directly to the center, because it sees it only through the mediation of the inner circle. At every point, the outer circle remains dependent on the inner circle in order to relate properly to the center. So it is with the state and the church. The state cannot relate to Christ apart from the church, nor can it fulfill its appointed role within the world apart from the church's witness. If the church were to be absorbed into the state, this witness would be lost and the state would no longer know its true Lord or the task for which it exists.

10. Barth's imagery of the concentric circles captures the dual nature of the church's existence as a people who are in but not of the world (John 17:11–17).

community under all circumstances (and therefore whatever the political form and reality it has to deal with concretely).[11] Luther's translation of Romans 13:1 speaks of "being subject," which is something dangerously different from what is meant here. The last thing this instruction implies is that the Christian community and the Christian should offer the blindest possible obedience to the civil community and its officials. What is meant is that Christians should carry out what is required of them for the establishment, preservation, and maintenance of the civil community and for the execution of its task, because, although they are Christians and, as such, have their home elsewhere, they also live in this outer circle (Rom. 13:6–7). Jesus Christ is still its center: they, too, are therefore responsible for its stability. "Subordination" means the carrying out of this joint responsibility in which Christians apply themselves to the same task with non-Christians and submit themselves to the same rule. The subordination accrues to the good of the civil community however well or however badly that community is defended, because the civil cause (and not merely the Christian cause) is also the cause of the one God.[12] In Romans 13:5 Paul has expressly added that this "subordination" is not optional but necessary, and necessary not merely "for fear of punishment," for fear of the otherwise inevitable conflict with an obscure commandment of God, but "for conscience sake": in the clear evangelical knowledge of the divine grace and patience, which is also manifested in the existence of the State and, therefore, in full responsibility towards the will of God which the Christian sees revealed in the civil community. The "subordination" will be an expression of the obedience of a free heart which the Christian offers to God in the civil sphere as in the sphere of the Church—although with a different purpose (he renders to Caesar what is Caesar's and to God what is God's—Matt. 22:21).[13] . . .

It is this reliance on a spiritual norm that makes the Christian community free to support the cause of the civil community honestly and calmly.

11. Here Barth offers a concrete account of the church's primary tasks in relation to the state. The church is to (1) clearly express the commitments it shares with the state; (2) pray for the state; (3) take responsibility before God for its role in relation to the state; (4) actively support the state in its divinely appointed task; and (5) submit to the authority of the state in the matters to which God has given the state authority.

12. In relation to various translations of Romans 13:1, Barth draws a distinction between being "subordinate" to the state and being "subject to" the state. In no sense does the church stand under the absolute authority of the state, as if Christians were subject to it. Christ is the only Lord of the church. Even so, because the church exists within the state and shares common God-ordained interests with it, it serves and submits to the state in order to serve these interests and live in obedience to God.

13. Barth sees the subordination that Christians show to the state as parallel to the humility and obedience Christ displayed during his incarnate life (see chap. 25).

In the political sphere the Church will not be fighting for itself and its own concerns. Its own position, influence, and power in the State are not the goal which will determine the trend of its political decisions. "My kingdom is not from this world. If my kingdom were from this world, my followers would be fighting to keep me from being handed over to the Jews. But as it is, my kingdom is not from here" (John 18:36). The secret contempt which a Church fighting for its own interests with political weapons usually incurs even when it achieves a certain amount of success is well-deserved. And sooner or later the struggle generally ends in mortifying defeats of one sort or another. The Christian community is not an end in itself. It serves God and it thereby serves man.[14] It is true that the deepest, ultimate, divine purpose of the civil community consists in creating opportunities for the preaching and hearing of the Word and, to that extent, for the existence of the Church. But the only way the State can create such opportunities, according to the providence and ordinance of God, is the natural, secular, and profane way of the establishment of law, the safeguarding of freedom and peace, "according to the measure of human insight and capacity." The divine purpose is therefore not at all that the State should itself gradually develop more or less into a Church. And the Church's political aim cannot be to turn the State into a Church, that is, make it as far as possible subservient to the tasks of the Church.[15] If the State grants the Church freedom, respect, and special privileges in any of the ways which are open to it (guarantees of one kind or another, a share in education and broadcasting, the defense of the Sabbath, financial reliefs or subsidies, and the like), the Church will not immediately start dreaming of a ChurchState. It will be thankful for the State's help, seeing in such help a result of the divine providence and ordinance: and it will show its gratitude by being a Church all the more faithfully and zealously within the broader frontiers that the State's gifts make possible, thereby justifying the expectation which the State evidently reposes in it. But it will not claim such gifts as a right. If they are refused, it will look in itself for the reason, not in the State. "Resist not evil!" is an injunction that applies here. The Church will ask itself whether it has already given proof to the State of the Spirit and the power of God, whether it has already defended and proclaimed Jesus Christ to the world to the extent that it can expect to

14. Barth believes that the church cannot live as a partisan interest group fighting for its own space within the world. To do so would be to deny the church's reason for being. The church exists to bear witness to Christ within the world. If and when it engages in political activity, it must do so strictly for the benefit of this mission and the world it exists to serve (see chap. 29).

15. Barth quotes from the affirmation of the fifth thesis of the Barmen Declaration and then summarizes its two negations.

be considered an important, significant, and salutary factor in public life. It will ask, for example, whether it is in a position to say the tremendous things that are certainly entitled to be heard in schools. It will first and foremost do penance—when and where would it not have cause for so doing?—and it will do that best by concentrating on its own special work in the, possibly, extremely small space left to it in public life, with all the more confidence and intensity and with redoubled zeal, "with the greatest force applied at the narrowest point."[16] Where it has first to advertise its desire to play a part in public life, where it must first establish its claim to be considered a factor of public importance, it only proves that its claim to be heard is irrelevant and it thoroughly deserves not to be heard at all, or to be heard in a way that will sooner or later afford it no pleasure. Whenever the Church has entered the political arena to fight for its claim to be given public recognition, it has always been a Church which has failed to understand the special purpose of the State, an impenitent, spiritually unfree Church.[17] . . .

The Church is based on the knowledge of the one eternal God, who as such became man and thereby proved Himself a neighbor to man, by treating him with compassion (Luke 10:36–37). The inevitable consequence is that in the political sphere the Church will always and in all circumstances be interested primarily in human beings and not in some abstract cause or other, whether it be anonymous capital or the State as such (the functioning of its departments!) or the honor of the nation or the progress of civilization or culture or the idea, however conceived, of the historical development of the human race. It will not be interested in this last idea even if "progress" is interpreted as meaning the welfare of future generations, for the attainment of which man, human dignity, human life in the present age are to be trampled underfoot. Right itself becomes wrong (*summum ius summa iniuria*) when it is allowed to rule as an abstract form, instead of serving the limitation and hence the preservation of man.[18] The Church is at all times and in all

16. This quotation comes from the poem "Breite und Tiefe" ("Breadth and Depth") by Friedrich Schiller (1759–1805).

17. With respect to religious freedom, two key principles guide the church's approach: (1) the church remembers that God's kingdom transcends earthly kingdoms; and (2) the church's mission is to serve the world by bearing witness to Christ. These two principles lead the church to adopt a posture of humility. The church does not expect special privileges or recognition in society, nor does it fight for its own rights within the political realm. When the church is able to act freely, it is thankful and commits to using its freedom to serve the world through its mission. If the state restricts the church's freedom, the church responds first by examining itself and then by focusing even more intensely on serving the world from within its limited space. At no point does the church make its own rights and privileges its focus.

18. The phrase *summum ius summa iniuria* means "supreme law, supreme injustice." It comes from Cicero's *De officiis* (*On Duties*) 1.10.33.

circumstances the enemy of the idol Juggernaut. Since God Himself became man, man is the measure of all things, and man can and must only be used and, in certain circumstances, sacrificed, for man. Even the most wretched man—not man's egoism, but man's humanity—must be resolutely defended against the autocracy of every mere "cause." Man has not to serve causes; causes have to serve man.[19] . . .

The Church is witness of the fact that the Son of man came to seek and to save the lost. And this implies that—casting all false impartiality aside—the Church must concentrate first on the lower and lowest levels of human society. The poor, the socially and economically weak and threatened, will always be the object of its primary and particular concern, and it will always insist on the State's special responsibility for these weaker members of society. That it will bestow its love on them, within the framework of its own task (as part of its service), is one thing and the most important thing; but it must not concentrate on this and neglect the other thing to which it is committed by its political responsibility: the effort to achieve such a fashioning of the law as will make it impossible for "equality before the law" to become a cloak under which strong and weak, independent and dependent, rich and poor, employers and employees, in fact receive different treatment at its hands: the weak being unduly restricted, the strong unduly protected. The Church must stand for social justice in the political sphere.[20]

19. Note how Barth frames the church's engagement in political matters with a concreteness that mirrors God's relationship with the world in Jesus Christ. The church is not interested in abstract political ideologies, institutions, or systems. Rather, it focuses its attention and action on the concrete realities and needs of humans.

20. In line with Jesus Christ's example, the church dedicates special attention to addressing the needs of the poor. It does not merely address immediate needs, but it also addresses structural issues that lead to systematic economic and social inequality. A church living in line with its mission will be a church that challenges the state to order its laws and bureaucracy so that every citizen is treated justly.

Conclusion

The Tradition of Karl Barth

I
f such a thing as a Barthian tradition exists in Christian theology, then Karl
Barth cannot be considered a member of it. The very idea runs against the
grain of his life and theology. It also contradicts the way theologians received
his work both during and after his career. However, Barth did establish a
particular method of doing theology, one focused more on the future than
the past. To gain a sense of this unique approach, the story of how and why
Barth ended up standing apart from every theological tradition must be told.

From Prophet to Theologian

Barth faced the unique challenge of becoming prominent as a theologian
before figuring out what he actually believed. He arrived on the scene as a
prophetic voice from the wilderness, a village pastor descending from the
Swiss mountains with a message of judgment for a century-old tradition of
academic theology. In most eras, Barth's message would have been ignored.
Indeed, many of his opponents tried this strategy. But Barth arrived at precisely the right moment in history. He gained a hearing because the world was
in crisis, and so was the discipline of theology. Many of its most prominent
thinkers had undermined their authority because they had helped usher in
the crisis. Barth had studied under many of them, and he knew how to strike
at the heart of their authority: he added an exclamation point to the crisis.

Barth's early theology performs this work by calling *everything* into
question. He challenges the tradition of his teachers by breaking from their

methods, rejecting their educational philosophy, and tossing aside their well-established conclusions. He then goes further by presenting a picture of a "wholly other" God who calls into question humanity's ability even to practice theology at all. In many times and places, this argument would have made little sense to theologians. But in that time and place, it made perfect sense to a great number of students, pastors, and thinkers for whom the old answers no longer worked. Barth knew that his claims resonated because he was writing primarily for himself. He wrote to address the disillusionment that comes with mounting the pulpit on a Sunday morning and no longer knowing what to say. He wrote to soothe the sting that comes with feeling betrayed by one's teachers. He wrote because he needed God to break into his life and set it on a new course. And he knew many others were in the same position.

It took a while for Barth to realize, however, that the prophets who draw the largest crowds often end up alone. The trajectory toward this isolation was set from the beginning.[1] Barth's break from his teachers and his push toward new ideas meant that he began his career by separating himself from the tradition in which he was trained. But what he lacked in tradition he made up for with theological allies—at least early on. Within just a few years, he had moved from a village pulpit to lecture halls packed with listeners who took his every claim seriously. He was given a chair in theology even though he had never earned a doctorate. He published widely discussed commentaries and books of sermons, and his essays regularly appeared in an academic journal that he had helped create. His work received substantive responses from scholars across the spectrum, and major figures engaged him in print as if they were equals.

Yet Barth knew that prophets need to proclaim grace as well as judgment. His early theology pruned the Protestant tradition down to its roots. Could he help it grow again? This question prompted another crisis for Barth, this time a personal one. By 1924, he realized that the theology of *The Epistle to the Romans* was inadequate. When he wrote the preface to the fourth edition that year, he noted that reviewers had pointed out significant deficiencies in his argument. While he did not fully agree with their criticisms, Barth acknowledged that they "displayed a genuine understanding of the point at issue" and conceded that "the book needs to be rewritten."[2] But he did not have time to take on the project. Barth was scheduled to present his own dogmatic

1. For an examination of the theme of isolation in Barth's theology, see Hans Anton Drewes, "In the Same Solitude as Fifty Years Ago," in *Karl Barth and the Making of Evangelical Theology: A Fifty-Year Perspective* (Grand Rapids: Eerdmans, 2015), 15–29.

2. Karl Barth, *The Epistle to the Romans*, 6th ed., trans. E. C. Hoskyns (Oxford: Oxford University Press, 1933), 20–21.

theology, and he had no idea what he was going to say. "I shall never forget the spring vacation of 1924," he recalled. "I sat in my study at Göttingen, faced with the task of giving lectures on dogmatics for the first time. No one can ever have been more plagued than I then was with the problem, could I do it? and how?"[3]

Engaging Tradition

Barth responded by turning to the Christian tradition for help. He initially drew mostly from the insights of the Reformed tradition, but soon he began to incorporate ideas from the church fathers, Anselm, Aquinas, Luther, and many others. His use of these traditional sources was eclectic because he was willing to draw from any person or idea if it helped him make his own argument better. On one page, Barth might appeal to a medieval theologian like Anselm to criticize his own Reformed tradition; then, a few pages later, he might use the theology of the Reformation as the basis for rejecting centuries of Catholic teaching. He then might apply his own reading of Scripture against the *entire* tradition in order to offer a new alternative. This approach left Barth standing both within and outside the Christian tradition at the same moment. He accepted what it taught and stood against it whenever and wherever he deemed it necessary.

Barth proceeded in this way on the basis of his theological method. He began with the premise that theology happens as a result of a personal encounter with the living God. God speaks to humans right now in and through his Word, and he demands a response of obedience. Theologians respond by telling the church what they hear so the church can think and speak about God more clearly. Since theologians' words come as the result of their encounter with God, Barth argues that they "cannot proceed by building with complete confidence on the foundation of questions that are already settled, results that are already achieved, or conclusions that are already arrived at."[4] Instead, they have to reconsider their conclusions every day by beginning again at the beginning in light of what they hear in the Word of God.

This reconsideration takes place primarily through an engagement with Scripture, which serves as the criterion for deciding which theological claims to embrace or reject. Scripture constantly presented Barth with new questions,

---

3. See Karl Barth, "Foreword," in Heinrich Heppe, *Reformed Dogmatics* (Grand Rapids: Eerdmans, 1978), v.

4. Karl Barth, *Evangelical Theology: An Introduction* (New York: Holt, Rinehart & Winston, 1963), 165.

prompted him to change his mind, revise prior formulations, and move in unexpected directions. His revision of the doctrine of election serves as an example in this regard. Even though he considered himself a Reformed theologian, Barth was willing to break from the traditional Reformed approach to election and predestination on the basis of his reading of Scripture. "I would have preferred to follow Calvin's doctrine of predestination much more closely, instead of departing from it so radically," he said. "But I could not and cannot do so. As I let the Bible itself speak to me on these matters, as I meditated upon what I seemed to hear, I was driven irresistibly to reconstruction."[5] Barth believed that Scripture gave theologians the ability to break from the Christian tradition precisely in order to remain faithful to God. This kind of faithfulness requires courage, Barth thought, because theologians face pressure to orient their claims not only around their own ideas, culture, and agendas but also around the claims of their tradition. Barth worried that theologians were often trained to operate like partisans whose primary task is to defend their position at all costs while looking for ways to show the deficiencies of their opponents. But such an approach distracts theologians from the reality that God is the true subject matter of theology. The only way to stay focused on God is to listen to God's Word and then test every claim—no matter its source—in light of what one hears. This approach grants "the free God room to dispose at will over everything that men may already have known, produced, and achieved."[6] Nothing in the church's tradition is off-limits for examination and revision because every claim must be brought into line with what God is saying to his people right now.

The ever-present possibility that one's theological claims might be revised gives theologians a sense of humility about their role and place in the church and its tradition. During an interview late in his life, Barth was asked about liberal theology and his own approach to dogmatics. He surprised his interviewer by saying that he himself was liberal in a certain sense. "Being truly liberal means thinking and speaking in responsibility and openness on all sides, backwards and forwards, toward both the past and the future, and with what I might call a total personal modesty." This modesty involves recognizing both the limits of one's theology and that, says Barth, "there have been and are other people before and alongside me, and that others still will come after me." This awareness brings peace because, as Barth says, "I do not think I always have to be right."[7] Barth's recognition of the provisional

---

5. See Karl Barth, *Church Dogmatics* II/2 (Edinburgh: T&T Clark, 1957), x.
6. Barth, *Evangelical Theology*, 166–67.
7. Karl Barth, *Final Testimonies* (Grand Rapids: Eerdmans, 1977), 34.

nature of his claims corresponds to his method. The fact that one's claims have to be tested again each day means that none of them can be considered permanent. "Rightly understood," he explains, "it is the material principle of dogmatics itself which destroys at its root the very notion of a dogmatic system."[8] This recognition also stems from Barth's understanding that he was just one of many theological voices in the history of the church. He believed that a commitment to the entire church, both living and dead, necessarily "precludes the possibility of a dogmatics which thinks and speaks, as it were, timelessly."[9] No single theologian or tradition can ever give the final theological answer for every Christian, and no specific era carries special authority over others. The stability of the theological tradition is found not in the consistency of the tradition but in the constancy of the God to whom the tradition testifies.

Each one of these characteristics of Barth's theological approach—his eclectic use of the tradition, the primacy he gives to Scripture, his willingness to revise prior claims, and his sense that every claim is both provisional and contextual—places Barth in a unique position with respect to his theological legacy. Nothing in his approach is conducive to linking him to a particular theological tradition or forming one in his name. Barth's approach carries exactly the opposite effect. As he sees it, the life of the theologian is marked by relentless self-criticism, constant revision of one's claims, and a willingness to adhere to God's Word—even if that means standing alone.

A Question of Principle

Among the many characteristics that shape Barth's theology, none leave Barth standing alone more often than his rejection of the idea that theologians need to justify their claims on the basis of general principles. These principles are "general" because they are universally accessible through the exercise of natural human capacities such as the operation of reason or the human conscience. A particular act of divine revelation is not necessary to establish or understand these principles, and they transcend any particular time or culture. They might be used to establish a philosophical framework or develop a natural theology that exists alongside, or perhaps in conjunction with, the insights provided by God's revelation in Jesus Christ. One of Barth's central convictions is that, if theologians utilize general principles in their theology, then their claims about God will be determined by their own creaturely ideals

8. Karl Barth, *Church Dogmatics* I/2 (Edinburgh: T&T Clark, 1956), 868.
9. Barth, *Church Dogmatics* I/2, 841.

rather than the reality of God. He developed this conviction as a result of events early in his career.

Barth's break from Protestant liberalism was prompted, in part, by the way that liberal theologians used general criteria to justify their theological judgments. When World War I began in 1914, Barth believed the war was immoral and unjust, and he could not fathom how a Christian could support it. Imagine his surprise, then, when many of his former teachers publicly endorsed the German war policy on the basis of their theology. This theology was shaped by its starting point. His teachers typically began with a general account of religious experience that then served as the basis for their particular description for Christianity. Now Barth saw them appealing to this same starting point in order to justify their support for the war. This argument greatly disturbed him. As he wrote at the time to his former professor Wilhelm Herrmann, "We learned to acknowledge 'experience' as the constitutive principle of knowing and doing in the domain of religion. . . . Now, however, in answer to our doubts [about the war], an 'experience' which is completely new to us is held out to us by German Christians, an allegedly religious war 'experience,' i.e., the fact that German Christians 'experience' their war as a holy war is supposed to bring us to silence, if not demand reverence from us."[10] Barth's remark implies that Herrmann has allowed his politics to shape his theology instead of allowing his theology to determine his politics. In Barth's view, the result borders on idolatry because human experience has determined the content of the theological description of God. As Barth later reflected, this event was the moment that Protestant liberal theology finally "unmasked itself" to him as a human-centered enterprise.[11]

Barth faced similar arguments nearly two decades later, during his confrontation with the German Christian movement. In their case, the German Christians appealed to a universally accessible natural law in order to justify their support for the Nazi government and its anti-Semitic policies. Barth thought history was repeating itself: theological ideas derived on the basis of general principles again were being manipulated to serve destructive political aims. He pointed out this problem when he criticized his former friend and ally Friedrich Gogarten for joining the German Christians. Gogarten had been utilizing generally derived historical and anthropological insights in his theology for years, and Barth was convinced this methodological error led directly to Gogarten's political

10. See Barth's letter to Hermann in *Karl Barth-Martin Rade: Ein Briefwechsel*, ed. Christoph Schwöbel (Gütersloh: Gütersloher Verlagshaus Gerd Mohn, 1981), 115.

11. Karl Barth, "Concluding Unscientific Postscript on Schleiermacher," in *The Theology of Schleiermacher: Lectures at Göttingen, Winter Semester of 1923/24*, ed. Dietrich Ritschl (Grand Rapids: Eerdmans, 1968), 264.

misjudgment. After years of placing creaturely ideas alongside the Word of God, it was not that great of a leap for Gogarten to place the claims of Adolf Hitler alongside God's Word as well. As Barth put it, "Gogarten's entire path has led him with the highest degree of consistency to condone everything."[12]

These situations taught Barth a crucial lesson about theological method: whenever general principles serve as the basis for theological reflection, the result will be an idolatrous view of God that is easily manipulated to serve human ideologies. No matter how well-intentioned or rigorous a theologian might be, if God's revelation in Christ is placed into a framework established on the basis of universally accessible ideas about the nature of reason or history, then the description of Christ that results will be determined by creaturely ideals rather than the reality of Christ's person and life. This distorted picture of Christ will correspond to—rather than challenge and correct—deceptive human ideologies. To avoid this problem, God's revelation in Jesus Christ as attested in Scripture must be the criterion by which every theological claim must be measured.

Debating the Question

As Barth argued for the priority of the Word of God in theology, the problem he faced is that nearly everyone disagreed with him about it in some form or another. This includes many of Barth's fellow dialectical theologians, the Protestant liberals, and Roman Catholics. Even Barth himself struggled to maintain this commitment at times.

The embrace of general principles by many of the dialectical theologians happened gradually throughout the decade of the 1920s. While they initially embraced Barth's arguments about the dangers of using natural theology or philosophical criteria as the basis for theology, many of them began to waver as they developed their own constructive theologies. Barth particularly worried about the development of Gogarten and Emil Brunner in this regard. Throughout the mid-1920s, they both attempted to draw connections between the insights of natural law and the biblical testimony about Christ. Barth soon recognized that Gogarten's theology was leading him down the path toward what would become the German Christian movement. He initially hoped that Brunner could be convinced that natural theology was a dead end, especially since he joined Barth in strongly opposing the German Christians.

12. Karl Barth, "Abschied," in *Karl Barth Gesamtausgabe*, vol. 49, *Vorträge und Kleinere Arbeiten 1930–1933*, ed. Michael Beintker, Michael Hüttenhoff, and Peter Zocher (Zurich: Theologischer Verlag Zürich, 2013), 503.

But Brunner still insisted that, even after the fall, humans retained the capacity to know something of God apart from God's revelation in Christ. Barth thought this mediating position compromised too much. Despite Brunner's good intentions, he still allowed general principles to shape his account of the content of God's Word. Eventually, after Brunner criticized Barth's approach for being too restrictive, Barth strongly rebuked Brunner and drew a stark line against any use of natural theology in dogmatics.[13]

Barth's strong response to Brunner's mediating position reflects lessons he learned from his own mistakes. After Barth published his first volume of dogmatic theology, *Die christliche Dogmatic im Entwurf* (Christian Dogmatics in Outline) in 1927, the book received criticism from many directions. But it was the positive responses that most worried Barth. He later recalled being surprised that Paul Tillich and Rudolf Bultmann—both of whom were now trying to bring the insights of theology into conversation with philosophical existentialism—thought "that they could welcome [him] as one of themselves" on the basis of the book.[14] This embrace helped Barth realize that, despite his intentions, his theology had not closed the door to the use of this kind of general criteria. When he offered a revised version of the argument in *Church Dogmatics* I/1, he noted, "I have excluded to the very best of my ability anything that might appear to find for theology a foundation, support, or justification in philosophical existentialism."[15] Decades later, he still blamed himself for the consequences of his 1927 "false start" and admitted that he "must bear a good deal of witting responsibility" for theology that followed.[16] He had learned that there was no room for compromise with respect to the starting point of theology or the criteria by which theologians make their judgments. If the integrity of theology is to be upheld, the priority and centrality of the Word of God must be maintained.

Barth emphasized this point in his early debates with Protestant liberal theologians. Their criticism of Barth's theology often was rooted in their assumption that theology must begin with general, universally acceptable principles in order to be considered rational. This is the perspective defended by Adolf von Harnack in his 1923 open letter to Barth.[17] In response to Barth's

13. See Karl Barth, "No! A Reply to Emil Brunner," in *Natural Theology: Comprising "Nature and Grace" by Dr. Emil Brunner and the Reply "No!" by Dr. Karl Barth*, trans. Peter Fraenkel (London: Centenary, 1946), 65–128.

14. Karl Barth, *Church Dogmatics* II/1 (Edinburgh: T&T Clark, 1957), 635.

15. Karl Barth, *Church Dogmatics* I/1, rev. ed. (Edinburgh: T&T Clark, 1975), xiii.

16. Karl Barth, *Church Dogmatics* III/4 (Edinburgh: T&T Clark, 1961), xii.

17. See Adolf von Harnack, "An Open Letter to Karl Barth," in *Revelation and Theology: An Analysis of the Barth-Harnack Correspondence* of 1923, ed. H. Martin Rumscheidt (Cambridge: Cambridge University Press, 1972), 35–39.

criticisms of the historical-critical method, Harnack insists that theology must maintain its scientific character lest it fall into irrelevance. His definition of "scientific" is shaped by the method of the natural sciences, where objectivity and critical judgment are prized above all. No alternative method can be permitted because "each age possesses only one science," and this science represents "the only possible way of mastering an object epistemologically."[18] If theologians are to be scientific, they must evaluate their subject matter objectively by standards of critical reason. "The task of theology," Harnack insists, "is at one with the task of science in general."[19] In line with this method, any belief grounded on a presupposed source of authority such as the Bible must be considered suspect until both the claim and the source are evaluated rationally and historically. Otherwise, anyone could "freely create their own understanding of the Bible."[20] Similarly, since moral and ethical claims are both culturally specific and historically contingent, any such claim must be assessed in light of universal principles. A failure to do so risks opening the door to an irrelevant occultism that leaves Christianity isolated among the world's religions.

Barth responded by insisting that theology should operate on the basis of its own unique starting point.[21] He questioned whether Harnack's generally based "scientific" approach is truly more rational than the revelation-centered approach of premodern figures like Paul or Luther. He also raises doubts about whether the modern approach actually produces superior results. Appealing to the theology of the past seems like a better option, Barth argues, because this theology is "more instructive than the chaotic business of today's faculties for which the idea of a determinative object has become strange and monstrous in the face of the determinate character of method."[22] In other words, at least the older theology said something about God; modern theology mostly talks about itself.

Nearly a decade later, Barth developed this argument further. He begins his *Church Dogmatics* by arguing that theology is a scientific discipline because it focuses on a definite object of knowledge and examines this object in a consistent, rational, and ordered way.[23] The question is not *whether* theology is scientific but *how*. The distinction between theology and every other science

18. Harnack, "Open Letter to Karl Barth," 39, 36.
19. Harnack, "Open Letter to Karl Barth," 36.
20. Harnack, "Open Letter to Karl Barth," 39.
21. For Barth's response to Harnack's letter, see chap. 4.
22. Karl Barth, "An Answer to Adolf von Harnack's Open Letter," in Rumscheidt, *Revelation and Theology*, 41–42.
23. Barth, *Church Dogmatics* I/1, 7–8.

is that theology uses a different criterion to make judgments: while other disciplines operate on the basis of general criteria such as human experience or natural reason, theology operates strictly on the basis of God's revelation in Jesus Christ. Theologians who turn from this particular revelation to operate on the basis of general criteria undermine the integrity of the discipline, because they are making judgments "in accordance with alien principles" that reflect creaturely ideals and ideologies.[24] The problem with this approach is that the subject matter of theology is God, and God's distinction from creation means that theologians can speak about him rightly only by reflecting on what God reveals to them. In this light, Barth argues that theology "does not have to justify itself" on the basis of general principles any more than God has to justify himself before a creature.[25] Nor does theology need to hold to both universal principles and divine revelation, as if it must "accept the obligation of submission to standards valid for other sciences" alongside its own standards.[26] The only criterion by which theological claims are to be judged is the Word of God.

Catholic theologians also affirmed the use of general principles in theology but for different reasons. They had little sympathy for Protestant liberalism, but they thought that Barth's alternative was untenable because he rejected the role of natural theology. Hans Urs von Balthasar summarizes Catholic criticism of Barth on this point. Although he is sympathetic to many of Barth's concerns, Balthasar argues that Barth's theological method is shaped by an unfortunate christological "narrowing" (*Engführung*). According to Balthasar, Barth prioritizes God's revelation in Christ to such an extent that he makes the created order meaningless, as if the creature can know nothing about God as a result of God's act of creation. The problem is that this approach is inconsistent with Barth's arguments about divine revelation. Balthasar explains that, whenever Barth talks about God's revelation, he fails to acknowledge that there is a "presupposition lying at its foundations that makes revelation possible."[27] This presupposition is God's prior act of creation. After all, God would not be able to reveal himself if he had not *already* created a human who can receive this revelation, and this revelation could not be received if God had not *already* given the human the capacity to receive it. This means that God's revelation in Christ presupposes an already-existing relationship between God and humanity established in and through God's act of creation.

24. Barth, *Church Dogmatics* I/1, 6.
25. Barth, *Church Dogmatics* I/1, 8.
26. Barth, *Church Dogmatics* I/1, 10.
27. Hans Urs von Balthasar, *The Theology of Karl Barth: Exposition and Interpretation*, trans. Edward T. Oakes, SJ (San Francisco: Ignatius, 1992), 112.

In Balthasar's view, it does not make sense for Barth to restrict the operation of theology to God's revelation in Jesus Christ if this revelation presupposes the existence of this prior relationship between God and humanity. Why not allow insights derived from reflecting on this prior relationship to stand alongside the insights gained from God's revelation in Jesus Christ?

This argument serves as the ground for the Catholic alternative to Barth's method. Catholic theologians argue that the intrinsic relationship between creation and salvation—between nature and grace—means that general ideas about God derived through natural revelation can and must relate to God's revelation in Jesus Christ. The two sources nevertheless provide distinct kinds of knowledge. As Thomas Aquinas argues, because the truth about God exceeds the capacity of human reason, any knowledge of God obtained by means of rational reflection on the created order is only "known by a few, and that after a long time, and with the admixture of many errors."[28] In other words, natural revelation only gets humans so far when it comes to the knowledge of God. But this limitation does not mean that the knowledge gained through this revelation is empty or meaningless. Rather, this knowledge simply needs to be perfected where it is in error and fulfilled by being brought to its completion. This is precisely what happens when God reveals himself in Jesus Christ: grace perfects and fulfills nature. In light of this grace, theologians should proceed on the basis that God's acts of creation and salvation *both* provide information about God because God is both Creator and Reconciler. Even though the natural knowledge must be perfected and fulfilled, it still is useful for theology because it helps clarify and enrich the truths revealed in Christ.

Barth took this Catholic criticism of his position seriously, and he developed his response to it over the course of his career. He rejects the idea that the axiom "grace perfects and fulfills nature" can serve as a fundamental principle for theology because he argues that it relies on an abstract view of God, humanity, and creation. It approaches God abstractly because it assumes that God can be known as Creator before and apart from God's revelation in Christ. Barth thinks this assumption is mistaken. Whenever God is defined solely on the basis of his act of creation, this definition will be governed by an account of the "supreme attributes"—those qualities that distinguish God from creation. These attributes are derived by the human act of reflecting on created being and then determining what must be true of God in light of God's distinction from creation. The problem is that this humanly derived account of God's being is put into place before God acts to

---

28. Thomas Aquinas, *Summa Theologiae* I, q. 1, a. 1.

reveal himself in Christ. The inevitable result is that God's revelation in Christ will be shaped by an account of deity determined by creaturely ideals derived from human reflection on created being. Once again, general human ideas about God will be allowed to determine the content of God's revelation. In contrast, Barth insists that the true God—the only God that Christian theologians can and should be talking about—is the God who has joined himself to humanity in Christ. This God, and not the God of supreme attributes, is the proper subject matter of theology. Theologians will speak rightly about God's deity only when they begin with what God reveals about his deity in Jesus Christ. "The meaning of His deity—the only true deity in the New Testament sense—cannot be gathered from any notion of supreme, absolute, non-worldly being," Barth insists. "It can be learned only from what took place in Christ. Otherwise its mystery would be an arbitrary mystery of our own imagining, a false mystery."[29]

Similarly, Barth thinks the notion that "grace perfects and fulfills nature" presupposes an abstract view of humanity because human capacities are described as if they were operating just as they were when they were created. But the reality is that humans are fallen, and their sin has left them incapable of discerning the truth about God on their own. Barth insists that any account of God that humans offer in their fallen state inevitably will be shaped their own sinful being and thus fall into idolatry. This means that the only way humans can know God is through the saving work of Jesus Christ. God's Word in Christ does not come as something that "only partially proclaims something new," as if it perfects and fulfills something that humans "basically already know" in and through creation. Rather, "God's Word announces something new to them. It comes to them as light into darkness. It always comes to them as sinners, as forgiving and thus as judging grace."[30] This approach emphasizes that human knowledge of God is established by God's action rather than an act of the human. "When we ask questions about God's being," Barth explains, "we cannot in fact leave the sphere of His action and working as it is revealed to us in His Word."[31]

Barth insists that Balthasar's argument—that God's revelation in Jesus Christ presupposes God's prior act of creation and the intrinsic capacity of humans to receive it—is built on an abstraction. It assumes that created being can be defined in distinction from Jesus of Nazareth. But Barth insists that both the created order and everything in it is intrinsically defined by

---

29. Karl Barth, *Church Dogmatics* IV/1 (Edinburgh: T&T Clark, 1956), 177.

30. Karl Barth, "Fate and Idea in Theology," in *The Way of Theology in Karl Barth: Essays and Comments*, ed. H. Martin Rumscheidt (Allison Park, PA: Pickwick, 1986), 39.

31. Karl Barth, *Church Dogmatics* II/1, 260.

God's decision to save humanity in and through the human Jesus. "It is not that [God] first wills and works the being of the world and man, and then ordains it to salvation," Barth says. "But God creates, preserves and over-rules man for this prior end and with this prior purpose, that there may be a being distinct from himself ordained for salvation, for perfect being, for participation in his own being."[32] Grace does not presuppose nature; rather, nature presupposes grace. God's covenant of grace is the internal basis of creation and thus the reason why it exists at all. "There is no such thing," Barth says, "as a created nature which has its purpose, being, or continuance except through grace, or which may be known in this purpose, being, and continuance except through grace."[33] On this basis, Barth argues that the act of reflecting on the created order in distinction from God's revelation in Christ does not even give humans true knowledge about creation, much less knowledge of God. Humans can know the truth about both God and creation only when God reveals this truth to them in the person of Jesus. Once humans receive this revelation, however, they can look back at creation and see that the "divine form of life is not alien" to creaturely being.[34] God and humanity are compatible not because humans possess a natural capacity for God but because everything in creation was made in, through, and for Christ and the covenant of grace fulfilled in him.

On the basis of these arguments, Barth rules out the use of any general principles to establish theological claims about God or God's relationship with humanity: "We cannot be sufficiently eager to insist, nor can it be sufficiently emphasized in the Church and through the Church, that we know God in Jesus Christ alone, and that in Jesus Christ we know the one God." Barth sees this claim as the key to practicing theology faithfully, and he argues that every theologian is summoned again and again to make a "decision on this point."[35] A theologian's claims either will be grounded in their own creaturely ideas about God or they will be grounded on what God has revealed in Christ. There is no compromise, nor is there any alternative. As Barth puts it, "Any deviation, any attempt to evade Jesus Christ in favor of another supposed revelation of God, or any denial of the fullness of God's presence in Him, will precipitate us into darkness and confusion."[36] To be a theologian is to stand before the Word of God and be called to obedience—and there is only one way of obedience.

32. Barth, *Church Dogmatics* IV/1, 9.
33. Barth, *Church Dogmatics* II/2, 92.
34. Karl Barth, *Church Dogmatics* III/1 (Edinburgh: T&T Clark, 1958), 185.
35. Barth, *Church Dogmatics* II/1, 318–19.
36. Barth, *Church Dogmatics* II/1, 319.

The Politics of Obedience

Barth's argument that theology proceeds strictly on the basis of God's revelation in Jesus Christ addresses the problem that originally prompted his message of judgment against the tradition in which he was trained. But it also enables him to confront the issue that created this problem in the first place: the tendency of theologians to shape their account of God according to their own political ideologies.

Barth presumes that dogmatic theology necessarily carries concrete political implications. Jesus Christ preached the kingdom of God, and any account of God's revelation in Christ involves a description of what that kingdom entails for the church's life in the world. "Scripture did not attest for us the existence and work and deeds and words of God in Jesus Christ, and yet leave open the question of the result of it all on the men whom it is supposed to reach."[37] Because Barth sees politics in relation to Christ's command in his Word, he approaches the topic within the context of his dogmatic account of ethics. He insists that theologians cannot consider ethics as a second or optional step; rather, dogmatics must have "the problem of ethics in view from the very first, and it cannot legitimately lose sight of it."[38] Theologians who respond to God's Word must also present an account of what obedience to this Word looks like, including within the realm of politics. This task requires caution, however, because theologians face the temptation to offer political judgments on the basis of general principles that can be applied universally within a society. Barth insists that ethical questions, including questions about politics, "cannot be asked and answered except within the framework, or at any rate, the material context, of dogmatics."[39] His opposition to the use of general principles remains intact even on the subject of politics, and this leaves Barth's account of the church's political engagement standing apart from many traditional Christian accounts. He does not base his account on the claims of natural law, the orders of creation, a general affirmation of human dignity, or a universal account of morality. Instead, he insists that all Christian ethics, including political action, must be based on the particularity of God's revelation in Christ. "It is this connection with dogmatics," Barth argues, "which guards ethics against arbitrary assertions, arguments or conclusions, and allows it to follow a secure path to fruitful judgments."[40]

37. Barth, *Church Dogmatics* I/2, 207.
38. Barth, *Church Dogmatics* III/4, 3.
39. Barth, *Church Dogmatics* III/4, 3.
40. Barth, *Church Dogmatics* III/4, 3.

Barth put this approach into practice during his lecture "The Christian Message and the New Humanism" delivered in September 1949. He had been invited to Geneva to address the delegates of the Rencontres Internationales, who had gathered to discuss the prospects of humanism in the years after World War II.[41] What would it look like to affirm the goodness and integrity of humanity in the midst of an atomic age and after the horrors of the war and the Holocaust? The organizers asked Barth to offer a Christian approach to the topic, but he begins his lecture by rejecting the premise of the conference. The discussion had been framed in terms of general principles of human dignity and value, but Barth insists that Christians can speak only on the basis of the particularly of God's revelation. "Any idea about God and man," Barth says, "according to which their relations with one another, self-explanatory by their very definition, might be grasped through an analysis of the conceptions of God or of man, would here be unbearable and would distort everything."[42] Instead, a proper account of humanism requires the Christian first to speak about the "humanism of God" that takes place in the incarnation. Jesus Christ reveals that God relates to humans freely rather than on the basis of any qualities or rights they possess. On this basis, Barth concludes that human dignity will not be found in a general account of human being. Rather, it will be found in an account of God's free grace toward humanity in Christ and the corresponding human response of gratitude and obedience that includes a commitment to live for the sake of one's neighbors in the pattern of Christ. A Christian approach to humanism "acknowledges human dignity, human duty, human rights," Barth says, "but only within the framework of the knowledge that the real [human] exists because of his free relationship with his fellow" humans.[43]

Barth then draws a contrast between his revelation-centered approach to humanism and those offered in both the political West and East. He argues that the visions of human life offered in the West and East are idealistic because, in both cases, they begin from a general description of human being. Human dignity is not found in one's individual rights or capacities, as the West affirms; nor is it found in an ideal human community, as the East proclaims. Rather, the truth about human dignity and value will be discovered only as humans hear and respond to God's Word. But this response requires that they acknowledge the reality of human sin—and *this* is what makes the Christian approach to humanism distinct from every other approach. As Barth puts it,

41. See Karl Barth, "The Christian Message and the New Humanism," in *Against the Stream: Shorter Post-War Writings* (New York: Philosophical Library, 1954), 183–91.
42. Barth, "Christian Message and the New Humanism," 186.
43. Barth, "Christian Message and the New Humanism," 188.

the church is not able "to shirk the unpopular task, set to it by the Christian message, of pointing to the fact that the danger to human existence is greater, very much greater, than one wishes to believe."[44] The problem with classical humanism is that it emphasizes the human dignity without accounting for the reality of human sin. This abstraction is exposed as inadequate whenever the effects of sin become overwhelmingly apparent, as they do in times of war and atrocity.

The inadequacy of the classical approach created the crisis that prompted the delegates of the Rencontres Internationales to gather. As Barth sees it, they face the stark choice of offering a vision for human life that is either abstract or concrete. Their temptation will be to overlook the reality of human sin, because they want to affirm the inherent goodness, dignity, and worth of every human by offering a general account that everyone can readily affirm. But this unity-in-abstraction will come at a cost. The vision for human life that results will fail to grapple with the true reality of the human situation, and so it will be easily manipulated by political ideologies predicated on the inherent goodness and potential of humans. The crisis will not be solved; instead, the cycle of violence will simply be reset.

In contrast, Barth argues, because the Christian approach to humanism affirms human dignity on the basis of God's defeat of sin in Christ, it accounts for the concrete realities of human sin and its effects. This recognition does not detract from human dignity but instead reinforces it because every human life is seen in light of the reality of the gospel. It testifies to the fact that humans need to evaluate every aspect of their lives on the particular basis of God's affirmation of human worth in Jesus Christ. The gospel "starts from the assumption that the Kingdom is not yet visible, although it has come, and that everything is accomplished," Barth says. "On the basis of that supposition it protests against pessimism, tragedy, and skepticism."[45] The risen Christ's victory over sin—and his proclamation of this victory to the world—serves as the ground for a concrete and specific vision for human existence that remains hopeful even in the face of the horrors perpetuated by humans. Christ gives the world "a message of hope, a hope which the wicked lost man may set, not on himself, but on God, in which he may love his neighbor—and this is the premise of all ethics."[46]

This lecture shows how the method Barth used to guard against the danger of general principles applies to his account of the church's engagement with

44. Barth, "Christian Message and the New Humanism," 189.
45. Barth, "Christian Message and the New Humanism," 190.
46. Barth, "Christian Message and the New Humanism," 190.

politics. Instead of finding a common starting point with his audience, Barth begins with the particular claims of the Christian message. He does so because he does not want the content of God's revelation in Christ—particularly about the reality of human sin and the need for repentance—to be distorted or silenced by general assumptions about the nature of reality and history. Barth instead places the concerns and goals of his listeners within his own Christ-centered account of created reality and history. This approach allows him to highlight the failures of classical approaches while also offering an alternative that affirms human dignity even in the face of human sin. As Barth sees it, the vision he sets forward is much less open to political manipulation. A vision for human life built around general affirmations of human dignity could serve as the basis for sweeping claims about the dictates of natural law, the order of creation, the progress of history, or the inalienable truths rooted in human experience. Barth had encountered such claims before, and he had seen them manipulated to serve destructive and violent ideologies. His account of political life—centered around the call to recognize human dignity and work through concrete acts of love and service to one's neighbors—stands as a stark challenge to all such ideologies.

Christians who begin their thinking about God in light of God's revelation in Jesus Christ will not provide a theological justification for wars or the isolation of particular racial and ethnic groups. They will not embrace any political party or ideology or use the mechanism of the state to serve their own interests. They will not fight for their own rights or space within the world or see themselves as an interest group with their own political agenda. But neither will they withdraw from political matters and allow the world to function on its own terms. They will engage the world directly, and they will do so on the basis of a commitment to the dignity and value of every human. This commitment will be based not on a general claim about human dignity but on the particular relationship God establishes with humanity in Jesus Christ. In the same way that Christ addressed the concrete needs of humans by living for their sake, so do the people who have been joined to him. The primary form of their political engagement is to live for the sake of the most vulnerable in society by defending their integrity, caring for their needs, and advocating for their well-being.

The Poverty and Riches of Solitude

This kind of political vision comes with a cost, as Barth makes clear in a short essay on "Poverty," composed a few months later, in December 1949.

Barth begins by noting that there are many kinds of poverty, including both spiritual and material poverty. While the existence of material poverty seems to reflect a "divine ordering of events," this providential order does not mean that God views the poor neutrally. Barth insists that Scripture unequivocally shows that God "is on the side of the poor" and that Christians must share this allegiance.[47] Indeed, the ongoing presence of the distinction between rich and poor serves as "the reflection, the likeness, the testimony of a much more comprehensive distinction"—the poverty of every human in relation to God. In this sense, the existence of poverty should be the basis not for an exercise of power over others but for humility before others. This claim is grounded in the life of Jesus. He became materially poor and lived in solidarity with the poor even to the point of his death. If anyone wants to follow Christ, therefore, they must also live in solidarity with the poor. "Those who are rich must cleave to them," Barth says, "if they would be close to Him." Salvation from spiritual poverty should lead the believer to align their interests with those living in material poverty precisely because the materially poor Christ is the one who saves. "Not wealth but poverty is the mark of Heaven," Barth says, "the mirror of eternal salvation."[48]

A political vision centered on a call to sacrificially align one's life and resources with the poor is not likely to prevail in many elections. Nor is this message conducive to building a large political following or establishing a successful political party. The same can be said for the theological vision that undergirds it. A theological method that requires a daily surrender of one's claims before the reality of Christ is not likely to be the basis of a large theological tradition. It is more likely to leave one living in theological isolation. Barth seemed to think that was the case with his own theology. He pointed this out in a lecture delivered during his tour of the United States in 1962. The subject of the lecture is the solitude that comes with a life spent practicing theology. After discussing both the church's tendency to reject its theologians and the challenges that come with facing criticism of one's views, Barth observes that "the theologian seems to stand and persevere alone."[49] He later applies this observation to himself in the preface to the final volume of the *Church Dogmatics*, where he notes that his argument likely would reinforce the "theological and ecclesiastical isolation which has been [his] lot for almost fifty years."[50] This comment reveals that Barth saw himself as a theologian without a tradition. But he did not think of this as a problem. As he puts it,

47. Karl Barth, "Poverty," in *Against the Stream*, 244.
48. Barth, "Poverty," 246.
49. Barth, *Evangelical Theology*, 115.
50. Karl Barth, *Church Dogmatics* IV/4 (Edinburgh: T&T Clark, 1969), xii.

"The Church never did well to attach itself stubbornly to one man. . . . And it was never at any time good for it to look back instead of forwards as a matter of principle."[51] Theologians who look forward write theology for the church that does not yet exist, the one that will gather some day before the throne of Christ. Their present solitude testifies not to their break from the church but to their loyalty to the Christ who stands as its Head. This living Lord continues to speak in and through his Word, and theologians need to be free to respond to his instruction. "I would not like my life to result in the founding of a new school," Barth says. "I would like to tell anyone who is prepared to listen that I myself am not a 'Barthian,' because after I have learned something, I want to remain free to go on learning."[52]

51. Barth, *Church Dogmatics* III/4, xiii.
52. Quoted in Eberhard Busch, *Karl Barth: His Life from Letters and Autobiographical Texts* (Grand Rapids: Eerdmans, 1994), 417.

Credits

The introduction to part 2 consists of a revised version of an essay originally published in the *International Journal of Systematic Theology*. See Keith L. Johnson, "A Reappraisal of Karl Barth's Theological Development and His Dialogue with Catholicism," *International Journal of Systematic Theology* 14, no. 1 (January 2012): 1–23.

Chapter 2 is drawn from Karl Barth, *The Epistle to the Romans*, 6th ed., trans. E. C. Hoskyns (Oxford: Oxford University Press, 1933), 29–31, 35–39, 44–45. It is used by permission of Oxford University Press.

Chapter 3 is drawn from Karl Barth, "The Word of God as the Task of Theology," in *The Word of God and Theology*, ed. and trans. Amy Marga (London: T&T Clark, 2011), 185–98. It is used by permission of Bloomsbury Publishing, PLC.

Chapter 4 is drawn from Karl Barth, "An Answer to Adolf von Harnack's Open Letter," in *Revelation and Theology: An Analysis of the Barth-Harnack Correspondence of 1923*, ed. H. Martin Rumscheidt (Cambridge: Cambridge University Press, 1972), 40–48, 50–52. It is used by permission of Wipf & Stock Publishers.

Chapter 5 is drawn from Karl Barth, *The Resurrection of the Dead*, trans. H. J. Stenning (New York: Revell, 1933), 107–9, 133–34, 151–52, 167–68, 201–2. It is used by permission of Wipf & Stock Publishers.

Chapter 6 is drawn from Karl Barth, *The Göttingen Dogmatics: Instruction in the Christian Religion*, vol. 1, trans. Geoffrey W. Bromiley (Grand Rapids: Eerdmans, 1991), 57–63. It is used by permission of William B. Eerdmans Publishing Co.

Chapter 7 is drawn from Karl Barth, *The Holy Spirit and the Christian Life: The Theological Basis of Ethics*, trans. R. Birch Hoyle (Louisville: Westminster John Knox, 1993), 5–7. It is used by permission of Westminster John Knox Press.

Chapter 8 is drawn from Karl Barth, *Church Dogmatics* I/1, rev. ed. (Edinburgh: T&T Clark, 1975), xi–xvi. It is used by permission of Bloomsbury Publishing, PLC.

Chapter 9 is drawn from Karl Barth, "Abschied," in *Karl Barth Gesamtausgabe*, vol. 49, *Vorträge und Kleinere Arbeiten 1930–1933*, ed. Michael Beintker, Michael Hütten- hoff, and Peter Zocher (Zurich: Theologischer Verlag Zürich, 2013), 492–515; original translation by Matthew J. Aragon Bruce. It is used by permission of Theologischer Verlag Zürich and the Karl Barth Archiv, Basel.

Chapter 10 is drawn from Karl Barth, *The Humanity of God* (Richmond: John Knox, 1960), 39–46. It is used by permission of Westminster John Knox Press.

Chapter 11 is drawn from Karl Barth, *Church Dogmatics* I/1, rev. ed. (Edinburgh: T&T Clark, 1975), 11–16. It is used by permission of Bloomsbury Publishing, PLC.

Chapter 12 is drawn from Karl Barth, *Church Dogmatics* I/1, rev. ed. (Edinburgh: T&T Clark, 1975), 118–21. It is used by permission of Bloomsbury Publishing, PLC.

Chapter 13 is drawn from Karl Barth, *Church Dogmatics* I/1, rev. ed. (Edinburgh: T&T Clark, 1975), 228, 238–47. It is used by permission of Bloomsbury Publishing, PLC.

Chapter 14 is drawn from Karl Barth, *Church Dogmatics* I/1, rev. ed. (Edinburgh: T&T Clark, 1975), 304–5, 307–8, 312, 375–76, 379–83. It is used by permission of Bloomsbury Publishing, PLC.

Chapter 15 is drawn from Karl Barth, *Church Dogmatics* I/2 (Edinburgh: T&T Clark, 1956), 1, 132–34, 147–56, 204, 246–48, 257–58, 265, 269–70. It is used by permission of Bloomsbury Publishing, PLC.

Chapter 16 is drawn from Karl Barth, *Church Dogmatics* II/1 (Edinburgh: T&T Clark, 1957), 3–26, 47–49. It is used by permission of Bloomsbury Publishing, PLC.

Chapter 17 is drawn from Karl Barth, *Church Dogmatics* II/1 (Edinburgh: T&T Clark, 1957), 275–81, 301–3. It is used by permission of Bloomsbury Publishing, PLC.

Chapter 18 is drawn from Karl Barth, *Church Dogmatics* II/2 (Edinburgh: T&T Clark, 1957), 4–11, 13–14, 25–27, 53–54. It is used by permission of Bloomsbury Publish- ing, PLC.

Chapter 19 is drawn from Karl Barth, *Church Dogmatics* II/2 (Edinburgh: T&T Clark, 1957), 101–17. It is used by permission of Bloomsbury Publishing, PLC.

Chapter 20 is drawn from Karl Barth, *Church Dogmatics* II/2 (Edinburgh: T&T Clark, 1957), 140–42. It is used by permission of Bloomsbury Publishing, PLC.

Chapter 21 is drawn from Karl Barth, *Church Dogmatics* III/1 (Edinburgh: T&T Clark, 1958), 42–51. It is used by permission of Bloomsbury Publishing, PLC.

Chapter 22 is drawn from Karl Barth, *Church Dogmatics* III/2 (Edinburgh: T&T Clark, 1960), 203–4, 207–9, 212–20. It is used by permission of Bloomsbury Publishing, PLC.

Chapter 23 is drawn from Karl Barth, *Church Dogmatics* III/3 (Edinburgh: T&T Clark, 1961), 289, 303–5, 310–12, 363. It is used by permission of Bloomsbury Publishing, PLC.

Chapter 24 is drawn from Karl Barth, *Church Dogmatics* IV/1 (Edinburgh: T&T Clark, 1956), 6–16. It is used by permission of Bloomsbury Publishing, PLC.

Chapter 25 is drawn from Karl Barth, *Church Dogmatics* IV/1 (Edinburgh: T&T Clark, 1956), 158–59, 177, 179–80, 183–84, 186–88, 192–93, 197–204. It is used by permission of Bloomsbury Publishing, PLC.

Chapter 26 is drawn from Karl Barth, *Church Dogmatics* IV/2 (Edinburgh: T&T Clark, 1958), 31–36, 268–74, 280–81. It is used by permission of Bloomsbury Publishing, PLC.

Chapter 27 is drawn from Karl Barth, *Church Dogmatics* IV/3.1 (Edinburgh: T&T Clark, 1961), 166–68, 180–82, 211. It is used by permission of Bloomsbury Publishing, PLC.

Chapter 28 is drawn from Karl Barth, *Church Dogmatics* IV/3.1 (Edinburgh: T&T Clark, 1961), 477–78. It is used by permission of Bloomsbury Publishing, PLC.

Chapter 29 is drawn from Karl Barth, *Church Dogmatics* IV/3.2 (Edinburgh: T&T Clark, 1962), 751–63. It is used by permission of Bloomsbury Publishing, PLC.

Chapter 30 is drawn from Karl Barth, "Zwischenzeit," *Kirchenblatt für die reformierte Schweiz* 118 (1962): 38–39; translation and annotation by Matthew J. Aragon Bruce. It is used by permission of Theologischer Verlag Zürich and the Karl Barth Archiv, Basel.

Chapter 31 is drawn from John Michael Owen, "Karl Barth's Sermon for Advent 2, 1933: Introduction and Translation," *Colloquium* 36, no. 2 (2004): 161–80. It is used by permission of John Michael Owen and *Colloquium*.

Chapter 32 is drawn from Douglas S. Bax's translation in "The Barmen Theological Declaration: A New Translation," *Journal of Theology for Southern Africa* 47 (June 1984): 78–82. It is used by permission of the *Journal of Theology for Southern Africa*.

Chapter 33 is drawn from Karl Barth, "A Letter to American Christians," in *The Church and the War* (Eugene, OR: Wipf & Stock, 2008), 19–20, 22–25, 28–34. It is used by permission of Wipf & Stock Publishers.

Chapter 34 is drawn from Karl Barth, "The Christian Community and the Civil Community," in *Community, State, and Church: Three Essays* (Eugene, OR: Wipf & Stock, 2004), 156–60, 165–67, 171–73. It is used by permission of Wipf & Stock Publishers.

Index

analogia entis (analogy of being), 7, 17–21, 69–73, 78, 222
analogia fidei (analogy of faith), 19–21, 111, 121–23, 148
analogia relationis (analogy of relation), 211, 222–23
Anselm, 5, 7, 19, 74, 76, 78, 349
apokastasis. *See* universalism
Aquinas, Thomas, 5, 7, 17, 63, 69, 74, 78, 84n7, 349, 357
Asmussen, Hans, 348n1
atonement, 247–64
Augustine, 70, 97n10

Barmen Declaration, 9, 320–24, 327n3, 330n12, 334n21, 338, 339n5, 340n6, 343n15
Barth, Johann Friedrich, 1
Barth, Karl
  in Basel, 9–12
  in Bonn, 8–10
  childhood of, 1–2
  critique of liberalism, 94–96
  development of, 13–22
  education of, 2
  and German Christianity, 8–10, 20, 79, 86–92, 306, 308–19, 320–24, 354–55
  in Göttingen, 4–5, 63–64, 304–7
  marriage of, 2, 6–7
  method of, 32–43, 75–80, 93, 175–77, 347–65
  in Münster, 5–8, 304–7
  and natural theology, 78, 84–86, 91
  and poverty, 363–65
  in Safenwil, 2–4, 304
  in the United States, 11
  and universalism, 288–89
  and war, 325–36
Barth, Katharina Anna, 1
Bavinck, Herman, 64
Blumhardt, Christoph, 3
Blumhardt, Johann, 3, 25, 27n11, 63, 95n6
Breit, Thomas, 321
Brunner, Emil, 81, 82, 84, 85n8, 353–54
Bultmann, Rudolf, 81, 89n25, 354

Calvin, John, 5, 42, 47, 54n22, 98, 193n6, 350
Cavert, Samuel McCrea, 325
church, 290–300, 308–19, 320–45
creation, 205–10, 238–39

decretum absolutum, 193
dialectical theology, 36–43, 79–80, 82–84
Die Christliche Welt, 2, 32, 38n14, 45–46
divine revelation, 64–68, 115–23, 135–36, 138, 144–48
divine wrath, 30–31
dogmatics, 109–14
dogmatism, 34–35
Dostoevsky, Fyodor, 55, 95
Drewes, Hans Anton, 348n1

election, 174–99
evil, 200–204, 224–32, 239–41

faith, 53–54, 120–25, 155
Fezer, Karl, 87
Foerster, Erich, 32, 38n14
Frank, Sebastian, 38

Geibel, Emanuel, 97n11
Gellert, Christian, 273n18
German Christians, 8–10, 20, 79, 86–92, 306,
    308–19, 320–24
Geyer, Christian, 85n9
God
    being of, 167–73, 236
    condescension of, 250–56
    decision of, 191–99, 235, 242–44
    freedom of, 172–73
    knowledge of, 149–66
    love of, 167–71, 185
    obedience of, 261–64
    participation in, 237–38
    self-determination of, 183–84
    triune, 126–36, 191–99, 256–64
Gogarten, Friedrich, 5, 8, 20, 46n5, 81–89, 91,
    338, 352–53
gospel, 24, 27–30, 184–87
    and law, 316n22
grace, 181–82, 238–39

Heidegger, Martin, 303
Heppe, Heinrich, 63, 349n3
Hermann, Wilhelm, 2, 96, 352
Hirsch, Emmanuel, 87, 91, 320
Hitler, Adolf, 8, 9, 10, 86n, 301, 303, 309, 320,
    326, 331–32, 335n23, 353
Hoffmann, Nelly, 2, 6–7
Holy Spirit, 54, 69–73, 144–48, 155, 296–300
Hossenfelder, Joachim, 86, 308
human being, 211–23, 234–36, 238–39, 244–45,
    277

Icarus, 274n19
idolatry, 31
imago Dei, 221–23
immutability, 251–56

Jaspers, Karl, 303
Jesus Christ
    and the church, 290–96
    death on cross, 247–64
    divine and human, 139–44, 251–56
    election of, 178–80, 190–99, 201–4
    exaltation of, 265–77
    and history, 51–53, 248–49, 269–70, 283–85
    and human being, 214–23
    humanity of, 101–2, 265–77
    humility of, 256–64
    Jewish blood of, 313–14
    obedience of, 256–64

resurrection of, 25–26, 57–62
    as revelation of God, 187–89
    self-declaration of, 278–86
Jewish people, 308–19
justification, 276–77

Kant, Immanuel, 2, 68n12
Keller, Gottfried, 91
Kierkegaard, Søren, 25, 26n8, 30n18, 55, 95, 306
Knittermeyer, Hinrich, 88n21
Kutter, Hermann, 24n3, 95

Liebe, Reinhard, 32, 38n14
Lüdemann, Hermann, 96
Luther, Martin, 18, 29, 34–35, 37–38, 42, 47, 49,
    53, 55, 70, 86, 90, 306, 316n22, 342, 349, 355

Marcionism, 38, 54–55
Melanchthon, Philip, 47
Merz, Georg, 6, 81–82, 84–85, 88n21, 89n23
mission, 299–300
modalism, 134–35
Mozart, 2
Müller, Hans Michael, 83n3, 87n18
Müller, Ludwig, 86n13, 87n18
mysticism. See self-criticism

Nestorianism, 141
nothingness, 224–32

objectivity, 157–61
    primary objectivity, 157–58
    secondary objectivity, 158–59
Otto, Rudolf, 96
Overbeck, Franz, 25, 95, 96n7

participation, 237–38, 267, 273–77
Paul, 3, 4, 14, 22, 27, 29, 40, 47, 56–58, 60n5,
    61, 142n11, 144n14, 198n16, 269n9, 270n11,
    271n12, 274n20, 294n11, 302, 310–11,
    313n15, 315, 316n22, 318n27–28, 342, 355
Paul VI (pope), 12
Platonism, 40, 70, 98
Polycarp, 87n19
predestination, 192, 196
Przywara, Erich, 7, 17–18, 20–21, 69–71, 74

Rade, Martin, 2, 32
Ragaz, Leonhard, 90, 95, 99
resurrection, 57–62
Ritschl, Albrecht, 77

Rittelmeyer, Friedrich, 85n9
Rothe, Richard, 340

salvation, 236–38, 247–64, 282–83
Sartre, Jean-Paul, 303
Schaeder, Erich, 96
Schelling, Friedrich, 38
Schleiermacher, Friedrich, 2, 294n11, 352n11
Schumann, Friedrich, 87
Schweitzer, Albert, 25n5
scientific theology, 46–56
Scripture, 50–54, 64–65, 113–14, 118, 127–28
Seeberg, Reinhold, 96
self-criticism, 35–36
sin, 239–41
Söhngen, Gottlieb, 20–21
Stephan, Horst, 96
Strauss, Friedrich, 2, 25n5, 53n19
subordinationism, 133–34
supralapsarianism, 200–204

Tertullian, 144n14
theologia crucis, 112

Thomas Aquinas, 5, 7, 17, 63, 69, 74, 78, 84n7, 349, 357
Thurneysen, Eduard, 3–5, 23, 46, 79, 81–82, 85nn10–11, 92
Trinity. See God: triune
Troeltsch, Ernst, 87, 96

universalism, 288–89

Vilmar, August, 96
Vischer, Eberhard, 45n2
von Balthasar, Hans Urs, 12, 98n14, 356
von Harnack, Adolf, 2, 16, 44–56, 98n13, 114n8, 354–55
von Kirschbaum, Charlotte, 6–7, 11

Wobbermin, Georg, 78n11, 79n12, 87n18, 96
Word of God, 115–19, 121–25, 127–28
World Council of Churches, 10

Zwingli, Huldrych, 47, 55, 86n15
Zwischen den Zeiten, 5, 8, 20, 81–92, 307